The Role of the Chantress (*Šmꜥyt*) in Ancient Egypt

Suzanne Lynn Onstine

BAR International Series 1401
2005

This title published by

Archaeopress
Publishers of British Archaeological Reports
Gordon House
276 Banbury Road
Oxford OX2 7ED
England
bar@archaeopress.com
www.archaeopress.com

BAR S1401

The Role of the Chantress (*Šmꜥyt*) *in Ancient Egypt*

ISBN 1 84171 840 8

Printed in England by The Basingstoke Press

All BAR titles are available from:

Hadrian Books Ltd
122 Banbury Road
Oxford
OX2 7BP
England
bar@hadrianbooks.co.uk

The current BAR catalogue with details of all titles in print, prices and means of payment is available free from Hadrian Books or may be downloaded from www.archaeopress.com

ACKNOWLEDGEMENTS

The author would like to thank a number of people for their help and support in the preparation of this monograph and the doctoral dissertation it is based upon. Friends and family are foremost on the list; my husband, Richard Sherman, my parents, Scott and Diane Onstine, and especially Diane Flores and Troy Sagrillo who have helped with editing, references, and moral support throughout. Diane Flores is also the illustrator of the cover art which is based on numerous images of New Kingdom Theban chantresses.

Thanks also go to my University of Toronto committee members, Dr. Ron Leprohon, Dr. Krzys Grzymski, and most especially the late Dr. Nick Millet of the Royal Ontario Museum who was a source of help, encouragement, and humor during all my years of study in Toronto. Thanks are additionally due to Dr. Gay Robins of Emory University for providing insightful commentary while acting as the outside reader on the committee. Dr. Richard Wilkinson of the University of Arizona was also of enormous assistance in the process of writing this work while away from Toronto's research library.

Other individuals who went out of their way to send me references for the database include Dr. Rene van Walsem of the University of Leiden, Drs. Federicco Rocchi of Bologna University, and Drs. Marleen De Meyer of the Katholieke Universiteit Leuven.

Financial assistance from the Society for the Study of Egyptian Antiquities' Missy Eldredge Scholarship Fund was also helpful.

TABLE OF CONTENTS

ACKNOWLEDGEMENTS i

CHAPTER 1: INTRODUCTION 1
1.I GOAL STATEMENT 1
1.II QUESTIONS TO BE ADDRESSED 2
1.III METHODOLOGY AND SOURCE MATERIALS 2
1.III.1 METHODOLOGY 2
1.III.2 TYPES OF SOURCE MATERIAL 2
1.III.2.A TOMBS 2
1.III.2.B STELAE 2
1.III.2.C STATUES 2
1.III.2.D PAPYRI 2
1.III.2.E FUNERARY EQUIPMENT 2
1.III.2.F LITERARY AND INSCRIPTIONAL MATERIAL 2
1.IV CONCLUSION 3

CHAPTER 2: UNDERSTANDING *ŠMꜤ* 4
2.I DEFINING THE TERM *ŠMꜤ* 4
2.I.1 LINGUISTIC CONSIDERATIONS 4
2.I.2 COMPARISON WITH OTHER LANGUAGES 4
2.II ICONOGRAPHY AND GESTURES 5
2.III TERMS RELATED TO *ŠMꜤ* THAT CLARIFY ITS DEFINITION 5
2.III.1 DISCUSSION OF *ḤSY* 6
2.III.2 DISCUSSION OF THE *ḪNR* 7
2.III.3 DISCUSSION OF THE "RHYTHM SECTION" OR *ŠSPT DḪN* 8
2.III.4 DISCUSSION OF THE SISTRUM PLAYERS 8
2.IV CONCLUSIONS 9

CHAPTER 3: THE ROLE OF WOMEN AND MUSIC IN CEREMONIES AND PROCESSIONS 11
3.I INTRODUCTION 11
3.II IMITATING THE GODDESS: CONNECTIONS TO MERET AND HATHOR 11
3.III TYPES OF PROCESSIONS AND FESTIVALS 12
3.III.1 *OPET* FESTIVAL 12
3.III.1.A *OPET* RELIEFS IN LUXOR COLONNADE 13
3.III.1.B TEMPLE OF RAMESSES III AT KARNAK 13
3.III.1.C THE FAMILY OF HERIHOR AT KARNAK 13
3.III.2 BEAUTIFUL FEAST OF THE VALLEY 13
3.III.2.A THE TOMBS OF MENKHEPERRASONB 14
3.III.3 FUNERARY CONTEXTS 14
3.III.3.A THE TOMB OF NAKHTAMUN 14
3.III.3.B THE TOMB OF KENAMUN 15
3.III.3.C THE TOMB OF RAMOSE 15
3.III.4 *SED* FESTIVAL 15
3.III.4.A THE TOMB OF KHERUEF TT 192 15
3.III.4.B THE FESTIVAL HALL OF OSORKON II 16
3.III.5 DIVINE APPEARANCES 16
3.III.5.A THE TOMB OF KHONSU TT 31 16
3.III.5.B THE TOMB OF AMENMOSE TT 19 17
3.III.5.C THE TOMB OF PANEHSY TT 16 17
3.III.6 ROYAL FAMILY PROCESSIONS 17
3.III.6.A GREAT COURT OF RAMESSES II AT LUXOR TEMPLE 18
3.III.7 TEMPLE RITUAL 18
3.III.7.A THE FESTIVAL TEMPLE OF TUTHMOSIS III AT KARNAK 18
3.III.7.B TOMB OF AMUNHOTEP-SA-SE TT 75 19
3.III.7.C TOMB OF MIN TT 109 19
3.IV CONCLUSIONS 19

CHAPTER 4: INSCRIPTIONAL EVIDENCE AND LITERARY SOURCES 20
4.I INTRODUCTION 20
4.II ROYAL DECREES 20
4.II.1 TUTANKAMUN'S RESTORATION STELA 20
4.II.2 CANOPUS DECREE 20
4.III LEGAL AND ADMINISTRATIVE DOCUMENTS 20
4.III.1 P. BERLIN 10021 20
4.III.2 AMARAH WEST STELA 20
4.III.3 TOMB ROBBERIES PAPYRI 21
4.III.4 ADOPTION PAPYRUS 21
4.IV STORIES 21
4.IV.1 SINUHE, P. BERLIN 3022 21
4.IV.2 P. WESTCAR, P. BERLIN 3033 22
4.IV.3 NEFER-KA-RE AND THE GENERAL 22
4.V PRAYERS 22
4.V.1 BANKES STELA NO. 3 22
4.V.2 AMARNA HYMN TO THE ATEN 22
4.VI LETTERS 23
4.VI.1 LETTERS CONCERNING THE FAMILY OF BUTEHAMON 23
4.VI.2 LETTERS CONCERNING HERERE 24
4.VII CONCLUSIONS 24

CHAPTER 5: HISTORICAL DEVELOPMENT OF THE TITLE *ŠMꜥYT* 25
5.I INTRODUCTION 25
5.II MIDDLE KINGDOM ATTESTATIONS 25
5.III CONCLUSIONS ABOUT THE EARLY USE OF *ŠMꜥ* 26
5.IV THE NEW KINGDOM 27
5.IV.1 THE 18TH DYNASTY 27
5.IV.1.A HATSHEPSUT THROUGH TUTHMOSIS IV 27
5.IV.1.B AMENHOTEP III THROUGH HOREMHAB 28
5.IV.1.C ANALYSIS 28
5.IV.2 THE RAMESSIDE ERA 29
5.IV.2.A THE 19TH DYNASTY 29
5.IV.2.B THE 20TH DYNASTY 30
5.IV.2.C ANALYSIS 30
5.V THE THIRD INTERMEDIATE PERIOD 31
5.V.1 STATISTICS AND DISCUSSION 31
5.V.2 ANALYSIS 31
5.VI THE LATE AND PTOLEMAIC PERIODS 32
5.VI.1 STATISTICS AND DISCUSSION 32
5.VI.2 ANALYSIS 32
5.VII CONCLUSIONS 32

CHAPTER 6: FAMILY INFLUENCE 34
6.I INTRODUCTION 34
6.II THE HEREDITARY STATUS OF FEMALE TITLES 34
6.III PATTERNS OF INFLUENCE 34
6.III.1 MOTHERS AND DAUGHTERS 34
6.III.2 MOTHERS-IN-LAW 35
6.III.3 FATHERS AND DAUGHTERS 35
6.III.4 HUSBANDS 35
6.III.4.A MARRIAGE AS A PRECONDITION OF THE TITLE 36
6.IV CONCLUSIONS 36
6.IV.1 INHERITANCE 36
6.IV.2 FAMILY STATUS 36
CHART 1 38
CHART 2 45
CHART 3 49
CHART 4 54

CHAPTER 7: THE ORGANIZATION OF THE *ŠMʿYWT* 68
7.I TEMPLE HIERARCHY 68
7.II RANK 69
CHART 5 70

CHAPTER 8: CONCLUSIONS 75
8.I REITERATION OF QUESTIONS RAISED 75
8.I.1 FAMILY 75
8.III THE TEMPLE 75
8.IV SUMMARY 76

APPENDIX A: MALE *ŠMʿW* 78
CHART 6 81
APPENDIX B: THE EVIDENCE FROM ABYDOS 82
APPENDIX C: LETTERS 84
APPENDIX D: CATALOGUE OF *ŠMʿYWT* KNOWN FROM THEBAN TOMBS 87
APPENDIX E: NOTES ON THE DATABASE AND REFERENCES LIST 98
CHART 7 99
CHART 8 141

LIST OF ABBREVIATIONS 150

BIBLIOGRAPHY 151

CHAPTER 1 INTRODUCTION

1.I GOAL STATEMENT

The goal of this study is to determine what it meant to be a *šmʿyt*, or chantress, in ancient Egypt. Very little is known about the specifics of the title or the types of people who held it. Both men and women held the title, but the female version is by far the more prevalent. It is the women who held this title that will be the focus of this study.

Studies investigating the status of non-royal women are a fairly recent phenomenon.[1] While the title "god's wife of Amun" and other high-ranking titles have received attention,[2] lesser positions such as that of the *šmʿyt* have remained uninvestigated. In fact, one recent work states: "Le titre de *šmʿyt* apparaît dès la 18e dynastie et malgré sa profusion n'a fait l'objet d'aucune étude approfondie" (Naguib, 1990: 236). Since so many of the women of the New Kingdom and Third Intermediate Period held the title, this lack of research neglects a large segment of the population. The role was neither obscure nor unusual in ancient times. The abundance of data from private tombs and monuments concerning the women who held the title *šmʿyt* makes these women ideal subjects for a study of the status of non-royal women within their cultural and historical contexts.

Blackman's "On the position of women in the ancient Egyptian hierarchy"[3] is one of the earliest studies to deal with a number of women's titles. It offers, however, little specific information about the role of the *šmʿywt*. No distinction is made between the various feminine musical titles of the New Kingdom. Indeed, because of the frequent use of the generic translations 'singer' and 'musician' that are applied to a variety of different Egyptian titles (e.g. *šmʿyt, ḥsyt, mrt, ḫnrt*), it is often difficult to determine when *šmʿyt* is the original title used in a text in works where the Egyptian terms are not provided. That this basic translation is applied to diverse feminine titles associated with music and the temple system is an indication of the present lack of understanding of the actual roles of women possessing these titles. The various titles must have meant more than just 'singer', or it seems likely that the Egyptians would not have used more than one title for this position in the temple hierarchy. Nor would they have put the differing titles in the same contexts and rubrics as complementary, yet separate, activities (e.g., the story of Pepi II and the General, the tomb of Kheruef, P.Westcar).[4] Chapter 2 further defines the differences between the various musical titles based on linguistic and iconographic evidence.

The material presented in Chapter 3 demonstrates that the role of the *šmʿywt* in religious ritual was to make music by singing, chanting, or shaking the sistrum and *menyt*, as they are frequently depicted doing this. In groups they are occasionally designated as a choir, or *šspt dḫn*, in the accompanying rubric (e.g., TT 86). It is also clear that women who were *šmʿywt* also held other musical and nonmusical titles.[5]

Although the title *šmʿyt* is best attested in the New Kingdom and the Third Intermediate Period, a few isolated Middle Kingdom examples have been documented (Ward, 1982: 175). *Šmʿywt* are also known from the Late and Ptolemaic Periods. A full discussion of the relevant social and historical contexts is found in Chapter 5.

1.II QUESTIONS TO BE ADDRESSED

- Does the title *šmʿyt* imply a religious vocation or was it an honorific title?
- How was the title obtained?
- Who were the families of the *šmʿywt* and what was their social status?
- What were the differences between *šmʿywt* and other musicians (e.g., *ḫnrwt, ḥsywt*)?
- Since the majority of cases documented were women, what was the male role?
- Which gods did they serve and at which cult centers?
- What were their responsibilities in cult practices?
- Did those holding the title usurp the duties or role of a previously existing office or offices?
- When did the title come into being and when did it cease to be used?
- Are there patterns in the depictions and descriptions of *šmʿywt* in art and writing (literature, private letters, tomb inscriptions) that give clues to the answers to any of these questions?

[1] See, for instance, recent works by Tyldesley (1994), Robins (1993b), Watterson (1991), Lesko (1987), Bryan (1985).
[2] See Naguib (1990), Gitton (1984, 1979), and Graefe (1981).
[3] *JEA* 7 (1921) p. 8-30.

[4] See Section 4.IV for the Pepi II story and P. Westcar. See Section 3.III.4.A for a description of the tomb of Kheruef (TT 192).
[5] E.g., Ipay and Neith (DB #472 and #481) were both *mnʿt nsw* as well as *šmʿyt*.

1.III METHODOLOGY AND SOURCE MATERIALS

1.III.1 Methodology

The issues just listed can be elucidated by a thorough investigation of the familial and cult affiliations of the individual *šmᶜywt* who have been documented. Information on the families of *šmᶜywt* derive from a variety of sources ranging in date from the late 12th Dynasty to the Ptolemaic Period. Data on 860 women from a wide variety of locales and time periods are included in the database constructed for this study. Among the characteristics charted are the titles of a woman's parents, husband, and children, as well as the provenience, date, and current location of the object from which the information is drawn, along with pertinent publication information. Due to the fact that women seldom had their own tombs or stelae, most genealogical data are provided by the monuments of their fathers, husbands, and sons. The titles held by these men, and in some cases by female relations, are an indication of the chantresses' social standing. The familial affiliations recorded in this way also contribute to a determination of whether or not the title *šmᶜyt* was inherited or otherwise influenced by a family's cult affiliations. An analysis of the data can be found in Chapter 6.

1.III.2 Types of Source Material

A wide variety of source material provide the raw data for this study. The portrayal of the *šmᶜywt* differed from context to context. Tomb inscriptions or stelae rarely depict individual *šmᶜywt* engaged in temple duties, emphasizing, rather, their role in the family. Literature, however, describes their activities, and temple reliefs portray the *šmᶜywt* as part of ceremonies that took place within the temple walls. It is only through an examination of various contexts that a complete picture can be obtained.

1.III.2.A Tombs

The decorated tombs of the New Kingdom are an excellent source of information on the *šmᶜywt* and their families. In some cases complex genealogies can be drawn, and relationships between important families traced based on the data available from this source. The tombs also occasionally depict the festivals in which the chantresses took part.

1.III.2.B Stelae

The extant stelae discovered at cult sites like Thebes, Abydos, and Memphis give clues to familial status and relationships. Occasionally, a woman dedicated a stela herself. However, men who included female relatives in the dedication of their stelae were more common. Most of the stelae recorded here were dedicated by fathers, brothers, husbands, or sons of *šmᶜywt*. Many stelae are unprovenienced, and of those that are provenienced, relatively few come from provincial sites. This situation creates a paucity of evidence about the role of the *šmᶜwyt* at secondary cult sites such as el Kab or the cities of the Delta.

1.III.2.C Statues

Statues carry inscriptions and exhibit iconography similar to those found on stelae. Many, however, are also unprovenienced. Occasionally, the individuals named in the inscription can be matched to known tomb owners or historical figures and thus tentatively placed geographically. When this is possible, the additional information on specific families and their titles can create a more complete account of individual families.

1.III.2.D Papyri

Papyri of the Book of the Dead represent another source where the *šmᶜywt* are attested. Among the 44 papyri in the British Museum where the title *šmᶜyt* is mentioned, the majority were owned by women (Quirke, 1993). Only a few of these examples, however, mention other members of the papyrus owner's family. Four papyri belonged to men who listed titles and other personal information along with a mention of their *šmᶜyt* wives. Information on both husband and wife are important for placing the wife in family and social contexts. The 21st Dynasty papyri documented by Niwiński (1989b) are an especially good source of information for determining that the title was popular during the Third Intermediate Period. These funerary papyri and the accompanying coffins are virtually the only source of information on family relationships in the Third Intermediate Period (see comments by Bierbrier, 1975: 45).

1.III.2.E Funerary Equipment

Shabtis and coffins provide valuable information on *šmᶜywt*. Niwinski's work on the 21st Dynasty coffins of Thebes demonstrates that the title was common during the Third Intermediate Period. Most of these coffins came from Deir el Bahari caches such as that at Bab el Gusus. These caches provide a wealth of information for the families of the High Priests of Amun. This concentration of large numbers of extant papyri and coffins from one location skews the evidence in favor of the title being considered a Theban phenomenon. Chapter 5 deals with the historical implications of this preponderance of Theban attestations during the Third Intermediate Period.

1.III.2.F Literary and inscriptional material (nonfunerary)

Individual *šmᶜyt* and groups of *šmᶜyw*(*t*) are known from a variety of document types such as letters, stories, and official decrees. Their inclusion in legal proceedings and stories gives depth to our knowledge of their activities. Letters also provide an idea of their social surroundings and concerns. In two official decrees (one from the 18th Dynasty and one from the Ptolemaic Period) an indication of the continuity of the title can be seen. Chapter 4 presents this evidence grouped by genre and Appendix C outlines the content of the letters discussed.

1.IV CONCLUSION

The forms of the available source materials have dictated the types of questions that can be answered. Since there is no extant rule book or guide explaining the requirements of the title *šmʿyt*, a research framework that takes into consideration the limitations of the source material must be constructed so that patterns of behavior may be inferred. The database used in this research is one such tool. Documenting all that is known about these women as individuals can shed light on their behavior as a group and, it is hoped, answer the questions posed here.

CHAPTER 2 UNDERSTANDING *ŠMꜤ*

2.I DEFINING THE TERM *ŠmꜤ*

2.I.1 Linguistic Considerations

An investigation of the term *šmꜤ* [1] begins with Gardiner's *Egyptian Grammar* and the *Wörterbuch*. The word is written with the Gardiner sign list sign M27 , the sedge plant crossed with an arm. *ŠmꜤ* is defined as either "Upper Egypt" (and the adjectives derived from that meaning) or "to sing" (and related derivatives). The two uses of the words seem to be unrelated homophones. The *Wörterbuch* defines *šmꜤ* as "to sing, to clap hands" (*Wb* IV, 478). Therefore a *šmꜤyt* can be loosely defined as a female singer or hand clapper (*Wb* IV, 479-480). The title *šmꜤyt,* often spelled without the final "*yt*", is customarily translated as "singer", "songstress", and "chantress".

Two early examples – one from the Old Kingdom and one from the Middle Kingdom – show the word *šmꜤ* clearly associated with music making and dancing. In the Old Kingdom tomb of Djau at Deir el Gabrawi (Davies, 1902: pt. 2 pl. VII) may be found the earliest reference to the *šmꜤw* as a group. Vignettes depicting the funeral cortege include two rows of dancers and chanters. The text between the two rows reads: *ḫbt in ḫnrt šmꜤ in šmꜤw.* This can be translated as "dancing by the *Khener*, chanting by the chanters". A row of women, depicted with rings at the end of their queues, are probably the *Khener*, since they are shown dancing. In the row below them, the men, who raise their hands as if clapping, are probably the *šmꜤw* since their actions resemble those of *šmꜤw* from other tombs where groups of individuals are clearly identified as such (e.g., Kenamun [TT 93], Davies, 1930: pls. XXXIX, XL and Chapter 3.III.3.B). In the Middle Kingdom tomb of Khety at Beni Hassan (Newberry, 1893: v.2, pl. 7) a scene depicting a row of men singing and dancing in the funeral procession is accompanied by a rubric naming the *šmꜤw* where it is spelled with uniliteral signs (Newberry, 1893: v.2, pl.7). A phonetic spelling of *šmꜤ* is once also used in the tomb of Djau (Davies, 1902: pt. 2 pl. VII). This contrasts with the later New Kingdom spelling of the word, which commonly uses as the primary phonetic element of the word.

The determinatives used at the end of *šmꜤ* or *šmꜤyt* often provide visual clues to the meaning of the word. In Old Kingdom and Middle Kingdom writings, a determinative is seldom used (Deir el Gabrawi, Beni Hassan, Vienna stela ÄS 132[2]). With the New Kingdom title, however, the determinative is usually a woman. The seated man with hand to mouth is also commonly used in conjunction with the seated woman when *šmꜤyt* is used as a title. When depicting groups of *šmꜤw*, may also appear with the indication for a plural word .[3] On one mid-21st Dynasty papyrus, the *šmꜤ* hieroglyph (Gardiner sign list sign M27) holds a sistrum (DB ref. #373). In an inscription at Edfu dating to the Ptolemaic Period, the determinative depicts a woman holding a circular frame drum[4] (de Rochemonteix and Chassinat, 1987: 329). A few examples use the tusk sign , which is usually associated with activities related to the mouth (DB #674, #375). The fact that the determinatives used are associated with the mouth and with music supports the idea that *šmꜤ* was a vocal and musical activity.

Ranke notes two Middle Kingdom instances where *šmꜤ* was used as a personal name (*šmꜤt*, CG 20458c, *PN* I, 327.26 and *šmꜤ*, CG 20737c, *PN* I, 327.25). Both references are to women, but neither held any musical titles.

2.I.2 Comparison with Other Languages

Independent evidence of the word's meaning can be obtained by comparing the Egyptian meaning of /*šmꜤ*/ with meanings in other related ancient languages. This comparison can make the nuances of a word clearer. This type of investigation, coupled with a study of the iconography and gestures associated with the word (see below), provides a broader base for interpretation.

Hebrew, Akkadian, and Arabic all use the same root verb *šmꜤ* in ways similar to that of the Egyptian *šmꜤ*. In Hebrew the most basic meaning of the verb *šmꜤ* is "to hear", but can also mean "to make music" (Hickman, 1958: 125; Kolari, 1947: 89-90). Kolari states that the Hebrew verb *šmꜤ* means "schallen lassen" (ibid., 21), "hören lassen" (ibid.: 89), "tönen lassen" (ibid.: 90), or

[1] This term used to be transliterated *kema-t* in the 19th century (e.g., in Mariette's Abydos publications, and in Erman, 1890) but was revised to *šmꜤ* as early as 1910 (Dévaud, 1910: 103ff).

[2] DB ref. # 690.

[3] Some examples of where this occurs: P.Abbott 3 17/18, the Restoration Stela of Tutankhamun line 21, P.Chassinat I, x+2, P.Northumberland I line 11, in the tomb of Tutu at Tell el Amarna-Aten hymn on left entrance wall. Spelling does not seem to vary based on the written medium.

[4] Teeter's argument that the instrument usually called "tambourine" in Egyptological literature is actually a drum since it has no jingles (1993: 238-239, n.1) is being followed here. A similar instrument called a *nadam* is still played in Egypt today (Blackman, 1927: 114).

"klingen lassen" (ibid.: 91). The word is associated with various instruments. A related root also occurs in Akkadian as shemû, with a basic meaning "to hear" (*Chicago Assyrian Dictionary* vol. 13, pt.2, 287-288). The Arabic word for "to hear" is *smʿ*, which, over time, may have undergone a phonetic shift from /*š*/ to /*s*/, but has the same root meanings. Each language has a variant passive participle meaning "one who is heard", which is probably the most basic underlying meaning for the ancient Egyptian word as well.

The Greek form of *šmʿywt* found in the Canopus Decree is Των ἱερῶν Παρθένων "the holy virgins"[5] (Urk. II, 150 Section 27, line 250). This may be why modern translations have read *šmʿyt n Ỉmn* as "virgin of Amun" (Wilkinson, 1883, ii: 107 n. 365). At the opposite end of the spectrum, the title *šmʿyt* has been occasionally translated as concubine or prostitute.[6] Both translations ignore its musical implications. This interpretation may originate from Devéria's use of the word "pallacide", or concubine, in his translation of the term *šmʿyt* for the catalogue of manuscripts in the Louvre (1881, reprint 1980).[7] Even Bonnet states the following about singers in general: "Manche von ihnen, wenn auch keineswegs alle, werden zugleich Pallakiden gewesen sein" (1952: 490, quoting Blackman, 1921: 15). Bonnet never cites any specific evidence of sexual activity or concubinage by this group of women, however. More recently, Naguib asserts that there were *šmʿywt* who were prostitutes or concubines. The evidence offered, however, does not support this assertion (1990: 236; see discussion below).

Perhaps the documented customs of ritual prostitution in Mesopotamia and sacred virginity in Greece and Rome have influenced scholarly interpretations of women's roles and led to the application of those concepts where they do not belong. In fact, there is no basis for associating either sexual activity or celibacy with the title *šmʿyt* (see below).

2.II ICONOGRAPHY AND GESTURES

The study of the iconography and gestures of musicians are a necessary part of any attempt to define the term *šmʿ*. As discussed above, these gestures often occur as determinatives for the word itself. The depiction of these gestures as a part of the musicians' iconography should contribute to a more precise understanding of the word.

In the context of this study there are two gestures that will recur: clapping– both arms held in front of the body with palms together, either straight or slightly bent ; and vocalizing– this gesture may represent calling, reciting, singing, or other vocal activity, where one arm is extended and the other is brought close to the ear. A variant of the latter consists of one hand outstretched while the other hangs at the side, as in the tomb of Kenamun (TT 93, Davies, 1930: pl. XL). Groups of *šmʿywt* are frequently depicted making these two gestures.

The clapping gesture of two outstretched, raised hands is usually interpreted as a way of directing or keeping rhythm (Müller, 1937: 87-90). It frequently appears in drum beating scenes.[8] It is also the characteristic gesture of Meret, a goddess associated with music (Guglielmi, 1991: 18ff; Kees, 1912: 103ff; see also Chapter 3.II). Due to the idiosyncrasies of artistic convention, in some scenes the gesture appears to involve only one arm. In these cases, however, the absence of the other arm and the body's posture make it clear that two arms are meant.[9] The words for some musical activities can also be determined by either Gardiner sign list sign D36 or D41 . Because the spelling of *šmʿ* usually includes the arm sign D36, it was apparently considered unnecessary to use either of these signs as a determinative for the word.

The vocalizing gesture, which positions one hand to the ear and one outstretched, is also known in modern Egyptian singing and recitation (Hickman, 1961: fig. 50; Blackman, 1927: 82, 289).[10] Individuals portrayed in this pose are frequently present in ancient scenes depicting music making and dancing. It is therefore assumed that the gesture represents singing or rhythmic vocalization accompanying music. This gesture occurs in pictures of harpists, clarinetists, and flautists, and it is different in form from the more detailed hand signing and finger positions associated with cheironomy (Guglielmi, 1991: 20, n. 116).[11]

2.III TERMS RELATED TO *ŠMʿ* THAT CLARIFY ITS DEFINITION

It is generally accepted that in addition to the priests there were various singers, musicians, and other employees

[5] There is some discussion as to what is really meant by "holy virgins". To the ancient Greeks, *parthenos* may have merely meant "young woman" to differentiate between married and unmarried women. The Egyptian word *nfrwt* which roughly corresponds to this is defined in P. Westcar as "one who has not yet given birth" and not "one who has not yet had sex". There is no Egyptian word identified as "virgin" (Lyn Green, personal communication).

[6] As Naguib does (1990: 236, n. 239a - erroneously called n. 239b).

[7] E.g., I.3, I.4, II.2, II.4 and others.

[8] See for example at Philae, 2nd pylon in Lepsius *Denkmaeler* Abt IV, Bl. 26; and at Dendera (Manniche 1991a: fig. 38).

[9] See Guglielmi (1991: pl. II and XVI) for evidence that two hands were used in the gesture even when only one is depicted.

[10] This practice is easily understood by trying it; cupping the ear with one hand improves the ability to hear what is being vocalized, and to hear the accompaniment (Brunner-Traut, LÄ, II, 580 cites this action as having an amplifying effect).

[11] Chieronomy gestures can be differentiated from simple gestures because they are meant to direct a specific action, not imply the general activity. They are generally composed of various positions of the individual fingers and the forearm.

who performed the daily tasks necessary to ensure the proper daily functioning of the temple (David, 1981: 17). In scholarship, the terms *ḥsy, ḫnr, dḫn, iḥyt, sššt,* and *sḫmyt* are often ambiguously translated as "musician" without further differentiation. This variety of titles suggests, however, that each was associated with a different activity. In addition, these titles may be found listed together in groups (e.g., the Canopus Decree and P. Westcar), further suggesting that distinct activities are indicated. The terms do have more specific meanings and each must be discussed briefly in order to clarify how they differ from the word *šmꜥ*.

2.III.1 Discussion of *ḥsy*

Until now, the difference between the two words most commonly translated as "singer", namely *ḥsyt* and *šmꜥyt,* has not been clear (Teeter, 1993: 243, n. 88). However, usage of *ḥsy* and *šmꜥ* reveals a subtle difference in meaning between the two words. Although both words refer to types of vocal music, they occur in different contexts and suggest different interpretations.

The word *ḥs* has two related yet separate meanings: "to praise" (*Wb* III, 156-158) and "to sing" (*Wb* III, 164-165, esp. 165.5). It is from this perspective that the problem of inconsistent translations in publications arises. The two meanings are usually orthographically indistinguishable by the Middle Kingdom (Brunner-Traut, 1992: 44) but may occasionally be differentiated by the use of the Gardiner sign (D41)  in contexts meaning singing (Troy, 1986: 88). This distinction, however, is not consistently made.[12] A person designated *ḥsy n* N may therefore be called "singer of N" or "praised/favorite/beloved of N". For example, compare the translations of this formula in Theban tombs 74 and 68. Brack and Brack (1977: 87-88) translate *ḥsyt* as "gelobte" in TT 74 while Seyfried (1991: 122) translates it as "Sängerin" in TT 68. Where *ḥsyt* is followed by *n pꜣ ꜥ n Mwt*, as in TT 68, it is usually rendered "singer" because *ꜥ* can be translated as either "choir" or "domain" (*Wb* I, 159; and, e.g., Piankoff, 1936: 58). The titles in TT 74, however, are more complex. The woman Mutiry was a "singer (or favorite) of Hathor, chantress of Nehemet-away in the midst of Khemenu, chantress of Thoth lord of Khemenu, and lady-in-waiting" (*ḥsyt n Ḥwt-ḥr, šmꜥyt nt Nḥmt ꜥwꜣy ḥrt-ib ḫmnw, šmꜥyt n ḏḥwty nb ḫmnw, ḫkrt nsw*) (Brack and Brack, 1977: 87-88; Whale, 1989: 192-193). Her titles indicate she was a chantress for the gods Thoth and Nehmet-away, and so a case could be made for translating *ḥsy* as either "singer" or "favorite" of Hathor. In scenes representing music the choice between the two translations is usually clear, but, as this example demonstrates, this is not so in titles.[13]

A cursory examination of the use of *ḥsy* suggests that it is more commonly used than *šmꜥ*, especially over a longer period of time. *Ḥsy* is the word used to describe music making in various contexts, especially scenes that involve harpists who sing to their own music, and scenes where singers accompany a harpist or mixed ensemble. The occurrence of the word *ḥsy* in conjunction with scenes depicting harpists and accompanying singers are known from the Old Kingdom, New Kingdom, and Late Period (Manniche, 1991a: figs. 11, 13, 30, 48, 73, pl. 3). The Ramesside tomb chapel of Raia, Overseer of Singers of Ptah (*imy-r ḥsw n Ptḥ*) at Saqqara shows him playing the harp before the god Ptah (Martin, 1985: pl. 22).[14] This supports the idea that *ḥsy* meant singing in accompaniment to a stringed instrument. The scenes in this tomb also demonstrate that *ḥsy* was used in a variety of settings. A number of men in Raia's funeral procession are labeled *ḥsy nfr Ptḥ*. These are probably the men of whom Raia was the overseer.

The word *ḥsy* is additionally used to describe the vocalists who accompany flutists and clarinetists (ibid.: fig. 15, 17, 19). Numerous examples confirm that the word *ḥsy* designates an activity that occurred in conjunction with musical performance involving a variety of instruments. P. Anastasi IV line 12.2-3 (Gardiner, 1937: 47) illustrates that the vocal accompaniment could be to another musician and not simply singing along to one's own playing: *sbꜣ.tw.k (r) ḥsy m-sꜣ wꜣḏni* "you were taught (to) sing with the flute" and *ḥsy m-sꜣ nꜣ-ṯꜣḫ* "sing with the [unknown wooden instrument]".[15] A block from East Karnak (Gohary, 1992: pl. CVII [3]) depicts a group of singers, one playing the lute, labeled *ḥsw*. *Ḥsy* is also seen in the Ramesside tomb of Tjay (TT 23) where a lutist is called *ḥsy n pꜣ ꜥ n Imn* (KRI IV, 114.6-.12).

Women are often identified as *ḥsyt nt Mwt* or *ḥsyt nt Ḥwt-ḥr* (cf., Troy, 1986: 88) where *ḥsyt* is consistently rendered "singer".[16] In most cases where the phrase *ḥsy n* applies to men it is translated as "favored by" or "favorite of" followed by the name of a deity.[17] For example, men are frequently designated *ḥsy n nṯr nfr* or *ḥsy n nb.f*. The

[12] Compare Manniche 1991a: figs. 11 and 30 where music is clearly the context. Fig. 11 consistently uses the arm determinative, but fig. 30 uses instead the man-with-hand-to-mouth in its place.

[13] Documenting such a widely used epithet/title would yield a database as large as the current work. Of course, the women noted in this database are already *šmꜥyt*, so there is every reason to presume that *ḥsy* could have meant musician as well. Yet, where the only title held by a woman was *ḥsy*, or where it appeared in combination with another nonmusical title, there was still the prevalence of using singer as the translation, a situation not true of men to whom *ḥsy* was applied.

[14] Raia's wife was also a *šmꜥyt* (DB #814).

[15] This unknown wooden instrument is discussed in Hoch (1994: n. 266).

[16] There is also an unpublished text in TT 96 that reads *it ḥtp ḥr irt ḥsyt m pr Imn in šmꜥyt n Imn Mryt:* coming in peace in order to praise in the temple of Amun, by the Chantress of Amun, Meryt (DB #273).

[17] Cf. Doxey (1995: 297) and index, where *ḥsy* is consistently rendered "praised by".

exceptions to this translation are the instances where men are actually portrayed making music. There they are called "singer", as in Raia's tomb. When the phrase is applied to women, however, it is most commonly translated as "singer", even when they are not shown holding sistra and are not implicated as musicians in other ways.

The term *ḥsy* is also found used in the phrase *ḥsy(t) n pꜣ ʿ n Mwt*, which can be translated as "singer of the domain of Mut", meaning the goddess' temple complex (Faulkner, 1991: 36). Seyfried (1991: 122), however, refers to *pꜣ ʿ n Mwt* as "the choir of Mut" (see also *Wb* I, 159.16).[18] With either interpretation of *pꜣ ʿ*, it is clear that *ḥsy* should be interpreted as "singer" rather than "favorite". The addition of *pꜣ ʿ* would have been unnecessary to show devotion to the goddess Mut, and the phrase does not occur with any other goddess. The fact that *pꜣ ʿ* does not usually occur paired with other deities supports the interpretation advanced by Seyfried that it refers to a choir.[19]

Clearly, *ḥsy* could be used in secular contexts as well as formal religious ones. Those scenes that use the term *ḥsy* as a description of activity (rather than a title) are mostly secular in nature – entertainment at banquets, and so on. This differs from the contexts where the word *šmʿ* or the title *šmʿyt* appear.

One further point may be relevant. Depictions of male and female *šmʿywt* as individuals are plentiful in tombs and on stelae, but when they are shown performing, they are always in a group. The *ḥsyw(t)*, on the other hand, may be depicted as part of a group of *ḥsyw(t)* or as soloists accompanied only by the playing of his or her own harp.

2.III.2 Discussion of the *ḫnr*

In the past, the term *ḫnr* has been inappropriately translated as "harem", and the women associated with it as concubines. *Wb* III, 297, defines *ḫnr* as a harem and its inhabitants, as does Blackman (1921: 5-16). Preconceptions and the "tendency to islamicize" cultural aspects of ancient Egypt (Nord, 1975: 142) have contributed to the assumptions and generalizations that formerly dominated characterizations of women in ancient Egypt. Recently, this subject has been treated quite extensively.[20] Although the application of the term "harem" has been shown to be completely inaccurate in the common, or modern sense of the word (i.e., a place for the wives and concubines of men to be held in strict seclusion apart from the rest of society [Ward, 1983; Nord, 1981]), the use of the term lingers. Musical troupe, as is now proposed, is the more accurate definition of the word *ḫnr*.[21]

The evidence for harems in the Old and Middle Kingdoms has been largely ruled out by the authors just cited. However, due to the fact that the New Kingdom exhibits a few of the elements that characterize a harem, the term is still widely used and often applied to *ḫnr* and *ipt-nsw* (the latter of which will not be dealt with here).

The New Kingdom use of the term *ḫnr* has not been studied as thoroughly as has its use in the preceding ages, perhaps because the issue of the harem is perceived as complicated due to those elements often associated with a modern harem. The introduction of what has been called New Kingdom "internationalism" brought about diplomatic marriages. Where there were multiple royal wives, especially due to those diplomatic marriages, there probably existed an institution for the women and children of the royal household (Ward, 1983: 68). The royal household was never referred to as a *ḫnr*, but it is clear that the *ḫnr* could be an institution associated with royalty, as evidenced by the administrative titles associated with it. Reiser has shown that the *ḫnr* was involved in business of some kind (1972: Chapter 4). There were members of the royal family who carried the title *wrt ḫnr* (Troy, 1986: 186-187, B1/22-B1/29) among them Ahmose-Nefertari, Tuya (wife of Seti I), Queen Nefertari, Tia (daughter of Tuya), and Bananit I (a daughter of Rameses II).[22] A number of wives and daughters of the 21st Dynasty high priests of Amun also held the title. In fact, during the Third Intermediate Period, the position of the *wrt ḫnrt nt Ỉmn-Rʿ nsw nṯrw* was usually held by the wife or daughter of the High Priest of Amun (Kitchen, 1973: 430f; Lefebvre, 1929: 34 ff).[23] Kitchen hypothesizes that there was an expansion of the office to accommodate more women of "sacerdotal families", and this resulted in the application of the phyle system (1973: 431).

Most of the New Kingdom non-royal women associated with the *ḫnr* were married and had children. There is no evidence for a non-royal harem, nor much clear evidence for polygamy.[24] Women who were part of the *Kheners* of

[18] One would like to be able to render ʿ as "procession", but that translation is not attested.

[19] An exception to this has already been noted in TT 23 where a lutist is called a *ḥsy n pꜣ ʿ n Ỉmn* (KRI IV, 114.6-.12)

[20] Most scholars rely on Nord's 1981 study, which is the best documented and most comprehensive. See also Ward (1983) and Fischer (1976). Fischer translates the term as harem but puts it in the category of singing and dancing, while Ward discusses the many terms commonly translated as harem including *ḫnr*, which he also believes refers to musical entertainment.

[21] See the discussion in Robins (1993b: 148-149).

[22] It is no surprise to learn that the mother, wife, sister, and a daughter of Rameses II all held this title. It seems that the women of Rameses II's family consciously sought to emulate Ahmose-Nefertari, the sole royal woman to hold the title previously. As she was a strong and respected historical figure, the Ramesside line looked to Ahmose-Nefertari in an attempt to link themselves with the pre-Amarna legitimacy (Thausing and Goedicke, 1971: 32).

[23] The wife of Herihor was a *wrt ḫnrwt n Ỉmn-Rʿ* and one daughter was a *šmʿyt n Ỉmn wrt ḫnr n Ḫnsw* (Epigraphic Survey, 1979: pl. 26).

[24] On this controversial topic see Robins (1993b: 64-67), Kanawati (1976), Simpson (1974a), and El-Amir (1964).

specific gods were occasionally members of the family of the high priest of that god. Two women listed in the database demonstrate that situation clearly. Sekhmetnefret (DB #612) was a *šmʿyt n Ỉmn-Rʿ* and a *wrt ḫnrt nt Ỉn-ḥrt* (great one of the Khener of Onuris). She was married to Onuris-mes, High Priest of Onuris. She and her husband are depicted in a Ramesside tomb representation at el Mashayikh (Ockinga and al-Masri, 1988: 11-12). Khatnesu (DB #758), a *šmʿyt n Ỉn-ḥrt* and *nbt pr wrt ḫnrwt n Ỉn-ḥrt* was married to Min-mes High Priest of Onuris, High priest of Shu, *Ỉmy-ist* of Shu and Tefnut, *Wr-mȝʿw* of Ra in Thinis. This Ramesside couple is known from material derived from el Mashayikh and Abydos (Bryan, 1986: 5-30).

The fact that a woman could be a *šmʿyt* of one god and also belong to the *Khener* of another god indicates that the one role was not integral to the other. For example, there does not seem to be any evidence to indicate that Sekhmetnefret (DB #612) was a *šmʿyt* of Amun within the *Khener* of Onuris. However, since there was no special title for a woman who was a member of the Khener, except for the lead woman who was the *wrt*, it may very well be that the women who made up the ranks of a *Khener* were *šmʿywt, ḥsywt*, or sistrum players.

It is perhaps this association of the *šmʿywt* with the god's "harem", however, that has led us to using the labels "concubine" and "prostitute" (as in Naguib, 1990: 236). Due to the frequent association of music in general with sexuality (e.g., the Turin Erotic papyri, which shows musicians engaged in sexual activity, and the relief from Mereruka's mastaba showing his wife playing the harp on their bed) this assumption has gone unchallenged. However, there is no connection between the title *šmʿyt* and any sexual behavior either in literary or epigraphic sources. Similarly, there is no evidence that the *Khener* had any sexual character. Their level of organization, the high status of the members, the fact that many members were married, and the fact that there were female *Kheners* of goddesses (also noted by Nord, 1981: n.10),[25] indicates a function other than sexual service for the *Khener* as an institution.[26]

It is clear that a *Khener* was perceived to be a special kind of entertaining group, probably made up of a variety of vocalists and dancers. For the sake of clarity, the word *ḫnr* will be rendered as *Khener* throughout this work.

[25] See Nefret-Mut (DB #578), the *wrt ḫnr n Nḫbt* from el Kab and Hebwynunes (DB #652) a *wrt ḫnrt n Bȝstt*.

[26] It has been suggested that a *Khener* may be attached to private estates (Ward, 1986: 22). Although Ward cites no evidence for specific musicians being attached to private estates, the following passage from a family archive confirms the existence of at least one such *Khener*. A man, *Pȝ-šri-n-Ptḥ*, states: *iw wn n.i ḫn(r)w nfrw*  "To me belongs a *ḫnr* of beautiful ones". The extended context implies that the king gave him the *ḫnr* as a token of his favor (Reymond, 1981: 143, text 18, line12). For the practice of dropping the "r" in Egyptian see Černý and Groll (1984: 6, section 1.9).

2.III.3 Discussion of the "Rhythm Section" or *šspt dḫn*

Dḫn designates the action of keeping the beat, and *šspt dḫn*, the group of people, often called a choir (*Wb* IV, 533), who direct the rhythm of the music. The individuals, both men and women, are characteristically shown clapping their hands or gesturing with one arm. One well-known example is the image of three men labeled *šspt dḫn* who accompany a harpist and a *Khener* depicted on the "acrobat block" from Hatshepsut's "Red Chapel" (Brunner-Traut, 1992: 52-53). Smith and Redford also translate *dḫn* as "rhythm makers" (1976: fig. 20.38 and pl. 40.4; see also Gohary, 1992: 163) where a rubric appears above a row of five bowed heads on a block from East Karnak.

Representations make it clear that a *šspt dḫn* could be comprised of men or women, and that these individuals might also be *šmʿ(y)w(t)*. Images in the tomb of Menkheperrasonb (TT 86) preserve both a male and a female group labeled respectively *šspt dḫn šmʿw* and *šspt dḫn šmʿwt* (Davies and Davies, 1933: pl. 17). In the tomb of Kenamun (TT 92) the image of three women is labeled *dḫn in šmʿwt*. They are depicted wearing the crossed chest-bands best known from the tomb of Kheruef (TT 192) where dancers are similarly attired, and two of the three extend one arm in a gesture of proclaiming or singing. Their text, "May your images endure in the Great House and in the Temple of Amun eternally" (Davies, 1930: pl. XL), is directed toward a statue of the deceased that is being pulled to the temple.

There is also preserved in TT 109 a scene of a *Khener*, a *šspt dḫn*, and a group of *šmʿwt* who may all be singing in harmony led by the *šspt dḫn* (Lüddeckens, 1943: 48f, abb. 17; and Virey, 1887: 29). This scene does nothing to resolve the question of what specific types of vocalists made up the *dḫn*, since each group is labeled separately. It does, however, illustrate that the different kinds of musicians occasionally worked together.

2.III.4 Discussion of the Sistrum Players: *iḥyt, sḫmyt, sššt, ssty*

These four terms are all defined as "sistrum player" and are not as commonly found as *šmʿyt* or *ḥsyt*.[27] The definitions usually followed are: *sḫm*, "loop sistrum", therefore *sḫmyt*, "sistrum player" (*Wb* IV, 252), and *sššt*, "a naos sistrum" and "to play the sistrum"[28] (*Wb* III, 486-87). Other terms include *iḥyt*, "musician" or "sistrum

[27] It is outside the scope of this research to further define these terms.

[28] For the differentiation between the two kinds of sistra see Troy (1986: 86). A recent paper challenges the common definition of *sḫm*, preferring to translate it as "divine appearance" or "Hathor manifestation", emphasizing its aspect as a divine symbol rather than as an instrument (Reynders, 1998: 1013-1026).

player”[29] (*Wb* I, 121-122), and *ssty*, “sistrum player (?)” (*Wb* IV, 279).

Based on the present research, it is known that a *šmꜥyt* could also hold the title “sistrum player” in one of these forms.[30] Perhaps to the point, all of these cases are derived from Ramesside or later Theban sources. Like *šmꜥyt*, the sistrum player titles are also compounded with the names of deities, usually the names of Amun or Mut, and in one case the whole Theban triad (DB #668, a *sḫmyt n Ỉmn, Mwt, Ḫnsw*). Some of these women also had additional titles such as *ḥsyt* or *wrt ḫnrt*. Women holding the title “sistrum player”, especially *iḥyt*, are far more common in the Late Period, while the title *šmꜥyt* is only rarely encountered.

2.IV CONCLUSIONS

When studied on a representational basis, groups labeled *šmꜥ* enact gestures that imply vocal music and its rhythmic accompaniment by hand clapping, sistrum rattling, or drum beating. Due to the fact that this is an oral and aural phenomenon, a more precise designation (chanting, rhythmic intonation, or melodic singing) is difficult to determine.

Examining numerous scenes and inscriptional passages where the verb *šmꜥ* occurs reveals that the word primarily appears in religious contexts, namely temple settings and funeral processions. *Šmꜥ* is only rarely found in secular contexts. When it does occur in such a context, it is always associated with other musical activities (see, for example, the story of Pepi II and the General,[31] and P. Westcar,[32] discussed here in Sections 4.IV.2 and 4.IV.3).

A recent work on women in ancient Egyptian religious hierarchy, Naguib's *Le Clergé féminin d'Amon Thébain à la 21e dynastie* (1990), puts forth the idea that there were two kinds of *šmꜥyt*: religious and secular. Of the secular type, not dealt with by Naguib, she states “il est évident que ce qualificatif s'appliquait aussi aux filles de joie ou prostitutées et aux courtisanes” (1990: 236). The evidence cited in support of this statement (1990: 236, n.239a – erroneously called 239b in the footnotes) derives from P. Westcar, the tale of Wenamun, and P. Turin 55001.

The tale of King Khufu and the magicians in P.Westcar (Blackman, 1988; Erman, 1890) contains a list of musical activities, not people: *ḥsy, šmꜥ, ḥbt, wꜣg* (line 12.1). In the context of the story, these refer to the noises emitted from a sack of barley left behind by the goddesses who, in the guise of a *Khener*, had assisted in the birth of the future kings. The noises are described as “all that is done for a king”. There is absolutely no sexual connotation to this passage. The activities of the goddesses who change themselves into *ḫn(r)yt* (line 10.1) have no sexual connotation in this story. The women in the story of Sneferu and the boating party from the same papyrus are not *šmꜥywt*, but simply *nfrwt*.[33]

The tale of Wenamun does not mention a *šmꜥyt*, but rather a *ḥsy n Kmt* (Gardiner, 1932:74.5-6 line [2.69]). She entertains Wenamun during his stay with the Tjeker prince. She is ordered to sing for him, and he is exhorted to eat, drink, and relax (“do not let your heart be anxious”). Here also there is no overt reference to sex, although one might be inferred.

P. Turin 55001, or the Turin Erotic Papyrus, does not contain a reference to a *šmꜥyt* but rather a *ḥsyt [n Ḥt-ḥr]* who has just dropped her lyre during a sexual encounter (Omlin, 1973: 70, recto 19). Since the woman is not a *šmꜥyt*, this example does not support Naguib's contention.

Because the references cited by Naguib in support of the *šmꜥywt* being prostitutes are not viable, one must conclude that this line of reasoning is false. There are no further references that could be interpreted in such a way. In fact, secular portrayals of musicians used the word *ḥsy* far more often and consistently than *šmꜥyt*.

The evidence reviewed above reveals that the term *ḥsy* can be used in a variety of ways: as part of religious titles such as *ḥsy nt ḫnw n Ỉmn,* usually translated as “Chantresses of the Residence (or interior) of Amun” (Yoyotte, 1961; Ritner, 1998: 85); as *ḥsy n pꜣ ꜥ n Mwt,* discussed above; as *ỉmy-r ḥsw* as in Raia's case; and as a rubric for musical performances in secular contexts involving wind and stringed instruments and, in one case, sex. It seems to be an all-purpose word indicating singing and music regardless of context.

In contrast, *šmꜥ* appears to have a more limited use, predominantly in sacred contexts such as processions of funerals and divine images and in titles compounded with the name of a god or temple. The few exceptions have already been noted. In addition, *šmꜥ* is most often used in scenes involving percussion: drums, sistra, and clapping hands.[34] The difference is subtle because *ḥsy* can appear in those same contexts alongside *šmꜥ*. *Ḥsy*, however, is

[29] All the *Wörterbuch* examples cited show a person holding a sistrum as part of the word. This probably accounts for it being translated as “sistrum player” more often than “musician”.

[30] Cf., DB #415, 569, 668, 726, 727.

[31] P. Chassinat I, X+2 (pl. 8) line x+8 and x+11,12. Here, *ḥsy, šmꜥ, tiꜣ, gꜣwꜣ* are used in a list of things happening at the court to distract the complainant. *gꜣ* “sing” *Wb* IV, 149; *tiꜣ* “to cry or jubilate” *Wb* Iv, 241. Posener translates this passage “chant des chant[eurs, par la musique] des musiciens, par la claimeur [des acclamateurs et par le sif] flement des sif[fleurs]” and notes that the exact sense of *tiꜣ* and *gꜣwꜣ* are not known (1957: 128 and n.3). Wente prefers the translation “clatter” (Epigraphic Survey, 1980: 71, n. *p*).

[32] On line 12.1 (Erman, 1890: 68; translated kma) *ḥsy, šmꜥ, ḥbt, wꜣg* are used together to describe sounds coming from the sack of barley left behind by the goddesses who posed as a *Khener*. (See Chapter 4.IV.2).

[33] Naguib does not specify where in the text *šmꜥyt* appears. Those episodes are the only two to which she could be referring.

[34] See, for example, the tombs of Kenamun (TT 93) and Kheruef (TT 192).

the word most often used in secular contexts like the Turin Erotic Papyrus, the story of Wenamun, and scenes of music involving stringed and wind instruments.

These differences lead to the conclusion that *šmꜥ* was a specialized kind of vocal music, probably more rhythmic than melodic, based on the prevalence of percussion accompaniment. The term "chantress", which is most often used in English translations of the title *šmꜥyt n Ỉmn*, is more than likely the correct sense of the word.

CHAPTER 3 THE ROLE OF WOMEN AND MUSIC IN CEREMONIES AND PROCESSIONS

"Observe the feast of your god... song, dance and incense are his foods" The Instructions of Any, 3.3-10

3.I INTRODUCTION

Music and dance played an integral role in temple liturgy (Naguib, 1990: 61). Music had symbolic importance and was critical in maintaining *Mꜣꜥt* and restoring balance at times of transition (Naguib, 1990: 61; Sauneron, 1968: 46f). The gods were believed to be fond of music and were frequently described in royal women's epithets as being "pacified by a woman's voice" (Troy, 1986: 192 examples B4/26-30). The Hellenistic historian Chaeremon records that the Egyptian priests sang hymns to their gods three or four times a day as part of the daily ritual (van der Horst, 1982: 69). Many private stelae portray an individual performing directly for his or her god.[1] The *šmꜥywt* are present in scenes that represent part of the daily temple liturgy found in the Festival Hall of Tuthmosis III at Karnak (corridor XL in PM II, 123-124, pl. XII.2). There the king offers to images of the gods and performs sacred rituals. He is accompanied by groups of priests and men and women chanters.

An examination of the representational evidence of the groups of people called *šmꜥw* is necessary in order to define what part these individuals played in ritual and society. Many scenes depict groups of male and female *šmꜥyw(t)* involved in various types of activities, detailed below. One such example is the scenes of Osorkon's *Sed* festival. These scenes are the only representations not dated to the New Kingdom. Thus, generalizations may be limited by the range of this material. As the title is most common in the New Kingdom and Third Intermediate Period, however, this paucity of evidence from other eras is not unexpected.

Processions rather than temple ritual, however, were probably the most common event in which the elite could participate and publicly worship through music.[2] There can be no doubt that women of the New Kingdom and later most commonly served their gods through providing music in these processions. The extensive reliefs depicting the *Opet* festival at Luxor Temple provide representations of celebrants making music and accompanying the barques of the gods. (See Section 3.III.1)

Religious festival processions gained a high degree of importance during the New Kingdom, particularly at Thebes (Spalinger, 1998: 248). Routes were paved, adorned, and equipped with rest stations. Processional routes connected Karnak and Luxor temples with the temples of the west bank, roughly delineating the boundary of "the Domain of Amun" (Kemp, 1989: 210 and Bell, 1997: fig. 65). The Festival of *Opet* and the Beautiful Feast of the Valley, both largely developed during the early New Kingdom, had processional components that followed these routes. Celebratory occasions, when provincial gods traveled from their temples, could also be accompanied by a procession (e.g., Hathor from Dendera, Bleeker, 1973: 84-101). In the Ramesside era, kings and commoners alike relied on oracles with processional components (Faulkner, 1975: 35). All of these processional types included music in which the *šmꜥywt* participated.

In their tombs, some individuals portrayed royal festivals in which they may have taken part during their life, such as the well-known reliefs of the *Sed* festival of Amenhotep III in the tomb of Kheruef (TT 192). Many of the scenes there include dancers, musicians, and wrestlers — entertainment befitting a royal festival — as well as ritualistic activities. Even the daughters (*msw nsw*) of Amenhotep III honor or praise (*swꜣš*) the raising of the *Djed* pillar with the shaking of sistra and *menywt*. Ceremonies involving private individuals could also warrant accompaniment by musicians and dancers. The depiction in the tomb of Kenamun (TT 93) of the statue procession of his image to the local temples and his tomb is an example. These private monuments are a valuable source of information relevant to this study.

3.II IMITATING THE GODDESS: CONNECTIONS TO MERET AND HATHOR

Naguib suggests that the *šmꜥywt,* when performing religious rituals, were identified with musical divinities, especially Meret and Hathor (1990: 237).[3] While Hathor is the recognized goddess of music and dance, Meret has been called "the personification of the priestess as singer" (Troy, 1986: 87-88). The iconography of the goddess Meret is very similar to that of the representations of musicians. The gesture associated with Meret consists of extended, raised arms brought together as if clapping (Guglielmi, 1991: 18ff).[4] It is a common gesture in musical scenes of all types and should be interpreted as a general way to denote vocal and rhythmic music (see Section 2.II).

[1] E.g., BM 22557 and Louvre N 3 657- both of male harpers called *ḥsy*. There is also a beautiful scene from a Memphite tomb showing Raia, the Overseer of Singers of Ptah, performing for a statue of Ptah, presumably in his temple (Robins, 1997: fig. 219). This piece is also discussed in Section 2.III.1.

[2] Assmann has identified processions and daily ritual as the main elements of cultic religion (1991a:105-22; see also Spalinger, 1998: 253 n. 77).

[3] Her evidence is not specific of *šmꜥywt*, but rather the *ḫnr* and general "prêtresses-musiciennes" (Naguib, 1990: Sections II.4.1.5.2 and I.2.1.5.2).

[4] Occasionally only one arm is shown, as in Troy (1986: fig. 60— OK Khufu fragment); see also comments in Section 2.II.

Representations of Meret from the Old Kingdom show her in a vulture headdress with the heraldic plants of Upper and Lower Egypt depicted behind her or nearby.[5] Due to the fact that the vulture headdress was reserved for goddesses and royal women in the Old Kingdom, the Meret figure clearly represents a goddess in these scenes, and not a priestess imitating the goddess.[6] The later iconography appears to have dropped the vulture headdress in favor of a headdress consisting of the plants symbolic of Upper and Lower Egypt.[7] Perhaps this change in iconography indicates that women who are impersonating the goddess are represented. The fact that the *šmꜥywt* and *rwtt* depicted in Osorkon's festival hall wear headdresses similar to Meret's suggests that the musicians were meant to be identified with the deity (Guglielmi, 1991: 20; Naville, 1892: pls. 14.1 and 25.VI).

Meret figures can be seen adorning the barques of the gods and kings. She repeats "(I) come, (I) bring" when she stands before the king in his pavilion (ibid.: 87; Borchardt, 1981: 102; Blackman, 1921: fig. 1), apparently part of a rite that welcomes the king. The Meret figures are also present in symbolic rites associated with the *Sed* festival.[8] There may be a relationship between the presence of Meret at the "announcement" of the king in his *Sed* festival (Guglielmi, 1991: 25-56; Baines, 1985: 252; Borchardt, 1981:102; Kees, 1912: 103ff) and the ubiquitous presence of singers in the *Sed* festival ceremonies. Various sources preserve representations of singers and dancers at the *Sed* festival (see Section 3.III.4), some of whom are called *šmꜥywt*. Perhaps the chantresses imitated the function of Meret by announcing or hailing the king.

Old Kingdom examples of women who are called the "*mrt* singers of Upper and Lower Egypt" are not common, but are known (Fischer, 1989: 12). Their role in temple services was to hail the king and as early as the Fourth Dynasty, these women were under the direction of a male overseer (ibid.). In the Ptolemaic Period they are described as playing the sistrum before the god's face (Guglielmi, 1991: 14; de Rochemonteix and Chassinat, 1987: 341).

The idea of musician-priestesses impersonating Hathor has previously been proposed by Blackman: "The musician-priestesses impersonated a goddess, namely Hathor, and in that capacity were able, as we have seen, to confer divine favors and graces on that divinity's devotees. To such an extent was this impersonation carried that the priestesses in the sun-temple at Heliopolis were actually spoken of as Hathors"(1921: 9, 23). Evidence for this association comes from a Ramesside text commonly referred to as the "Blessing of Ptah".[9] The text describes the *wrw*, or "great ones", of the temple of Ptah and the Hathors (*Ḥwt-ḥrwt*) 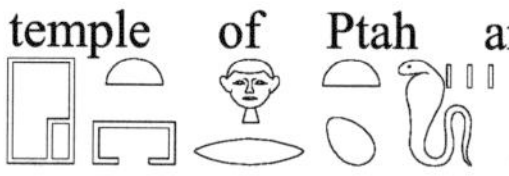 of the temple of Atum who are in festival (*m ḥb*), rejoicing and playing drums on account of seeing the king (KRI II, 264). Iconographic support for this comes from the Ptolemaic Period. Female musicians playing frame drums commonly wear horned headdresses in imitation of Hathor.[10]

It is quite possible to suppose that priestesses of all periods, even where they are not called Merets or Hathors, were engaged in representing the activities of the goddesses. They acclaimed, praised, announced, and appeased the king and the gods with music at public appearances and in more private ritual settings. Hathor was, after all, the goddess of music and dance. An analogous example exists in the case of the women who impersonated Isis and Nephthys in funerary contexts.[11] Similarly, in temple ritual, the *šmꜥywt* may have acted the roles of Meret and Hathor in an effort to recreate a mythic drama reenacted by mortals.

3.III TYPES OF PROCESSIONS AND FESTIVALS

3.III.1 *Opet* festival[12]

The *Opet* festival was a celebration of the renewal of the royal *kꜣ* that took place in the second month of Inundation. A festival of great religious significance, it was the focal point for the "regeneration of the Creator, Amun of Luxor, the rebirth of Amun-Re of Karnak, and the recreation of the cosmos" (Bell, 1997: 157 and n. 91). Its celebration was first recorded by Hatshepsut at Karnak Temple on blocks now reconstructed in the so-called "Red Chapel", once a barque shrine in the temple (Lacau and Chevrier, 1977, vol. II: pl. 9). It seems likely that she developed the rites into what is now recognized as the *Opet* festival (Bell, 1997: 161). The length of time for its celebration varied from reign to reign, but it was undoubtedly the longest feast in the Egyptian calendar, ranging from 11 to 27 days (Bell, 1997: 158).

During the festival a procession of the cult statues of the king, Amun, Mut, and Khonsu moved from Karnak Temple to Luxor Temple, stopping at barque stations along the way, and then returned (Bell, 1997: fig. 65). This procession was accompanied by musicians and dancers, as well as by many kinds of priests and offering

[5] E.g., the fragment from the funerary temple of Khufu (Troy, 1986: fig. 60; Guglielmi, 1991: pl. 1b).
[6] E.g., a fragment from the mortuary temple of Sahure in Borchardt (1981: vol II, bl. 22); also in Guglielmi, (1991: pl. 1a).
[7] E.g., Guglielmi (1991: pl. II) shows a relief of Amenhotep III with twin Merets behind him from his temple at Soleb.
[8] Images are plentiful at Karnak and Luxor (PM II, 567 - index entry for "Meret"). See also the temple of Rameses II at Abydos (Kees, 1912: 272 Nr. 15, pl. II, Abb. 4; Guglielmi, 1991: pls. VIII-IX).
[9] The original of this text by Rameses II is at Abu Simbel, with a copy by Rameses III at Medinet Habu. This text is published by Naville (1882) and KRI II, 258-281.
[10] See *LD* IV, 26 Philae, 2nd pylon; Manniche, 1991a, fig. 38- Dendera.
[11] See Robins (1993b: 164); D'Auria, Lacovara, and Roehrig (1988: 56-57); Spencer (1982: 51); Tosi and Roccati (1971-1972: n. 50053).
[12] This topic is dealt with extensively by Bell (1997: 157-176), Bell (1985: 251-294), and Wolf (1931).

bearers. Originally, the images of the gods were carried on land, but later they were borne by riverboats towed by gangs of men along the banks (Kemp, 1989: 206f). The following descriptions of processions demonstrate that the *šmʿywt* participated in the ceremonies of the *Opet* festival as ritual specialists.

3.III.1.A Opet Reliefs in Luxor Colonnade (PM II, 314 [77-86]; Epigraphic Survey, 1994)

The celebration of the *Opet* festival was one of the major functions of Luxor Temple. It was the mythological center of the living divine king and an important national shrine for his cult (Bell, 1997: 157). Luxor Temple's colonnade hall is decorated with scenes of the *Opet* festival dating mainly to the reigns of Tutankhamun through Seti I. The decorative program in the temple emphasizes the relationship between the divinity of the king and Amun, here as the ithyphallic creator (Bell, 1985: 254, n. 5).

The procession scenes portray groups of singing women and men following the barques of the gods on the riverbank. The men are clearly labeled *šmʿw nty ḥr šmʿ ḥr ḥ3t nṯr pn špsy 'Imn nb nsw t3wy:* "the chanters who are chanting before this noble god, Amun, lord of the Thrones of the Two Lands" (Epigraphic Survey, 1994: pls. 91, 99). Before them is a group of Libyan musicians with clappers called [*ḥsw*] *n ṯmḥw* "[singers] of Libya", and a group of lutists called *ḥsw n ḫpšyt* "singers of Khepeshyt".[13] The words of the songs they sing are also recorded nearby (ibid.: pls. 26 and 97).

Unlabeled[14] female singers and dancers are depicted performing at a gateway, and the presence of the butchers and offering pavilions suggest that the group has arrived at the doors of Luxor Temple (Epigraphic Survey, 1994: pl. 38). The lead woman's leg overlaps the doorway, suggesting that the group is entering the building, or performing in the gateway.[15] The outer courtyards of temples were frequently decorated with *rḫyt* birds, demarking the extent of public access (Wilkinson, 1994: 68, and fig. 49) and doorways were often the sites of popular shrines (Nims, 1957: 79f) since the average person could go no further. Perhaps, then, this was the terminus for the bulk of the entourage, who did not have access to the ceremonial rites. Due to the facts that the women are unlabeled and that they may be either entering the building or stopping at the entryway, it is unclear what ritual status, if any, these women held.

[13] *Ḫpšyt* was a district in the fourth nome of Upper Egypt, near modern El Rizeiqat (Hannig, 1995: 1374).

[14] There seems to be room for a rubric although the scene is rather small and crowded. Damage does not appear to be the cause of the omission.

[15] For more on performers in gateways, kiosks, and porches, see Badawy (1975). Ptolemaic reliefs in temple entrances at Philae (Daumas, 1969: 1-17) the Mut complex, and at Medamud may further indicate that this was where some performances took place.

3.III.1.B Temple of Rameses III at Karnak (PM II, 34 [121])

The south wall of Rameses III's temple at Karnak preserves scenes of an *Opet* procession being met by *šmʿywt* (Epigraphic Survey, 1936, v. II: pl. 88; KRI V, 186-189). The exterior west wall displays scenes of the barques of the gods on the river, with two rows of female worshippers standing on the bank. They hold sistra, *menywt*, and large papyrus umbels. A queen who wears a modius and vulture crown as well as upturned sandals leads the whole company. The two women who immediately follow her also seem to be high ranking, as they are wearing large, round earrings, like the queen, while the rest do not. This first row of celebrants is very orderly. The second row, led by a woman playing a circular frame drum, is characterized by a feeling of movement rather than order.

3.III.1.C The Family of Herihor at Karnak (PM II, 230 [17-18])

An *Opet* procession of the sons and daughters of Herihor led by Herihor's wife, Nedjmet, appears on the west wall of the forecourt of the Temple of Khonsu (Epigraphic Survey, 1979: pl. 26), below the scene of the river procession of the divine barques. The first of the four named daughters is identified as *s3t nsw* [*mrt.f*] *šmʿyt n 'Imn wrt ḫnrt n ḫnsw* [name lost]: "the King's Daughter, His Beloved, Chantress of Amun, Great One of the Khener of Khonsu [name lost]". Her mother, shown above, is the *wrt ḫnrt n 'Imn-Rʿ nsw nṯrw* (Great one of the Khener of Amun-Re, king of the gods), an office commonly held by the wife of the high priest of Amun (Wente, 1967b: 157, n. 16). The daughters carry sistra and bouquets of flowers.

3.III.2 Beautiful Feast of the Valley

The Beautiful Feast of the Valley consisted of a procession of Amun's image from Karnak to the west bank of the Nile, where it stopped at the various mortuary temples of the kings to pay homage. The procession's final west bank destination was the upper terrace of Hatshepsut's mortuary temple. The festival gave families an occasion to gather at the tombs of their dead relatives, where they feasted and watched the procession of the god. Families wanted the deceased to take part in the blessings of the god's presence so they may have taken statues of their loved ones with them along the processional route (Bleeker, 1973: 43). The deceased's image was returned to the tomb, where there were further festivities including singing and a banquet, all for the benefit of the dead person's *k3* (Bleeker, 1967: 137-139; Schott, 1952; Foucart, 1930). Offerings of food and flowers to the divine image became imbued with life-renewing essence, and family members would take these to back to the tomb for the benefit of the deceased (Siliotti, 1996: 111). This popular practice of honoring deceased ancestors at their tombs mirrored the official celebration honoring the dead kings at their mortuary temples (Spalinger, 1998: 251).

One of the earliest depictions of the festival can be found on blocks from the north side of the so-called "Red Chapel" (Bell, 1997: 103). The blocks depict part of the procession to the west. Here the group of women are called *ḫnr n ḥwt nṯr* "the *Khener* of the temple"; the men are designated *šspt dḫn* "choir". They are accompanied by acrobats and a harpist (Lacau and Chevrier, 1977, vol. II: pl. 9).

Although a number of Theban tombs (TT 39, TT 55, TT 77, TT 78, TT 86, TT 112, TT 182)[16] record the words of the song sung by the choirs accompanying the festival, only one, that of Menkheperrasonb (TT 86), identifies the women singing it as *šmᶜywt*. The tomb of Horemhab (TT 78) depicts two such groups of male and female singers along with the words of their song, but they are not explicitly identified as *šmᶜyw(t)* (*Urk.* IV, 1590-1596; Brack and Brack, 1980: 29-30). Horemhab's wife is identified as a "chantress of Amun of Karnak" (*šmᶜyt n Ỉmn-m-ipt-swt*).[17] This aspect of Amun was the principal figure of the Beautiful Feast of the Valley. Perhaps she was a member of one of the choirs that participated in the annual procession.

3.III.2.A The Tombs of Menkheperrasonb; TT 112 and TT 86

Menkheperrasonb's tomb (TT 86) contains representations of both men and women acting as *šmᶜyw(t)* in an offering scene. The women play sistra and *menyt*, while the men clap. The inscription accompanying them consists of praise for the king (Manniche, 1991a: 71-72) as part of the Feast of the Valley procession. The text also mentions the presentation of sistra and *menywt* of Amun in Deir el Bahari (Davies and Davies, 1933: pl. XVII).

In the earlier tomb of Menkheperrasonb (TT 112), there is a scene of four women bearing sistra and *menywt* (Davies and Davies, 1933: pl. XXIV) making an address to the king parallel in content to the one seen in TT 86 (ibid.: 21).[18] Although no titles are indicated, the women depicted here are so similar to those in TT 86 that they may have been *šmᶜywt* as well.

Three men in this tomb of Menkheperrasonb (TT 112) (Davies and Davies, 1933: pl.XVII) are labeled *dḫnt šmᶜw:* "choir of chanters". [19] They hold their arms out in a clapping gesture while the text of their hymn is spelled out before them (ibid.: 14; *Urk.* IV, 935.5-.14). The text of their song makes it clear that these representations depict part of the Beautiful Feast of the Valley procession or festivities (see also Manniche, 1991a: 71-72).

3.III.3 Funerary Contexts

Scenes of funeral processions were a common topic represented in the tombs of ancient Egypt. A description of the funeral procession in the Tale of Sinuhe (see Section 4.IV.1) paints a verbal picture similar to what was visually portrayed on the walls of the tombs. According to Sinuhe's story, a proper funeral included musicians leading the procession, the body being borne on a sledge to the tomb, and dancers waiting at the entrance of the tomb. A fragment of relief from Saqqara (Vandier, 1964, pt. 2: pl. XXI) is one of the liveliest portrayals of such a funerary procession. A group of women dancing and playing circular drums and clappers leads the cortege to the final resting place.

The examples included here are singled out because of the use of the term *šmᶜywt* to denote the group of women who take part in the funerary procession. Many more examples exist where the musicians and mourners are not specifically labeled. Although it may be safe to infer that many of those unidentified individuals were also *šmᶜywt* participating in the rites of burial, only those explicitly identified as such will be discussed.

3.III.3.A The Tomb of Nakhtamun TT 341

Nakhtamun seems to have been a lover of music despite his nonmusical title "Head of the Altar in the Ramesseum". From his tomb come scenes of a harpist and a young lyre-player who has Bes tattoos on her legs. These figures were intended to entertain Nakhtamun for his pleasure in the afterlife (Davies and Gardiner, 1948: pl. XXVIII).

He appears to have had a professional mourner who headed "the ones who wail in front" at his funeral (Davies and Gardiner, 1948: 36, pl. XXVI). The woman who performed this service is identified as *nbt pr, šmᶜyt n Ỉmn-Rᶜ, Rᶜỉꜣ*. She was apparently not a relative, as she is nowhere identified as such and only appears in this scene depicting the funeral procession.[20] Perhaps it was the case that the *šmᶜywt* could hire themselves out for private funerals in addition to their temple duties.

In another scene, Nakhtamun is shown taking part in a ritual at the Ramesseum that consists of making offerings to Sokar on the king's behalf. A troupe of male musicians also participated (Davies and Gardiner, 1948:

[16] For publication information on these tombs, see Appendix D.
[17] DB #287
[18] Similar texts exist in TT 39, TT 182, TT 95, and TT 86.
[19] Three women with the same rubric stand above in the first register.

[20] Professional mourners in Egypt were known from ancient times (Spencer, 1982: 51; Robins, 1993b: 164) up until at least the beginning of this century. Blackman recounts the use of female professional mourners in the villages of Upper Egypt (1927: 109f, 122f). These women accompanied the female family members and friends in the profuse expression of grief: shrieking, screaming, wailing, slapping their own cheeks, crying, waving handkerchiefs, covering their heads and breasts with mud, and making noise.

35, pl. XXIV). The first three men in the row are identified as *sḏm ˁš* or "servants".[21] The last two in the group are *šmˁ n ḥwt wsr-mȝˁt-rˁ stp-n-rˁ, Ỉmn-nsw-niwt,* "Chanter of the Ramesseum, Amun-nesu-niwt" and *šmˁ n Ptḥ-Skr, Nfr-ˁḥˁ* "Chanter of Ptah-Soakr, Nefer-aha". Behind them sit a lutist and a man or boy who claps his hands. The words of the hymn above the seated men implore the god Ptah-Sokar-Osiris to provide for and protect Rameses II.

3.III.3.B The Tomb of Kenamun TT 93

Scenes in this tomb show a procession of people dragging statues of Kenamun to the temples and his tomb (Davies, 1930: pls. XXXIX, XL).[22] A nearby text describes the scene as "accompanying the statues of the Overseer of the Cattle of Amun, Kenamun to the temple [of Amun in Karnak,] to the entrances of the temples [of north and] south in complete peace and to his tomb of the necropolis according to the favor of the king; made by this servant while all his relations, gathered into a crowd, jubilate at the head of them [the statues]" (Davies, 1930: 39, pl. XXXVIII). This rite is accompanied by an entourage of many singers and dancers of both genders and priests who purify the statue with incense. A group of men bear the rubric *ḫbt in šmˁw* "dancing by the *šmˁw*" while a group of women are *dḫn in šmˁwt* "rhythm making by the *šmˁwt*".

Another scene shows a young girl playing the lute while two others serve the young king who sits on the lap of his nurse, Kenamun's mother. The scene is damaged, but another musician can be inferred by traces of a harp finial, which can be seen in the lower left (Davies, 1930: 17, pl. IX). The song of the girls is recorded in the caption above them: *šḫm-ib mȝȝ bw nfr ḥs ḫbt šmˁ ḥˁyt ršwt m ib mȝȝw* [...] *ḥm.f* : "Be entertained at seeing prosperity — singing, dancing, chanting, being joyful with gladness of heart at seeing [...] his Majesty ..."

3.III.3.C The Tomb of Ramose TT 55

Three men labeled *šspwt* [*dḫn*] *nt šmˁ(w)*: "a choir of chanters" (Davies, 1941: pl. XIII) are depicted in the tomb of Ramose. They are dressed in normal short kilts with shaven heads. Their song, recorded in front of them, is a prayer to Amun and the gods of the Underworld. This scene is not part of the funerary procession recorded on the south wall. They flank the entrance to the tomb (the east wall), paired with offering bearers on the opposite side, both beneath scenes of Ramose standing before heaps of offerings. They seem to greet anyone who enters the tomb, similar to the scene described in the Tale of Sinuhe (Section 4.IV.1).

3.III.4 *Sed* Festival

The *Sed* festival was an important ceremony usually held for the reigning king after 30 years of rule, and subsequently more often (Hornung, 1997: 310; Hornung and Staehelin, 1974: 12). The main purpose seems to have been a symbolic renewal of the king's vitality and power. Only fragments of information survive about the totality of rites conducted during the festival, but it is clear that music was an integral part. The depiction of singers and dancers is common in the festival representations of Amenhotep III,[23] Amenhotep IV,[24] and Osorkon II. Earlier representations of the *Sed* festival also include depictions of musicians and dancers in similar poses, but these scenes are outside the temporal focus of this study and the individuals depicted therein were not explicitly called *šmˁywt*.

3.III.4.A The Tomb of Kheruef TT 192

The tomb of Kheruef contains many depictions of musicians and dancers that are an important source of information for interpreting both the *Sed* festival and music in ancient Egypt. On a badly fire-damaged section of the north wall of the west portico there are reliefs depicting both male and female chanters. The content of these scenes is the raising of the *Djed* pillar during the *Sed* festival ceremonies of Amenhotep III. The King and Queen Tiye are followed by princesses who worship Ptah-Sokar-Osiris in the form of the *Djed* pillar by shaking sistra and *menywt* necklaces.

In two registers below this scene groups of vocalists (*ḥsyw* and *šmˁw*), dancers, stick fighters, and offering bearers are depicted participating in the raising of the *Djed* pillar. The first register shows a group of three male *šmˁw* who are chanting an invocation to the god Ptah, the lyrics of which are preserved next to the men[25] (Epigraphic Survey, 1980: 62, pls. 47, 59-63; Fakhry, 1942: 481). The second register has four groups of two women each. The women of the first group play circular frame drums. Their rubric reads *šmˁywt n(t)y ḥr šmˁ ḫft* [*irt irrw*][26] *n sˁḥˁ ḏd*: "Chanters who chant at the time of [performing the ceremonies of] raising the *Djed* pillar". The rest of the women are shown clapping their hands. Presumably all the women join in the men's invocation to Ptah. Behind the *šmˁywt* are four Oasis women (*ḥmwt inw ḥr wḥȝt*) who appear to be dancing and are wearing garments similar to those depicted on acrobatic women

[21] Two of these men may be foreigners (Davies and Gardiner, 1948: 35). Although dressed like Egyptians, they wear cone shaped hats normally associated with Levantine peoples (Manniche, 1991b: 63).

[22] Davies mentions a statue of Kenamun found in situ in the temple of Mut that described the attendance of the female choir (Davies, 1930: 39 n.3). This is incorrect. The statue in question, Cairo 935, makes no reference to a choir (PM II, 262; Benson and Gourlay, 1899: 326-328; Borchardt, 1911-1936, vol. III: 163-164, pl. 158; *Urk.* IV, 1407 [422]).

[23] The *Sed* festival of Amenhotep III is known from both Soleb and TT 192 (Gohary, 1992: 11-18), but detailed information on the Soleb reliefs is not available.

[24] Many blocks with depictions of musicians on them are known from East Karnak (Smith and Redford, 1976; Gohary, 1992), but none have preserved the title or word *šmˁ(yt)* in any form.

[25] The group of *ḥsyw* address a chorus to Sokar.

[26] Restoration of lacuna by Epigraphic Survey (1980: pl. 59).

pictured elsewhere in the tomb. Their rubric states that they were brought for the raising of the *Djed* pillar. The two registers of singers, dancers, and other celebrants were probably meant to be seen as one continuous group taking part in the same scene.

On the southern half of the west portico wall, in the reliefs depicting the towing of the night barque, the princesses are followed by a group of *šmꜥywt* who are chanting and setting the rhythm (Epigraphic Survey, 1980: pl. 45). This scene is badly damaged, but the chantresses seem to be wearing floral crowns, similar to, but more elaborate than those worn by the *šmꜥywt* represented on the blocks depicting Osorkon's *Sed* festival (see below).[27] These women also carry the same gazelle-headed wands as the *šmꜥywt* of Osorkon's reliefs. The proximity of the chantresses to the royal children is important to note: "The royal children (*msw-nsw*) play sistra together with the chantresses of Amun" (Wente, in Epigraphic Survey, 1980: 51-53 and pl. 44-45). Only women of the noblest of families could have been so close to the royal family. One of the chantresses appears to be labeled *snt.f mrt.f* "his sister, his beloved". This may refer to Kheruef's sister as it is believed Kheruef was not married (Wente, in Epigraphic Survey, 1980: 53, note *w*).

3.III.4.B The Festival Hall of Osorkon II

The order of the *Sed* festival scenes found on the blocks from the great temple of Bubastis has been reconstructed in the works of Naville (1892) and Uphill (1965). These blocks show the participation of various musicians, dancers, offering bearers, and supplicants in the *Sed* festival rites. This reconstructed context of scenes is divided into areas that show ceremonies accessible to the general public, and ceremonies that were restricted to ritual personnel. This allows the content of those scenes, namely the musical activities, to be more fully interpreted.

One block fragment shows a group of three women labeled *šmꜥywt* (Naville, 1892: pl. XXV.VI). This block comes from an area depicting private ceremonies (north wall of the inner gateway, wall E; Naville, ibid.; Uphill, 1965: 366). This places the *šmꜥywt* in a restricted ritual context where ordinary citizens were not allowed. The *šmꜥywt* each hold *ꜥnḫ* signs and wear tall, floral headdresses. They also each hold either a gazelle-headed wand or a naos-sistrum (see Wente, 1969: 84) The text to the right of the *šmꜥywt,* and presumably chanted by them, reads "Hail to the festival, hail the festival of Ptah takes place". The text to the left reads: "Horus rises, he has received the two plumes, he is the King Osorkon". This behavior is reminiscent of the function of the goddess Meret (see Section 3.II).

Musicians and dancers are prominent throughout the reliefs, but especially so on the outer face of the entrance, which would have represented a public area (Naville, 1892: pls. I[6], XIII[V], XIV, XVI[10]). Uphill suggests that these upper registers depict a large public reception, such as those seen on the walls of Theban tombs (1965: 381). One scene involving the *šspt dḫn,* however, is located on the innermost face of the gate, wall C, which was reserved for representations of private ceremonies not to be witnessed by the public (Naville, 1892: pl. XL[6]). In various places, groups of male *šspt dḫn* (choir) appear, occasionally leading men who shout *r tꜣ:* "to the ground" (ibid., pl. I[6], XL[6]) or follow men with a giant frame drum (ibid., pl. XL[6], XVI[10]) and in one case they lead an incense bearer (ibid., pl. XIII[V]). These men clearly precede the entourage and announce it.

3.III.5 Divine Appearances

Oracle processions, a god's journey, and the procession of sacred vases are all contexts in which the *šmꜥyw(t)* occur.

3.III.5.A The Tomb of Khonsu TT 31

The scenes in this 19th Dynasty tomb include many references to *šmꜥywt.* Khonsu's mother, wife and daughters were all *šmꜥywt.* Two scenes in particular show the participation of *šmꜥywt* in religious ritual. Scenes portraying the god Montu's journey to Tod depict members of Khonsu's family forming the procession, which includes a number of *šmꜥywt* (Davies and Gardiner, 1948: pl. XII).[28] In the first scene, a group consisting of priests and members of Khonsu's family await the arrival of the god by boat at kiosks that are filled with offerings of food and flowers. One woman is of particular interest. A Priestess of Tjenenet of On (*ḥmt nṯr n Ṯnnt n Ꞽwnw*) named Ru, most likely a daughter of Khonsu and Mutia, dedicates a pile of offerings herself.[29] Her head is shaven like a priest and she wears sandals on her feet. Another figure in the same group is dressed similarly, and therefore is probably also a priestess. One of the three lines of text over the heads of this group of women reads *sꜣt.s ḥmt nṯr* [*ṯnt*[30]] *mꜣꜥt ḫrw*: "her daughter, priestess [Tjenet?], true of voice" and may apply to this last figure.

The second scene (ibid.: pl. XV) involves some of the same women making offerings at a kiosk outside the mortuary temple of Tuthmosis III. On the kiosk is a fragmentary text reading "... *n šmꜥyt n Mwt nbt Ꞽšrw nb(t)*

[27] For information about the headdresses see Wente's note * in Epigraphic Survey (1980: 52).

[28] The group includes Khonsu's mother, wife, and daughters.

[29] The goddess Tjenenet of On was the consort of Montu, and had rooms dedicated to her at the temples of Tod and Armant (Davies and Gardiner, 1948: 14-15).

[30] The name of the individual is worn and difficult to read but may be *Ṯnt*.

t3wy n p3..."[31](of the Chantress of Mut Lady of Isheru, Lady of the Two Lands, of the...) followed by the titulary of the king. Three of them present sistra and flower bouquets while a larger group appears to mourn for the king.[32] The women involved are mainly called chantresses of Montu and Amun in the rubrics above each individual's head, but by their actions, they also seem to have been attached to the funerary cult of Tuthmosis. This may have been due to Khonsu's position as the High Priest of that cult.

Not only do the scenes in this tomb provide information about the participation of women in religious rituals, they also show the influence of a family's cultic ties on the chosen cult affiliations of a younger generation. Since there is no evidence that *šmˁyt* was an inherited title, its prevalence in this family might be attributed to the influence of a family member or members. The men were involved in the cults of Montu, Sobek, and the funerary estates of various deceased kings, while the women were *šmˁywt* of Montu and Amun, in addition to the two priestesses of Tjennenet.

3.III.5.B The Tomb of Amenmose TT 19

A scene in this 19th Dynasty tomb depicts the cult statue of Amenhotep I being carried before tables of offerings and groups of people (Foucart, 1935: pl. XXXII).[33] Since Amenmose was a *ḥm-nṯr* in the cult of "Amenhotep-of-the-forecourt", he would have been intimately involved in this procession. One of the priests in front turns back to the group with a hand over his mouth in the same gesture as the *wˁb* priests depicted on the walls of the *3ḫ-mnw* at Karnak (corridor XL in PM II, 123-124, pl. XII.2). At least one of the women in the procession is identified as a *šmˁyt* (DB # 674). She is depicted as part of a group of women who play sistra, clappers, a drum, and a double reed flute. The group of women was meant to represent acquaintances of Amenmose, but due to the ruined condition of the scenes, only one name and title are preserved. The purpose of this procession was probably oracular.

In another scene where a statue of Ahmose-Nefertari is shown being pulled in a procession outside a temple precinct, two men dressed in long gowns at the head of the group extend their arms in the gesture associated with singing or other vocal recitation (Foucart, 1935: pl. IV).[34] Similar costumes can be seen at Medinet Habu, worn by men leading the Min and Sokar festivals. There they are usually identified as *šspt dḫn*: "choir" or *imy-r ḥsw*: "overseer of singers" (PM II, 498 [93-95] and 499-500 [96-98]; Epigraphic Survey, 1930, v. IV: pl. 197, 203, 209, 226). If the men depicted in this way can be identified as a *šspt dḫn*, and if *šmˁw* made up the *dḫn*,[35] then it is reasonable to assume that wherever there are such depictions the possibility that the men represented might be *šmˁw* must be considered. The unlabeled men in TT 19 are one such case.

3.III.5.C The Tomb of Panehsy TT 16

The tomb of Panehsy preserves an interesting scene of the procession of the sacred vases of Amun (Baud and Drioton, 1928: fig. 16).[36] This ritual is led by priests, who burn incense, and men including Panehsy and his brother Pahesy, who sing. The brothers are both labeled as *šmˁ wdḥw n Imn.*: chanters of the offering table of Amun. This scene clearly depicts a public procession; part of the scene is a representation of the front of the pylon of Karnak outside the temple enclosure in public space.

Elsewhere in the tomb Panehsy is identified as a priest (*ḥm-nṯr*) in the cult of Amenhotep-of-the-forecourt, as was his near contemporary Amenmose in TT 19. Panehsy's title *ḥry šmˁ wdḥw n Imn* ("overseer of the chanters of the offering tables of Amun") suggests that there was a group of *šmˁ n wdḥw n Imn* serving the temple. Although this is a rare title, it is also known from papyrus BM 10052, one of the Tomb Robberies Papyri. There, a man called Hori, the father of a suspect being questioned, is identified as a *šmˁt* (sic) *wdḥw*.[37]

3.III.6 Royal Family Processions

"The royal women participate as sistrum players and singers in the rituals of the gods" (Troy, 1986: 89).

Royal women were known to have held the title *šmˁyt*, but not in large numbers. The exception to this was the family of Rameses II. In addition to many of his daughters (detailed below), a sister[38] named Tia was also a *šmˁyt* (DB # 813; Cooney, 1956: 27). She is known from a number of monuments including a block that is presumed to have come from a chapel at Tanis (now in Toronto, ROM 955.79.2) that shows the mother of Rameses II followed by the well known official Tia, and his wife Tia.[39] The inscription above the wife reads: *nbt*

[31] The title *šmˁyt n Mwt* is surprisingly rare. Only four examples can be cited from the database; DB #30, #434, #550, #672. Three others were *šmˁyt* for the whole Theban triad, Amun, Mut, and Khonsu (DB #120, #664, #704).

[32] It seems clear that the mourning is for the king and not Khonsu as the scene does not involve the funerary rites of Khonsu, but rather the estate of the dead king.

[33] The representation of the statue is now disintegrated, but was seen and documented by Hay (PM, I.1, 1960: 33).

[34] Hannig uses a similar figure to illustrate an *imy-r ḥsw* (1995: 59).

[35] As shown by the rubric *dḫn in šmˁyt* in TT 86 and TT 93 (see Section 2.III.3).

[36] The purpose of this kind of procession is unknown. For discussion of the vessels and the procession see Radwan (1985) and Traunecker (1972).

[37] The feminine "t" is present. More information on this and TT 16 is given in Appendix A.

[38] Cooney has interpreted her relationship to the king as that of a former concubine (Cooney, 1956: 27).

[39] Information on Tia is found in PM III, pt. 2, 654-55; Martin (1983 and 1984); Málek (1974); Helck, (1960, vol. II: 188 n. 143a).

pr šmʿyt n Ỉmn, snt nsw, špswt nsw, ṯỉꜣ: "Mistress of the House, Chantress of Amun, Royal Sister and Noble Favorite of the King, Tia" (Cooney, 1956: 27-28, pl. 51). She is also known from Pi-Ramesse where "the Chantress of Amun of 'great of victories', Royal Sister, Tia" is attested (Kitchen, 1973: 428).[40]

Even when they are not shown taking part in a procession, royal women still included musical epithets in their titulary. A statuette of Ahmose-Nefertari dating to the reign of Rameses II may reflect that queen's interest in music as far back as the beginning of the 18th Dynasty. Her epithets recorded on the piece include *wʿb ʿwy ẖr sššt mrt ḫrw ḥr šmʿw*; "pure of hands carrying the sistra, beloved of voice in chanting" (Berlin 6908: KRI III, 657.9-.10; see also Troy, 1986: 161-162, B4/23).

3.III.6.A Great Court of Rameses II at Luxor Temple (PM II, 308 [28])

The inscription accompanying the scenes of the king is a dedication of the monument to Amun-Re, king of the gods, lord of heaven, chief of his sanctuary [i.e. Luxor temple] (*ḫnty ipt.f*) (KRI II, 606; Abd el-Razik, 1974, 1975). Scenes on the upper portion of the north half of the western wall depict Rameses II with various deities. Queen Nefertari, three nome gods, and some of the royal children appear in a procession depicted in the register below. Eleven daughters can be identified as *šmʿywt*, and the one at the head of the line is a *wrt ḫnr n Ỉmn*. In most cases the names of the daughters and the deities they served are preserved.[41] Three served Hathor in three different manifestations, two served Amun, and one each served Isis, Mut, Sekhmet, Re, and Ptah. The south wall of the pylon also seems to preserve traces of the princes and princesses. Very little remains of the titles and names of the individuals, but they probably represent the same group of people (see PM II, 306 [17]; KRI II, 919-920; Kuentz, 1971: scene 16d). Some of the same princesses are also depicted in the first court of Rameses II's temple at Abydos (PM VI, 3 [13-18]; KRI II, 918-919). Although identified as *šmʿywt* at Luxor, their titles are omitted at Abydos. Perhaps the integral role of Luxor temple in the *Opet* festival influenced the princesses' use of the *šmʿyt* title on this particular monument. As has been shown previously, music played an important and visible part in the *Opet* festivities.

3.III.7 Temple ritual

Included in this category are scenes depicting temple rituals. They may be found on the actual temple walls or in the tomb of a person who participated in the rites.

3.III.7.A The Festival Temple of Tuthmosis III (ꜣḫ-mnw) at Karnak[42]

An east-west corridor (XL in PM II, 123-124, pl. XII.2) of the *ꜣḫ-mnw* contains well preserved reliefs of a procession[43] of *šmʿyw(t)*, and priests (*ḥm-nṯr* and *wʿb*). The scenes occupy the space between two episodes of the king performing rites before statues of the god Amun. Three women *šmʿywt* lead the procession of men that consists of three *šmʿw*, three *wʿb ḥsw,* and a group of eight *ḥm-nṯr* priests bearing vases, vessels, and in one case, a small royal statue. The two groups of *šmʿyw(t)* bear the additional caption *šspt-dḫn* and hold their hands outstretched as if clapping. The *wʿb ḥsw*[44] priests behind them also seem to be vocalizing as they hold one hand to their mouths in the gesture usually associated with speaking (Brunner-Traut, LÄ II, 574 ff). This procession of offerings moves toward the western vignettes of the king offering incense to a statue of Amun, and purifying another statue of Amun with water. The statues stand next to small shrines with *shen* signs on top and a lotus pad or a papyrus umbel growing from them.

The eastern scene is described by Myśliwiec as "extinguishing torches in lakes of milk" (1985: 33, pl. XVI). It consists of the king offering incense and a purifying libation (*snṯr* and *swʿb*) before piles of offerings being presented to a seated figure of Amun, "Lord of Thrones". A *ḥm-nṯr*-priest holding two torches approaches two tubs probably containing milk (Myśliwiec, 1985: 18). Two Nile-god figures seem to act as candelabra (ibid.). This rite may be associated with the Beautiful Feast of the Valley (Myśliwiec, 1985: 18; Altenmüller, LÄ III, 1078-79). However, the presence of light-bearing servants and heaps of food and drink indicate the morning ceremony of the god, conducted at dawn when artificial light would have been necessary.[45] These two offerings are often presented simultaneously, or in immediate succession (Blackman, 1912: 69), exactly as portrayed in the festival hall; on the west side the successive presentation of water and incense is represented, and on the east, the simultaneous presentation of them. If the scenes depicting the *šmʿw* are related to the eastern vignette as well as the western one, it can be deduced that the *šmʿw* participated in both the morning and evening ritual.

[40] The tomb of Tia and Tia is known at Saqqara, and is being excavated by a joint project of the Egypt Exploration Society-Rijksmuseum van Oudheden. She is DB #813.

[41] See also KRI II, 916-921 and Lieblein (1979: 802, #2092) for the names of the princesses.

[42] The building has been associated with the *Sed* festival (Uphill, 1965: 368), but the particular scenes discussed do not seem to have any relation with the *Sed* festival.

[43] Above the complete register described here is another that preserves only the legs of a procession of men going in the opposite direction. They are probably part of the same group as that depicted below them.

[44] The use of the word *wʿb* in this context may be adjectival and not part of a title. It may have been important to distinguish these "pure" singers from the secular kind.

[45] See Sauneron's description of the morning ritual, including the sprinkling of water and purifying with incense (1960: 80-90). Also see Moret (1988: 171) who includes purification with resin and incense in the daily ritual, as well as purification with water.

The inclusion of female and male *šmʿyw(t)* in a procession in close proximity to the king and the cult statue of the god lends weight to their status. They must have been considered ritually pure as were the *wʿb* and *ḥm nṯr* they accompanied. Only priests and other initiates could be so near the image of the god (Spalinger, 1998: 241; Assmann, 1984: 14-16; Bleeker, 1967: 52; Sauneron, 1960: 80-90). Therefore, the *šmʿyw(t)* must have been ritual specialists.

Further evidence of the privileged status of the *smʿywt* lies in a statement about female musicians in the tomb of Kheruef. There, the song sung by female musicians was said to "open the doors of heaven that the god may go forth pure" (Teeter, 1993: 85).[46] It is commonly thought that the doors of the wooden shrines of the gods were called "the doors of heaven" (Bell, 1997: 134). This places the chantresses at the ceremony in which the god's shrine was opened for the daily rites.

3.III.7.B Tomb of Amunhotep-sa-se TT 75

Amunhotep's induction ceremony as the second prophet of Amun is depicted here (Davies, 1923b: 9, pl. XIV). An entourage enters the garden in front of the temple and is greeted by a group of chantresses of Amun, consisting of his wife[47] and three daughters. They carry sistra and *menywt*. Their importance is shown by their larger scale compared with that of the other figures in the entourage. This, however, is probably due to their relationship to the deceased, and not their office. The presence of other people greeting Amunhotep and the event's location just outside the walls of Karnak indicate that this was an official ceremony and not just a family affair.

3.III.7.C Tomb of Min TT 109

The scene under consideration does not clearly depict a procession, but is comprised of three groups of musicians: two female, one male (Virey, 1887: 29; Virey, 1891: 364, fig.1; Lüddeckens, 1943: 49, abb. 17). The top register shows three women holding fly whisks that are labeled with the rubric *ḏd mdw in ḫnryt*: "words spoken by the *Kheneryt*" followed by three lines of text addressed to the deceased. The middle register shows three men with the rubric *šsp dḥn iit m ḥwt nṯr*: "the choir coming from the temple" and three more lines of song. The bottom register contains three women with sistra, the simple label *šmʿ(y)wt,* and a further three lines of text. The other scenes on this wall deal with the offering of vases, incense, and meat by the deceased on behalf of Tuthmosis III (PM I.1.226[3]).[48] This offering and the accompanying musical performance may have been carried out at the mortuary temple of Tuthmosis III. This cannot be ascertained, however, based on the available information.

3.IV CONCLUSIONS

The depictions of *šmʿywt* in diverse ritual contexts demonstrate that they had actual duties and a place in the religious hierarchy. The title was not merely honorific. Although more women than men held the title, men are occasionally identified as *šmʿw*, especially in groups participating in processions and ritual contexts. As named individuals, only a few men can be documented.[49] Nevertheless, this shows that being a chanter or chantress was not a gender specific role. For that reason it cannot be tied to a woman's marital status.

The *šmʿyw(t)*'s association with *wʿb* priests, offering bearers, and other temple personnel in graphic representations demonstrates their relative place in the religious hierarchy. It is clear that this specialized grade of ritualist was an essential part of the daily routine of the temple as well as being necessary for public displays and festivals. They were also an important part of funerary rites carried out by the general populace, and perhaps hired themselves out for those occasions (see Section 3.III.3.A). Since actual service was involved, it seems doubtful that the title was bestowed upon noble women and men as a reward or honorific.

The role of non-royal women in the New Kingdom religious hierarchy seems to have been limited to the performance of music for the gods in some temple services and in processions meant for public viewing. With the new popularity of processions during the New Kingdom, the public had the opportunity to become more involved in state religion, and it seems to have provided the opportunity for more women to participate. Being a *šmʿyt* seems to have been one of the only avenues of service left open to women in an age where the priesthood was becoming exclusive and professionalized (Spalinger, 1998: 245). Perhaps the redirection of women into musical specialization was part of this process.

---

46 This rubric accompanies the scenes of two groups of women seated near the acrobats. A similar scene is also found in the tomb of Antefoker, TT 60 (Davies and Gardiner, 1920: pl. XXIII) which preserves the phrase *wn ʿ3 pt pri nṯr* (opening the doors of heaven that the god may go forth) in association with singers and dancers.

47 She was also a *ḫkrt nsw* (lady-in-waiting).

48 Another scene of musicians exists in the tomb, but is unpublished except for general descriptions by Virey (1887: 31f; 1891: 369-70) and (PM I.1, 227[9]). It is described as an offering scene including a female lutist, flutist, clapper, and dancer as well as a male harpist.

49 For the New Kingdom, only eight men were found who included *šmʿw* among their titles (see Appendix A).

CHAPTER 4 INSCRIPTIONAL EVIDENCE AND LITERARY SOURCES

4.I INTRODUCTION

Šmᶜywt are mentioned in a number of stories, letters, legal documents, and royal decrees. The sources provide evidence for the presence of *šmᶜywt* in a variety of contexts, making it clear that the title was held by a diverse group of women. *Šmᶜywt* are grouped with servants in Tutankhamun's Restoration Stela, with temple personnel in the Canopus Decree, and they are wives and mothers in their correspondence with loved ones. The literary sources give depth to our perceptions of the lives and activities of the *šmᶜywt* because a narrative can paint a more vivid picture of a woman, or group of women, than mere funerary epithets or captions can.

4.II ROYAL DECREES

4.II.1 Tutankhamun's Restoration Stela

> *iw swᶜb.n ḥm.f ᶜnḫ(.w), wḏ3(.w), snb(.w) ḥmw ḥmwt šmᶜw(y)t ḫbywt wn m nḏtyw m pr nsw ip.tw b3kw.sn*[1] *r ᶜḥ r pr-ḥḏ n nb t3wy* (*Urk.* IV, 2030.6-8; Bennett, 1939: 10, line 22 of text).

> His majesty, l.p.h., has purified/consecrated men and women servants, chantresses and dancers, who are as dependents in the house of the king; and their work/wages are to be charged to the palace, and to the treasury of the lord of the two lands.

In the decree, the king declared his intentions concerning the restoration of the temples. He ordered new images of the gods and endowed the temples with property and priests. The consecration of servants, chanters, and dancers falls into the same category of endowment. According to the decree, their wages were to be charged to the palace as a personal donation of the king. Because the *šmᶜw(y)t* are listed with servants (*ḥmw, ḥmwt*) and not with the priests mentioned in the preceding portion of the text (line 17), it seems likely that their status was considered closer to that of a servant than that of a priest, even though evidence presented elsewhere in this study demonstrates that the *šmᶜywt* enjoyed a certain amount of prestige and were of a higher social class than servants would have been.

[1]The use of the term *b3kw* here fits the sense of the word "wages" (*Wb* I, 428; Leprohon, 1985: 99) or "rations" (Bleiberg, 1988: 163).

4.II.2 Canopus Decree

In 238 B.C., a synod of priests issued the Canopus Decree honoring Ptolemy III and his Queen, Berenice. In it they set up a fifth phyle of priests and also arranged for the postmortem deification of Ptolemy III's daughter, the princess Berenice. The section detailing the cult activities to be performed in honor of the princess contains a reference to the *šmᶜywt*, who in the Greek text are called ἱερῶν παρθένον: "holy virgins".

> When the early corn comes up, the *šmᶜywt* should praise the deified princess and honor her image with jewelry (Urk. II, 150.10ff; line 250; Spiegelberg, 1922: 75).

This quote defines the role of the *šmᶜywt* in a specific religious service. It demonstrates that those who held the title had actual responsibilities, implying that even as late as the Ptolemaic Period the title had not entirely become an honorific. The text following the one just quoted (Urk. II, 151.5ff) deals with the *ḥsyw* who are instructed to sing daily in honor of the *k3* of the princess. The assignment of two different activities to individuals holding two different titles is indicative of the differentiation between the titles *ḥsywt* and *šmᶜywt* (as discussed in Sections 2.III and 2.IV). This decree, along with two references in the database (DB #427, 662), constitute the entire corpus of available evidence for the title *šmᶜyt* during the Ptolemaic Period.

4.III LEGAL AND ADMINISTRATIVE DOCUMENTS[2]

4.III.1 P. Berlin 10021

This Middle Kingdom document from Illahun appears to have been an administrative list of individuals and contains a reference to a *šmᶜyt* named *S3-tp-iḥw* who was in the *ḫnrt* of Illahun (Scharff, 1924: autographed text 9, line 5). If *ḫnrt* here refers to an institution whose activities included music (as proposed in Chapter 2), then this example shows that *šmᶜywt* held positions within it.[3]

4.III.2 Amarah west stela

This Ramesside text was inscribed on a sandstone stela that was found in the temple at Amarah (Fairman, 1938). It is an agreement in which a mother and her son renounce all claims to the property of the boy's father in favor of her daughter, a *šmᶜyt n Ḫnm ỉry-tḫ* (DB #513), on the condition that she look after her mother, a *šmᶜyt n*

[2] It is interesting to note that there are no *šmᶜywt* mentioned in the Wilbour Papyrus. The common designation *ᶜnḫ.t n niwt* seems to be the only title used for women in this document.

[3] An alternate translation for *ḫnrt* is "workhouse" or "prison" (Ward, 1986, 153 and 1983, 71, n. 29).

Ḥr, nb Miꜥm, TꜢ-mḥyt (DB #514) in her old age.[4] This property was extensive and included male and female servants, fields, pastures, and trees and was originally meant to be passed on from father to son. The sides of the stela carry a curse against anyone who disputes the agreement (Fairman, 1938: 155). The lunette scene shows the dedicator, the son, worshipping Amun in ram form (ibid.: pl. 11.3).[5] The relevance of this text to the present study is that it provides additional evidence for the participation of the *šmꜥywt* in local cults. Amarah is in Nubia, and accordingly, the gods whom mother and daughter served, Khnum and Horus of Aniba, were gods of the south.

4.III.3 Tomb Robberies Papyri

In the accounts of the trials associated with the tomb robberies of the 20th Dynasty, the inspection of the tombs of four *šmꜥywt n pr dwꜢt nṯr n Ỉmn-rꜥ nsw nṯrw* (chantresses of the domain of the divine adoratrice of Amun Re, king of the gods) is related (Peet, 1930: P. Abbott 3, 17-18; KRI VI, 468-481).[6] They are included at the end of a list of royal tombs that were searched as well. These *šmꜥywt* may be regarded as an independent group in the employ of the Divine Adoratrice (Peet, 1930: 48). No other *šmꜥywt* associated with the office of the divine adoratrice are known.

In a separate account of the tomb robberies, P. British Museum 10052 (KRI VI, 767-803) provides a further attestation of the title. A list of individuals examined in this matter includes the name of one of the suspects' fathers, a *šmꜥt* (sic) *n wḏḥw, Ḥri* (Chanter of the Offering Table, Hori).[7]

4.III.4 Adoption Papyrus

The text of the Adoption Papyrus dates to the reign of Ramesses XI.[8] Naunefer,[9] a chantress of Seth of Spermeru, and her husband, the Stablemaster Nebnefer, had this document drafted in order to legally adopt her as his heir, thereby giving her explicit rights of inheritance over and above the claims of any other relative, especially his sisters and brothers. The mere fact that a legal document was drawn up to protect the wishes of a man and his wife concerning their property suggests that this property was of some consequence.

Seventeen years later an addition was made to this document. The new clause involved the adoption of the three children of a slave the couple had purchased together. The adoption made them freemen. She also adopted her younger brother, Padiu, as a son. This may have been motivated by the fact that he married one of the aforementioned slave's children who was adopted in the same document. Perhaps because Padiu was biologically related to her, Naunefer reserved for him role of executor of the will over the other three.

Two of the witnesses to the second part were the *šmꜥyt n Stḫ, TꜢy-ḥryt,* and the *šmꜥyt n Nmty, Tnt-nbt-ḥwt.*[10] They are listed alongside the names of a stablemaster, a farmer, and a woman with no title. The witnesses of the first part were four stablemasters, a Sherden and his wife, and Nebnefer's sister. The variety of witnesses, from stable masters to a woman with no title, reveals no specific pattern for choosing witnesses. The witnesses may have been people with whom the couple were in regular contact, namely their neighbors or friends.

The location of the family's residence in Middle Egypt, the man's title, and the presence of many military men as witnesses to the document, suggest that this was a military family resettled as part of a military pension. There are two possibilities for the wife's attachment to the local cult. Nebnefer may have married a local woman after arriving there, or his wife may have become active in the local cult after moving there. Both options demonstrate that being involved with the local cult was part of being in the elite class of society during the Ramesside era. It seems that the women wished to participate in whatever institution was socially and economically powerful in their area.

This example also demonstrates that a woman could be a *šmꜥyt* without being a member of the hereditary aristocracy. Her husband belonged to that portion of the middle class where men were not courtiers, but were important enough to make a comfortable living and amass sufficient wealth to pass on to their heirs.

4.IV STORIES

4.IV.1 The Tale of Sinuhe, P. Berlin 3022

The story of Sinuhe provides a description of a group of *šmꜥywt*[11] that is helpful for determining in which types of ritual settings they were present (P. Berlin 3022, line 194;

[4] The legal aspects of this document are dealt with by Théodoridès (1964: 45ff).

[5] See also Helck (1960: 239).

[6] The location of these tombs is unknown, but they are now suspected to be in the Dra Abu el Naga region (Graefe, 1981, vol. 2: 48).

[7] For *šmꜥ n wḏḥw*, see Traunecker (1972). See also Appendix A dealing with the men in TT 16 and TT 19 who held the title *šmꜥ n wḏḥw*.

[8] The main publication is Gardiner (1940: 23-29); see also discussions by Eyre (1992: 207-221), Cruz-Uribe (1988: 220-223), and Allam (1990, 189-191).

[9] Her name is also spelled Rennefer. This alternate spelling is commented on by Eyre (1992: 208) and Groll (1984: 61).

[10] For another example of a *šmꜥyt* acting as a witness to a legal proceeding, this time an oracular judgment, see *LRL*, 31, Wente (1967a: 199). There, a *šmꜥyt n Ỉmn* and a scribe witness a decision made by the oracle of Khnum.

[11] The reference is plainly to a plural group, and not a single man as implied by Ward (1982, #1514). Text B appears to refer only to men because of the absence of the feminine *t*,  and any female determinative. This may, however, be a peculiarity of the hieratic text. The Ashmolean version of the text reads  (Barns, 1952: vs. 16).

Koch, 1990: 62). In the last part of the story, Sinuhe receives a message from the King asking him to return to Egypt. He reminds Sinuhe of the necessity of a proper Egyptian burial, which includes a funerary procession. The relevant portion of the text describes an ox-drawn hearse led by the chantresses and chanters. When the cortege arrives, *Muu-* dancers perform at the entrance of the tomb and offerings are made.

4.IV.2 P. Westcar, P. Berlin 3033

In one story recorded in P. Westcar, the verb *šmʿ* is used in a list of terms describing the noise emanating from the sack of barley left behind by goddesses who had disguised themselves as *ḫnryt* ("entertainers of the *Khener*") (Blackman, 1988: 15; Erman, 1890: 68). *Ḥsi, šmʿ, ḫbt, wꜣg* are the terms used to describe these noises which were stated to be "all that is done for a king". Presumably these were the activities performed by the *Khener*, since they were the ones who left behind the sack of barley.

> *ʿḥʿ.n sḏm.n.s ḫrw ḥsi šmʿ ḫbi.t wꜣg irr.t nb.t n nsw m tꜣ ʿ.t* (line 12.1)
> Then she heard the noise of music-making, chanting, dancing, and jubilation (?), all the things usually done for a king, in the room.

Here again is an example of the words *ḥsi* and *šmʿ* apparently used together to indicate different types of vocal music. Since the activities are described as "what is done for a king", it would seem that *ḥsyw* and *šmʿw* were employed by the palace. This assumption is further supported by the story of Nefer-ka-re and the General.

4.IV.3 Nefer-ka-re and the General

Different parts of this story are known from two New Kingdom tablets[12] and are also recorded on P. Chassinat I (Louvre n. E 25351) which may date to the 25th Dynasty (Posener, 1957: 120-121). According to the story, a complainant who goes to make his case at King Nefer-ka-re's court, is distracted by the activity there, namely the commotion of singing singers (*ḥsy ḥsyw*), chanting chanters (*šmʿ šmʿw*), screaming screamers (*tiꜣ tiꜣw*),[13] and whistling whistlers (*gꜣwꜣ gꜣwꜣw*)[14] (Posener, 1957: 126,128, P Chassinat I, x + 2). In fact, it is so impossible to be heard that the complainant begins to cry [and tear at his hair?]. The text is quite broken in this initial section, but the extant portion suggests that the musicians have been employed as an intentional distraction. Unfortunately, the text breaks here. The use of two different words in this passage of the story demonstrates that there were two different kinds of performance activity associated with the words *šmʿ* and *ḥsy*. Both of the groups of people who held these titles were apparently employed in the palace for secular purposes.

4.V PRAYERS[15]

4.V.1 Bankes Stela No. 3

A stela dedicated during the reign of Ramesses II associates yet another goddess, besides Hathor and Meret, with music. Here the goddess Mut is invoked. A prayer to her that comprises the body of the text reads: "Giving praise to Mut, mistress of heaven and mistress of the house of Amun, the hand that carries the sistrum, sweet of voice. Chantresses, content your heart with all she says, [...] at the fore of the heart. May she give life, prosperity, health, intelligence, favor, and love to the *kꜣ* of the scribe in the place of truth, Ramose, revered with the great god" (Černý, 1958: n.3; KRI III, 619-620).[16] Since the word *ḥsy* is much more commonly associated with this goddess, as in the title *ḥsyt n pꜣ ʿ n Mwt* (discussed in Section 2.III.1), it is interesting that here it is the *šmʿywt* who are mentioned as being in the service of the goddess.

4.V.2 Amarna Hymn to the Aten

The tombs of three nobles at el Amarna preserve a hymn dedicated to the Aten.[17] A passage in the hymn describing the activities taking place in the Court of the House of Benben confirms that singing and music were part of the cult of the Aten.[18]

> *di.n.k stwt.k [...] m ḥb sḏfw sḥḏ.k sw ḥsw šmʿ(w) nhmw ršwt m wsḫt n ḥwt bnbn ḥwt nṯr.k m ꜣḫt-itn st mꜣʿt...* (line 9-111)
> When you give your rays [every land] is in festival and is provisioned when you illuminate it; singers and chanters shout with joy in the court of the Benben house and your temple in Akhet-aten, place of truth... (Davies, 1908, v.6: pl. XVI, lines 9-11).

---

[12] T. Oriental Institute #13539 and T. IFAO (no number).

[13] *tiꜣ* has also been translated as "clatter" by Wente in Epigraphic Survey (1980: 71, n. p). Parkinson renders it "acclamation" (1991:54-56).

[14] Or is this a misspelling of *wꜣg* as seen in P. Westcar above? Neither have a clear translation.

[15] In Coffin Text Spell 301 (as seen in B3L and B1L), the reading *pr šmʿtt* [] may be a mistake. "I have passed by the house of the singer, and it was an *ibꜣyt*-bird which brought you to me ..." (de Buck, 1951, vol. 4; Faulkner, 1973, vol. 1: 221). Another text of spell 301 (L1Li) has a variant reading *pr nsw*. Spell 301 corresponds to BD 76, in which *šmʿtt* is consistently replaced by *pr nsw*, "the house of the king" or "palace" (Allen, 1974; Faulkner, 1972). A reading of *pr-nsw* is favored, if only because it makes more sense. *Pr-šmʿtt* is not known in the Pyramid texts, nor is it present in the Book of the Dead.

[16] Ramose has been identified as the owner of three tombs at Gurnah; TT 7, TT 212, TT 250 (PM I.1, 309).

[17] The tombs are those of Mahu, Tutu, and Meryra at Tell el Amarna (Davies, 1908, v. 6: pl. XVI, and 1906, vol. 4: 28f). Minor variations occur in each text.

[18] For a good summary of musical activity in the Amarna era, see Manniche, 1991b and Leprohon in Redford, 1988, 49.

It is evident that musicians continued to be used for religious purposes, even during the religious reformations of Akhenaten, and are a prominent feature of the Amarna cult activities. Although most of the graphic evidence for the participation of musicians in the cult of the Aten does not identify the individuals or groups by title, some information does exist. For example, one block confirms the presence of the *šmᶜywt* at the Aten temple of Karnak (Smith and Redford, 1976: fig. 20.35).

4.VI LETTERS

A number of extant letters from the Ramesside Period are either addressed to or sent by *šmᶜywt*.[19] The content of the letters is usually mundane — an inquiry after someone's health, instructions for a business transaction, and other personal concerns. They provide glimpses into the real-life situations of the chantress and her family. Here she can be seen in her true social context, and not one artificially created by the traditional, idealized funerary requirements of the tomb or stela.

It should be noted that the women in these letters chose to be identified by their title, and not simply by name or relationship, even when the recipient was a relative. This reflects a degree of pride in and status conferred by the title that would not be expected if it were simply an empty designation.

The existence of potentially literate *šmᶜywt* has been documented by Bryan in her work on female literacy (1985, passim).[20] Four of the five Theban women documented with scribal equipment under their chairs were *šmᶜwyt*. Similarly, most of the women encountered in this section on letters were from the wealthy, Theban middle class whose male family members were scribes and priests. They could have had access to writing instruction, and they were often responsible for business dealings, as is shown in two of the letters[21] detailed in Appendix C. These letters illustrate the capacity women had for acting on others' behalf in business matters, which may have necessitated the ability to read. The writer of the letters, Nesamenope, must have known men who could have carried out his wishes, but he trusted two different women to act in his place.

Moreover, in their role as *šmᶜwyt* they were engaged in cult activities that would have required instruction and perhaps a sort of apprenticeship to receive the requisite knowledge of rites and ceremonies. Musical notation did not exist before the Ptolemaic Period, but a written script of the songs used in various rituals would have been useful in this instruction. Although Egypt had a strong oral tradition, the homogeneity among the recorded texts of the Beautiful Feast of the Valley hymn (Manniche, 1988: 30) suggests that the words to the song may have been transcribed in order to be passed on from one generation to the next.

Evidence for the written transmission of hymns does not appear until the Ptolemaic Period. The religious festivals in Alexandria during this era must have required that at least some women be literate, for female choirs had to be able to read words and musical notation (Pomeroy, 1984: 59 see also 20, 48). During the Ptolemaic Period, royal women were not only literate, but patrons of literature. The education of the princesses led to the opportunity for court women to be educated as well (ibid.: 59).[22] Although this situation describes the Ptolemaic court, it might be reasonable to assume that noble women of the Pharaonic era also enjoyed the same opportunity.

4.VI.1 Letters concerning the family of Butehamon

The series of letters concerning the Scribe Butehamon and his father Thutmose are a good source of information about the life of one family that included *šmᶜywt*. Of the extant letters relating to Butehamon, he wrote five, 11 others were addressed to him, and he is named as a third person in five others.[23] The main correspondence is between him and his father. The two women mentioned most often are Shedemdua and Hemisheri, possibly a second wife and a sister in-law respectively of Butehamon (Niwiński, 1984: 143). It is also possible that these two women were the second wives of Butehamon and his father. Not enough evidence exists, however, to further clarify their relationships. Shedemdua and Hemisheri are most often found addressed along with Butehamon when he is in Thebes. In the one letter where Butehamon was absent from Thebes (*LRL* 8), they are addressed in the care of Thutmose. Another woman, the Chantress of Amun Akhtay, is known to have been a wife of Butehamon who predeceased him (Bierbrier, 1982b: 36) and is not mentioned in these letters.

The scribe Butehamon is a well-known figure from Deir el Medina. He lived at the end of the 20th Dynasty and the beginning of the 21st. Bierbrier has placed him in the family of the Scribe Amennakht whose descendants can be traced for six generations at Deir el Medina (1975: 39ff). They were an established scribal family, with a history of holding the title "Scribe of the Necropolis" (*sš pꜣ ḫr*) dating back to the reign of Ramesses III. Butehamon was one of those responsible for the reburial of the royal mummies in the Deir el Bahari cache after the civil unrest and the rise to prominence of the High Priesthood of Amun in the early 21st Dynasty (Bierbrier, 1982b: 121). Butehamon's house at Medinet Habu, where the Deir el Medina villagers relocated because of

[19] See Appendix C.
[20] Women were depicted with scribal equipment under their chairs in Theban tombs 55, 69, 147, and 162.
[21] *LRL* 37- P. Geneva D191 (Wente, 1967a: 71-74 and 1990: 174-75) and *LRL* 36- P. British Museum 10412 (Wente, 1967a, 70-71 and 1990: 175-76).
[22] See also Cole (1981: 219-245).
[23] Letters dealing with Butehamun and the women frequently mentioned in conjunction with him are briefly summarized in Appendix C.

war with Nubia and Libyan raiders, was wealthy enough to have a stone-columned central hall (ibid.: fig. 80).

Since Butehamon's quality of life is known, considerably more is known about the lifestyle of Shedemdua and Hemisheri than most other women of the period. Although Butehamon's family were not from the hereditary nobility, they epitomize the wealthy middle class. In general, the picture these letters paint is one of close family ties. Concern for the welfare of the women and children is always expressed, and the addressees are always reassured concerning the condition of the writer. Other villagers are also exhorted to take care of them in the absence of Butehamon or Thutmose (*LRL* 7 and *LRL* 31).

4.VI.2 Letters concerning Herere

A series of letters concerning a woman named Herere[24] illuminates the state of unrest in Thebes at the time when Butehamon and Thutmose were corresponding. Herere's activities recorded in these letters indicate a level of importance and personal power, possibly derived from her marriage to the High Priest of Amun Piankh (who is referred to as "general" [*imy-r mšᶜ*] in *LRL* 14 and *LRL* 17). She conducts military business for her husband in Thebes (*LRL* 30) and accompanies him to Elephantine on campaign (*LRL* 38). In *LRL* 38 and 39 she also takes on the role of administrator, making sure that people do as they have been ordered to, namely, give rations to the necropolis workmen. Her titles *wrt ḫnr n Ỉmn-rᶜ nsw nṯrw*[25] and *šmᶜyt n Ỉmn-rᶜ* alone do not suggest such secular power. However, one may assume that the status these titles conferred commanded respect because she uses them regularly to identify herself in her correspondence. She never refers to herself as the wife of the General Piankh.

4.VII CONCLUSIONS

The evidence discussed above allows a few important points to be made. The difference between the terms *ḥsy* and *šmᶜ* has been discussed in Chapter 2, and many of the examples here support the conclusion made there that the two titles denote different activities and therefore the translation "singer" for both of them is inaccurate.

The evidence cited here also indicates the classes represented by the women who held the title. Their social status is varied, ranging from the wife of General Piankh down to the wives of provincial landowners and Deir el Medina villagers. They worked in the palace and in the temple. *Šmᶜywt* are also demographically dispersed throughout the country, from Amarah West in Nubia to Pi-Ramesses in the Delta, and they served the full range of local deities. The common ground these women shared was access to wealth. Some were wealthier than others, but the minimum requirement seems to have been belonging to a family that held property.

[24] Goff (1979: 53), Bierbrier (1973: 311), and Kitchen (1973: 45) have refuted the suggestion that she was the mother of Nedjmet, Herihor's wife.

[25] Here there is some support for Wente's theory that the title *wrt ḫnr n Ỉmn* was the prerogative of the wife, sister, or daughter of the high priest (1967a: 157 n. 16) since Piankh was the High Priest of Amun.

CHAPTER 5 HISTORICAL DEVELOPMENT OF THE TITLE *ŠMʿYT*

5.I INTRODUCTION

The preceding chapters have, for the most part, examined the context and activities of impersonal groups of *šmʿyw*(*t*). Now that the generalities of the title have been presented, specific women may be discussed. The database constructed for this study has been a useful tool for sorting the 860 women examined, and grouping them into meaningful data sets, including a chronological examination.

After considering the evidence from the many attestations of *šmʿywt*, it is clear that the title underwent changes in status from the earliest Middle Kingdom attestations through the Ptolemaic Period. What social and historical conditions affected the title's use? Why did the title appear to become commonplace in the early New Kingdom, with a noticeable increase in the numbers of women holding the title from the 19th through 21st Dynasties? The answers must not be sought in a single theory or model, for societal forces are multifaceted.

It is apparent that changes in administrative titles indicate larger historical developments (Kemp, 1983: 107-8). The application of this concept need not be restricted to the context of the male administrative structure to which Kemp was referring. The origin and development of the title *šmʿyt* in the Middle Kingdom and its widespread use thereafter can be seen as part of historical developments and social changes that shaped each era.

Non-royal women's titles from the New Kingdom and later dynasties are characterized by roles that pertain to music and music making. The early New Kingdom marks the start of a trend toward a more specialized, visible, and accessible role in religion for women of wealthy families than had been previously available to them during the Middle Kingdom. For a time the title *šmʿyt* was quite common. This trend continued through the 19th Dynasty and into the Third Intermediate Period where there are significant increases in the number of documented cases of women who held the title *šmʿyt*. Afterwards, however, there appears to have been a sharp decline in the title's usage. The historical context behind the evolution of the title over time is explored and supported by data from the database.

5.II MIDDLE KINGDOM ATTESTATIONS

Before examining the material that dates to the New Kingdom or later, the few cases that date to the Middle Kingdom and Second Intermediate Period must be dealt with.[1]

5.II.1. A late 12th Dynasty statue excavated at Saqqara in the valley temple of Unas, a king of the 5th Dynasty, bears the name and titles of a man from Memphis: *imy-r pr-ḥsb it mḥy m ʿnḫ-tꜣwy šmʿw n Ptḥ rsy inb.f nb tꜣwy, Sr-mꜣʿt iri n Ḫty*: Steward of the Granary of Lower Egyptian Barley in Memphis, Chanter of Ptah- South-of-his-wall, Lord of the Two Lands, Sermaat, born of Kety (Ward, 1982: #164 and #1515; Moussa and Altenmüller, 1975: 94). The masculine title *šmʿw n Ptḥ* is not otherwise known, but a similar title, *ḥry šmʿw n pr Ptḥ,* (supervisor of chanters of the temple of Ptah) dates to the reign of Amenhotep III (Moussa and Altenmüller, 1975: 95).

5.II.2. In the story of Sinuhe (text B 194), a description of an Egyptian funeral contains a reference to a group[2] of *šmʿw*  who are followed by the *Muu*-dancers and offering bearers (Ward, 1982: #1514; see also Section 4.IV.1).

5.II.3-4. A late 12th Dynasty stela in Cairo (CG 20216) from the northern necropolis at Abydos, [3] Mariette's "cemetery of singers", mentions one man and one woman who held the title (Ward, 1982, #1514,#1516). Although the placement of the hieroglyphs makes it difficult to determine to whom on the stela the titles apply, the spelling and determinatives of the two instances are different, suggesting a gender distinction was intended. The first man is *šmʿw Sbk-sʿnḫ* (the Chanter Sobek-sankh). The feminine title *šmʿyt,* mistakenly written in front of the man following Sobek-sankh, may apply to the woman after him who is referred to as the *nbt pr, Bby* (Lady of the House Beby) (Mariette, 1880: n. 986; Lange and Schäfer, 1902, vol I: 238f, vol IV: pl. XVII).

5.II.5. Another late 12th Dynasty stela from Abydos (CG 20142) mentions a *šmʿyt* named Senet-ankh (DB #580). The *wʿb n Wp-wꜣwt Nfrw* (*Wʿb*-priest of Wepwawet, Nefru) named on the stela may have been her husband or son (Mariette, 1880: n. 909; Lange and Schäfer, 1902, vol. I: 167f, and vol. IV: pl. XIII; Ward, 1982: # 1516). No definite relationship, however, can be defined based on the inscription.

5.II.6. Lines 5 and 6 of an unprovenienced Middle Kingdom stela (CG 20777) mention a mother daughter pair; (line 5) *ḥbyt t.w-nwt mꜣʿt ḫrw irt.n* (line 6) *ii-ib mst.n šmʿyt*  *Snbt*: the Dancer Tuniwt, true of voice,

[1] Ward lists various *šmʿywt* in his index of Middle Kingdom titles (1982: n. 1514-1516), although one reference listed in the index (CG 20023) did not contain the word *šmʿ* in any form.

[2] Ward seems to imply the reference is to an individual rather than a group (Ward, 1982: #1514), which is apparently not the case.

[3] The Abydos material is dealt with as a group in Appendix B.

fathered by Ii-ib and born of the Chantress Senbet (Lange and Schäfer, 1902, vol. II: 406; Ward, 1982: #1516).

5.II.7-8. A further Middle Kingdom stela from Abydos[4] (Vienna ÄS 132) contains a references to a mother, *šmʿt* (sic) *n Mnṯw n Mꜣdu, Sꜣ-ꞽmn* (DB #690) and daughter, *šmʿ* (sic) *nt Mnṯw n Mꜣdu, Wꜣḏ-hꜣ* (DB #691). They were both chantresses Montu of Medamud (Hein and Satzinger, 1989: 34-38; von Bergmann, 1892: 16; Ward, 1982: #1516).

5.II.9. A letter fragment from the Illahun archives (P.Berlin 10.081 a,b,c) mentions the *šmʿw* () *S-nḫt sꜣ Ḥtpi*. (Kaplony-Heckel, 1971, vol. 1: 36-37, reference 64; Ward, 1982: #1514).

5.II.10-11. Another fragment from Illahun (P.Berlin 10021) is a short text listing a number of individuals (Scharf, 1924: autographed text). It provides one of the rare attestations of an individual male chanter: *šmʿw ꞽtiti ḥnʿ pꜣ kty nty m ẖnrt pn: sꜣ Sn-wsrt*: the Chanter Ititi together with the other one who is in this *Kheneret*: Sasenusert (lines 6-7). This text also lists a woman: *šmʿyt Sꜣt-tp-iḥw ntt m ẖnrt nt R-n-š-Sbk*: the Chantress Sattepihu who is in the *Kheneret* of Illahun (line 5) (DB ref. #581; Ward, 1982: #1514).

5.II.12. Only one Second Intermediate Period *šmʿyt* is known. A stela of unknown provenience from the Petrie collection (UC 14419) depicts Mes, a *šmʿyt* of Osiris (DB #497; Stewart, 1979: 33, pl. 34.3). The fact that all of the provenienced examples of the title *šmʿyt n Wsr* in the database are from Abydos suggests that this stela came from that site as well.

5.III CONCLUSIONS ABOUT THE EARLY USE OF *Šmʿ*

There are a few patterns in the title's usage made apparent by these Middle Kingdom examples. The first point is that the role was not gender specific. From the inception of the title it is clear that women and men were participating in cult activities as chantresses and chanters. The second pattern demonstrates a period of transition from the use of the word *šmʿ* as a verb, to its use in the title. Only four of the 12 Middle Kingdom references are modeled on the *šmʿyt n* [deity] paradigm, the rest being simply *šmʿyt* without any affiliation to a deity. This suggests that the title may not have been well established or defined at this early stage. None of the Middle Kingdom title-holders served Amun, the most common form of the title in subsequent years. Ptah, Osiris, and Montu are represented instead.

These early examples demonstrate that the title was connected to important cult sites; the masculine title *šmʿw n Ptḥ* was documented at Saqqara, the women's stelae come from Abydos, and the papyri are from Illahun. These areas were important Middle Kingdom seats of government. The proximity of the individuals to government supported state cults suggests that the role of chanter/chantress developed in association with the official state religious hierarchy. The relative rarity with which it is found, however, indicates that it was not entirely formalized yet. The significance of the provenience of the women and the involvement of the official state religious apparatus will be discussed further below and in Chapter 6.

The first use of the title *šmʿyt* developed against a backdrop of apparently declining public status for women. In the Old Kingdom, priestesses (*ḥmt nṯr*) of Hathor and Neith, were common (Begelsbacher-Fischer: 1981). Women also held a variety of administrative positions, although far less commonly than men.[5] During the Middle Kingdom the title *ḥmt nṯr nt Ḥwt-ḥr* and some administrative titles continued to be used, but the documented occurrences are far fewer than during the previous dynasties. The general scholarly consensus regarding this phenomenon is that the women of the Middle Kingdom were less frequently involved in the religious and administrative institutions of their day than the women of the Old Kingdom had been (Robins, 1993b: 116; Fischer, 1976: 79; Guest, 1926: 48). Occurrences of the common title *ḥmt nṯr* further decline and almost completely disappear during the New Kingdom. It is at this exact point when these other titles decline that the title *šmʿyt* becomes common. This apparent decline in recorded occurrences of the *ḥmt nṯr* title coincides with the increased occurrence of the *šmʿyt* title. This seems to suggest that the role of the *šmʿyt* replaced the role of *ḥmt nṯr*. The common association of music with the priestesses of Hathor contributes to this implication. Whether or not the role of the *ḥmt nṯr* was in fact the antecedent of the *šmʿyt* is an open question, but one that has some tentative indications.

There are similarities between the two titles. Both titles were associated with the primary economic institution in the region for the time periods considered.[6] The cults of Hathor at Dendera and Amun at Thebes represent the dominant economic forces of the regions, and the dominant religious hierarchies of the ruling class for the Old and New Kingdoms respectively.[7]

It is a reasonable hypothesis that the *ḥmt nṯr n Ḥwt-ḥr* at Dendera during the Old Kingdom set a precedent for the role that economically advantaged women of the New

[4] Although this stela comes from Abydos, no reference is made by the publishers to Mariette's numbering system nor to the question of whether or not it came from his area of excavations there.

[5] For a thorough study of Old Kingdom women, see Fischer (1989); for the Middle Kingdom see Ward (1986).

[6] For a discussion of the cult of Hathor as a primary economic force, see Gillam (1991: 222) and Galvin (1984: 42ff).

[7] This theme is also expanded upon in Chapter 6.

Kingdom played in the dominant institution of their day, namely the cult of Amun at Thebes.[8] The sudden appearance of Hathoric titles for both men and women during the 6th Dynasty leads Gillam to conclude that the sponsorship of the Memphite court, especially Pepi I, was the key factor in Cusae's economic development (1991: 244). A similar situation existed at Dendera (Fischer, 1968: 55). Only a few *ḥmt nṯr* are known from before the time of Pepi I's patronage of the cults of Hathor at these sites. This royal interest in a cult can be compared to New Kingdom Thebes and the spread of the cult of Amun. There were only a limited number of chantresses before Thebes controlled the government and the resulting ascendancy of Amun. These Middle Kingdom attestations represent this time of transition. Once the hegemony of Amun was established, the title *šmʿyt* flourished. The fact that Thebes dominated the religious and political arenas of the New Kingdom by no means presupposes that there were not women who served other gods in other cult centers. These women usually lived in provincial seats and were serving the dominant cult of that region, following the model of the economically advantaged taking part in whatever cult was economically and politically preeminent in the area.[9]

5.IV THE NEW KINGDOM: A chronological and statistical breakdown by reign

The next step is to consider the historical events that may have directly or indirectly influenced the use of the title during its peak of popularity along with the collected data on women from each era. As will be seen, there are periodic spikes in the numbers of women who held the title. Understanding the various societal forces at work may make it possible to infer the significance of this phenomenon and the role of the women who held the title *šmʿyt*.

The New Kingdom must be broken down into two eras: the 18th Dynasty and the Ramesside Period. The reason for this will be clear when the statistics are reviewed. Five hundred eighty-nine references are classified as New Kingdom. Of those, only about 103 are positively dated to the 18th Dynasty, while 317 date to the 19th Dynasty, and only 85 date to the 20th Dynasty. Sixty-one were classified as either 19th or 20th Dynasty. Twenty-three could not be dated more precisely than New Kingdom.

[8] Sadek hypothesizes that the cult of Hathor at Dendera may have been transplanted to Deir el Bahari at Thebes as early as the Middle Kingdom (1987: 48-49) thus setting the stage for a specific type of women's participation in cult activities.

[9] Women who do not fit that model can occasionally be shown to have family connections to a specific province or cult.

5.IV.1 The 18th Dynasty

5.IV.1.A Hatshepsut through Tuthmosis IV: Statistics and discussion

One hundred and three women in the database are classified as having lived during the 18th Dynasty. Of those who could be identified with a specific reign,[10] that of Hatshepsut's was the first where the *šmʿyt n* [deity] paradigm appeared on a regular basis. During her reign, four daughters of the High Priest of Amun, Hepuseneb (TT 67), bore the title *šmʿyt n Ỉmn* (DB #s 257-260).[11] A fourth daughter was also the earliest non-royal *dwꜣt nṯr* (DB #260). Another *šmʿyt* attested from the reign of Hatshepsut (DB #261) was the daughter of User, a vizier, also a high ranking position.

Eighteen women are documented as having held the title *šmʿyt* during the reign of Tuthmosis III. With the exception of three women (DB #s 254[12], 265[13], 795), all of them are known from Theban tombs.[14]

Eight women who lived during the reign of Amenhotep II are recorded in the Database. All but two of the women are known from the Theban tombs of their husbands or fathers. The exceptions are known from a statue now in the British Museum (DB #487) and graffito (DB #830). One of the women was a *šmʿyt wrt* (DB #273) indicating a hierarchy or ranking system in place.

Ten women are attested from the reign of Tuthmosis IV including one *šmʿyt n Ỉn-ḥrt* (DB #576) known from a stela of her husband, a Priest of Onuris. He may also be the owner of the now-lost Theban tomb A19 (Van Siclen, 1979: 17-20).

The majority of women who lived during the reigns of Hathshepsut, Tuthmosis III, Amenhotep II, and Tuthmosis IV served Amun if a deity was mentioned at all as part of their title. Interestingly, of the women documented from Thebes during this period, two served the god Thoth, not Amun (DB #s 276 and 283). This

[10] Women whose lives encompassed more than one reign have been counted in the earlier reign for the sake of convenience.

[11] These women are actually known from their father's monument at Gebel el Silsila, Shrine 15, and not from his Theban tomb (Whale, 1989: 25-27). In the database, the daughter who was a *dwꜣt nṯr* (DB #260) is classified as having lived in the reign of Tuthmosis III, and not Hatshepsut, since the monument in which her *šmʿyt* title was found (TT 39) is dated to that reign.

[12] DB #254 is a *šmʿyt n Sbk(?)* mother of the High Priest of Sobek in the Sobek temple at Dahamsha. The text does not include a reference to a deity, but as can be seen in other cases, provincial nobility most often served the local god. This is especially true when they are represented on monuments dedicated to that god or depicted making offerings to that god.

[13] DB #265 is known from a statue now in Cairo (CG 42125), which may mention the mother of Menkheperresoneb (TT 112 and TT 86). The relationship between the two is uncertain. The statue may have originally come from his tomb.

[14] These are TT 42, TT 53, TT 74, TT 78, TT 82, TT 85, TT 88, TT 98, TT 100, TT 224, TT 345. For the details in each case, see Appendix D.

suggests that the women may originally have come from Hermopolis (Whale, 1989: 175f, 192f). Another Theban woman (DB #269) is the only *šmꜥyt* documented to have served both a pharaoh, in this case *ꜥꜣ-ḫpr-kꜣ-rꜥ* [Tuthmosis I] and Amun. One woman from Dahamsha may have served Sobek (DB #254).

5.IV.1.B Amenhotep III through Horemhab: Statistics and discussion

Thirteen women are dated to the reign of Amenhotep III. In contrast to the previous group of references, many of the sources that mention *šmꜥywt* are stelae and statues. The tombs of Ramose (TT 55), Kheruef (TT 192),[15] and the recently rediscovered A24[16] are the only tombs that have depictions of *šmꜥywt* from this time. Very little information about individual women remains for this time period because of the trend away from depicting private scenes during the Amarna interlude, and the geographical shift of the court from Thebes to Tell el Amarna where far fewer tombs are preserved for study. The decoration of the tomb of Ramose (TT 55) is a valuable source of information about the transitional years at the end of Amenhotep III's reign and the beginning of that of his son. Construction of the tomb was begun during the reign of Amenhotep III, and it continued to be decorated during the reign of Akhenaten. It exemplifies the transition from the traditional Egyptian artistic canon to that of the new early-Amarna style. Ramose's wife and other women depicted in the tomb are portrayed in the earlier decorative phase at banquets and in the funeral procession in the customary manner. Some of these women held the title *šmꜥyt n Ỉmn*, but the name of Amun was carefully erased at a later time. The women are not present in the later phase of the decorative program, which concentrates on Ramose and his relationship to the king.

Other sources of information for the occurrence of the title from the reign of Amenhotep III include a stela from Memphis (DB #575) and another from Bubastis that bears the name of a *šmꜥyt n Bꜣstt* (DB #492). Further evidence derives from a coffin found in the undecorated tomb of Hatiay (no number) at Qurnah (DB #443). The coffin's owner, Henutwedjebu, was a *šmꜥyt n Ỉmn*, despite the fact that the man who was likely her husband was already in the service of Aten as a granary overseer of the mansion of Aten.[17] There was also a *šmꜥyt* from Balansurah who served Khnum (DB #697). One reference from this reign provides information on the organization of the *šmꜥwyt*. A woman (DB #493) depicted on a stela from Abydos belonged to the fourth phyle, indicating the *šmꜥywt* were organized in the same manner as the priesthood.

There are fewer references documented from the reign of Akhenaten. Only five women could be attributed to his reign[18] and only two were associated with his reign exclusively. Three others are known from the transitional period at the end of Akhenaten's reign and during the reigns of Tutankhamun and Aye. The two women who are known from the Amarna period proper were both identified as *šmꜥyt nt pꜣ Ỉtn* (DB #s 446, 447). The other women served Amun, presumably since the monuments from which they are known were decorated during the restoration phase directly following Akhenaten's reign. With fewer gods to serve in cultic settings during the Amarna interlude, fewer personnel were needed. Music was part of the new religion, however, as the cultic scenes from Amarna (Leprohon in Redford, 1988: 47-51) and on the Talatat from east Karnak demonstrate (Manniche, 1991b: 62ff; Gohary, 1992: e.g., Pl. L, LI, CVII).

The demise of Akhenaten and the return to orthodoxy are evidenced by the numerous women who held the title *šmꜥyt nt Ỉmn* in the short time period encompassing the reigns of Tutankhamun, Aye, and Horemhab. The tomb of Huy (TT 40), dating to the reign of Tutankhamun, yields one reference (DB #699). The tomb of Neferhotep (TT 49), which was decorated during the reigns of Tutankhamun and Aye, contains depictions of two women (DB #s 648, 649). The tomb of Amenmose (TT 254), which is dated to the reigns of either Aye or Horemhab, contains representations of four *šmꜥywt* (DB #s 588-592). One reference (DB #692) attests to the presence of the cult of Amun at Diospolis Parva during the reign of Horemhab. The tomb of another man named Neferhotep (TT 50) dating to the reign of Horemhab, depicts nine *šmꜥywt*; in fact, most of the women in this Neferhotep's family were *šmꜥywt n Ỉmn* (DB #s 615-622). Approximately 16 additional occurrences of the *šmꜥyt* title were classified as late 18th or early 19th Dynasty. Perhaps these families are an early indication of the new, outward religious piety that will be displayed by the people of the Ramesside Period.

5.IV.1.C Analysis

It was during the reign of Hatshepsut that officials began to be buried in the necropolis at Qurnah. It is from these tombs that we glean a great deal of information about the women of the New Kingdom. It should be understood, however, that the apparent sudden popularity of the title in the society of 18th Dynasty Thebes could be a result of our dependence on these tombs as a source of information

[15] This tomb is discussed fully in Section 3.III.4.A.

[16] An expedition sponsored by Waseda University, Japan located this "lost" tomb during their 1988-89 season; their designation for it is W-6 (Egyptian Culture Center, Waseda University, Japan, 2000: www.waseda.ac.jp/projects/egypt/sites/TT-E.html).

[17] She, with two other women, were found buried with him in the undecorated tomb. Her coffin was decorated in a manner similar to his while the other two women had very simple coffins (Kozloff, Bryan, and Berman, 1992: 312). It is therefore assumed that she was his wife.

[18] Six women from the reign of Amenhotep III lived into the reign of Akhenaten, but are counted with the initial reign in which they are attested.

about the occurrences of the title.[19] It seems likely that, since the title is known from earlier times, albeit uncommonly, there were probably a few women who held the title *šmʿyt* during the reigns of the earlier 18th Dynasty monarchs, even though they cannot presently be identified in the archaeological record.

Nevertheless, there are many factors that come into play during the reigns of Hatshepsut and Tuthmosis III, which form a kind of temporal nexus of activity with regard to the title-holders. There was a "rapid, major alteration in the political-theological constellation at this time" (Spalinger, 1998: 251; see also Assmann, 1989: 71-82). There were a number of changes, or innovations, which may be responsible for the formation and character of the *šmʿyt* as a distinct class of priestess.

A characteristic feature of the 18th Dynasty was the distinguished role played by women in the monarchy (Myśliwiec, 1985: 2). There is no doubt that during the early 18th Dynasty there were many influential royal women, and that the concurrent development of the title God's Wife was an important step in empowering women in the political sphere. Although there is no direct evidence for a women's movement, many authors have noted a more "female-friendly" environment during Hatshepsut's reign (Tyldesley, 1996: 57; Roberts, 1997: 128; Whale, 1989: 241f). It is tempting to see the reign of a woman, Hatshepsut, as a catalyst for the greater appreciation of women in general as revealed by the increasing status afforded to women in tomb scenes (Whale, 1989: 241). The previous influence of Ahmose Nefertari, Ahhotep, and Tetisheri may also have been felt. Although no specifics can be brought forward to demonstrate that the powerful 18th Dynasty royal women intentionally caused any societal changes, it may be suggested that their existence alone was enough to initiate a reexamination by Egyptian society of the value of women in public roles.

It has also been noted that there was a "secularization of ritual" between the reigns of Hatshepsut and Tuthmosis IV (Myśliwiec, 1985: 30) suggesting a conscious role in the alteration of religious practices. This secularization of ritual may have allowed for many more people to participate in ritual, and the new, elaborated festivals requiring musical specialists probably played an important role in the popularization of the title.[20] It was Hatshepsut who elaborated the Opet festival, which included female singers, chantresses, musicians, and acrobats (see Section 3.III.1). The new processional route that included Hatshepsut's temple at Deir el Bahari may have been partly created for the purpose of having musicians accompany the god on his journey during the Beautiful Feast of the Valley celebrations.

Hatshepsut's reign coincides with a trend during the 18th Dynasty toward a more active role of the wife in tomb scenes. This becomes especially clear during the reign of Tuthmosis III (Whale, 1989: 241). Ritual and offering scenes that previously had been predominantly male now begin to include women and other members of the family. It is suggested that the "almost continuous military campaigns of the reign of Tuthmosis III necessitated women playing a more active role in family affairs and this was reflected in their role in the tomb" (Whale, 1989: 275). Taken at face value, this "active role" would appear to be solely in funerary contexts. By examining non-funerary evidence, however, it is clear that the women's participation extended beyond the familial funerary roles. Specifically, with regard to the chantresses, evidence from Tuthmosis III's Festival temple at Karnak demonstrates that the *šmʿywt* played a role in temple activity (see Section 3.III.7.A). Many other monuments attest to the participation of all kinds of female musicians in religious rites.[21] If there were fewer men available to serve in temple ceremonies, as Whale suggests, it would have been natural for the women to step in.

The professionalization of the priesthood in the 18th Dynasty (Spalinger, 1998: 245; Allam, 1970: 78-79) may have also contributed to the character of women's participation in cultic activities. This process of excluding women from the common priestly roles (e.g. *wʿbt, ḥmt nṯr*) left only few opportunities for women to participate. This participation took the form of musical accompaniment. These subsidiary musical roles had to be filled, but were not prestigious in the traditional administrative sense, and therefore were not of interest to men building careers.[22] These duties could be sporadically and episodically carried out by women.[23]

5.IV.2 The Ramesside Era

5.IV.2.A The 19th Dynasty

Two hundred seventy-four women recorded in the database lived during the 19th Dynasty. Fifty-eight entries could not be dated more specifically than 19th Dynasty. There were three entries classified as "early 19th Dynasty" and an additional 26 attributed specifically to the reign of Seti I.[24] One hundred ninety women lived

[19] The bias toward Theban material is a serious consideration, but unavoidable with limited source material. Eighteenth Dynasty material from elsewhere was consulted but did not reveal the wealth of information that the Theban tombs did.

[20] The new emphasis on processions has also been dealt with in Chapter 3.

[21] E.g., six unlabeled women bearing sistra depicted in the area of the Tuthmosis III Karnak Annals (PM II, 97 [281.I]), and the famous *Khener* women and acrobats on blocks from Hatshepsut's "Red Chapel" (Lacau and Chevrier, 1977, vol. II: pl. 9).

[22] The men who held the title *šmʿ* were few in number and are documented in Appendix A.

[23] The episodic nature of participation is also noted in Naguib (1990: 238).

[24] Four of those women lived into the reign of Ramesses II, but are counted in the reign of Seti I.

during the reign of Ramesses II. There are more *šmʿywt* known from this time than any other New Kingdom reign. During the reign of his successor Merneptah, 53 women held the title. Two others can be dated to the late 19th Dynasty. Sixty-three are classified as 19th or 20th Dynasty.

Amun was by far the most common deity with which these women were affiliated. A variety of others, however, were also represented. The most common provenience of the source material documenting these *šmʿywt* was Thebes, but there were a number of objects recorded from Nubian sites such as Buhen, Sehel, Faras, and Amarah West. The latter objects may reflect increased civilian activity in Lower Nubia, which accompanied the official activities of Ramesses II.[25] Middle Egypt is represented by sources from Abydos, el Mashayikh, Coptos, Sedment, Gurob, Zwayet el Sultan, Asyut, and Hermopolis. Even a stela from Serabit el Khadim in the Sinai provides information on two women (DB #s 99-100). The North is represented by sources from Bubastis, Heliopolis, Qantir, and Saqqara, perhaps reflecting the renewed importance of Lower Egypt brought about by Ramesside building projects there.

5.IV.2.B The 20th Dynasty

The 20th Dynasty exhibits a marked decline in the numbers of women who were *šmʿywt*. Eighty-five cases dated to the 20th Dynasty but 26 of these could not be assigned to a specific reign. Twenty women dated to the reign of Ramesses III. An additional 12 could not be dated more specifically than to the reign of Ramesses III or a later 20th Dynasty king. Four are attributed to the reign of Ramesses IV, three to that of Ramesses VI, one to Ramesses VII, seven to Ramesses VIII, seven to Ramesses IX, and five to Ramesses XI. This decrease in documented instances of the title may be the result of a smaller number of decorated Theban tombs attributable to the 20th Dynasty from which to draw information. In fact, the majority of 20th Dynasty information comes from stelae. Other sources include literary documents and shabtis.

Over half of the women documented for the 20th Dynasty served Amun. Osiris and Wepwawet were also very common, however. Out of the total of 23 individuals who were chantresses of Osiris, 15 can be dated to the 20th Dynasty. The gods Herishef, Nemty, Seth, Montu, Mehyt, Hathor, (*P3*) Re, Mut, Horus, and Isis are all also represented by small numbers of devotees. Abydos and Thebes are the most common provenience, though items from Herakleopolis Magna, Bubastis, and Heliopolis are represented as well.

[25] Simplistically, this may be construed as evidence of the translocation of Egyptian populations to an area being actively colonized. This idea is debatable, however (Kemp, 1978b: 34). It may simply reflect the influence of Egyptian ideals on the local population.

5.IV.2.C Analysis

The aftermath of the Amarna Period saw a resurgence of personal and state piety. In fact, the Ramesside Period has been described as pervaded by piety (Assmann, 1989: 68-69).[26] The state's campaign to rebuild and restore temples neglected during Akhenaten's reign began under Tutankhamun (Robins, 1997: 158) and was maintained into the reign of Horemheb (Grimal, 1992: 243). The prolific restoration and building by Seti I and Ramesses II can be seen as a continuation of this effort (Faulkner, 1975: 221). This new state religiosity was probably a result of a desire to connect with the legitimacy and glory of the pre-Amarna 18th Dynasty. This increase in religious piety may be seen as a theological response to Akhenaten's "revolution", which evolved in the Ramesside period; this included a strong role for the God's Wife of Amun, a post held by Rameses II's wife, Nefertari, and later princesses (Grimal, 1992: 313).

The Ramesside nobles' tombs reflect this increased religiosity as well. The emphasis of the decorative themes shifts away from the personal to the eternal. Scenes from the Book of the Dead play a much larger role in the decorative programs of the 19th and 20th Dynasty tombs than they had previously (Aldred, 1987: 161 and 170). Additionally, the tomb owner is no longer frequently shown in daily life pursuits. He is now depicted offering to the gods, while his family participates in offering rituals for the benefit of the deceased (Manniche, 1987: 64, 80; Abdul-Qader, 1966: 251ff). Fortunately, the tombs still provide the names and titles of family members and close associates, providing a continuing source of information on genealogy and the institutions of the day.

With this increasing emphasis on religion, one may expect to see a rise in religious titles. And indeed there was an increase in the numbers of women who held the title *šmʿyt*. Since the numbers of hereditary nobility did not necessarily increase, the title now appears to have been more accessible to members of the wealthy middle class. A correlation can be drawn between the higher number of 19th Dynasty *šmʿywt* and the less illustrious positions of their families. While the women of higher nobility are still present in the sample, more and more simple *wʿb* priests have *šmʿyt* wives.[27]

A side effect of this increasing piety and a conciliatory attitude toward the cult of Amun[28] may have resulted in

[26] Breasted also generally agrees with this characterization (1959: ch. 10; 1967: Chapter 20). Sadek, however, has shown that "popular religion", sometimes linked with levels of personal piety, was more widespread than previously thought, both temporally and geographically (1987: 293ff.).

[27] This type of diversity was also noted by Galvin (1981: 250) with regard to the priestesses of Hathor in the Old Kingdom.

[28] "The Ramessides were an upstart line of rulers, and it was important for them to have the support of the powerful corporation which served the god of Thebes" (Faulkner, 1975:222).

the prolific use of the title *šmʿyt n Ỉmn*. The title may have been cultivated by Ramessside rulers as part of a program of "buying support" from the nobles, on the same model as Kanawati's theory concerning the Old Kingdom proliferation of officials and new titles (1977: 69ff).[29] Since the first regular use of the title occurs during the reign of Hatshepsut, it is conceivable that she also used this idea of "buying support" to consolidate the power base of her unusual reign.

5.V THE THIRD INTERMEDIATE PERIOD: 21st-22nd Dynasties

5.V.1 Statistics and discussion

The Third Intermediate Period is represented by a total of 252 women who held the title *šmʿyt*. Eighteen women were dated unspecifically to the Third Intermediate Period. Two hundred and six women could be attributed to the 21st Dynasty with 34 of those dating to the late 21st or early 22nd Dynasties. Twenty-eight references were dated to the 22nd Dynasty.

Only five women from the Third Intermediate Period in this survey did not serve Amun (DB #s 74, 215, 451, 566, 759). One (DB #74) served Montu, Lord of Thebes, another (DB #215) served the goddess Khnumet, and a third (DB #451) served Thoth. A stela from Dakhla made during the reign of Sheshonq I contains references to two *šmʿywt n Stḫ* (DB #s 566, 759; Gardiner, 1933). Only two women served other gods in addition to Amun (DB #s 149, 120). The first (DB #149) served Amun as well as an unknown institution, *pꜣ grg wʿb n Ptḥ*, "the pure foundation of Ptah." The other (DB #120) was a *šmʿyt* of Amun, Mut, and Khonsu.[30]

5.V.2 Analysis

Most of the material preserved from this era is funerary equipment; coffins, cartonage, and papyri. The 21st Dynasty data set is mainly from Thebes.[31] The provenience of the material from the 22nd Dynasty is largely unknown, but probably Theban as most of it is of the same style as the 21st Dynasty objects.[32] Thus, the Third Intermediate Period data demonstrate how pervasive the title and the cult of Amun had become in Thebes.

Examples of children holding the titles *wʿb*, *it-nṯr* (god's father), and *šmʿyt* come from the Bab el Gusus cache and include a girl named Ankhesenaset who was a *šmʿyt n Ỉmn* (DB #144; Niwiński, 1989b: 39).[33] The unusual practice of giving titles to children during the Third Intermediate Period may reflect a desire on the part of the Amun priesthood to strengthen their power base by involving more families in the temple's hierarchy. This strategy may also be indicated by the numbers of Third Intermediate Period women who were *šmʿywt*. There is a disproportionate increase in the numbers of women who held the *šmʿyt* title between the time of the late 20th Dynasty and the middle of the 21st. Such an artificial increase may have been the effect of active recruitment. Significantly, the majority of those women are attributed to the middle or late years of the 21st Dynasty. It was at exactly that time that the High Priests of Amun had usurped power. By creating a cadre of people loyal to the priesthood, a foundation of political support could be forged.

The effect of this practice seems to have been the further diminishment of the title's status. It seems that almost every noblewoman in Thebes could claim having the title *šmʿyt*.[34] The title itself may still have held prestige because of its former associations, but was probably becoming more of an honorary title during the Third Intermediate Period. This phenomenon has been noted in Old Kingdom contexts, where a number of honorific court titles of the late Old Kingdom were based on older offices in order to associate the honorific with the previous legitimacy of the title (Grimal, 1992: 90). The Third Intermediate Period also saw the greatest number of *šmʿywt*, yet none of them were associated with a phyle, supporting the conclusion that the title no longer always entailed serious duty. The proliferation of *šmʿywt* in the Theban area during the 21st Dynasty can be seen as a predominantly political development, rather than an expression of personal piety by increasing numbers of women. The societal and political forces of the Ramesside age that fueled widespread female participation in cult activity were simply resurrected during the Third Intermediate Period and used to the Theban priesthood's advantage.

---

[29] Kanawati's theory is generally that the creation of new titles may have been a way for the king to compensate officials and gain their support (1977: 69ff).

[30] A more common combination is *šmʿyt n Ỉmn, ḥsyt n Mwt, mnʿt n pꜣ ẖrd Ḫnsw*: chantress of Amun, singer of Mut, nurse of the child Khonsu (e.g. DB #s 143, 304, and the partial formula in DB #s 128, 402, 116).

[31] It must be pointed out that information on the Third Intermediate Period depends on a largely biased sample. The Bab el Gusus cache alone provides an immense sample size: about 20 percent of Third Intermediate Period references. This bias for Theban material in the Third Intermediate Period may be largely a matter of preservation. Because of preservation problems in the Delta, where there was significant political activity in the Third Intermediate Period, there is little or no comparative information on wealthy private individuals.

[32] Niwiński's two studies on Theban papyri (1989b) and coffins (1988) explain the typology and seriation of the types.

[33] DB #144. Two other children (one female- D.L. A.79, and one unidentified) had coffins at Bab el Gusus, but held no titles (Niwiński, 1988: ref. nos. 127, 130, 131, 154).

[34] Unfortunately, very little familial information survives from this time so it is impossible to make generalizations about the economic status of the *šmʿywt* from the Third Intermediate Period. The only facts that are certain are that the families of the Amun priesthood (Second, Third and Fourth prophets) are represented and that the women were wealthy enough to have burial equipment.

5.VI LATE AND PTOLEMAIC PERIODS

5.VI.1 Statistics and discussion

Ten database entries were dated to periods after the 22nd Dynasty. Six entries (DB #s 558, 679, 680, 243, 568, 569) can dated to either the "Late" or Saite Periods. The three women classified as "Late Period" were from Abydos, and of those, two served Osiris, and the other served Amun. One of the Saite women served in the temple of Hathor at Dendera;[35] the other two were in the service of Amun and are known from the tomb of Padiamenipet (TT 33). One unprovenienced statue mentions a woman named Taibhet-Re (DB #427) and is tentatively dated to the 30th Dynasty. An unprovenienced stela now in Athens bears a reference to a woman (DB #766) who was a *šmˁyt n Ỉmn* and is dated to a time period covering Dynasties 22-30. Two individuals are known from the Ptolemaic period: Ta-amun (DB #662) is known from her Book of the Dead and Ta-imenet-seneb (DB #784) is portrayed on a stela with her son.

5.VI.2 Analysis

For the Saite, and Ptolemaic Periods, there are very few women known to have held the title *šmˁyt* and information about them is scanty. This is partly due to the fact that decorated tombs from this period are not common. Additionally, the Egyptians almost completely stopped making stone sculptures of women at the beginning of the 6th century B.C. (Bothmer, de Meulenaere, and Müller, 1960: 116). In contrast to the absence of statuary during this period, stelae were quite popular,[36] and many women dedicated them on their own behalf. These stelae were most often simple affairs representing the dedicator before a god with a few lines of praise. When a woman dedicated a stela, she rarely recorded the names and titles of her family members. This is due to the rules of compositional hierarchy that governed such matters (Robins, 1994: 33-40). Therefore we know little about their families. The best example of an extended family in the database is that of Padiamenipet (TT 33), Chief Lector Priest of Nekhbet. His wife Tadi (DB #568) was a *šmˁyt n Ỉmn* as was his mother Namenekhaset (DB #569), who, in addition to being a *šmˁyt n Ỉmn*, was also an *iḥyt*, or sistrum player. *Ỉḥyt* and *ḥsyt* (sometimes with *n ḫnw n Ỉmn*) were the most commonly found titles on Late Period monuments.[37]

Official texts are more informative than those few private attestations of the title. *Šmˁywt* are among the temple priestesses mentioned in the Canopus Decree.[38] The goddess Hathor is described as *šmˁyt n pr ḳ3* (Chantress of the Sanctuary of Hathor at Abydos) in a Ptolemaic inscription at Behbeit el Hagar (Montet, 1949: 47).[39] At Edfu, *šmˁywt* are mentioned along with *ḫn(r)yt* in a Ptolemaic scene of the king adoring Horus (de Rochemonteix and Chassinat, 1987: 329). These texts demonstrate that the title was still in use and considered a religious duty. The small numbers of women who held the title suggest that it may have resumed its original character, one that reflects personal devotion and ability rather than the politics of appeasement or a popular fad.

The Ptolemaic Period in general may have seen another increase in the number of women involved in cult activities (Johnson, 1998: 1410; de Cenival 1977: 29-30), although this is not true for the title *šmˁyt*. De Cenival also questions "whether this increase was favoured by the government for political or economic reasons" (Johnson, 1998: 1410 citing de Cenival, 1977: 29). If so, it would fit the pattern documented for the periods discussed in this study.

5.VII CONCLUSIONS

From the material collected in the database, a trend emerges revealing a pattern of intermittent increases in the number of women who held the title *šmˁyt*. This eventually culminated in the large number attributable to the 21st Dynasty. After the 22nd Dynasty, however, the number dropped dramatically.

The pattern of punctuated increases observed here seems to have been fueled by political need and trends in personal piety. During the reigns of Hatshepsut and Ramesses II, as well as the ascendancy of the Theban High Priests of Amun, there were increases in the numbers of women who held the title *šmˁyt*. These eras were particularly vulnerable to image problems because some of the rulers could be considered as usurpers and were in need of legitimizing circumstances and support. The Ramesside Period and the Third Intermediate Period were also times of great religiosity.

It seems that cultivating a group of women who were tied to the religious hierarchy served the advantage of the ruling bodies in each case. This scenario roughly parallels Kanawati's theory that the proliferation of Old Kingdom titles was directly linked to a royal program of buying support (1979: 69ff). Establishing an "official" organization of female devotees connected to the state religious hierarchy ensured that not only the women support the state system, but also that their children are influenced by this loyalty. Since women traditionally provide most of the child care, including the teaching of values and belief systems, children raised by a woman

[35] The stela does not actually say Hathor of Dendera, but as its provenience is Dendera, it is a reasonable assumption.

[36] See, for example, the extensive corpus in Munro (1973).

[37] Unfortunately, Munro's work is inconsistent with the translation of such titles. Anyone whom he rendered as *sängerin* or *musikantin* was checked against the original publications to ensure only *šmˁyt* were counted in this study.

[38] See Section 4.II.2.

[39] The *pr-kˁ* is the *Hieligtum der Hathor in Abydos* (Hannig, 1995: 1339).

loyal to the cult of Amun (or other local power structure) would consequently be more likely to be part of that system as well.

CHAPTER 6
FAMILY INFLUENCE

6.I INTRODUCTION

"Rank creates its rules: A woman is asked about her husband, a man is asked about his rank" Instruction of Any, 6.14-15

This sentiment is found in a variety of contexts in ancient Egypt. In art, we see the man holding the insignia of office, while the woman holds her man. In funerary epithets, a man is clever, useful, and admired by his peers; a woman is beloved of her man.[1] Men are portrayed interacting with the public sphere, whereas women usually interact with their family members. In tomb representations, a woman may play a part in public life, but her husband or other family members accompany her.

The Egyptian family was a close one, probably best demonstrated by the numerous family scenes on tomb walls and the numbers of relatives often included on stelae. Those who could afford monuments portrayed family life as desirable. On a regular basis, men included depictions or references to their wives, daughters, sisters, mothers, and female relatives in their tombs, and on their stelae and statuary. Another reflection of this familial closeness was the use of first-degree kinship terms for extended family members and for those who married into the family. Even wives were called "sister" from the 18th Dynasty onward (Whale, 1989: 239; Robins, 1979: 203-204).

It is through a woman's family relationships that some conclusions about the title *šmˁyt* can be reached. Since women were traditionally outside the "power hierarchy", ultimately their social status was defined by their families or husbands. Based on the assumption that the Egyptians chose their partners from the same social circle – a man and his wife's father often had similar occupations[2] (Pestman, 1961: 4) – knowledge regarding the family of a *šmˁyt* makes placing her in a larger social context possible, and thus helps to define the character of its holders and hence the title.

6.II THE HEREDITARY STATUS OF FEMALE TITLES

The issue of inherited titles for women has only rarely been studied. The most commonly examined title in this respect is "Priestess of Hathor".[3] By breaking down the data into relationships (mother/daughter; father/daughter; mother-in-law/daughter-in-law; husband/wife) and comparing the level of similarity between the two individuals' titles, it is possible to speculate about what factors influenced a woman's decision to become a *šmˁyt*. Galvin's results with the priestesses of Hathor suggest that there was no consistent pattern to suggest the inheritance of a Hathoric title from any family member. Rather the data reflect the importance of the title for noble women. As will be seen, the title *šmˁyt* exhibits some traits similar to the title *ḥmt nṯr nt Ḥwt-ḥr*.

6.III PATTERNS OF INFLUENCE

6.III.1 Mothers and daughters

Only 84 out of the 860 women investigated left evidence of their mother's titles.[4] The majority of mothers recorded on their *šmˁyt* daughter's monuments apparently held no titles. There were more women who recorded the names of their mothers who had no titles than those whose mothers had titles. This clearly suggests that the title did not pass from mother to daughter. Of those 84, however, 74 shared the *šmˁyt* title with their mothers. The majority of mother-daughter pairs are from the New Kingdom.

Some women served different gods than their mothers. A good example of this is the family of Tjay (TT 23). Mutnefret (DB #719) was a chantress of Amun and the mother of two chantresses of Bastet and a chantress of Amun (DB #627, 721, 722). This example demonstrates that several women in one family could hold the title *šmˁyt* concurrently. In fact, in one documented case (BM 161) a woman is depicted with her mother, mother-in-law, daughter, and daughter-in-law, all of whom were *šmˁywt*. There are a number of cases where three or more generations are known, and the women of each generation held similar titles (e.g., the families of Tjanefer in TT 158 and Khonsu in TT 31 – see Appendix D). This demonstrates that the title was not held by a single person in the family and transferred in a single line of inheritance. In fact, there was a tendency for the title to run in families. For instance, if a mother and at least one daughter were *šmˁywt*, chances are that some of the other daughters were *šmˁywt* as well (e.g., DB #s 85-88, #s 45-47, #s 704-710, #s 503, 506-511). This tendency is borne out by the fact that although 84 women claimed mothers who were *šmˁywt*, the number of mothers with daughters recorded in the database is 46 (see Chart 1.) Not all the women in a family necessarily held the title, however; many sisters of *šmˁywt* were not *šmˁywt* themselves.

[1] Doxey characterizes the use of Middle Kingdom women's epithets as usually focusing on either the afterlife (*mȝˁt-ḫrw*) or the principal male figure of the monument (*mrt.f*) (1995: 287).

[2] Unfortunately, where we know about the husband, the woman's father is not usually included on the monuments, and vice-versa.

[3] The title *ḥmt nṯr* of Hathor and the women who held that title have been dealt with by Galvin (1981, 1984) and Gillam (1991). Galvin's methodological framework is followed in this chapter.

[4] Only mothers with titles were recorded.

The fact that a mother and her daughters could all hold the title underscores the title's desirability in some families and perhaps the influence of family tradition. It in no way implies a hereditary position passed on from mother to daughter. It must be remembered that the majority of women in this study did not include the title *šmꜤyt* in the information about their mothers.

6.III.2 Mothers-in-law

The relationship between a woman and her mother-in-law provides insight into the structure of the Egyptian family. Fifty of the women recorded in the database provided information about the titles held by their mothers-in-law[5] (see Chart 2). Of those 50, all but four shared the title *šmꜤyt* with their mothers-in-law.[6] Other titles held in varying combinations by the mothers-in-law include *mnꜤt nsw* (royal nurse) or *mnꜤt wrt* (great nurse), *wrt ḫnrt nt sꜣt nsw* (great one of the *Khener* of the king's daughter), *šdt nṯr* (nurse of the god), *ḥsyt n nṯr nfr* (singer/beloved of the good god), *ẖkrt nsw* (lady-in-waiting). They are all clearly from the upper echelon of society. In a few cases, more than one woman claimed the same mother-in-law due to either the remarriage of a son or the marriage of several sons to women who were *šmꜤywt*. Consequently, there are only 38 women in the database who were mothers-in-law to those 50 *šmꜤywt* instead of an equal number of both mothers-in-law and daughters-in-law.

A total of 88 references is too small a sample from which to draw many conclusions. It is interesting to note, however, that these women were largely Theban and exclusively New Kingdom.[7] The evidence presented in this section is somewhat reminiscent of the results of Galvin's research (1981: 282), which demonstrated that the relationship between mother-in-law and daughter-in-law had a higher level of correlation in the titles held than other relationships. Where both individuals were known, nearly 50 percent of that sample group both shared Hathoric titles. The conclusion drawn was that these correlations were a result of close knit communities of hereditary nobility in major Hathoric cult centers such as Cusae, Dendera, and Giza (Galvin, 1981: 281f). The evidence also suggests that the mother's social circle provided a community from which she chose a bride for her son (ibid.). Because nearly all of the women in the present study who recorded mothers-in-law shared the title *šmꜤyt* with their mothers-in-law, it seems likely that a similar situation existed here.

[5] There were a number of women who had mothers-in-law without titles, but they are not counted here.

[6] A fifth woman may have been either the mother-in-law or grandmother of DB #919, but their relationship cannot be ascertained.

[7] There may have been many more women who shared the title with their mothers-in-law, but often relationships are undefined, especially on stelae or small objects.

6.III.3 Fathers and daughters

One hundred sixteen women listed the titles of their fathers (see Chart 3). Many of the fathers held priestly titles connected to the cult of Amun (e.g., *ḥm nṯr* (priest), *ḥm nṯr tpy* (high priest) *ḥm nṯr 2-nw* (second priest), *ḥm nṯr 3-nw* (third priest), *ḥm nṯr 4-nw* (fourth priest), *wꜤb* (*wꜤb*-priest), *it nṯr* (god's father)). The rest held administrative titles. Of those who held priestly titles, there was a correspondence between the god served by father and daughter. This, however, is mostly reflective of the popularity of the cult of Amun, as only 25 (37 percent) *šmꜤywt* documented in this chart did not serve that deity. Two of those served other gods in addition to Amun (DB #s 120, 603). A further woman (DB #269) served the funerary cult of Tuthmosis I and Amun, and 14 listed no deity at all.

There is very little correlation between the daughter's and father's service besides those cases where they both served the cult of Amun. Those cases where the father and daughter served Amun should probably be seen as indicative of the popularity of the cult of Amun. Because the cult of Amun was very popular, especially in Thebes where most of the source material originated, little can be said about the significance of this phenomenon except that familial exposure must have played a large role in what temple the woman eventually served.

6.III.4 Husbands

Two hundred eighty-seven women recorded in the database were associated with husbands who held at least one title (see Chart 4). The majority of these men held administrative titles. Perhaps one-third held priestly titles alone or in combination with those representing a variety of administrative posts. A wide range of jobs are represented in this sample; charioteers, stablemasters, military men of various rank, doorkeepers, mayors, overseers of cattle and granaries, fan bearers, metal engravers, kitchen staff, an overseer of singers, and above all, scribes of all sorts. In fact, scribe was the most common title. Among the priestly titles were some of the highest, *ḥry sštꜣ*, first, second, third, and fourth priests of Amun, high priests of Osiris, Onuris, Bastet, Sobek, and *wꜤb* and *ḥm nṯr* priests of Amun (in his various manifestations).

The women who were married to men with priestly titles did not always serve the same deity as their husbands. The wife of the high priest of Osiris (DB #251) was a *šmꜤyt* of Isis; a priest of Amun and Ptah had a wife who served Bastet (DB #515); and several high priests of Onuris had wives who served Amun (DB #s 611, 612, 284, 872, 873). Most of the rest of the couples were affiliated with the cult of Amun at Thebes during the New Kingdom and the Third Intermediate Period. The predominance of the cult during these eras, and the nature of the material dealt with (tombs, coffins, and papyri from Thebes) makes it difficult to evaluate how much influence should be ascribed to the cultural climate or to a husband.

Generally the *šmʿywt* of the 18th Dynasty were married to men of privileged status. There was, however, a slight change in the status of the women who held the title *šmʿyt* during the Ramesside Period. More often, their families now included scribes of the army, stable masters, chief washermen, chiefs of fattened fowl, charioteers, and *wʿb* and *ḥm nṯr* priests. These individuals seem to have been part of a wealthy middle class, no longer closely associated with the king, but not simple laborers either. This pattern of the title's gradual assimilation by a more diverse population from its previously elite context is a phenomenon perhaps best described as the "trickle-down effect". The Third Intermediate Period material documented here is characterized by husbands who held titles connected with the cult of Amun at all levels, reinforcing the idea that the title *šmʿyt* had become "democratized" by this time, and not purely an elite designation.

6.III.4.A Marriage as a precondition of the title

There is no reason to assume that the fact that most *šmʿywt* seem to have been married was in some way relevant to their cultic status. Marriage was normal for all adult Egyptians. Further, in the 21st Dynasty there is some evidence that children (DB #144) held the title. Thus being a chantress was not dependent on marital status, at least by that time.[8]

In fact, only one woman included in the database seems to have received the title *šmʿyt* after marriage. Senseneb (DB #260) was one of the two wives of Puimre depicted in TT 39 (Urk. IV, 520-527; Whale, 1989: 50ff; Davies, 1923a). She bore the titles *dwꜣt nṯr* and *šmʿyt nt Ỉmn*. She is probably the same woman as one of Hepuseneb's daughters, depicted in his Gebel el Silsila shrine (DB #15) where she is only identified as a *dwꜣt nṯr*. As mentioned previously, three of her sisters were *šmʿywt* and her father was a High Priest of Amun and a powerful official under Hatshepsut (Grimal, 1992: 212, 219). Puimre was his subordinate during the building of Hatshepsut's mortuary temple at Deir el Bahari. The connection between the two men makes it likely that Puimre married the daughter of his superior. It is possible that preservation conditions have obliterated traces of her *šmʿyt* title at Gebel el Silsila. Or perhaps there was only space in the inscription for one title and *dwꜣt nṯr* was considered the more important of the two. She may have adopted the title *šmʿyt* late in life as an expression of personal devotion. These various possibilities prohibit a definitive statement about when Senseneb became a *šmʿyt*.

[8] See also Section 5.V.2.

6.IV CONCLUSIONS

6.IV.1 The Issue of Inheritance

The women included in the database do not seem to have inherited the office from their mothers. Nor did they become *šmʿywt* due to any specific titles that their fathers held.[9] There does not appear to be any consistent connection between a woman's possession of the title *šmʿyt* and any other family member's cult affiliations. Rather, a pattern of exposure to the cult, or family participation in cult activities seems relevant. As most subjects in this study served Amun at Thebes during the New Kingdom or the Third Intermediate Period, it is not surprising nor a coincidence that many members of one family could all be affiliated with the cult of Amun. The predominance of family members in the service of Amun probably had more to do with the popularity of Amun as the state god than any specific family tradition. The cult of Amun's economic and social importance resulted in the active participation of many citizens, which may statistically appear to be the inheritance of the title. This is not the case, however, since the pattern is not sufficiently consistent to remove all doubts. Similarly, Galvin (1981: 281) and Gillam (1991: 222) agree that the economic and social importance of the cult of Hathor at Cusae resulted in that cult's dominance by a few families and that this "monopoly" of cult positions cannot be interpreted as inheritance.

The decision of a woman to participate as a *šmʿyt* in a specific cult seems to have been governed by three factors. Firstly, the family's involvement in a particular cult seems to have been important, but not overriding in all cases. Secondly, the influence a particular cult had in the local community was also a consideration. These two factors were usually related because the small community of elite officials and wealthy members of the middle class were usually involved in the dominant state religious institutions of their time. The third factor was personal piety, or the individual's desire to carry out religious duties. This last factor must not be overlooked since it most likely explains why some women chose to become *šmʿyt* where there was no family history of religious service, and why others chose different deities to serve than the ones their mothers or other relatives chose.

6.IV.2 Family Status

It is clear that much more is known about the family of the *šmʿywt* of the New Kingdom than of the later periods. This may be due to the fact that the decorated nobles' tombs at Thebes record scenes of family life and the lifestyle of the officials. These monuments, as well as the other sources, demonstrate that the title *šmʿyt* was a common part of the lives of the elite.

[9] This seems to be the case for the title *wrt ḫnrt nt Ỉmn* in the Third Intermediate Period where wives and daughters of the high priest of Amun commonly held this title (Wente, 1967b: 157, n.16)

The 18th Dynasty definitely saw an increase in the status of the families of *šmʿywt*.[10] Some were from the families of the highest officials in Egypt including high priests, second, third, and fourth priests of Amun, mayors, seal bearers, judges, overseers of goldsmiths, senior scribes, and guardians of the treasury of the two lands. Women's designations included *ẖkrt nsw* (lady-in-waiting) and *mnʿt nsw* (royal nurse) as well as *šmʿyt*. These families were of an educated noble class.

As mentioned previously, the *šmʿywt* of the Ramesside age were of a slightly less elite social class. Despite the fact that a few royal women were *šmʿwyt* during this era, the families of the chantresses were more often characterized by men who held titles of lesser distinction such as scribe, priest (*ḥm nṯr* and *wʿb*), stablemaster, standard bearer, fan bearer, and charioteer.

For the periods after the New Kingdom, there are far fewer decorated tombs and other monuments documenting the families of secular and religious officials. Most information about the *šmʿywt* of the Third Intermediate Period derives from their coffins and papyri, largely of Theban origin. Information from these artifacts is primarily limited to the families of the High Priests of Amun. The majority of the remaining evidence is from objects that simply omit any mention of husbands or other family members. Occasionally these omissions were for reasons of space. However, where a monument was dedicated by a woman, or was for her specific funerary use, the husband was omitted due to the artistic conventions that dictated "compositional dominance" of the male figure whenever it was present (Robins, 1994: 33ff).

It is probably accurate to assume that women who were allowed to participate in the official religious hierarchy of Egypt were of at least a middle class background. In fact, the total data-set suggests that the women who held the title *šmʿyt* did belong to the economically advantaged middle and upper classes of society. It should be remembered that the daughters of Ramesses II were *šmʿywt*, as were the daughters of some of the highest officials. These women would not have wanted to serve as *šmʿywt* alongside common peasants. Nor would the average woman have had time for responsibilities outside her home and family.

With the issue of heredity ruled out, what were the deciding factors for becoming a *šmʿyt*? The evidence demonstrates that in some families, only a few of the women were chantresses, while others in the family were not. The family of User (TT 61) is a good example of this. Of User's numerous daughters, only one held the title *šmʿyt n Ỉmn*. His wife, sister, and mother did not (see Appendix D for details). The fact that there is no consistent pattern as to who held the title within a family strongly suggests that holding the title was a matter of personal piety.

The family of Khonsu (TT 31) demonstrates a mixture of family influence and personal piety. One scene, in which many family members take part, depicts the feast of Montu that was celebrated when the god journeyed between Armant and Tod (Davies and Gardiner, 1948: pl. XII). Two registers of women holding flowers, sistra, and incense wait on the shore for the sacred barque of Montu to dock. Male relatives attend the god on his boat and at offering piles near the women awaiting the god's arrival. The most important detail about this scene is that it illustrates women taking part in an important religious event with the men of the family. That they are participating as a family is demonstrated by the presence of a young girl with her mother. Her inclusion may indicate that the involvement of women in religious festivals began at an early age.

The participation of Khonsu's female family members in cultic activities can be traced back to his mother, a *šmʿyt* of Montu (DB #585). Her daughter (DB #927), daughters-in-law (DB #586, 602), and granddaughters (DB #s 603-605) were also involved in cult activity. It is clear that there was a deep family tradition concerning the post *šmʿyt n Mnṯ* as all of the women served in this capacity. Two of them, however, also claimed to serve Amun (DB #s 586, 603). The fact that they were attached to an additional cult outside the family tradition suggests a personal choice made by these two women.

A combination of personal piety and family influence, such as that illustrated in TT 31, coupled with an atmosphere receptive to female participation in religious ritual, perhaps due to periods of state encouragement or sponsorship of the title *šmʿyt* (as discussed in Chapter 5), adequately accounts for the distribution patterns of the title encountered in this study.

[10] An Abydene stela from the Middle Kingdom mentions two chantresses of Montu of Medamud who were mother and daughter. A number of other individuals are mentioned on the stela, but their relationships to one another are mostly unspecified. Most male titles represent humble professions, e.g., sandal maker, baker, builder, *wʿb* priest of Khnum, and cattleman. Likewise, the only 17th Dynasty stela documented in this study records a *šmʿyt* of Osiris whose son was an overseer of cattle.

CHART 1: Mothers and Daughters

Ref. #	NAME	DEITY	OTHER TITLES	MOTHER	FAMILY	PROV.	DATE
691	*W3ḏ-h3w*	Montu of Medamud		#690		Abydos	Middle Kingdom
690	*S3t-Ỉmn*	Montu of Medamud			daughter #691	Abydos	Middle Kingdom
270	*T3-ḫˁt*	Amun		*ḫkrt nsw, nbt pr, Mryt*		TT100	Tuthmosis III
271	*M3ˁt-nfrt*	Amun?		*ḫkrt nsw, nbt pr, Mryt*		TT100	Tuthmosis III
272	*Mwt-nfrt*	Amun		*ḫkrt nsw, nbt pr, Mryt*		TT100	Tuthmosis III
273	*Mryt*	Amun	*nbt pr, šmˁyt wrt, ḥsyt n Mwt m Ỉšrw*		one daughter and one sister are *ḫkrt nsw*; daughter #277; step-daughter #480	TT224, TT96 & KV40	Tuthmosis III
267	*Ḥnwt-t3wy*	Amun	*nbt pr, ḫkrt nsw*		daughters # 268, 269; mother-in-law, *mnˁt wrt nt Nb-Ỉmn*	TT98	Tuthmosis III
268	*Ỉmn-m-ipt*	Amun		#267		TT98	Tuthmosis III
269	*Mwt-nfrt*	pharaoh *ˁ3-ḫpr-k3-Rˁ*, Amun		#267		TT98	Tuthmosis III
480	*Mwt-nfrt*	Amun		*mnˁt nsw wrt, Snt-n3y*	step-mother #273	Karnak (also in TT96?)	Amenhotep II-Tuthmosis IV
277	*Mwt-twy*	Amun		#273		TT162 (and TT96)	Amenhotep II-Tuthmosis IV
278	*R3y*	Amun	*ḫkrt nsw*		daughters #279, 280, 281	TT75	Tuthmosis IV
279	*Mwt-nfrt*	Amun		#278		TT75	Tuthmosis IV
280	*Ḥnwt-t3wy*	Amun		#278		TT75	Tuthmosis IV
281	*Ṯ3-ti*	Amun		#278		TT75	Tuthmosis IV
491	*Mryt-Ptḥ*	Amun Re	*nbt pr, ḫkrt nsw, ḥsyt nt ...*	#701		TT55	Amenhotep III-Amenhotep IV
701	*Mˁy*	Amun	*nbt pr, ḥsyt n nbt t3wy*		daughter #491	TT55	Amenhotep III-Amenhotep IV

CHART 1: Mothers and Daughters

588	*Dwꜣt-nfrt?*	Amun of Karnak	*nbt pr*		daughter #589	TT254	Horemheb
589	*Mwt-m-wiꜣ*	Amun		#588		TT254	Horemheb
584	*Rnwtt*	Amun		#616	mother-in-law #618	TT50	Horemheb
616	*Mwt-nfrt*	Amun			daughter #584	TT50	Horemheb
618	*Tꜣ-ḫꜤt*	Amun	*wrt ḫnrt n Ỉmn*		daughters # 619, 620; daughter-in-law # 584; aunts #621, 622	TT50	Horemheb
619	*PikꜤ?*	Amun		#618	sister of Neferhotep (TT50)	TT50	Horemheb
620	*Ṯꜣpwy?*	Amun		#618	sister of Neferhotep (TT50)	TT50	Horemheb
768	*Mryt*	Amun			daughter #769	probably Thebes?	late Dyn.18-early Dyn. 19
769	*Tꜣ-ḫꜤt*	Amun		#768	other daughters are not *šmꜤyt*	probably Thebes	late Dyn.18-early Dyn. 19
58	*Ꜥšꜣt-nbw*	Khnum	*nbt pr*		daughters #60, 61; mother-in-law #812; daughter-in-law #59		Dyn. 19
60	*Wrt-nfrt*	Khnum		#58	sister in law #58; grandmother #812; others #62-65		Dyn. 19
61	*BꜤktiꜣ*	Khnum		#58	sister-in-law #58; grandmother #812; others #62-65		Dyn. 19
49	*Ḥnwt-ḏww*	Amun		#50	daughter #51; mother-in-law #48; daughter-in-law #52	Abydos?	Dyn. 19
49	*Ḥnwt-ḏww*	Amun		#50	daughter #51; mother-in-law #48; daughter-in-law #52	Abydos?	Dyn. 19
50	*NsꜤ*	Amun			daughter #49; granddaughter #51	Abydos?	Dyn. 19
51	*Tꜣ-wrt*	Amun		#49	sister-in-law #52; grandmothers #48, 50	Abydos?	Dyn. 19
824	*Sḫmt*	Amun	*nbt pr*		mother-in-law #826; daughter #825		Seti I

CHART 1: Mothers and Daughters

623	*Ḥ3t-špswt*	Amun	*nbt pr, ḥsyt n Ḥwt-ḥr, nbt pt t3*	#756	mother-in-law #624; daughter-in-law #4	TT51	Seti I
756	*Ḥnwt-t3wy*	Amun Re	*nbt pr, ḥsyt nt Ḥwt-ḥr*		daughter # 623	TT51	Seti I
847	*T3-n*[...]			#849		Buhen (Wadi Halfa)	Rameses II
848	*Mryt-nbw*			#849		Buhen (Wadi Halfa)	Rameses II
849	*?ḥ-di.s*		*nbt pr*		daughters #847, 848	Buhen (Wadi Halfa)	Rameses II
26	*Wrnr*	Hathor, lady of the southern sycomore			daughter #27	Memphis?	Rameses II
27	*Yy*	Hathor, lady of the southern sycomore		#26		Memphis?	Rameses II
643	*Ḥnwt-mtr*	Amun	*wrt ḫnrt n Ỉmn*		daughters #628, 629, 633; daughters-in-law #635, 634	Sehel, (TT158)	Rameses II
724	*Nʿw-šʿʿt*	Amun Re			daughter #725	TT138	Rameses II
725	*Bʿkt-Mwt*	Amun		#724		TT138	Rameses II
835	*Bʿkt-wr-n-r*	Amun		#836		TT156	Rameses II
836	*Mʿi3*	Amun			daughter #835	TT156	Rameses II
663	*Nḏm-Mwt*	Amun	*nbt pr*	#702	mother-in-law #664	TT194	Rameses II
702	*?*				daughter #663	TT194	Rameses II
736	*Nfrt-iry*	Amun, Mut, Khonsu	*nbt pr, ḥsyt ʿ3 n Ḥwt-ḥr*		daughters (or step daughters) #738, 832, 833	TT296	Rameses II
737	*Nḏm-Mwt*	Amun, Mut, Khonsu	*sḫmyt*		daughters (or step daughters) #738, 832, 833	TT296	Rameses II
738	*3st*	Amun		may be #836, 837, or 839		TT296	Rameses II
739	*K3ḥ*	Amun	*nbt pr*		daughters (or step daughters) #738, 832, 833	TT296	Rameses II
832	*Ḥr-pry*	Amun		may be #836, 837, or 839		TT296	Rameses II

CHART 1: Mothers and Daughters

833	*Ḥuy-n-r*	Amun?	*nbt pr*	may be #836, 837, or 839		TT296	Rameses II
585	*Tꜣ-wsrt*	Montu			daughter #927; daughters-in-law #586, 602; granddaughters #603-605	TT31	Rameses II
586	*Mwtiꜥy* (*Mꜥy*)	Montu, Amun	*nbt pr, ḥsyt ꜥꜣ n Ḥwt-ḥr nbt Ỉwnt*		daughters #604, 605; mother-in-law #585	TT31	Rameses II
602	*Rwiꜣ*	Montu			daughter # 603; mother-in-law #585; step-daughters #604, 605	TT31	Rameses II
603	*Wiꜣy*	Montu, Amun		#602	half-sisters #604, 605; step-mother #586; grandmother #585	TT31	Rameses II
604	*ꜥꜣti*	Montu		#586	sister #605; half-sister #603; step-mother #602; grandmother #585	TT31	Rameses II
605	*Ns-nb*	Montu		#586	sister #604; half-sister # 603; step-mother #602; grandmother #585	TT31	Rameses II
927	*Tnt-iwnt*	Montu		#585		TT31	Rameses II
881	*Nḏmt*	Amun	*nbt pr, ḥsyt ꜥꜣ n imntt wꜣst*	#882	mother-in-law #880	TT41	Rameses II
882	*Mꜥy?*	Amun	*nbt pr*		daughter #881	TT41	Rameses II
503	*Ỉsw-mwt*	Amun of Karnak, *ḥr sꜣ šmꜥ*			daughters #506-511; daughters-in-law #504, 505?	TT44	Rameses II
506	*?*			#503	sisters #507-511; sisters-in-law #504, 505	TT44	Rameses II
507	*Nfrt-iry*			#503	sisters #506,508-511; sisters-in-law #504, 505	TT44	Rameses II
508	*Tꜣ-my(t)*			#503	sisters #506, 507, 509-511; sisters in law #504, 505	TT44	Rameses II
509	*Ỉryt-nfrt*			#503	sisters #506-508, 510-511; sisters-in-law #504, 505	TT44	Rameses II

CHART 1: Mothers and Daughters

510	*?*			#503	sisters #507-509, 511; sisters-in-law #504, 505	TT44	Rameses II
511	*?*			#503	sisters #507-510; sisters-in-law #504, 505	TT44	Rameses II
704	*Bʿk-ḫnsw*	Amun, Mut, Khonsu	*nbt pr*		daughters #705-706, 708-710; mother-in-law # 703; granddaughter #707	TT45	Rameses II
705	*Ty-m-ḥb*	Amun		#704		TT45	Rameses II
706	*Nḫt-Mwt*	Amun		#704		TT45	Rameses II
708	*Ḥnwt-tꜣwy*	Amun		#704		TT45	Rameses II
709	*wr-[nfr]*	Amun		#704		TT45	Rameses II
710	*ꜣst-nfrt*	Amun		#704		TT45	Rameses II
778	*Tꜣy-sn-nfr*	Wepwawet			daughters #779-781; mother-in-law #782	Asyut?	Rameses II or Merneptah
779	*Mhyt-ḫʿṯ*	Wepwawet		#778		Asyut?	Rameses II or Merneptah
780	*Nfr-ꜣst*	Wepwawet		#778		Asyut?	Rameses II or Merneptah
781	*Wnp*	Wepwawet		#778		Asyut?	Rameses II or Merneptah
39	*Ḥnwt-Ỉwnw*	Bastet			co-wife with #40; daughters #41, 42; mother-in-law #38; sisters-in-law #43, 37		Merneptah
41	*Tꜣ-ḫʿ(t)*	Bastet		#39 or 40	grandmother #38; aunts #37, 43		Merneptah
42	*Nfrt-iiṯ*	Bastet		#39 or 40	grandmother, #38; aunts, #37, 43		Merneptah
43	*Tꜣriꜣ*	Bastet		#38	sisters-in-law #37, 39; nieces, #41, 42		Merneptah
627	*Nbt-tꜣwy*	Amun	*nbt pr*	#719	mother-in-law #625; sisters #721-722; grandmother #720	TT23	Merneptah
719	*Mwt-nfrt*	Amun		#720	daughters #627, 721, 722	TT23	Merneptah
719	*Mwt-nfrt*	Amun		#720	daughters #627, 721, 722	TT23	Merneptah
720	*Mhyt-ḫʿṯ*	Amun			daughter #719; granddaughter #627	TT23	Merneptah

CHART 1: Mothers and Daughters

721	*Ḥuy-n-r*	Bastet		#719	sisters #627, 722; grandmother #720	TT23	Merneptah
722	*Mwt-nfrt*	Bastet		#719	sisters #627, 721; grandmother #720	TT23	Merneptah
85	*Wrt-wꜣḥ-sw*	Amun	*nbt pr*		daughters #86-88; mother-in-law #89		Dyn. 19-20
86	*Nfrt-iry*			#85			Dyn. 19-20
87	*ꜣst*			#85			Dyn. 19-20
88	*Ḥʿt-bꜣḫt*			#85			Dyn. 19-20
97	*Tꜣ-nfrt*	Amun			daughter #98		Dyn. 19-20
98	*Bꜣk-wrn*	Montu		#97			Dyn. 19-20
101	*Tꜣ-wrt*	Wepwawet			daughter #102?		Dyn. 19-20
102	*Sḫmt*	Wepwawet	*nbt pr*	?#101			Dyn. 19-20
513	*Ỉry-tḫ*	Khnum		#514		Amarah West, temple	Dyn. 19-20
514	*Tꜣ-mḥyt*	Horus of Aniba			daughter #513	Amarah West, temple	Dyn. 19-20
99	*Tꜣy-bs*	Thoth			daughter #100	Serabit el Khadim	Dyn. 19-20
100	*Tꜣy-ʿḳy*	Thoth		#99		Serabit el Khadim	Dyn. 19-20
682	*?*	Amun		#681		Medinet Habu	Rameses III
653	*Ḥnwt-mtr*	Amun	*nbt pr*		daughter #653	TT267	Rameses III
654	*Nbw-iiy*	Amun	*m sꜣw tpy?*	#654		TT267	Rameses III
785	*Tꜣ-mryt*	Amun of Karnak	*wrt ḫnrt...*	*wrt ḫnrt Ỉmn*, Adjetau	mother-in-law #634	TT148	Rameses III or later
786	*Tꜣ-mit*	Amun		*wrt ḫnrt n Ỉn-ḥrt*	mother-in-law #634	TT148	Rameses III or later
628	*Ḥnwt*	Amun		#643		TT158	Rameses III or later
629	*Šri(t)-Rʿ*	Amun		#643		TT158	Rameses III or later
630	*(Ḥ?)krt*	Amun		#634	many sisters and aunts were *šmʿyt*	TT158	Rameses III or later
632	*Tꜣy-ḥnwt-pꜣ-mtr*	Amun		#634	many sisters and aunts were *šmʿyt*	TT158	Rameses III or later
634	*Nfrt-iry*	Amun of Karnak	*nbt pr, wrt ḫnrt n Ỉmn*	*wrt ḫnrt n Ỉmn*	daughters #630, 632; mother-in-law #643; daughters-in-law #785, 786; sister-in-law #681	TT158	Rameses III or later

CHART 1: Mothers and Daughters

634	*Nfrt-iry*	Amun of Karnak	*nbt pr, wrt ḫnrt n Ỉmn*	*wrt ḫnrt n Ỉmn*	daughters #630, 632; mother-in-law #643; daughters-in-law #785, 786; sister-in-law #681	TT158	Rameses III or later
633	*T3y-nḏmt*	Amun	*nbt pr*	#643		TT158, TT148	Rameses III or later
639	*Mꜥi3y*	Montu, Amun	*wrt ḫnrt n Mnṯw*	*wrt ḫnrt n Ỉmn, T3-ḫꜥ*	mother-in-law # 637	TT331	Rameses VII
45	*T3-wsr(t)*	Wepwawet	*nbt pr*		daughters #46, 47		Rameses IX
46	*3st*	Wepwawet		#45			Rameses IX
47	*T3-ꜥky*	Wepwawet		#45			Rameses IX
789	*Mwt-m-mr.s*	Amun Re, Mut, Knonsu	*ḥsyt n ḥwt-ḥr*	#791	daughter-in-law #726; mother-in-law #790	TT65	Rameses IX
791	*T3-mt…*	Amun Re			daughter #789	TT65	Rameses IX
9	*Ṯnt-Ỉmn (T3-nt-Ỉmn)*	Amun Re	*nbt pr, ḥsyt n p3 ꜥ n Mwt wrt nbt Ỉšrw; ḥsyt ꜥ3t n nbw w3st Ỉmn, Mwt, Ḫnsw*		daughter #341?		mid Dyn. 21
341	*T3yw-ḥryt*	Amun Re	*nbt pr, ḥsyt ꜥ3t ꜥ n nbw ḥḥ*	#9?			mid Dyn. 21
150	*Ḥryw-wbn*	Amun Re	*nbt pr, wrt ḫnrt n Ỉmn m s3 4-nw, wrt ḫnrt tpt, ḥm(t) nṯr 2-nw n Mwt, ḥm(t) nṯr 2-nw n Mwt n pr ms*	priestess, Asetemak-heb, daughter of HP Menkheper-re		Bab el Gusus	late Dyn. 21
164	*Nsy-Mwt*	Amun		temple singer of Amun, Djedkhons-uiwsankh		TT83	late Dyn. 21-early Dyn. 22
181	*(Nsy)t3-nbt-išrw*	Amun		#787			early Dyn. 22
194	*Nsy-Mwt*	Amun		#788			early Dyn. 22
787	*Ḏd-ḥr-iw.s-ꜥnḫ*	Amun			daughter #181		early Dyn. 22
788	*Nsy-t3-nb-išrw*	Amun			daughter #194		early Dyn. 22
566	*?*	Seth	*nbt pr*		daughter #759	Dakhla	Sheshonq I
759	*?*	Seth		#566		Dakhla	Sheshonq I

CHART 2: Mothers-in-law and Daughters-in-law

Ref. #	NAME	DEITY	OTHER TITLES	FAMILY	PROV.	DATE
481	*Nyt*	Amun	*mnʿt wrt n nb t3wy ḥsyt n nṯr nfr šdt nṯr nfrt snḳ, ḫnm.n ḥr šnbt*	mother-in-law, *mnʿt wrt*	TT88	Tuthmosis III-Amenhotep II
267	*Ḥnwt-t3wy*	Amun	*nbt pr, ḫkrt nsw*	daughters # 268, 269; mother-in-law, *mnʿt wrt nt Nb-Ỉmn*	TT98	Tuthmosis III-Amenhotep II
276	*Mryt*	Thoth		daughter-in-law, *ḥsyt n Ḥwt-ḥr*	TT92	Amenhotep II
275	*T3-ddt.s*	Amun		mother-in-law, *mnʿt nsw*	TT93	Amenhotep II
493	*Bʿt3*	Amun *ḥr s3 4-nw*		mother-in-law, *Nbt-k3bny-wrt ḫnỉyt nt s3t nsw, mnʿt wrt, šdt nṯr ḥsyt n nṯr nfr*, born of *ḫkrt nsw, ʿḥms*	Abydos	Amenhotep III
584	*Rnwtt*	Amun		mother-in-law #618	TT50	Horemheb
618	*T3-ḫʿt*	Amun	*wrt ḫnrt n Ỉmn*	daughters # 619, 620; daughter-in-law # 584; aunts #621, 622	TT50	Horemheb
58	*ʿš3t-nbw*	Khnum	*nbt pr*	daughters #60, 61; mother-in-law #812; daughter-in-law #59		Dyn. 19
58	*ʿš3t-nbw*	Khnum	*nbt pr*	daughters #60, 61;mother-in-law #812; daughter-in-law #59		Dyn. 19
59	*Ty*	Khnum	*nbt pr*	mother-in-law #58		Dyn. 19
812	*Wrt-nfrt*	Khnum	*nbt pr*	daughter-in-law #58; granddaughters #60-61		Dyn. 19
48	*Ỉpt-nfrt*	Amun		daughter-in-law #49	Abydos?	Dyn. 19
49	*Ḥnwt-ḏww*	Amun		daughter #51; mother-in-law #48; daughter-in-law #52	Abydos?	Dyn. 19
49	*Ḥnwt-ḏww*	Amun		daughter #51; mother-in-law #48; daughter-in-law #52	Abydos?	Dyn. 19
52	*Ỉy-nfr.ti*	Amun		mother-in-law #49; sister-in-law #51	Abydos?	Dyn. 19
762	*T3-k3-mn-(wḏ3?)*	Amun		mother-in-law #763	Thebes?	Dyn. 19
763	*Ḥuy-n-r*	Amun		daughter-in-law #762	Thebes?	Dyn. 19
824	*Sḫmt*	Amun	*nbt pr*	daughter #825; mother-in-law #826		Seti I
826	*Ḥnt-iwnw*	Amun		daughter-in-law #824		Seti I
783	*Rnnwtt*	Amun Re, Wepwawet	*nbt pr*	daughter-in-law #444	Asyut, tomb of Amen-hotep	Seti I

CHART 2: Mothers-in-law and Daughters-in-law

444	*Rnnwtt*	Amun Re, Wepwawet, Hathor of Medjedny	*wrt ḫnrt Ḥwt-ḥr, nbt Mddny*	mother-in-law #783	Asyut?	Seti I
919	*Tiy*	Amun	*wrt ḫnrt n Ỉmn, ḥsyt n nsw, ḥsyt n pr nsw*	grandmother or mother-in-law, *wrt ḫnrt n Ỉmn, Mryt-rꜥ*	TT106	Seti I
4	*?*	Amun	*ḥsyt n Ḥwt-ḥr*	mother-in-law #623	TT51	Seti I
623	*Ḥꜣt-špswt*	Amun	*nbt pr, ḥsyt n Ḥwt-ḥr, nbt pt tꜣ*	mother-in-law #624; daughter-in-law #4	TT51	Seti I
624	*Tꜣ-wsrt*	Montu?		daughter-in-law #623	TT51	Seti I
608	*Mwt-nfrt*	Amun	*wrt ḫnrt n Ỉmn-Rꜥ nb Ỉw-rd*	mother-in-law #609	Zawyet el Sultan	Seti I
609	*Ḳꜣ [ḳꜣ]*	Amun		daughter-in-law #608	Zawyet el Sultan	Seti I
578	*Nfrt-Mwt*	Nekhbet, Amun	*wrt ḫnrt n Nḫbt, wrt ḫnrt n Ỉmn*	mother-in-law #607	Faras, Qasr Ibrim, TT289, Sehel	Rameses II
607	*ꜥ-n-wḏꜣ*	Amun		daughter-in-law #578	Kom el Ahmar?	Rameses II
643	*Ḥnwt-mtr*	Amun	*wrt ḫnrt n Ỉmn*	daughters #628, 629, 633; daughters-in-law #635, 634	Sehel, TT158	Rameses II
876	*Wiꜣy*	Amun	*nbt pr*	daughter-in-law #877	TT111	Rameses II
877	*Ỉwy*	Bastet, lady of Ankh-tawy	*nbt pr*	mother-in-law #876; daughter-in-law #878	TT111	Rameses II
852	*Bꜥkt-Mwt*	Amun	*nbt pr*	mother-in-law #853	TT183	Rameses II
853	*Twiꜣ*	Amun		daughter-in-law #852	TT183	Rameses II
663	*Nḏm-Mwt*	Amun	*nbt pr*	mother-in-law #664	TT194	Rameses II
664	*Mwt?*	Amun, Mut, Khonsu	*ḥryt šmꜥywt*	daughter-in-law # 663	TT194	Rameses II
585	*Tꜣ-wsrt*	Montu		daughter #927; daughters-in-law #586, 602; granddaughters #603-605	TT31	Rameses II
586	*Mwtiꜥy (Mꜥy)*	Amun, Montu	*nbt pr, ḥsyt ꜥꜣ n Ḥwt-ḥr nbt Ỉwnt*	daughters #604, 605; mother-in-law #585	TT31	Rameses II
602	*Rwiꜣ*	Montu		daughter # 603; mother-in-law #585; step-daughters #604, 605	TT31	Rameses II
693	*ꜣst*	Amun	*nbt pr, ḥsyt n Ḥwt-ḥr*	mother-in-law #723	TT32	Rameses II
723	*Ḥnwt-wꜣḏbt*	*Nbt-ww, ꜣmun*	*nbt pr*	daughter-in-law #693	TT32	Rameses II
804	*Rꜥiꜣy*	Amun Re, Mut	*nbt pr*	mother-in-law #805	TT409	Rameses II
805	*Twt-wiꜣ*	Amun		daughter-in-law #804, 806	TT409	Rameses II
806	*Tꜣ-smnt*	Amun		mother-in-law #805	TT409	Rameses II
880	*Ỉny*	Amun, Mut, Khonsu	*nbt pr*	daughter-in-law #881	TT41	Rameses II

CHART 2: Mothers-in-law and Daughters-in-law

881	*Nḏmt*	Amun	*nbt pr, ḥsyt ʿ3 n imntt w3st*	mother-in-law #880	TT41	Rameses II
503	*ỉsw-mwt*	Amun of Karnak *ḥr s3 šmʿ*		daughters #506-511; daughters-in-law #504, 505?	TT44	Rameses II
504	*Ḥwt-ḥr*	Amun		mother-in-law #503?; sisters-in-law #506-511	TT44	Rameses II
505	*?*	Amun	*nbt pr*	mother-in-law #503?; sisters-in-law #506-511	TT44	Rameses II
703	*3st*	Amun	*nbt pr*	daughter-in-law #704	TT45	Rameses II
704	*Bʿk(t)-Ḫnsw*	Amun, Mut, Khonsu	*nbt pr*	daughters #705-706, 708-710; mother-in-law #703; granddaughter #707	TT45	Rameses II
778	*T3y-sn-nfr*	Wepwawet		daughters #779-781; mother-in-law #782	Asyut?	Rameses II or Merneptah
782	*T3-kt*	Wepwawet		daughter-in-law #778	Asyut?	Rameses II or Merneptah
37	*Ḳ3-nḥbt*	Amun		mother-in-law #38?		Merneptah
38	*Bʿk-wrnr*	Bastet		daughter-in-law #37?		Merneptah
39	*Ḥnwt-ỉwnw*	Bastet		daughters #41, 42 shared with #40; mother-in-law #38; sisters-in-law #43, 37		Merneptah
902	*3st-nfrt*	Amun	*nbt pr.f*	mother-in-law #903	Abydos	Merneptah
903	*ʿwrti*	Amun		daughter-in-law #902	Abydos	Merneptah
625	*T3-miw*	Amun		daughter-in-law #627	TT23	Merneptah
626	*Rʿỉ3*	Amun of Karnak	*nbt pr, wrt ḫnrt n Sbk*	mother-in-law #625	TT23	Merneptah
627	*Nbt-t3wy*	Amun	*nbt pr*	mother-in-law #625; sisters #721-722; grandmother #720	TT23	Merneptah
641	*Wi3y(?)*	Amun		daughter-in-law #642	TT163	mid-late Dyn. 19
642	*Nḏmt-niwt*	Amun		mother-in-law #641	TT163	mid-late Dyn. 19
85	*Wrt-w3ḥ-sw*	Amun	*nbt pr*	daughters #86-88; mother-in-law #89		Dyn. 19-20
89	*ỉni-h3y*			daughter-in-law #86		Dyn. 19
595	*S3-kt*	Thoth		step-mother-in-law #596?		Dyn. 19
596	*Nsw-m-ḥʿb*	Thoth		step-daughter-in-law #595		Dyn. 19
66	*ỉs3y (Ḥn3y)*	Banebdjed		daughter-in-law #67	Mendes or Hermopolis Parva?	Dyn. 19
67	*T3-b3-s3*	Thoth, arbitrator of the two combatants	*nbt pr*	mother-in-law #66	Mendes or Hermopolis Parva?	Dyn. 19
68	*T3-bw-b3*	Pre	*nbt pr*	mother-in-law #69		Rameses III
69	*Mwt-m-wi3*	Hathor, lady of the southern sycomore		daughter-in-law #68		Rameses III

CHART 2: Mothers-in-law and Daughters-in-law

891	*Tꜣ-kꜣrt (ḫꜥ-Bꜣstt)*	Amun	*nbt pr*	mother-in-law #892		Rameses III
892	*ꜥnḫ-iꜣ-iw-nbw*	Amun		daughter-in-law #891		Rameses III
785	*Tꜣ-mryt*	Amun of Karnak	*wrt ḫnrt...*	mother-in-law #634	TT148	Rameses III or later
786	*Tꜣ-mit*	Amun		mother-in-law #634	TT148	Rameses III or later
634	*Nfrt-iry*	Amun of Karnak	*nbt pr, wrt ḫnrt n Ỉmn*	daughters #630, 632; mother-in-law, #643; daughters-in-law #785, 786; sister-in-law #681	TT158	Rameses III or later
634	*Nfrt-iry*	Amun of Karnak	*nbt pr, wrt ḫnrt n Ỉmn*	daughters #630, 632; mother-in-law, #643; daughters-in-law #785, 786; sister-in-law #681	TT158	Rameses III or later
635	*Sḫmt*	Khnum		mother-in-law #643	TT158	Rameses III or later
631	*Ḥnwt-tꜣwy*	Amun	*nbt pr*	mother-in-law #634	TT158, TT148	Rameses III or later
637	*Ỉwy*	Montu, Amun		daughter-in-law #639	TT324, Sehel	Rameses VI
639	*Mꜥiꜣy*	Montu, Amun	*wrt ḫnrt n Mnṯw*	mother-in-law # 637	TT331	Rameses VII
726	*Ṯnt-pꜣ-sṯꜣ*	Amun Re	*sḫmyt n Mwt m Ỉšrw, ḥsy ꜥꜣ n Ḥwt-ḥr ḥr ib ḏrst*	mother-in-law #789	TT65	Rameses IX
789	*Mwt-m-mr.s*	Amun Re, Mut, Knonsu	*ḥsyt n Ḥwt-ḥr*	mother-in-law #790; daughter-in-law #726	TT65	Rameses IX
789	*Mwt-m-mr.s*	Amun Re, Mut, Knonsu	*ḥsyt n Ḥwt-ḥr*	mother-in-law #790; daughter-in-law #726	TT65	Rameses IX
790	*Wiꜣy*	Amun Re		daughter-in-law #789	TT65	Rameses IX
568	*Tꜣ-di*	Amun		mother-in-law #569	TT33	Saite
569	*Nꜣ-mnḫ-ꜣst*	Amun	*iḥyt n Ỉmn*	daughter-in-law #568	TT33	Saite

CHART 3: Fathers

Ref. #	NAME	DEITY	FATHER	PROV.	DATE
412	3sty	Bastet	imy-r mšʿ, Ḥri		New Kingdom
413	T3-rnnt	Amun	imy-r mšʿ, Ḥri		New Kingdom
257	T3-m-rsfy	Amun	ḥm nṯr tpy n Ỉmn, Ḥpw-snb	TT67 and Gebel el Silsila, shrine 15	Hatshepsut
258	Ḥnwt-t3wy	Amun?	ḥm nṯr tpy n Ỉmn, Ḥpw-snb	TT67 and Gebel el Silsila, shrine 15	Hatshepsut
259	Ḥnwt-nfrt	Amun?	ḥm nṯr tpy n Ỉmn, Ḥpw-snb	TT67 and Gebel el Silsila, shrine 15	Hatshepsut
261	B3kt	Amun?	imy-r niwt ṯ3ty, Wsir	(TT61, TT131) TT82, TT100, Gebel el Silsilah shrine 17	Hatshepsut-Tuthmosis III
260	Sn-snb	Amun	ḥm nṯr tpy n Ỉmn, Ḥpw-snb (TT67)	TT39	Hatshepsut-Tuthmosis III
270	T3-ḫʿt	Amun	imy-r niwt ṯ3ty, Rḫ-mi-rʿ	TT100	Tuthmosis III-Amenhotep II
271	M3ʿt-nfrt	Amun?	imy-r niwt ṯ3ty, Rḫ-mi-rʿ	TT100	Tuthmosis III-Amenhotep II
272	Mwt-nfrt	Amun	imy-r niwt ṯ3ty, Rḫ-mi-rʿ	TT100	Tuthmosis III-Amenhotep II
268	Ỉmn-m-ipt	Amun	ḥm nṯr 3-nw n Ỉmn, K3-m-ḥry-ib.sn	TT98	Tuthmosis III-Amenhotep II
269	Mwt-nfrt	pharaoh ʿ3-ḫpr-k3-Rʿ, Amun	ḥm nṯr 3-nw n Ỉmn, K3-m-ḥry-ib.sn	TT98	Tuthmosis III-Amenhotep II
480	Mwt-nfrt	Amun	ḥ3ty-ʿ n niwt rsyt, Sn-nfr	Karnak (also may be in TT96)	Amenhotep II-Tuthmosis IV
277	Mwt-twy	Amun	ḥ3ty-ʿ n niwt rsyt, Sn-nfr	TT162 (and TT96)	Amenhotep II-Tuthmosis IV
279	Mwt-nfrt	Amun	ḥm nṯr 2-nw n Ỉmn, Ỉmn-ḥtp-s3-s	TT75	Tuthmosis IV
280	Ḥnwt-t3wy	Amun	ḥm nṯr 2-nw n Ỉmn, Ỉmn-ḥtp-s3-s	TT75	Tuthmosis IV
281	T3-ti	Amun	ḥm nṯr 2-nw n Ỉmn, Ỉmn-ḥtp-s3-s	TT75	Tuthmosis IV
491	Mryt-Ptḥ	Amun Re	ḥm nṯr Wrt ḥk3w, imy-r ḥmw-nṯr m ḥwt sḫmt, sš nsw, Ỉmn-ḥtp	TT55	Amenhotep III-Amenhotep IV
589	Mwt-m-wi3	Amun	ḥry iry pr-ḥd n pr Ỉmn-Rʿ, sš pr-ḥd Ỉmn, sš it nṯr Ỉmn, iry n pr Tiy m pr Ỉmn, Ỉmn-ms	TT254	Horemheb
619	Pikʿ?	Amun	it nṯr n Ỉmn, s3b, Ỉmn-m-int	TT50	Horemheb
620	T3pwy?	Amun	it nṯr n Ỉmn, s3b, Ỉmn-m-int	TT50	Horemheb
621	Ty	Amun	imy-r sd3wty?, Tʿḥ-msw	TT50	Horemheb
622	Ỉmn-sʿḥ	Amun	imy-r sd3wty?, Tʿḥ-msw	TT50	Horemheb
769	T3-ḫʿt	Amun	ḥm nṯr tpy n Ptḥ, Ỉmn-ḥtp	probably Thebes	late Dyn. 18-early Dyn. 19
51	T3-wrt	Amun	idnw imy-r mnmnwt, Nb-ms	Abydos?	Dyn. 19

CHART 3: Fathers

60	*Wrt-nfrt*	Khnum	*imy-r ssmt, Pˁy*		Dyn. 19
61	*Bˁkti3*	Khnum	*imy-r ssmt, Pˁy*		Dyn. 19
825	*Rnnwt*	Amun	*imy-r pr wr n nsw, imy-r ssmt n nb t3wy, stm m t3 ḥwt mn-m3ˁt-Rˁ ḥry-ib, Rwrw*		Seti I
251	*Mˁi3ny*	Osiris, Isis	*ḥm nṯr Wsr, Ṯ3*	Abydos	Seti I-Rameses II
496	*Tiy*	Osiris, Isis	*Ỉmy-r šnwty, Ḳny-nḫt*	Abydos	Seti I-Rameses II
847	*T3-n*[...]		*imy-r ḥmw-nṯrw n nbw t3 šmˁ, imy-r ḥmww, Mr-nḏm*	Buhen (Wadi Halfa)	Rameses II
848	*Mryt-nbw*		*imy-r ḥmw-nṯrw n nbw t3 šmˁ, imy-r ḥmww, Mr-nḏm*	Buhen (Wadi Halfa)	Rameses II
840	*Mrwt-t3-dy*	Amun	*imy-r ḥmwt n pr Ḥr nb Miˁm, R-k3*	Buhen or Aniba?	Rameses II
841	*Ḥnwt-n-m3ˁt*	Amun	*imy-r ḥmwt n pr Ḥr nb Miˁm, R-k3*	Buhen or Aniba?	Rameses II
842	*Ḥnwt-bw-tm-mt.s*	Amun	*imy-r ḥmwt n pr Ḥr nb Miˁm, R-k3*	Buhen or Aniba?	Rameses II
843	*Ḥˁt-špst*	Amun	*imy-r ḥmwt n pr Ḥr nb Miˁm, R-k3*	Buhen or Aniba?	Rameses II
844	*Ỉi-m-wnwt*	Amun	*imy-r ḥmwt n pr Ḥr nb Miˁm, R-k3*	Buhen or Aniba?	Rameses II
845	*Ḥwt-ḥr*	Amun	*imy-r ḥmwt n pr Ḥr nb Miˁm, R-k3*	Buhen or Aniba?	Rameses II
27	*Yy*	Hathor, lady of the southern sycomore	*ḥry rḫty n nb t3wy, Ḥwy*	Memphis?	Rameses II
851	*Ỉni-hty*	Hathor, lady of the sycomore	*ḥˁty-ˁ, sš nsw pr ḥd, imy-r pr wr m pr Ptḥ, wr m inb ḥd, Ptḥ-ms*	Saqqara	Rameses II
713	*3st*		*wpt nswt r ḫ3st nb, ḥri ssmt n nb t3wy, Mn-ḫpr*	Sehel	Rameses II
714	*Mˁi3*		*wpt nswt r ḫ3st nb, ḥri ssmt n nb t3wy, Mn-ḫpr*	Sehel	Rameses II
715	*3st-nfrt*		*wpt nswt r ḫ3st nb, ḥri ssmt n nb t3wy, Mn-ḫpr*	Sehel	Rameses II
928	*Ty*	Amun Re	*wˁb n ḥˁt n Ptḥ, ḥry nbyw n Ptḥ, Ṯi3*	Saqqara, tomb of Mose	Rameses II
725	*Bˁkt-Mwt*	Amun	*imy-r ḫnty ḥri Mw m t3 ḥwt-wsr-m3ˁt-rˁ-stp-n-rˁ m pr Ỉmn, Nḏm-gr*	TT138	Rameses II
835	*Bˁkt-wr-n-r*	Amun	*ḥry-pḏt, imy-r ḫ3swt rsywt, Pn-nswt-t3wy*	TT156	Rameses II

CHART 3: Fathers

663	*Nḏm-Mwt*	Amun	*ḫry ḳrst n imi-wrt ḫry iḥw tpy n nb tꜣwy, ?*	TT194	Rameses II
738	*ꜣst*	Amun	*sš nsw, idnw n pr-ḥḏ, Nfr-sḫrw*	TT296	Rameses II
832	*Ḥr-pry*	Amun	*sš nsw, idnw n pr-ḥḏ, Nfr-sḫrw*	TT296	Rameses II
833	*Ḥuy-n-r*	Amun?	*sš nsw, idnw n pr-ḥḏ, Nfr-sḫrw*	TT296	Rameses II
603	*Wiꜣy*	Montu, Amun	*ḥm nṯr tpy n Mn-ḫpr-rꜤ* (Tuthmosis III), *Ḫnsw*	TT31	Rameses II
604	*Ꜥꜣti*	Montu	*ḥm nṯr tpy n Mn-ḫpr-rꜤ* (Tuthmosis III), *Ḫnsw*	TT31	Rameses II
605	*Ns-nb*	Montu	*ḥm nṯr tpy n Mn-ḫpr-rꜤ* (Tuthmosis III), *Ḫnsw*	TT31	Rameses II
927	*Tnt-iwnt*	Montu	*ḥm nṯr tpy n Mn-ḫpr-RꜤ* (Tuhmosis III), *Nfr-ḥtp*	TT31	Rameses II
506	?		*wꜤb n ḥꜤt Ỉmn, sš ḥwt nṯr Ỉmn, Ỉmn-m-ḥb*	TT44	Rameses II
507	*Nfrt-iry*		*wꜤb n ḥꜤt Ỉmn, sš ḥwt nṯr Ỉmn, Ỉmn-m-ḥb*	TT44	Rameses II
508	*Tꜣ-my(t)*		*wꜤb n ḥꜤt Ỉmn, sš ḥwt nṯr Ỉmn, Ỉmn-m-ḥb*	TT44	Rameses II
509	*Ỉryt-nfrt*		*wꜤb n ḥꜤt Ỉmn, sš ḥwt nṯr Ỉmn, Ỉmn-m-ḥb*	TT44	Rameses II
510	?		*wꜤb n ḥꜤt Ỉmn, sš ḥwt nṯr Ỉmn, Ỉmn-m-ḥb*	TT44	Rameses II
511	?		*wꜤb n ḥꜤt Ỉmn, sš ḥwt nṯr Ỉmn, Ỉmn-m-ḥb*	TT44	Rameses II
705	*Ty-m-ḥb*	Amun	*ḥr mrw n pr Ỉmn, ḥr ir nfr sšr n pr Ỉmn, Ḏhwty-m-ḥb*	TT45	Rameses II
706	*Nḫt-Mwt*	Amun	*ḥr mrw n pr Ỉmn, ḥr ir nfr sšr n pr Ỉmn, Ḏhwty-m-ḥb*	TT45	Rameses II
708	*Ḥnwt-tꜣwy*	Amun	*ḥr mrw n pr Ỉmn, ḥr ir nfr sšr n pr Ỉmn, Ḏhwty-m-ḥb*	TT45	Rameses II
709	*wr-[nfr]*	Amun	*ḥr mrw n pr Ỉmn, ḥr ir nfr sšr n pr Ỉmn, Ḏhwty-m-ḥb*	TT45	Rameses II
710	*ꜣst-nfrt*	Amun	*ḥr mrw n pr Ỉmn, ḥr ir nfr sšr n pr Ỉmn, Ḏhwty-m-ḥb*	TT45	Rameses II
872	*Wiꜣy*	Amun	*imy-r pr n ḥwt-Ptḥ*		Rameses II
779	*Mhyt-ḫꜤt*	Wepwawet	*ḥm nṯr?, Ḫnsw*	Asyut?	Rameses II or Merneptah
780	*Nfr-ꜣst*	Wepwawet	*ḥm nṯr?, Ḫnsw*	Asyut?	Rameses II or Merneptah
781	*Wnp*	Wepwawet	*ḥm nṯr?, Ḫnsw*	Asyut?	Rameses II or Merneptah
656	*Šrit-RꜤ*	Amun	*sḏm Ꜥš m st mꜣꜤt, Pꜣ-nb*	TT211	Merneptah

CHART 3: Fathers

906	*Ỉwy*	Amun	*?sš nsw tp, sš nsw šꜥt n pr ꜥ3, rpꜥt, ḥꜥty-ꜥ, Ṯ3y*	TT23	Merneptah
41	*T3-ḫꜥ(t)*	Bastet	*kḏn tp n ḥm.f wpwty nsw r t3 nb, Wnn-nfr*		Merneptah
42	*Nfrt-iiṯ*	Bastet	*kḏn tp n ḥm.f wpwty nsw r t3 nb, Wnn-nfr*		Merneptah
43	*T3ri3*	Bastet	*ṯꜥy-sryt, Ry*		Merneptah
513	*Ỉry-tḫ*	Khnum	*imy-r šnwty, P3-sr*	Amarah West, temple	Dyn. 19-20
100	*T3y-ꜥḳy*	Thoth	*sš nsw, Swtḫ-nḫt*	Serabit el Khadim	Dyn. 19-20
86	*Nfrt-iry*		*sš wḏḥw n ꜥt irp, Bꜥk-n-Ỉmn*		Dyn. 19-20
87	*3st*		*sš wḏḥw n ꜥt irp, Bꜥk-n-Ỉmn*		Dyn. 19-20
88	*Ḫꜥt-b3ḥt*		*sš wḏḥw n ꜥt irp, Bꜥk-n-Ỉmn*		Dyn. 19-20
98	*Bꜥk-wrn*	Montu	*?sš mšꜥ, sš nfrw, Ỉmn-m-ḥb*		Dyn. 19-20
654	*Nbw-iiy*	Amun	*idnw n t3 ist m st m3ꜥt, ḥmw wr n nb t3wy m st m3ꜥt ḥr imntt w3st, ms sšmw n nṯrw nbw m ḥwt nbw, Ḥ3y*	TT267	Rameses III
785	*T3-mryt*	Amun of Karnak	*ḥm nṯr tpy n Ỉmn, Rꜥ-mss-nḫt* (TT293)	TT148	Rameses III or later
786	*T3-mit*	Amun	*ḥm nṯr tpy n Ỉn-ḥrt,* (no name)	TT148	Rameses III or later
628	*Ḥnwt*	Amun	*ḥm nṯr Ỉmn, Ỉmn-ḥtp*	TT158	Rameses III or later
629	*Šri(t)-Rꜥ*	Amun	*ḥm nṯr Ỉmn, Ỉmn-ḥtp*	TT158	Rameses III or later
630	*(Ḥ?)ḳrt*	Amun	*ḥm nṯr 3-nw n Ỉmn, Ṯ3-nfr*	TT158	Rameses III or later
632	*T3y-ḥnwt-p3-mtr*	Amun	*ḥm nṯr 3-nw n Ỉmn, Ṯ3-nfr*	TT158	Rameses III or later
633	*T3y-nḏmt*	Amun	*ḥmt nṯr Ỉmn, Ỉmn-ḥtp*	TT158, TT148	Rameses III or later
728	*Mwt-m-wi3*	Amun	*wꜥb, ḥry-ḥb, ḥry-sšt3 n Ỉmn m ipt-swt, Ky-nbw*	TT113	Rameses VIII
729	*ꜥ-n-wḏ3-mst*	Amun	*ḥry-ḥb, ḥry-sšt3 n Ỉmn-m-ipt-swt, Ky-nbw*	TT113	Rameses VIII
730	*Mwt-m-ipt*	Amun	*ḥry-ḥb, ḥry-sšt3 n Ỉmn-m-ipt-swt, Ky-nbw*	TT113	Rameses VIII
46	*3st*	Wepwawet	*ḥm nṯr tpy n Ỉmn Rꜥ-mss, s3 nsw Kš, Wn-t3w3t*		Rameses IX
47	*T3-ꜥḳy*	Wepwawet	*ḥm nṯr tpy n Ỉmn Rꜥ-mss, s3 nsw Kš, Wn-t3w3t*		Rameses IX
111	*Ỉw.s-ꜥnḫ*	Amun	*ḥm nṯr tpy, Mn-ḫpr-Rꜥ*	Bab el Gusus	Dyn. 21
246	*T3-šryt-n(t)-3st*	Amun	*ḥm nṯr pr Ỉmn (n) ḫpw, imy-r imi-wt n pr-ꜥ3, ꜥnḫ.f-n-Ỉmn*	Thebes?	Dyn. 21
170	*Ṯnt...*	Amun	*wꜥb Ỉmn-m-ipt, Ỉmn-ḫꜥ*		Dyn. 21

CHART 3: Fathers

448	*Ỉr-mwt-p3-nfr*	Amun Re	*ḥm nṯr pr Ỉmn (n) ḫpw, imy-r imi-wt n pr-ˁ3, ˁnḫ.f-n-Ỉmn*		Dyn. 21
384	*N3w-ny*	Amun Re	*ḥm nṯr tpy n Ỉmn, Ḥri-ḥr*	TT358	early Dyn. 21
152	*Ḥnwt-t3wy*	Amun	*ḥm nṯr tpy n Ỉmn, P3y-nḏm* (I)	TT 60	mid Dyn. 21
120	*Ḥnwt-t3wy*	Amun Re, Mut, Khonsu	*ḥm nṯr tpy n Ỉmn, Mn-ḫpr-Rˁ*	TT60	mid Dyn. 21
341	*T3yw-ḥryt*	Amun Re	*it nṯr n Ỉmn Rˁ , it nṯr, sš ḥwt nṯr n pr Mwt, ḥry s3wty sšw pr ḥḏ n pr Ỉmn, imy-r ḥwt nbw n Ỉmn*		mid Dyn. 21
298	*Mˁ3t-k3-Rˁ*	Amun	*ḥm nṯr tpy n Ỉmn, P3y-nḏm* (II)	Bab el Gusus	late Dyn. 21
304	*Mryt-Ỉmn*	Amun Re	*ḥm nṯr tpy n Ỉmn, Mn-ḫpr-Rˁ*	Bab el Gusus	late Dyn. 21
305	*G3t-sšn*	Amun	*ḥm nṯr tpy n Ỉmn, Mn-ḫpr-Rˁ*	Bab el Gusus	late Dyn. 21
128	*?*	Amun Re	*ḥm nṯr tpy*	Bab el Gusus?	late Dyn. 21
335	*Bw-irw-ḥˁr-Mwt?*	Amun Re	*it nṯr n Ỉmn Rˁ , B3k-n-mwt*		late Dyn. 21
391	*Nsy-Ḫnsw-p3-ḫrd*	Amun Re	*it nṯr n Ỉmn, Ns-p3-spy-t3wy*		late Dyn. 21
402	*T3-nḏm-Mwt*	Amun Re	*it nṯr mry, Ỉˁḥ-ḫrw?*		late Dyn. 21
366	*Špst-ns-Mwt-ˁnḫ-ti*	Amun (Re)	*ḥm nṯr 4-nw n Ỉmn Rˁ , Ḏd-Ḫnsw-iw.f-ˁnḫ*		late Dyn. 21-early Dyn. 22
371	*Nsy-Ḫnsw*	Amun Re	*it nṯr n Ỉmn, B3k-n-Mwt*		Dyn. 22
759	*?*	Seth	*ḥm nṯr n Swtḫ, Nsy-B3stt*	Dakhla	Sheshonq I
74	*Ns-ṯr-n-m3ˁt*	Montu, lord of Thebes	*ḥry k3t n pr Ỉmn, ˁnḫ-p3-ḫrd*	Thebes	Third Intermediate Period
418	*Ḏd-Mwt-iw.s-ˁnḥ*	Amun	*ḥm nṯr 4-nw n Ỉmn, smr wˁt, imy-r pr-ḥḏ n nb t3wy, irty nsw, msḏrty bity, Nḫt.f-Mwt?*	Ramesseum	Third Intermediate Period?
680	*Ḏd-3st-n-imw*	Osiris	*ḥm nṯr Wsir, Ỉ-y*	Abydos	Late Period
784	*T3-imnt-snb*	Khenti-amentiu	*ḥskw, ḥm nṯr Wrt-ḥk3w, Ḥr-wn-nfr*	Akhmim	Ptolemaic Period

CHART 4: Husbands

REF. #	NAME	DEITY	OTHER TITLES	HUSBAND	PROV.	DATE
580	*Snw-ʿnḫ*			*wʿb n Wpw3wt, Nfrw*	Abydos	Middle Kingdom
497	*Ms*	Osiris	*nbt im3ḫ*	*imy-r mnmnt, Ḏd-nb*	Abydos?	Second Intermediate Pierod
646	*Nwbt-nṯr-nfr*	Sobek		*sš nfr, Sny*	El Kab	New Kingdom
695	*Mwty*	Isis	*nbt pr*	*sš wʿb n ḫ3t 3st ḥ3ty-ʿ, Nḫt-mnw*		New Kingdom
685	*Mwt-nfrt*	Atum	*nbt pr*	*sš nsw, imy-r pr-ḥḏ n nb t3wy, Ḥwy*		New Kingdom?
686	*Sḫmt*	Atum		*sš nsw, imy-r pr-ḥḏ n nb t3wy, Mʿḥw*		New Kingdom?
579	*Ḥr-iy*	Amun	*nbt pr, ḥsyt n nṯr nfr*	*imy-r 3ḥt n Ỉmn, Nfr-ḥb*	Abydos	Dyn. 18
775	*Bi3t*	Amun	*nbt pr*	*ḫry-ḥb ḥry-tp imi pr-mḏ3t, sš nsw ʿnn n ḫft-ḥr, S3-mwt*	Abydos, near Portal Temple of RII	Dyn. 18
515	*Ỉw-ns-nb-t3wy*	Bastet, lady of Bubastis	*nbt pr*	*ḥm-nṯr Ỉmn nb nswt, ḥm nṯr Ptḥ, N3-nfr-ḫprw*		Dyn. 18
260	*Sn-snb*	Amun	*dw3t nṯr*	*ḥm nṯr 2-nw n Ỉmn, Pwy-m-rʿ*	TT39	Hatshepsut-Tuthmosis III
263	*Rn3y*	Amun	*ḥmt.f, nbt pr*	*wʿb s3 nswt tpy n ʿ3-ḫpr-k3-r3, Ỉmn-ḥtp*	TT345	Tuthmosis III
264	*Tti-m-nṯr*	Amun		*imy-ist-ʿ n Ỉmn, Ỉt.f-nfr*	TT53	Tuthmosis III
262	*Mryt-Ỉmn*	Amun		*imy-r pr n ṯ3ty, sš ḥsbw it n Ỉmn, Ỉmn-m-h3t*	TT82	Tuthmosis III
265	*?*	Amun		*s3b im3ḫy, Ỉmn-m-h3t*		Tuthmosis III
795	*Mryt-rʿ*			*ḥm nṯr 2-nw n Mn-ḫpr-Rʿ*		Tuthmosis III
254	*Ỉy3*	Sobek?	*nbt pr*	*ḥm nṯr tpy n Sbk, Piʿ*	Dahamsha - Sobek temple	Tuthmosis III?
273	*Mryt*	Amun	*nbt pr, šmʿyt wrt, ḥsyt n Mwt m Ỉšrw*	*ḥ3ty-ʿ n niwt rsyt, Sn-nfr*	TT224, TT96 & KV40	Tuthmosis III-Amenhotep
266	*Ḥnwt-t3wy*	Amun	*nbt pr, ḥsyt nt nbt Ỉwnt*	*rpʿt, ḥ3ty-ʿ, irty nsw, ʿnḫwy sḏmwy bity, ḫr ḥ3st Rṯnw, ḫst ḥry pḏt, Ỉmn-msw*	TT42	Tuthmosis III-Amenhotep II
831	*B3k*	Amun	*ḫkrt nsw, mnʿt wrt n nb t3wy, ḥsyt nṯr nfr, šdt nṯr, nfrt snḳ, ḫnm n ḥr šnbt.s*	*idnw n mšʿ, ḫrd n k3p, Ỉmn-m-ḥb*	TT85	Tuthmosis III-Amenhotep II

CHART 4: Husbands

481	*Nyt*	Amun	*mnˁt wrt n nb t3wy ḥsyt n nṯr nfr šdt nṯr nfrt snḳ, ḫnm.n ḥr šnbt*	*idnw nswt ṯ3y-sryt, Pḥ-sw-ḫr*	TT88	Tuthmosis III-Amenhotep II
267	*Ḥnwt-t3wy*	Amun	*nbt pr, ẖkrt nsw*	*ḥm nṯr 3-nw n Ỉmn, K3-m-ḥry-ib.sn*	TT98	Tuthmosis III-Amenhotep II
283	*Mwt-iry*	Thoth, lord of Hermopolis, Nemet-away who is in Hermopolis	*ẖkrt nsw, nbt pr, ḥsyt nt Ḥwt-ḥr*	*sš nswt imy-r mšˁ, Ṯ3-nny*	TT74	Tuthmosis III-Tuthmosis IV
287	*Ỉṯwy*	Amun	*nbt pr*	*sš nswt, sš nfrw, Ḥr-m-ḥb*	TT78	Tuthmosis III-Amenhotep III
482	*Mryt?*	Amun?	*ḥsyt n Ḥwt-ḥr nbt iwnt*	*sš nsw, imy-r pr ḥḏ?, Ḏḥwty-nfr*	TT80	Amenhotep II
276	*Mryt*	Thoth		*ḥ3ty-ˁ n Nfrwsy, Ỉ3m-nfr*	TT92	Amenhotep II
275	*T3-ddt.s*	Amun		*imy-r pr wr n nswt m Prw-nfr, Kn-Ỉmn*	TT93	Amenhotep II
487	*Ḥnwt-wrt*	Amun		*ḥry mrw s3w ˁt imy-r pr-ḥḏ wˁb n Ỉmn, Ỉṯw*		Amenhotep II
830	*Mryt.f*	Thoth	*ḥsyt n nbt...*	*wˁb, ḥ3ty-ˁ, sš n wḏḥw ḏḥwty, Ỉ3mw-nfr*		Amenhotep II
277	*Mwt-twy*	Amun		*ḥ3ty-ˁ n niwt rsyt, Ḳn-Ỉmn*	TT162 (and TT96)	Amenhotep II-Tuthmosis IV
288	*Rnwtt*	Amun	*ḥsyt nt Mwt*	*ḥry sšt3 m hn Ỉnpw, Ḏḥwty-ms*	TT295	Amenhotep II-Tuthmosis IV?
567	*Ḥnwt*	Onuris	*nbt pr*	*ḥm nṯr tpy n Ỉn-ḥrt, Ỉmn-ḥtp*	Thebes, TTA19?	Tuthmosis IV
284	*Sn-snb*	Amun	*ẖkrt nsw*	*ḥm-nṯr tpy n Ỉn-ḥrt, Nb-sny*	TT108	Tuthmosis IV
2	*T3wy*	Amun		*wnwty n Ỉmn, sš, Nḫt*	TT52	Tuthmosis IV
285	*Rn-n3y*	Amun		*imy-r niwt ṯ3ty, Ḥpw*	TT66	Tuthmosis IV
286	*Ḥnwt-t3wy*	Amun		*imy-r 3ḥwt n nb t3wy, Mnn3*	TT69	Tuthmosis IV
278	*R3y*	Amun	*ẖkrt nsw*	*ḥm nṯr 2nw n Ỉmn, Ỉmn-ḥtp-s3-s*	TT75	Tuthmosis IV
683	*Mryt*	Amun		*ẖrd n k3p, imy-r k3wt n Ỉmn, imy-r 3ḥwt n Ỉmn, ṯ3y ḫw n nb t3wy, rpˁt, ḥ3ty-ˁ, Ptḥ-m-ḥ3t*	TT77	Tuthmosis IV
493	*B3t3*	Amun *ḥr s3 4-nw*		*sš ḥwt-nṯr n Wsr, Ḥk3-nfr*	Abydos	Amenhotep III
492	*Mˁnwn3*	Bastet	*nbt pr*	*ḥry pḏt, imy-r ḫ3swt mḥyt, spry? m ḥb-sd tpy n ḥm.f, Ḫˁ-m-w3st*	Bubastis	Amenhotep III

CHART 4: Husbands

652	*Ḫbwy-nw-ns*	Bastet	*nbt pr, ḥsyt n Sḫmt, wrt ḫnrt n Bꜥstt*	*ḥry pḏt, imy-r ḫ3swt mḥyt, spry? m ḥb-sd tpy n ḥm.f, Ḫꜥ-m-w3st*	Bubastis	Amenhotep III
575	*Ỉ-pw-y*	Amun	*nbt pr*	*ṯꜥy sryt, ḥry pḏt, Wsy*	Memphis	Amenhotep III
443	*Ḥnwt-wḏbw*	Amun	*nbt pr*	*sš, imy-r šnwt n pr Ỉtn, Ḥ3t-ty3*	Thebes, tomb of Hatiay, no TT number	Amenhotep III
792	*Bꜥky*	Amun	*nbt pr, ḫkrt nsw*	*ḥm nṯr 2-nw n Ỉmn, imy-r pr ḥḏ nbw , S3-mwt*	TTA24 (Waseda designation W-6), Mut temple at Karnak	Amenhotep III
827	*Mwt-nfrt*	Amun	*nbt pr*	*s3 nsw ḥꜥt Ỉmn, wꜥb, Nḫt-Ỉmn*		Amenhotep III?
697	*Mwt-nfrt*	Khnum, lord of Her-weret		*ḥꜥty-ꜥ n Nfrwsy, Ỉwny*	Balansurah	Amenhotep III-Amenhotep IV
700	*Typwy*	Amun		*imy-r mšꜥ, Pꜥ-itn-m-ḥb*	Saqqara	Amenhotep III-Amenhotep IV
698	*Nfrt-ḫꜥ*	Ahmose-Nefertari, the Aten	*ḥsyt Ḥwt-ḥr*	*sš nsw m3ꜥ, mr.f, imy-r šnwty nw šmꜥ mḥw, imy-r pr n t3 ḥwt p3 Ỉtn, rpꜥt, ḥꜥty-ꜥ, ṯꜥy sryt nsw, Rꜥ-ms*	TT46	Amenhotep III-Amenhotep IV
491	*Mryt-Ptḥ*	Amun Re	*nbt pr, ḫkrt nsw, ḥsyt n ...*	*ṯꜥty, Rꜥ-msw*	TT55	Amenhotep III-Amenhotep IV
701	*Mꜥy*	Amun	*nbt pr, ḥsyt n nbt t3wy*	*ḥm nṯr Wrt Ḥk3w, imy-r ḥmwt-nṯr m ḥwt Sḫmt, sš nsw, Ỉmn-ḥtp*	TT55	Amenhotep III-Amenhotep IV
828	*Ṯwyw*	Amun	*ḫkrt nsw, ḥsyt n Ḥwt-ḥr*	*rpꜥt, ḥꜥty-ꜥ, smr wꜥt, it nṯr, ḥm nṯr Mnw, Ỉ33*		Amenhotep III-Amenhotep IV
699	*Knr*	Amun	*ḥsyt n nṯr nfr*	*?s3 nsw n Kš, Ḥwy*	TT40	Tutankhamun
648	*Mryt-Rꜥ*	Amun of Karnak	*nbt pr, ḥsyt n Ḥwt-ḥr nbt Ḳis, ḥsyt n Mwt*	*sš wr, imy-r mnmnt, Nfr-ḥtp*	TT49	Amenhotep IV-Aye
649	*Ỉwy*	Amun	*nbt pr*	*sš, Nby*	TT49	Amenhotep IV-Aye
692	*Mwt-nfrt*	Amun of the lake, Amun of Diospolis Parva	*nbt pr*	*ḥm nṯr tpy n Ỉmn n p3 š; ḥm nṯr tpy n Ỉmn m sm3-bḥdt, Nb-wꜥ*	Diospolis Parva	Horemheb

CHART 4: Husbands

588	*Dw3t-nfrt?*	Amun of Karnak	*nbt pr*	*ḥry iry pr-ḥḏ n pr Ỉmn-Rˁ, sš pr-ḥḏ Ỉmn, sš it nṯr Ỉmn, iry n pr Tiy m pr Ỉmn, Ỉmn-ms*	TT254	Horemheb
675	*Nbt-t3wy*	Amun	*nbt pr, wrt ḫnrt Mwt, ḥsy ˁ3 n Ḥwt-ḥr*	*sš nsw, imy-r pr m pr Ḥr-m-ḥb m pr Ỉmn, Ry*	TT255	Horemheb
676	*Bwy*	Amun	*nbt pr, wrt ḫnrt Mwt*	*ḥm nṯr tpy ˁḥms-nfrt-iry, Ḏḥwt*	TT255	Horemheb
677	*Mwty*	Amun	*nbt pr*	*sš nsw, imy-r šnwty n nb t3wy, Ỉmn-m-ipt*	TT255	Horemheb
584	*Rnwtt*	Amun		*it nṯr n Ỉmn, Nfr-ḥtp*	TT50	Horemheb
615	*Bˁk-mwt*	Amun		*ḫry-ḥb, it nṯr n Ỉmn, P3-rn-nfr*	TT50	Horemheb
616	*Mwt-nfrt*	Amun		*sš m3ˁt m Ỉwnw, Rˁ-msw*	TT50	Horemheb
618	*T3-ḫˁt*	Amun	*wrt ḫnrt n Ỉmn*	*it nṯr n Ỉmn, s3b, Ỉmn-m-int*	TT50	Horemheb
472	*Ỉp3y*	Amun	*mnˁt nsw, ḥsyt n Ḥwt-ḥr, nbt pr*	*rpˁt, ḥˁty-ˁ smr ˁ3 n mrt, ḥˁty-ˁ n Mn-nfr, Ṯ-nw-r3*	Saqqara	late Dyn. 18
661	*Ỉwy*	Amun	*nbt pr*	*sš nsw, imy-r pr wr Mn-nfr, Ni3*	Saqqara	late Dyn. 18
803	*Nfrt-iry*			*imy-r ḥmwwt n nb t3wy, imy-r nbyw n nṯr nfr, Ỉmn-m-int*	Saqqara, tomb of Ameneminet	late Dyn. 18
767	*Ryˁ*	Amun	*nbt pr*	*i3wtw n imj-prwj, Ỉmn-nḫtw*	unknown, probably Thebes	late Dyn. 18
772	*Pwy*	Amun		*imy-r ḫtm, Ḥwy*		late Dyn. 18
829	*Nfrt-iry*	Amun	*nbt pr, ḥsyt n Ḥwt-ḥr*	*sš nsw, Wsr-ḥˁt*		late Dyn. 18
696	*Bi3*	Amun	*nbt pr*	*it nṯr n Wsr, sš ḥwt nṯr n Wsr, Ḥk3-nfr*	Abydos	late Dyn. 18-early Dyn. 19
577	*Mrwt-ti*	Hathor		*wr, Ḥ3ti3*	Faras, temple at Hathor rock	late Dyn. 18-early Dyn 19
768	*Mryt*	Amun		*ḥm nṯr tpy n Ptḥ, Ỉmn-ḥtp*	probably Thebes?	late Dyn. 18-early Dyn. 19
797	*Ty*	Hathor, lady of the (southern) sycomore		*sš nsw?*	Saqqara	late Dyn. 18-early Dyn. 19
798	*Mˁi3*	Amun Re	*nbt pr*	*wt (?) ḥry pḏt, imy-r ssmt, Ry*	Saqqara	late Dyn. 18-early Dyn. 19
760	*Wrty*	Thoth		*šms ḥr, Nḫt*		late Dyn. 18-early Dyn. 19?
49	*Ḥnwt-ḏww*	Amun		*idnw, imy-r mnmnwt, Nb-ms*	Abydos?	Dyn. 19
52	*Ỉy-nfr.ti*	Amun		*sš nsw, imy-r pr wr, Ršpw*	Abydos?	Dyn. 19

CHART 4: Husbands

770	*Nfrt-iry*	Amun	*nbt pr*	*ḥsy ꜥꜣ n Mnw nb ipw, Mry-mꜣꜥt*	probably Thebes?	Dyn. 19
763	*Ḥuy-n-r*	Amun		*ṯꜥy mḏꜣt, Mꜥy*	Thebes?	Dyn. 19
58	*ꜥšꜣt-nbw*	Khnum	*nbt pr*	*imy-r ssmt, Pꜥy*		Dyn. 19
59	*Ty*	Khnum	*nbt pr*	*ḥry iḥw tp n nb tꜣwy, wpwty r tꜣ nb, Nꜥyꜥ*		Dyn. 19
106	*Dwꜣt*	Amun	*ḥsyt n Ḥwt-ḥr*	*imy-r kꜣwt n Ỉmn-m-ipt-swt, Mꜥḥw*		Dyn. 19
812	*Wrt-nfrt*	Khnum	*nbt pr*	*Ỉmy-r mnmnwt, Nꜥyꜣ*		Dyn. 19
587	*Ḥwt-ḥr*	Amun	*nbt pr*	*wꜥb n Ỉmn-rꜥ, Rmꜥ*	TT294	early Dyn. 19
773	*Tꜣ-wsr*	Amun		*ḥm nṯr, wꜥb, ẖry-ḥb, wbꜣ-nsw, Ptḥ-pꜣ-tnr*		early Dyn. 19
783	*Rnnwtt*	Amun Re, Wepwawet	*nbt pr*	*sš nsw, ẖry-ḥb ḥry-tp, imy-r wꜥbw, wr swnw, Ỉmn-ḥtp*	Asyut, tomb of Amenhotep	Seti I
444	*Rnnwtt*	Amun Re, Wepwawet, Hathor of Medjedny	*wrt ḫnrt Ḥwt-ḥr, nbt Mddny*	*sš nsw, ẖry-ḥb ḥry-tp, imy-r wꜥbw, imy-r pr ꜣst, sš šꜥt, Ỉwny*	Asyut?	Seti I
823	*Mꜥyꜥ*	Isis		*imy-r ipt-nsw n Mn-nfr, imy-r ḫtm, Ḥr-mn*	Saqqara	Seti I
657	*Ḥuy-n-r (Ḥwt-ḥr)*	Hathor?, Amun	*nbt pr, ḥsyt n Mwt*	*sš nsw m st mꜣꜥt, imy-r isw m st ḥḥ, Ỉmn-m-ipt*	TT215	Seti I
4	*?*	Amun	*ḥsyt n Ḥwt-ḥr*	*ḥm nṯr tpy kꜣ nsw ꜥꜣ-ḫpr-kꜣ-Rꜥ, Ḏḥwty*	TT51	Seti I
623	*Ḥꜣt-špswt*	Amun	*nbt pr, ḥsyt n Ḥwt-ḥr, nbt pt tꜣ*	*ḥm-nṯr tpy n kꜣ nsw nfr-ḫpr-kꜣ-Rꜥ, Wsr-ḥꜥt*	TT51	Seti I
624	*Tꜣ-wsrt*	Montu?		*ḥm nṯr tpy n Ỉmn, Ḫnsw-m-ḥb*	TT51	Seti I
608	*Mwt-nfrt*	Amun	*wrt ḫnrt n Ỉmn-Rꜥ nb Ỉw-rd*	*sš nsw, imy-r pr, Nfr-sḫrw*	Zawyet el Sultan	Seti I
609	*Ḳꜣ [ḳꜣ]*	Amun		*imy-r mnmnt n Ỉmn, Nfr-ḥtp*	Zawyet el Sultan	Seti I
6	*Nꜣšꜣ*	Amun	*nbt pr*	*imy-r pr n nsw Mn-mꜣꜥt-Rꜥ, imy-r mnmnwt n nsw nb tꜣwy, sš nsw, Ḥw-nfr*		Seti I
818	*Tꜣ-ḳꜣ*	Amun	*nbt pr*	*ḥm nṯr n Mn-mꜣꜥt-rꜥ, Ḥr-nfr*		Seti I
822	*Ṯw-iw*	Amun	*nbt pr*	*sš nsw, imy-r mšꜥ, Nḫt*		Seti I
824	*Sḫmt*	Amun	*nbt pr*	*imy-r pr wr n nsw, imy-r ssmt n nb tꜣwy, stm m tꜣ ḥwt mn-mꜣꜥt-Rꜥ ḥry-ib, Rwrw*		Seti I
251	*Mꜥiꜣny*	Osiris, Isis	*nbt pr*	*ḥm nṯr tpy n Wsr, imy-r ḥmw nṯrw n ꜣbḏw, Mry*	Abydos	Seti I-Rameses II
496	*Tiy*	Osiris, Isis	*nbt pr, wrt ḫnrt n Wsr*	*ḥm nṯr tpy n Wsr, Wn-nfr*	Abydos	Seti I-Rameses II

CHART 4: Husbands

582	*Ỉwy*	Amun *ḥr s3 2-nw*	*nbt pr*	*imy-r sš ḳd n Ỉmn-m-ipt-swt, Ddi3*	statue from Karnak cachette	Seti I-Rameses II
816	*Nfrt-iry*	Amun	*nbt pr*	*sš ḳd n Ỉmn m ḥwt Skr, P3-šdw*	TT323	Seti I-Rameses II
846	*T3-bs*		*nbt pr*	*wꜤb, Ḥuy*	Abu Simbel?	Rameses II
76	*Ḥwt-ḥr*	Horus of Behdet, Amun	*nbt pr*	*kḏn nb t3wy, Ỉmn-ms*	Abydos	Rameses II
659	*Wrt-nfrt*	Isis	*nbt pr*	*wꜤb, ḫry ḥb n Wsr* (at the temple of RII at Abydos), *Mn-m3Ꜥt-rꜤ-m-ḥb*	Abydos	Rameses II
834	*Nwb-mt*	Amun	*nbt pr*	*ḥry pḏt n nṯr nfr, Ḥ3i3*	Abydos	Rameses II
869	*Ntibp3rti3?*	Amun		*kḏn ḥr-tp n ḥm.f, Swti-m-ḥb*	Abydos	Rameses II
870	*T3-wsrt*	Amun	*nbt pr.f*	*kḏn n ḥm.f, Ḥḥ (w3ḥ?)*	Abydos	Rameses II
837	*T3-nḏmt*	Amun	*nbt pr*	*ḥꜤty-Ꜥ n MiꜤm, idnw n W3-w3t, Ḥr-nḫt*	Aniba	Rameses II
839	*Nb-m-wsḫt*		*nbt pr*	*ḥꜤty-Ꜥ (n MiꜤm), Ḏḥwty-ms*	Aniba	Rameses II
849	*?ḥ-di.s*		*nbt pr*	*imy-r ḥmw nṯrw n nbw t3 šmꜤ, imy-r ḥmww, Mr-nḏm*	Buhen (Wadi Halfa)	Rameses II
502	*?*		*nbt pr*	*imy-r ḥmw nṯrw nbw, T3-nḏm*	Buhen, temple pavement of south temple	Rameses II
758	*ḪꜤt-nsw*	Onuris	*nbt pr, wrt ḫnrt n Ỉn-ḥrt*	*ḥm nṯr tpy n Ỉnḥrt, ḥm nṯr tpy n Šw, imy ist Šw Tfnwt, wr m3w n RꜤ m ṯny, r ḥryw m ḫnyt Wsir..., Mn-msw*	el Mashayikh, Abydos	Rameses II
578	*Nfrt-Mwt*	Nekhbet, Amun	*wrt ḫnrt n Nḫbt, wrt ḫnrt n Ỉmn*	*s3 nsw n kš, imy-r ḫ3swt rsyt, St3w*	Faras,(also Qasr Ibrim, TT289, Sehel)	Rameses II
433	*Tnt?-ipt*	Montu-m-tawy		*ṯꜤy ḫw n Mnṯw-m-tꜤwy, ḪꜤ-m-w3st*	Horbeit or Qantir?	Rameses II
884	*?*		*nbt pr*	*sš nsw, imy-r pr m pr Wsr, Tw-ry*	Mashayikh	Rameses II
23	*Nbt-t3wy*	Pre		*ḥry-iḥw, BꜤk-Ꜥ3*	Memphis?	Rameses II
26	*Wrnr*	Hathor, lady of the southern sycomore		*ḥry rḫty n nb t3wy, Ḥwy*	Memphis?	Rameses II
423	*3st-m-ḥb*	Amun	*nbt pr*	*iry-Ꜥ3, Pn-nꜤyt*	possibly Qantir or Ramesseum	Rameses II
857	*Twy*	Hathor, lady of the (southern) sycomore		*rpꜤt, ḥꜤty-Ꜥ, sš nsw, imy-r pr m t3 ḥwt wsr-MꜤꜤt-RꜤ-stp-n-RꜤ m pr Wsr, imy-r k3t m st ṯs, Ḥ3t-i3y*	Qurnah	Rameses II
417	*Nfr(t)-iy*	Isis		*sš mšꜤ n nb t3wy, Wbw-rmṯ?*	Ramesseum	Rameses II

CHART 4: Husbands

855	*Ty*	Amun	*nbt pr*	*imy-r pr n t3 ḥwt-wsr-m3ʿt-Rʿ-stp-n-Rʿ m pr Ỉmn, Ḥr-m-ḥb*	Saqqara	Rameses II
808	*3ḫ.s?*	Hathor?	*nbt pr*	*sš ḥtp n nṯrw nbw sš pr ḥd n Ỉmn, Ỉw-rwḏ.f*	Saqqara, tomb of Iurudef	Rameses II
643	*Ḥnwt-mtr*	Amun	*wrt ḫnrt n Ỉmn*	*ḥm nṯr Ỉmn, Ỉmn-ḥtp*	Sehel, (TT158)	Rameses II
77	*Nfrt-iry*	Amun		*ḥmww wr n nb t3wy, Rʿ-msw*	Thebes? TT149	Rameses II
814	*Mwt-m-wi3*	Amun	*nbt pr*	*imy-r ḥsw nb m3ʿt, ḥry ḥsw Ptḥ nb m3ʿt, ḥsw n Ptḥ nb m3ʿt, Rʿi3*	Saqqara, tomb of Raia	Rameses II
929	*Mwt-nfrt*	Bastet, lady of Ankh-tawy	*nbt pr*	*imy-r pr ḥd n Ptḥ, Ms*	Saqqara, tomb of Mose	Rameses II
876	*Wi3y*	Amun	*nbt pr*	*ḥry sš ḳd n nb t3wy m mnw nb n Ỉmn-m-ipt-swt, S-mwt*	TT111	Rameses II
877	*Ỉwy*	Bastet, lady of Ankh-tawy	*nbt pr*	*sš mḏ3t-nṯr m pr Ỉmn, Ỉmn-w3ḥ-sw*	TT111	Rameses II
879	*Ḥnwt*	Amun Re	*nbt pr*	*idnw n pr Ỉmn, Ỉb-ḫʿy?*	TT111	Rameses II
878	*Bʿkt-wr-n-r*	Amun	*nbt pr*	*sš mḏ3t-nṯr n nb t3wy, Ḫʿ-m-ipt*	TT111?	Rameses II
724	*Nʿw-šʿʿt*	Amun Re		*imy-r ḫnty ḥri Mw m t3 ḥwt-wsr-m3ʿt-rʿ-stp-n-rʿ m pr Ỉmn, Nḏm-gr*	TT138	Rameses II
836	*Mʿi3*	Amun		*ḥry-pḏt, imy-r ḫ3swt rsywt, Pn-nswt-t3wy*	TT156	Rameses II
757	*T3-ḫʿt*	Isis	*wrt ḫnrwt n Ỉmn, wrt ḫnrwt n Ḥwt-ḥr, sḫmyt n Mwt*	*ḥm nṯr tpy n Ỉmn, ḥm nṯr tpy n Ḥwt-ḥr, nbt Ỉwnt, imy-r ḥmw nṯrw n Nbw w3st, Nb-wnn.f*	TT157	Rameses II
678	*T3-rnwt*	Amun	*nbt pr*	*ḥm nṯr n Ỉmn-ḥtp n p3 wb3, ḥry šmʿ wḏḥw n Ỉmn, P3-nḥsy*	TT16	Rameses II
875	*Mry-nbw*	Amun of Karnak	*nbt pr*	*it nṯr n Ỉmn-m-ipt-swt, wʿb ʿwy, ḥry-ḥb stp n nb nṯrw, 3nwy*	TT168	Rameses II
670	*Mwt-m-wi3*	Amun	*nbt pr*	*sš n pr ḥd n Ỉmn, Nfr-rnpt*	TT178	Rameses II
852	*Bʿkt-Mwt*	Amun	*nbt pr*	*imy-r pr wr, Nb-sw-mnw*	TT183	Rameses II
853	*Twi3*	Amun		*ḥʿty-ʿ n niwt rsyt, P3-sr*	TT183	Rameses II
854	*3st*	*Nbt-ww*	*nbt pr*	*imy-r 3ht m ʿ rsyt, ḥʿt-ʿ, Ḏḥty-ms*	TT183	Rameses II
850	*Mry(t)*	Amun	*nbt pr*	*ḥʿty-ʿ n niwt rsyt, sš nsw, imy-r šnwty, Nfr-mnw*	TT184	Rameses II
732	*Niwt-m-ḥb*	Amun		*imy-r ḥmww (p3 š mḥty) n Ỉmn, ḥry nbw m pr Ỉmn, Nḫt-ḏhwty*	TT189	Rameses II
733	*Tnt-p3-ipt*	Amun		*imy-r ḥmww (p3 š mḥty) n Ỉmn, ḥry nbw m pr Ỉmn, Nḫt-ḏhwty*	TT189	Rameses II
674	*Ỉwy*	Amun Re of Karnak	*wrt ḫnrt n Ỉmn-ḥtp*	*ḥm nṯr tpy n Ỉmn-ḥtp n p3 wb3, Ỉmn-msw*	TT19	Rameses II

CHART 4: Husbands

663	*Nḏm-Mwt*	Amun	*nbt pr*	*imy-r sẖtyw n pr Ỉmn, imy-r h3mw n pr Ỉmn, sš ḥwt nṯr n pr Ỉmn, sš nswt, Ḏḥwty-m-ḥb*	TT194	Rameses II
664	*Mwt?*	Amun, Mut, Khonsu	*ḥryt šmᶜywt* (full title)	*sš ḥwt nṯr m pr Ỉmn, wᶜb n ḥᶜt n Ỉmn, sš ḥtp-nṯr, Nb-nfr*	TT194	Rameses II
665	*Nfr-Mwt*	Amun		*imy-r ḫntyw, Ỉmn-ḥtp?*	TT194	Rameses II
702	*?*			*ḥry ḳrst n imi-wrt ḥry iḥw tpy n nb t3wy*	TT194	Rameses II
583	*T3-wrt*	Amun	*nbt pr*	*idnw n t3 ḥwt Wsr-m3ᶜt-rᶜ-stp-n-rᶜ m pr Ỉmn-Rᶜ ḥr imnt w3st, Mᶜḥw*	TT257	Rameses II
735	*Wbḫt*	Amun		*ḥry šnᶜw n Ỉmn m ḫnm w3st ḥr ib ḥwt Wsr-m3ᶜt-rᶜ-stp-n-rᶜ, sš n rw? pr n Ỉmn?, Pi3y*	TT263	Rameses II
645	*?*	Amun		*ṯᶜy ḫw ḥr imnt n nsw, wpwty r ḫ3st nb, ḥry pḏt n kš, Ỉn-ḥr-nḫt*	TT282?, Sehel	Rameses II
736	*Nfrt-iry*	Amun, Mut, Khonsu	*nbt pr, ḥsyt ᶜ3 n Ḥwt-ḥr*	*sš nsw, idnw n pr-ḥḏ, Nfr-sḫrw*	TT296	Rameses II
737	*Nḏm-Mwt*	Amun, Mut, Khonsu	*sḫmyt*	*sš nsw, idnw n pr-ḥḏ, Nfr-sḫrw*	TT296	Rameses II
739	*K3ḥ*	Amun	*nbt pr*	*sš nsw, idnw n pr-ḥḏ, Nfr-sḫrw?*	TT296	Rameses II
585	*T3-wsrt*	Montu		*ḥm nṯr tpy n Mn-ḫpr-Rᶜ, Nfr-ḥtp*	TT31	Rameses II
586	*Mwtiᶜy (Mᶜy)*	Amun, Montu	*nbt pr, ḥsyt ᶜ3 n Ḥwt-ḥr nbt Ỉwnt*	*ḥm nṯr tpy n Mn-ḫpr-rᶜ, Ḫnsw*	TT31	Rameses II
602	*Rwi3*	Montu		*ḥm nṯr tpy n Mn-ḫpr-rᶜ, Ḫnsw*	TT31	Rameses II
693	*3st*	Amun	*nbt pr, ḥsyt n Ḥwt-ḥr*	*imy-r pr wr n Ỉmn, sš nsw, imy-r šnwty n Ỉmn, ḥᶜty-ᶜ Ỉwny.t, Ḏḥwty-ms*	TT32	Rameses II
723	*Ḥnwt-w3ḏbt*	*Nbt-ww, 3mun*	*nbt pr*	*imy-r 3ht n nb t3wy, ḥᶜty-ᶜ n Ỉwnyt, Ỉmn-ms*	TT32	Rameses II
742	*Kmnᶜ*	Amun		*ḥry wḏḥw m ḥwt Wsr-m3ᶜt-rᶜ-stp-n-rᶜ m (pr) Ỉmn, Nḫt-Ỉmn*	TT341	Rameses II
886	*Twy*	Amun	*nbt pr*	*ḥri ist m st Mᶜᶜt, Ḳ3ḥ3*	TT360 Deir el Medina	Rameses II
748	*T3-iwnw*	Amun	*nbt pr*	*ḥm nṯr tpy n Ptḥ, ḥm nṯr 3-nw n Ỉmn, K3-m-w3st*	TT369	Rameses II
668	*Mwt-m-int*	Amun	*sḫmyt n Ỉmn, Mwt, Ḫnsw*	*s3b, P3-n-ḏrty*	TT373	Rameses II
751	*Bᶜkt-sḫmt*	Amun of the Ramesseum		*[ḥm nṯr m pr] Ỉmn m ḫnm w3st, ᶜ3 ᶜḳ m ḥwt skr, Nb-mḥyt*	TT384	Rameses II
752	*Nhty*	Amun	*nbt pr*	*ḥᶜty-ᶜ n niwt rsyt, imy-r šnwty n nṯr ḥtpw n Ỉmn, Hw-nfr*	TT385	Rameses II

CHART 4: Husbands

753	*Nb[-ḫni?]-tw*	Amun	*nbt pr*	*sš nsw (n) wḏḥw n nb tꜣwy, Mry-ptḥ*	TT387	Rameses II
804	*Rꜥiꜣy*	Amun Re, Mut	*nbt pr*	*ỉmy-r sš ḥsb ỉḥw n pr Ỉmn, Sꜣ-mwt (Kyky)*	TT409	Rameses II
805	*Twt-wiꜣ*	Amun		*sš ḥsb ỉḥw n nbw wꜣst, Mryt-rꜥ*	TT409	Rameses II
806	*Tꜣ-smnt*	Amun		*ỉmy-r sš ḥsb ỉḥw n pr Ỉmn, Sꜣ-mwt (Kyky)*	TT409	Rameses II
880	*Ỉny*	Amun, Mut, Khonsu	*nbt pr*	*sꜣb, Nfr-ỉw*	TT41	Rameses II
881	*Nḏmt*	Amun	*nbt pr, ḥsyt ꜥꜣ n ỉmntt wꜣst*	*ỉmy-r pr wr n Ỉmn, Ỉmn-m-ỉpt*	TT41	Rameses II
503	*Ỉsw-mwt*	Amun of Karnak, *ḥr sꜣ šmꜥ*		*wꜥb n ḥꜥt Ỉmn, sš ḥwt nṯr Ỉmn, Ỉmn-m-ḥb*	TT44	Rameses II
504	*Ḥwt-ḥr*	Amun		*wꜥb, sš ḥwt nṯr n pr Ỉmn, ꜥꜣ-Ỉmn*	TT44	Rameses II
505	*?*	Amun	*nbt pr*	*sš wḏhw nsw n nb tꜣwy, ỉmy-r n nw n Ỉmn, Ỉmn-ms?*	TT44	Rameses II
703	*ꜣst*	Amun	*nbt pr*	*ḥr ỉr nfr sšr n pr Ỉmn, Wn-nfr*	TT45	Rameses II
704	*Bꜥk(t)-Ḫnsw*	Amun, Mut, Khonsu	*nbt pr*	*ḥr mrw n pr Ỉmn, ḥr ỉr nfr sšr n pr Ỉmn, Ḏḥwty-m-ḥb*	TT45	Rameses II
716	*Ỉy*	Khnum, Satis, Anukis	*ḥsyt ꜥꜣt n Ḥwt-ḥr*	*ꜥꜣ n ỉst m st mꜣꜥt (ḥry ỉst), Nb-nfr*	TT6	Rameses II
25	*Mrt-Rꜥ*	Pre		*ỉt nṯr n pꜣ Rꜥ, Hꜣw-nfr*		Rameses II
31	*Ỉniw-hꜣy*	Hathor		*sš nsw ỉpt pr-ḫnrt(?) m Mn-nfr, Bꜣ-n-ꜥꜣ*		Rameses II
247	*Tꜣ-miꜣt*	Amun	*nbt pr*	*sš wḏḥw n nb tꜣwy, Nfr-ḥtp*		Rameses II
253	*Twy*	Amun	*nbt pr, ḥsyt ꜥꜣt Ḥwt-ḥr*	*ỉmy-r pr m pr Ỉmn ḥwt-wsr-mꜣꜥt-rꜥ-stp-n-rꜥ, Ỉw-r-ḫy-y*		Rameses II
598	*Sḫm-nfr*	Amun		*wꜥb n ḥꜥt Ỉmn, ḫry-ḥb wrt, Ỉmn-m-ḥꜥt*		Rameses II
813	*Ṯiꜣ*	Amun, great of victories	*snt špst nsw*	*sš nsw, ỉmy-r pr ḥḏ n nb tꜣwy, Tiꜣ*		Rameses II
838	*Bꜥkti*	*Mn-ḫpr-Rꜥ* (no cartouche)		*sš wḏḥw n Kš, Pn-nst-tꜣwy*		Rameses II
856	*Twy*	Hathor, lady of the southern sycomore	*nbt pr*	*sš nsw, ỉmy-r mšꜥ, ỉmy-r pr m ḥwt-Wsr-mꜣꜥt-rꜥ-stp-n-Rꜥ m pr Ỉmn ḥr ỉmnt wꜣst, Rꜥ-ms-nḫt*		Rameses II
871	*Ḥnwt-mḥyt*	Amun		*ỉmy-r pr n ḥwt-Ptḥ*		Rameses II
872	*Wiꜣy*	Amun		*ỉmy-r kꜣwt, wr n mḏꜥy, ḥm nṯr tpy n Ỉn-ḥrt, Ỉmn-m-ỉnt*		Rameses II
873	*Nfrt-ỉry*	Amun		*?ỉmy-r kꜣwt, wr n mḏꜥy, ḥm nṯr tpy n Ỉn-ḥrt, Ỉmn-m-ỉnt*		Rameses II

CHART 4: Husbands

874	*T3-k3-ʿnti*	Pre	*nbt pr*	*imy-r k3wt* (with various institutions), *Mʿy*		Rameses II
778	*T3y-sn-nfr*	Wepwawet		*ḥm nṯr?, Ḥnsw*	Asyut?	Rameses II or Merneptah
782	*T3-kt*	Wepwawet		*sm, Rʿ-msw*	Asyut?	Rameses II or Merneptah
902	*3st-nfrt*	Amun	*nbt pr.f*	*wʿb ʿwy, Pn-t3-wrt*	Abydos	Merneptah
917	*3st-[...]*	Isis		*ḥry pḏt, K3-nḫt*	Abydos	Merneptah
16	*Pry*	Pre		*ḥm nṯr n Mry-Imn-rʿ-msw ḫnt.f Imn, Rʿ-msw*	Abydos or Memphis?	Merneptah
910	*T3-wrt-hrṯ*	Amun Re *nb nswt t3wy*		*imy-r pr ḥḏ n nb t3wy m t3 sty, Mry*	Aniba, tomb SA.7	Merneptah
911	*Nsy-Mwt*	Amun		*ḥm nṯr Ḥwt-ḥr, Nb-b3k-wr*	Aniba, tomb SA.7	Merneptah
611	*T3-wrt-ḥtpt*	Amun		*ḥm nṯr tpy n In-ḥrt, In-ḥrt-msw*	el Mashayikh	Merneptah
612	*Sḫmt-nfrt*	Amun Re	*wrt ḫnrt nt In-ḥrt*	*ḥm nṯr tpy n In-ḥrt, In-ḥrt-msw*	el Mashayikh	Merneptah
916	*Nfrt-Mwt*	Amun		*ḥry sʿš3, Rʿ-m-ḥb*	Gurob	Merneptah
915	*Kʿt*	(Hathor) lady of the southern sycomore		*sm, wr ḫrp ḥmwt, Ḥri*	Memphis	Merneptah
918	*Ir...*			*sm n Ptḥ, Ii-ry*	Memphis, tomb	Merneptah
734	*Bdty*	Amun Re		*sš n st m3ʿt, Inpw-m-ḥb*	TT206	Merneptah
655	*Wʿbt*	Amun	*nbt pr*	*sḏm ʿš m st m3ʿt, P3-nb*	TT211	Merneptah
625	*T3-miw*	Amun		*sš nfrw, Ḫʿ-m-tri*	TT23	Merneptah
626	*RʿI3*	Amun of Karnak	*nbt pr, wrt ḫnrt n Sbk*	*sš nsw tp, sš nsw šʿt n pr ʿ3, rpʿt, ḥʿty-ʿ, Ṯ3y*	TT23	Merneptah
627	*Nbt-t3wy*	Amun	*nbt pr*	*sš nsw tp, sš nsw šʿt n pr ʿ3, rpʿt, ḥʿty-ʿ, Ṯ3y*	TT23	Merneptah
38	*Bʿk-wrnr*	Bastet		*ṯʿy-sryt, Ry*		Merneptah
39	*Ḥnwt-Iwnw*	Bastet		*kḏn tp n ḥm.f, wpwty nsw r t3 nb, Wnn-nfr*		Merneptah
40	*Iwy*	Amun		*kḏn tp n ḥm.f, wpwty nsw r t3 nb, Wnn-nfr*		Merneptah
905	*3st*	Amun	*nbt pr*	*ṯʿy nsw, wḥm nsw tp n ḥm.f, Rʿ-mss-m-pr-Rʿ*		Merneptah
907	*Ḥwt-ḥr*			*ṯʿy-ḫw, Ḥwy*		Merneptah
908	*Nfrt-iry*	Amun of Karnak	*ḥs(yt) n Mwt nbt Isrw*	*sš nsw, imy-r ḫtm n nb t3wy, Ḥri*		Merneptah
909	*T3-miw*	Amun	*nbt pr*	*ḥry nby, P3-Rʿ-m-ḥb*		Merneptah
641	*Wi3y(?)*	Amun		*ḥʿty-ʿ n niwt, Imn-ḥtp*	TT163	mid-late Dyn. 19
642	*Nḏmt-niwt*	Amun		*ḥʿty-ʿ niwt rsy, sš nsw, Imn-m-ḥʿt*	TT163	mid-late Dyn. 19

CHART 4: Husbands

84	*Twy*	Hathor, lady of the (southern) sycomore		*sš nṯr šʿt, sḏꜣwt nṯr, it nṯr n Rʿ-Ỉtm m pr ʿnḫ, Pꜣ-n-Ỉmn*	Abydos	Dyn. 19-20
514	*Tꜣ-mḥyt*	Horus of Aniba		*imy-r šnwt, Pꜣ-sr*	Amarah West, temple	Dyn. 19-20
500	*Wrt...*	Amun	*nbt pr*	*ḥm nṯr tpy n Ỉmn (n Bhn), Pꜣ-n-mḥyt*	Buhen, block B- courtyard B	Dyn. 19-20
689	*Ḥwt-ḥr*	Amun		*ḥꜣty-ʿ n Gbtyw, Rʿy*	Coptos	Dyn. 19-20
614	*Wr-n-r*	Amun		*ḥry wsḫt n pꜣ mšʿ*	Faqus region	Dyn. 19-20
57	*Bʿk(t)-ʿnḫt*	Isis		*ṯꜣy ḫw ḥr imnt n nsw, sš nsw, imy-r pr-ḥḏ, ḥm nṯr ꜣst, nbt ḥbyt, Nb-ms?*	Memphis/ Saqqara or Iseum	Dyn. 19-20
66	*Ỉsꜣy (Ḥnꜣy)*	Banebdjed		*ḥry ḳrʿw, Rʿiꜣ*	Mendes or Hermopolis Parva?	Dyn. 19-20
67	*Tꜣ-bꜣ-sꜣ*	Thoth, arbitrator of the two combatants	*nbt pr*	*ḥry ḳrʿw n ḥm.f, Smn-tꜣwy*	Mendes or Hermopolis Parva?	Dyn. 19-20
99	*Tꜣy-bs*	Thoth		*sš nsw, Swtḫ-nḫt*	Serabit el Khadim	Dyn. 19-20
83	*Tꜣ-ʿnt-ḥr-twy-st?*	Amun		*ḥryw* [obscure military title], *Nḫt-mnw*		Dyn. 19-20
85	*Wrt-wꜣḥ-sw*	Amun	*nbt pr*	*sš wḏḥw n ʿt irp, Bʿk-n-Ỉmn*		Dyn. 19-20
90	*Ḥnr*	Amun		*ir wꜣt šwy n tꜣ wʿbt n pr ʿꜣ, Ḫꜣr*		Dyn. 19-20
96	*Ḥnwt-tꜣ-nb*	Amun		*ṯꜣy bsnt pr Ỉmn, Twnn-nḫb-Ḫnsw*		Dyn. 19-20
97	*Tꜣ-nfrt*	Amun		*sš mšʿ, sš nṯrw, Ỉmn-m-ḥb*		Dyn. 19-20
594	*Kʿiꜣ*	Pre		*wʿb, Ḫʿ-m-ti-r*		Dyn. 19-20
636	*Nfrt-iry*	Montu, Amun	*ḥsyt n Ḥwt-ḥr*	*ḥm nṯr tpy n Ḫnm, Stṯ, ʿnḳt, Pꜣ-n-ḏrty*		Dyn. 19-20
638	*Tꜣ-mwt-nfrt*	Khnum, lord of the cataract		*ḥm nṯr tpy Ḫnm, Stṯ, ʿnḳt, Mn m Gbtw, Nb-wnn.f*		Dyn. 19-20
640	*Mwt-ir-di.s*	Anukis	*nbt pr*	*sš, wʿb n ḫnm, Ḏḥwty-m-ḥb*		Dyn. 19-20
416	*Tꜣ-wrt-m-ḥb*	Amun		*sš nsw n nb tꜣwy, imy-r prwy ḥḏ m ꜣḫty ḥḥ?, imy-r ḫrw m pr ḏt, imy-r kʿt m pr dwꜣt, Ỉmn-nḫt-m-tꜣwy*	Ramesseum	Dyn. 19-20?
667	*...?*	Amun	*ḥsyt n Ỉmn-Rʿ*	*wʿb n Ỉmn Mwt m Ỉsrw, [Pꜣ]-n-ḫnm*	TT68	Dyn. 20
498	*Sḫꜣ-nfr*	Re	*nbt pr*	*ḥry? ʿḥʿw n Ỉmn, Pꜣ-wr-m-wiꜣ*		Dyn. 20
650	*Ḫʿyt*	Mehyt		*sꜣ nsw n Kš, Ḥri*	Bubastis	Rameses III

CHART 4: Husbands

887	*T3-nḏmt*	Amun		*sš n pr Ḫnsw n Ἰmn-n-ipt, ʿšʿ-ḫt*	Deir el Bahari	Rameses III
681	*Ṯ3-tiy*	Herishef	*nbt pr*	*ḥʿty-ʿ n niwt, P3-sr*	Medinet Habu	Rameses III
890	*3st-nfrt*	(Hathor) lady of the sycomore		*?it nṯr n Bʿstt, Ḥri?*	Qantir	Rameses III
888	*Rny*	Mut		*imy-r k3wt m ḥwt Ἰmn ḥr imntt w3st, sš nṯr šʿt m pr ʿnḫ, Rʿ-mss-nḫt*	Sehel	Rameses III
815	*Ḥwt-ḥr*	Amun		*ḥry ḫ3w n t3 šnwty (n) pr Ἰmn, Wsr-ḥʿt*	TT A17	Rameses III
653	*Ḥnwt-mtr*	Amun	*nbt pr*	*idnw n t3 ist m st m3ʿt, ḥmw wr n nb t3wy m st m3ʿt ḥr imntt w3st, ms sšmw n nṯrw nbw m ḥwt nbw, Ḥ3y*	TT267	Rameses III
749	*Nfrt-iry-m-ḥb*	Amun		*imy-r ḥmww m pr nsw, Ἰmn-ḫʿw*	TT372	Rameses III
68	*T3-bw-b3*	Pre	*nbt pr*	*ḥry mʿš3k3bw, ḫni Rʿ-mss-ḥk3-Ἰwnw, Ἰmn-m-wi3 (Kʿr)*		Rameses III
69	*Mwt-m-wi3*	Hathor, lady of the southern sycomore		*it nṯr, ḥry sšt3 nt ḥwt Mr-n-pth m pr Rʿ, Ḥwy*		Rameses III
891	*T3-k3rt (ḫʿ-Bʿstt)*	Amun	*nbt pr*	*sš wdḥw, Ḥwri3*		Rameses III
892	*ʿnḫ-i3-iw-nbw*	Amun		*kḏn, Nfr-rnpt*		Rameses III
893	*W3ḏyt-m-ḥb*	Amun	*nbt pr.f*	*ḥry iḥw, H3w-nfr*		Rameses III
744	*Wʿbt*	Amun Re		*ʿ3 n ist n nb t3wy m st m3ʿt, Ἰn-ḥr-ḫʿ*	TT359	Rameses IV
445	*Ἰʿy*	Wepwawet	*nbt pr*	*imy-r mšʿ?, sš nsw, rḫ nsw?, Ḏḥwty-m-ḥb*	Asyut?	Rameses III or later
785	*T3-mryt*	Amun of Karnak	*wrt ḫnrt...*	*ḥm nṯr tpy n Mwt, ḥm nṯr 3-nw n Ἰmn, Ἰmn-m-ipt*	TT148	Rameses III or later
786	*T3-mit*	Amun		*ḥm nṯr tpy n Mwt, ḥm nṯr 3-nw, Ἰmn-m-ipt?*	TT148	Rameses III or later
634	*Nfrt-iry*	Amun of Karnak	*nbt pr, wrt ḫnrt n Ἰmn*	*ḥm nṯr 3-nw n Ἰmn, Ṯ3-nfr*	TT158	Rameses III or later
631	*Ḥnwt-t3wy*	Amun	*nbt pr*	*imy-r mnmnwt m t3 ḥwt Wsr-m3ʿt-rʿ-mry-imn, Bʿk-n-Ḫnsw*	TT158, TT148	Rameses III or later
637	*Ἰwy*	Montu, Amun		*ḥm nṯr tpy n Sbk, Mnṯw, Ἰnpw, Ḫnsw, Ḥ3t-i3y*	TT324 among others	Rameses VI
639	*Mʿi3y*	Montu, Amun	*wrt ḫnrt n Mnṯw*	*ḥm nṯr tpy n Mnṯw nb Ἰwny, P3-n-niwt*	TT331	Rameses VII
727	*3st*	Amun Re	*ssty (sḫmyt) n Mwt*	*wʿb, ḥry-ḥb, ḥry-sšt3 n Ἰmn-m-ipt-swt, Ky-nbw*	Thebes? (temple or TT113)	Rameses VIII

CHART 4: Husbands

726	*Ṯnt-pꜣ-stꜣ*	Amun Re	*sẖmyt n Mwt m Ỉsrw, ḥsy ꜥꜣ n Ḥwt-ḥr ḥr ib ḏrst*	*idnw n pr-ḥḏ n Ỉmn-m-ipt-swt, ḥry ẖꜣ n sš n pr Ỉmn, Ỉmi-sbꜣ*	TT65	Rameses IX
789	*Mwt-m-mr.s*	Amun Re, Mut, Knonsu	*ḥsyt n Ḥwt-ḥr*	*ḥry sš ḥwt nṯr n pr Ỉmn-m-ipt-swt, Ỉmn-ḥtp*	TT65	Rameses IX
790	*Wiꜣy*	Amun Re		*ḥry sš ḥwt nṯr n Ỉmn-Rꜥ nsw nṯrw m ipt-swt, Ḫꜥ-m-ipt*	TT65	Rameses IX
791	*Tꜣ-mt...*	Amun Re		*idnw n pr-ḥḏ n Ỉmn-m-ipt-swt, ḥry ẖꜣ n sš n pr Ỉmn, Ỉmi-sbꜣ*	TT65	Rameses IX
45	*Tꜣ-wsr(t)*	Wepwawet	*nbt pr*	*ḥm nṯr tpy n Ỉmn Rꜥ-mss, sꜣ nsw Kš, Wn-tꜣwꜣt*		Rameses IX
539	*Tꜣ-mr-pn-ꜥs*	Osiris		*wꜥb n Wsr, sš, Ḥri?*	Abydos	Rameses XI
428	*Nꜣ-nfr; Rn-nfr*	Seth		*ḥry iḥw, Nb-nfr*	Herakleopolis Magna (Ihnasya el Medina)	Rameses XI
666	*Tꜣ-bꜣk-n-Mwt*	Amun	*ḥsyt n pꜣ ꜥ n Mwt*	*ḥm nṯr n Ỉmn-Rꜥ nsw nṯrw, ḥry šsw ḥwt-nṯr n pr Ỉmn, ḥry sš wḏḥw n pr Ỉmn, Nsy-Pꜣ-nfr-ḥr*	TT68	Dyn. 21
170	*Ṯnt...*	Amun		*ḥm nṯr n Ỉmn, Ỉw-n-Ḫnsw?*		Dyn. 21
448	*Ỉr-mwt-pꜣ-nfr*	Amun Re	*hry šmꜥyt n Ḫnsw m wꜣst nfr-ḥtp, ḥsy n pꜣ ꜥ n Mwt wrt nbt Ỉsrw, mnꜥt nsw*	*it nṯr n Ỉmn, sš nsw, imy-r šnwty n šnwt pr-ꜥꜣ, it nṯr n Ḫnsw, ꜥꜣ n pr-ḳnt* (Psusennes), *Siꜣ*		Dyn. 21
385	*Ḥnwt-nṯrw*	Amun	*nbt pr*	*ḥry sšw ḥwt nṯr n pr Ỉmn, ḥry ḥmwwt wꜥb ḥry pr ḥmt sšw ḥwt nṯr m ipt-swt, ḥry sꜣwty sšw n prwy-ḥḏ n pr Ỉmn-Rꜥ nsw nṯrw, Šwty-ms*		early Dyn. 21
342	*Tꜣ-r-stit*	Amun	*nbt pr*	*it nṯr n Ỉmn-Rꜥ nsw nṯrw m ipt-swt m wꜣst, ḥsy ꜥꜣ n nṯr.f Ỉmn, wꜥb ꜥ-wy m ipt swt, it nṯr n Ỉmn m ir ḳd.f nb kk , Pꜣ-sr*		early-mid Dyn. 21
327	*Ḥnwt-tꜣwy*			*it nṯr n Ỉmn, Pꜣ-diw-Ỉmn*	Bab el Gusus	mid Dyn. 21
339	*Miꜣꜥ-nḥm*	Amun		*wꜥb n Ỉmn nb nswt tꜣwy, ꜥꜣ nḫt, ḥry-ḥb n Ỉmn-m-ipt-swt pꜣ smn tꜣwy, Bꜥk-n-wr-n*	Thebes?	mid Dyn. 21

CHART 4: Husbands

9	*Ṯnt-Ỉmn (T3-nt-Ỉmn)*	Amun Re	*nbt pr, ḥsyt n p3 ᶜ n Mwt wrt nbt Ỉšrw; ḥsyt ᶜ3t n nbw w3st Ỉmn, Mwt, Ḫnsw*	*?it nṯr n Ỉmn Rᶜ nsw nṯrw, it nṯr, sš ḥwt nṯr n pr Mwt, ḥry s3wty sšw pr ḥḏ n pr Ỉmn, imy-r ḥwt nbw n Ỉmn*		mid Dyn. 21
373	*Ỉnh3y*	Amun	*wrt ḫnrt n nb wt Ḫnm, s3 3-nw, nbt pr*	*ḥry iḥw* (of the Residence), *Nb-sw-mnw*		mid Dyn. 21
319	*G3t-sšn*	Amun	*nbt pr, wrt ḫnrt, tp n 3-nw n Ỉmn, ḥsyt ᶜ3 n Mwt*	*it nṯr mry, ḥry sšt3, ḥry t3 wnnwt pr, ḥry m? ipt-swt, ḥm nṯr 3-nw n Ỉmn Rᶜ nsw nṯrw, ḥm nṯr n Mnṯw nb w3st, imy-r mnmnwt n pr Rᶜ tp ḥwt n Ỉmn Rᶜ ḥm nṯr n Ḫnm nb ḳbḥw, Ṯ3-nfr*	Bab el Gusus	mid-late Dyn. 21
244	*Ns-Ḫnsw-p3-ḫrd*	Amun	*nbt pr*	*wᶜb-ᶜḳ Ỉmn, Ns-p3-ḥr-ᶜn*	Thebes	Dyn. 22
380	*Ḥnwt-t3wy*	Amun	*nbt pr*	*ḥry ᶜt n Ỉmn-n-pr, Diw-Ḫnsw-iry*		Dyn. 22 or later
227	*Nsy-Ḫnsw*	Amun	*nbt pr*	*Ỉt nṯr n Ỉmn-Rᶜ, it nṯr n mr-wnnw, Ḏd-ḥr-iw-ᶜnḫ*		early Dyn. 22
566	*?*	Seth	*nbt pr*	*ḥm nṯr Swtḫ, Nsy-b3stt*	Dakhla	early Dyn. 22
442	*Ns-ḥnsw-p3-ḫrd*	Amun	*nbt pr*	*mr-nṯr, wn ᶜwy pt m Ỉpt-swt, ḳbḥw n Bnbn, Ns-pr-nwb*	Thebes?	late Dyn.22
559	*Ỉ-t3wy*	Amun	*nbt pr*	*s-ᶜšᶜt n pr Ỉmn, Tᶜ-ḥr-iᶜwt.f*	Abydos	Third Intermediate Period
72	*Š...*	Amun	*nbt pr*	*wᶜb n Ỉmn, Nḫt.f-Mwt*		Third Intermediate Period
73	*T3y-iw-šri*	Amun	*nbt pr*	*imy-r ḥst, Ns-Mntw*		Third Intermediate Period
558	*T3-mwt-nfrt*	Amun	*nbt pr.f*	*3ḫ iḳr n Rᶜ, P3-dg3-r-dn?*	Abydos	Late Period
679	*Ṯ3y-nb-nḫt-rw*	Osiris		*ḥm nṯr Wsir, Šw, Tfnwt, ᶜnḫ-ḥr-s3-3st*	Abydos	Late Period
568	*T3-di*	Amun		*rpᶜt, ḥ3ty-ᶜ, sš nsw, ḥry-ḥb ḥry-tp Nḫbt, P3-di-Ỉmn-ipt*	TT33	Saite Period
784	*T3-imnt-snb*	Khenti-amentiu		*ḥm nṯr n Ḥr p3 Rᶜ ḥry-ib ᶜbḏw, ḥm nṯr n ḥ.t n pr Rᶜ-ms, ḥskw, imy ist rḫ nswt, ḥpt wḏ3t, Ḥr-ḥb*	Akhmim	Ptolemaic Period

CHAPTER 7
THE ORGANIZATION OF THE *Šmʿywt*.

7.I TEMPLE HIERARCHY

The most common assertion made concerning the organization of the *šmʿywt* is that they formed a subordinate level of auxiliary personnel, often serving in the ranks of the god's wife or divine adoratrice (Naguib, 1990: 238-239; Graefe, 1981: 48; Gitton, 1976: 88). According to the textual account of the 20th Dynasty tomb robberies investigations recorded on P. Abbott, there were four *šmʿywt* serving the estate of the divine adoratrice (*pr dwꜣt nṯr*) (Peet, 1930), but these are the only women documented as such. The chantresses' link to the god's wife, however, is entirely speculative since no evidence for a title such as "chantress of the god's wife" or "chantress of the estate of the god's wife" (*šmʿyt n ḥmt nṯr* or *šmʿyt n pr ḥmt nṯr*) has been documented.

The *šmʿywt* were divided into phyles in much the same fashion as the male orders of priests[1] (Naguib, 1990: 236; Lefebvre, 1929: 34). Four of the women documented in the database illustrate this clearly (DB #s 493, 503, 582, 654). One of the women, the lady Bata (DB #493; CG 34117), is documented on a stela from Abydos that dates to the reign of Amenhotep III. She was a *ḫkrt nsw šmʿyt n Ỉmn ḥr sꜣ 4-nw:* "lady-in-waiting, chantress of Amun on the fourth phyle". Since the male phyle system was divided into four groups, the fact that she belonged to the fourth phyle suggests that the hierarchy of the *šmʿywt* was based on the traditional model. A further case supports this suggestion. A woman named Iwy (DB #582, CG 42122) is known from a Ramesside inscription on a block statue found in the Karnak cachette. The statue refers to her as *nbt pr šmʿyt n Ỉmn ḥr sꜣ 2-nw*: lady of the house, chantress of Amun on the second phyle.

The third woman, Isumut (DB #503), had a curious title. On the walls of her husband's tomb (TT 44), she was given the title *šmʿyt n Ỉmn-m-ỉpt-swt ḥr sꜣ šmʿ*: chantress of Amun of Karnak on the *sꜣ šmʿ*. This last phrase has been taken to mean that she belonged to the "south phyle" (El-Saady, 1996: 43), but no other accepted attestations of the phrase *sꜣ šmʿ* have surfaced. Roth (1991: 148) discounts an early dynastic reading of *sꜣ šmʿw,* "Upper Egyptian phyle", by Kaplony (1963: v. 3, pl. 39, #134) on paleographic and grammatical principles. She suggests that the use of a cardinal direction such as *šmʿ* may simply be a reflection of the four-part division inherent in the phyle system (A. M. Roth, personal communication, 1998). Another possibility, however, may be that *sꜣ šmʿ* means "phyle of singers" as both the words "south" and "singer" can use the same hieroglyph.

From the tomb of Hay at Deir el Medina (TT 267) comes another curious piece of evidence. The name and title of Hay's daughter-in-law Nebu-iy (DB #654) was reconstructed from painted plaster fragments found on the floor of the tomb (Valbelle, 1975: 28 II F.8-9). She was a *nbt pr šmʿyt n Ỉmn m sꜣw tpy*: "lady of the house, chantress of Amun from the head phyles". The phrase *m sꜣw tpy*  is an unfamiliar construction, but may simply be a variant form or misspelling of "on the first phyle".

Four other women bore titles indicative of a ranking system or hierarchy among the *šmʿywt*. One woman, Meryt (DB #273), lived during the reigns of Hatshepsut and Tuthmosis III, and held the title *šmʿyt wrt,* or "head chantress". Three others held the title *ḥry(t) šmʿywt,* or "overseer of chantresses". Mut (DB #664) was a *ḥryt smʿywt* of Amun who lived in the time of Ramesses II and two women who lived during the Third Intermediate Period also were supervisors. Irmutpanefer (DB #448) was a *ḥry(t) šmʿywt* of Khonsu, and Nestjerenmaat (DB #74) was a *ḥry(t) šmʿywt* of Montu, lord of Thebes.

It is known that the *wrwt ḫnr(t)*, "great ones of the *Khener*", were also divided into phyles in the Third Intermediate Period (Kitchen, 1973: 67 n. 332, 430-431). At least five references from the database show that women could be organized on the phyle system with respect to the *wrt ḫnr* title (DB #397, 373, 150, 201, 305). These women, in addition to being *šmʿywt*, also bore the title *wrt ḫnr*.

It is tempting to try to place the *šmʿyt* in the *ḫnr* itself,[2] that is to say that the members of the *ḫnr* were *šmʿyt* or *ḥsyt* or *sḫmyt*. It is clear that as an individual a woman could serve one god in the role of *wrt ḫnrt* and concurrently serve the same god or another one as a *šmʿyt* (Section 2.III.2). More concrete evidence for their precise role in the *Khener* is lacking.

The most important conclusion that can be drawn about the organization of the *šmʿywt* is that during the New Kingdom they were organized along the same lines as other temple functionaries such as *wʿb*-priests who provided occasional or intermittent service.[3] If their organization was indeed modeled on the organization of

[1] Fischer states that they were "attached to the various phyles of priests" (Fischer, LÄ IV, 1102). This, however, is not demonstrated by the source quoted by Fischer, which merely states that the *šmʿyt* were divided into phyles like priests, not "attached to them" (Blackman, 1921: 29).

[2] Gillam has done just that (1995: 211), as has Niwiński (1989a: 81), but neither supply specific evidence to support that claim.

[3] The existence of phyles for the *šmʿywt* may have prompted Naguib's statement that they participated episodically in the liturgy (1990: 241). She was aware that the *šmʿyt* could belong to phyles, (ibid.: 236f) but only offers a secondary source as evidence (Bonnet, 1952, 490), which also does not provide specific examples.

the priesthood, it would seem that the *šmʿywt* formed a functioning part of temple service.

7.II RANK

A preliminary attempt at placing the *šmʿyt* title into a ranking system with the various other titles of women was unsuccessful. There were only a limited number of women in the database who held titles other than "chantress" and "mistress of the house" (see Chart 5). A further complication is a result of the nature of the source material. Quite often the full complement of a woman's titles was drawn from a variety of sources so that no single inscription encompassed all the titles. Therefore, the titles could not be used in the same manner as Baer's study of Old Kingdom titles (1960) where their relative rank was assessed based on how they appeared together. There was a definite trend for the title *nbt pr* to occur first[4] and for titles of similar natures to appear together (e.g., musician's titles appeared close to each other in the inscription). Beyond that there appears to be no internal order, nor any indication as to why a woman carried certain titles on one monument and different titles on another.

One woman's titles, however, may provide insight into the matter. Gatseshen (DB #319), is known from her own funerary papyrus as well as from that of her husband. On her papyrus she received a full list of titles – *nbt pr, wrt ḫnrt, tp n 3-nw n ỉmn, ḥsyt ʿ3 n Mwt* (lady of the house, great one of the *Khener*, head of the third <phyle> of Amun, great singer of Mut)– whereas her husband received only the most important of his titles, *ḥm nṯr 3-nw n ỉmn* (third prophet of Amun). The situation is reversed on his papyrus (Niwiński, 1989b: 264, 281-282). His lengthy string of titles is fully expressed – *it nṯr mry, ḥry sšt3, ḥry t3 pr wnnwt, ḥry m* [lost] *ipt-swt, ḥm nṯr 3-nw n ỉmn Rʿ nsw nṯrw, ḥm nṯr n Mnṯw nb w3st, imy-r mnmnwt n pr Rʿ tp ḥwt n ỉmn Rʿ ḥm nṯr n Ḫnm nb ḳbḥw* (beloved god's father, master of secrets, master of the priestly house, master of [lost] in Karnak, third priest of Amun-re king of the gods, priest of Montu lord of Thebes, overseer of cattle of the temple of Re-on-the-Roof, priest of Khnum lord of the cataract region) while Gatseshen's titles are abbreviated to *nbt pr, šmʿyt n ỉmn*. If it is safe to assume that each of them was represented by their most important title on the other's papyrus, then the *šmʿyt* title outranks the other two held by Gatseshen. This seems contrary to the ideas that the *wrt ḫnrt* was the head of a troupe in which the *šmʿywt* were subordinates. Other motivations may explain the choice of titles included on her husband's papyrus. The *šmʿyt* title may have been the title she held at her death and not necessarily the highest ranking title she had held in her lifetime. Or perhaps it was her favorite position among the three she held.

[4] The *nbt pr* title was found to be the most consistently used title where more than one monument was consulted for an individual woman. Often the title *šmʿyt* appeared on only one of the monuments.

CHART 5: Other Titles

REF. #	NAME	DEITY	OTHER TITLES	PROV.	DATE
579	*Ḥr-iy*	Amun	*nbt pr, ḥsyt n(t) nṯr nfr*	Abydos	Dyn. 18
260	*Sn-snb*	Amun	*dwꜣt nṯr*	TT39	Hatshepsut-Tuthmosis III
273	*Mryt*	Amun	*nbt pr, šmꜥyt wrt, ḥsyt nt Mwt m Ἰšrw*	TT224, TT96 & KV40	Tuthmosis III-Amenhotep II
266	*Ḥnwt-tꜣwy*	Amun	*nbt pr, ḥsyt nt nbt Ἰwnt*	TT42	Tuthmosis III-Amenhotep II
831	*Bꜣk*	Amun	*ẖkrt nsw, mnꜥt wrt nt nb tꜣwy, ḥsyt nṯr nfr, šdt nṯr nfrt snḳ ẖnm n ḥr šnbt.s*	TT85	Tuthmosis III-Amenhotep II
481	*Nyt*	Amun	*mnꜥt wrt n nb tꜣwy ḥsyt n nṯr nfr šdt nṯr nfrt snḳ ẖnm n ḥr šnbt*	TT88	Tuthmosis III-Amenhotep II
267	*Ḥnwt-tꜣwy*	Amun	*nbt pr, ẖkrt nsw*	TT98	Tuthmosis III-Amenhotep II
283	*Mwt-iry*	Thoth lord of Hermopolis, Nehemet-away who is in Hermopolis	*ẖkrt nsw, nbt pr, ḥsyt nt Ḥwt-ḥr*	TT74	Tuthmosis III-Tuthmosis IV
482	*Mryt?*	Amun?	*ḥsyt n Ḥwt-ḥr nbt Ἰwnt*	TT80	Amenhotep II
830	*Mryt.f*	Thoth	*ḥsyt n nbt* [lost]		Amenhotep II
288	*Rnwtt*	Amun	*ḥsyt nt Mwt*	TT295	Amenhotep II-Tuthmosis IV
284	*Sn-snb*	Amun	*ẖkrt nsw*	TT108	Tuthmosis IV
278	*Rꜣy*	Amun	*ẖkrt nsw*	TT75	Tuthmosis IV
652	*Ḫbwy-nw-ns*	Bastet	*nbt pr, ḥsyt n Sḫmt, wrt ḫnrt n Bꜣstt*	Bubastis	Amenhotep III
792	*Bꜣky*	Amun	*nbt pr, ẖkrt nsw*	TTA24 (Waseda Univ. W-6), Mut temple at Karnak	Amenhotep III
698	*Nfrt-ḫꜥ*	Ahmose-Nefertari, the Aten	*ḥsyt Ḥwt-ḥr*	TT46	Amenhotep III-Amenhotep IV
491	*Mryt-Ptḥ*	Amun Re	*nbt pr, ẖkrt nsw, ḥsyt n* [lost]	TT55	Amenhotep III-Amenhotep IV
701	*Mꜥy*	Amun	*nbt pr, ḥsyt n nbt tꜣwy*	TT55	Amenhotep III-Amenhotep IV
828	*Ṯwyw*	Amun	*ẖkrt nsw, ḥsyt n Ḥwt-ḥr*		Amenhotep III-Amenhotep IV
699	*Knr*	Amun	*ḥsyt n nṯr nfr*	TT40	Tutankhamun
648	*Mryt-Rꜥ*	Amun of Karnak	*nbt pr, ḥsyt n Ḥwt-ḥr nbt Ḳis, ḥsyt n Mwt*	TT49	Amenhotep IV-Aye
675	*Nbt-tꜣwy*	Amun	*nbt pr, wrt ḫnrt Mwt, ḥsy ꜥꜣ n Ḥwt-ḥr*	TT255	Horemheb
676	*Bwy*	Amun	*nbt pr, wrt ḫnrt Mwt*	TT255	Horemheb
618	*Tꜣ-ḫꜥt*	Amun	*wrt ḫnrt n Ἰmn*	TT50	Horemheb
472	*Ἰpꜣy*	Amun	*nbt pr, mnꜥt nsw, ḥsyt n Ḥwt-ḥr*	Saqqara	late Dyn. 18
829	*Nfrt-iry*	Amun	*nbt pr, ḥsyt n Ḥwt-ḥr*		late Dyn. 18
106	*Dwꜣt*	Amun	*ḥsyt n Ḥwt-ḥr*		Dyn. 19

CHART 5: Other Titles

533	*W3ḏt-rnpt*	Amun	*wrt ḫnrt*	Abydos	Seti I
444	*Rnnwtt*	Amun Re, Wepwawet Hathor of Medjedny	*wrt ḫnrt Ḥwt-ḥr nbt Mḏdny*	Asyut?	Seti I
919	*Tiy*	Amun	*wrt ḫnrt n Ἰmn, ḥsyt n nsw, ḥsyt n pr nsw*	TT106	Seti I
657	*Ḥuy-n-r (Ḥwt-ḥr)*	Hathor?, Amun	*nbt pr, ḥsyt n Mwt*	TT215	Seti I
4	*?*	Amun	*ḥsyt n Ḥwt-ḥr*	TT51	Seti I
623	*Ḥ3t-špswt*	Amun	*nbt pr, ḥsyt n Ḥwt-ḥr, nbt pt t3*	TT51	Seti I
756	*Ḥnwt-t3wy*	Amun Re	*nbt pr, ḥsyt nt Ḥwt-ḥr*	TT51	Seti I
608	*Mwt-nfrt*	Amun	*wrt ḫnrt n Ἰmn-Rˁ nb Ἰw-rd*	Zawyet el Sultan	Seti I
496	*Tiy*	Osiris, Isis	*nbt pr, wrt ḫnrt n Wsir*	Abydos	Seti I-Rameses II
758	*Ḫˁt-nsw*	Onuris	*nbt pr, wrt ḫnrt n Ἰn-ḥrt*	el Mashayikh, Abydos	Rameses II
578	*Nfrt-Mwt*	Nekhbet, Amun	*wrt ḫnrt n Nḫbt, wrt ḫnrt n Ἰmn*	Faras, Qasr Ibrim, TT289, Sehel	Rameses II
15	*Ḥwnry*	Hathor, lady of the southern sycomore	*nbt pr, wrt ḫnrt n Ḥršf*	Sedment	Rameses II
643	*Ḥnwt-mtr*	Amun	*wrt ḫnrt n Ἰmn*	Sehel, TT158	Rameses II
757	*T3-ḫˁt*	Isis	*wrt ḫnrwt n Ἰmn, wrt ḫnrwt n Ḥwt-ḥr, sḫmyt n Mwt*	TT157	Rameses II
674	*Ἰwy*	Amun Re of Karnak	*wrt ḫnrt n Ἰmn-ḥtp*	TT19	Rameses II
664	*Mwt?*	Amun, Mut, Khonsu	*ḥryt šmˁywt*	TT194	Rameses II
736	*Nfrt-iry*	Amun, Mut, Khonsu	*nbt pr, ḥsyt ˁ3 n Ḥwt-ḥr*	TT296	Rameses II
737	*Nḏm-Mwt*	Amun, Mut, Khonsu	*sḫmyt*	TT296	Rameses II
586	*Mwtiˁy (Mˁy)*	Amun, Montu	*nbt pr, ḥsyt ˁ3 n Ḥwt-ḥr nbt Ἰwnt*	TT31	Rameses II
693	*3st*	Amun	*nbt pr, ḥsyt n Ḥwt-ḥr*	TT32	Rameses II
668	*Mwt-m-int*	Amun	*sḫmyt n Ἰmn, Mwt, Ḫnsw*	TT373	Rameses II
881	*Nḏmt*	Amun	*nbt pr, ḥsyt ˁ3 n imntt w3st*	TT41	Rameses II
716	*Ἰy*	Khnum, Satis, Anukis	*ḥsyt ˁ3t n Ḥwt-ḥr*	TT6	Rameses II
253	*Twy*	Amun	*nbt pr, ḥsyt ˁ3t Ḥwt-ḥr*		Rameses II
813	*Ṯi3*	Amun, great of victories	*snt špst nsw*		Rameses II
612	*Sḫmt-nfrt*	Amun-Re	*wrt ḫnrt nt Ἰn-ḥrt*	el Mashayikh	Merneptah

CHART 5: Other Titles

626	*Rʿỉ3*	Amun of Karnak	*nbt pr, wrt ḫnrt n Sbk*	TT23	Merneptah
908	*Nfrt-iry*	Amun of Karnak	*ḥs(yt) n Mwt nbt Ỉsrw*		Merneptah
673	*S3t-Rʿ*	Atum-Re	*wʿbt n Ỉmn n Ṯkw, rpʿt*	Heliopolis-Matareyyeh	19.9
636	*Nfrt-iry*	Montu, Amun	*ḥsyt n Ḥwt-ḥr*		Dyn. 19-20
551	*Pr-ms-m-?*	Osiris	*nbt pr, ḥsyt n 3st*	Abydos	Dyn. 20
562	*Šrit-Rʿ*	Osiris	*t3.s? nbt pr*	Abydos	Dyn. 20
564	*T?-s3???ṯ*	Osiris	*snwy n?*	Abydos	Dyn. 20
667	*...?*	Amun	*ḥsyt n Ỉmn-Rʿ*	TT68	Dyn. 20
785	*T3-mryt*	Amun of Karnak	*wrt ḫnrt...*	TT148	Rameses III or later
634	*Nfrt-iry*	Amun of Karnak	*nbt pr, wrt ḫnrt n Ỉmn*	TT158	Rameses III or later
740	*Nfrt-iry*	Amun	*ḥsy n Ḥwt-ḥr*	TT324	Rameses VI
639	*Mʿi3y*	Montu, Amun	*wrt ḫnrt n Mnṯw*	TT331	Rameses VII
727	*3st*	Amun Re	*ssty (sḫmyt) n Mwt*	Thebes? (temple or TT113)	Rameses VIII
726	*Ṯnt-p3-sṯ3*	Amun Re	*sḫmyt n Mwt m Ỉsrw, ḥsy(t) ʿ3(t) n Ḥwt-ḥr ḥr ib ḏrst*	TT65	Rameses IX
789	*Mwt-m-mr.s*	Amun Re, Mut, Knonsu	*ḥsyt n Ḥwt-ḥr*	TT65	Rameses IX
111	*Ỉw.s-ʿnḫ*	Amun	*ḥsyt Mwt wrt nbt Ỉsrw, mnʿt n Ḫnsw p3 ...*	Bab el Gusus	Dyn. 21
235	*T3-šd-Ḫnsw*	Amun Re	*ḥsyt n p3 ʿ n Mwt, špst*	Bab el Gusus	Dyn. 21
666	*T3-b3k-n-Mwt*	Amun	*ḥsyt n p3 ʿ n Mwt*	TT68	Dyn. 21
448	*Ỉr-mwt-p3-nfr*	Amun Re	*hry šmʿyt n Ḫnsw m w3st nfr-ḥtp, ḥsy n p3 ʿ n Mwt wrt nbt Ỉsrw, mnʿt nsw*		Dyn. 21
384	*Nʿw-ny*	Amun Re	*nbt pr, ḥsyt n nbw w3st, Ỉmn, Mwt, Ḫnsw, s3t nsw*	TT358	early Dyn. 21
141	*Ḏd-Mwt-iw.s-ʿnḫ*	Amun Re	*ḥsyt ʿ3t n Mwt*	Bab el Gusus	early-mid Dyn. 21
210	*Ṯnt-n3w-ḥrrw*	Amun	*nbt pr, ḥsyt ʿ3t ʿ n Mwt nbt Ỉsrw, ḥryt mnʿwt*		early-mid Dyn. 21
133	*Nsy-t3-nb-tʿwy*	Amun Re	*ḥsyt n p3 ʿ n Mwt*	Bab el Gusus	mid Dyn. 21
137	*My-šm-rdwy-sktb?*	Amun Re	*ḥsyt ʿ3t* [lost], *ḥsyt ʿ3t n Mwt, ḥsyt n p3 ʿ n Mwt*	Bab el Gusus	mid Dyn. 21
149	*T3-wḏ3t-Rʿ*	the pure foundation of Ptah, Amun	*nbt pr, ḥsyt ʿ3t ʿ n Mwt nbt pt, mrt n Ḥwt-ḥr, wsrt.s, ḥsyt n p3 ʿ n Mwt*	Bab el Gusus	mid Dyn. 21
182	*Šd-sw-t3-ipt*	Amun Re	*nbt pr, ḥsyt n p3 ʿ n Mwt wrt nbt Ỉsrw*	Bab el Gusus	mid Dyn. 21
208	*Ns-t3-wḏ3t-3ḫ*	Amun	*nbt pr, ḥsyt n p3 ʿ n Mwt wrt nbt Ỉsrw*	Bab el Gusus	mid Dyn. 21
310	*Ḥnwt-t3wy*	Amun Re	*špst*	Bab el Gusus	mid Dyn. 21

CHART 5: Other Titles

323	*Ꜥnḫ.s-n-Mwt*	Amun Re	*nbt pr, ḥsyt n pꜣ* Ꜥ *n Mwt*	Bab el Gusus	mid Dyn. 21
115	*Tꜣyw-ḥrt*	Amun Re	*nbt pr, ḥsyt n pꜣ* Ꜥ *n Mwt ḥsyt n Ỉmn*	Thebes	mid Dyn. 21
120	*Ḥnwt-tꜣwy*	Amun Re, Mut, Khonsu	*wrt ḫnrt n Ỉmn-R*Ꜥ	TT60	mid Dyn. 21
204	*Ty*	Amun Re	*ḥsyt n pꜣ* Ꜥ *n Mwt*	TT60	mid Dyn. 21
9	*Ṯnt-Ỉmn (Tꜣ-nt-Ỉmn)*	Amun Re	*nbt pr, ḥsyt n pꜣ* Ꜥ *n Mwt wrt nbt Ỉsrw, ḥsyt Ꜥꜣt n nbw wꜣst Ỉmn, Mwt, Ḫnsw*		mid Dyn. 21
219	*Nsy-Ḫnsw*	Amun Re	*nbt pr, ḥsyt n pꜣ* Ꜥ *n Mwt wrt nbt Ỉsrw*		mid Dyn. 21
341	*Tꜣyw-ḥryt*	Amun Re	*nbt pr, ḥsyt Ꜥꜣt* Ꜥ *n nbw ḥḥ*		mid Dyn. 21
361	*Mwt-ḥtp-ti*	Amun	*nbt pr, ḥsyt n pꜣ* Ꜥ *n Mwt*		mid Dyn. 21
373	*Ỉnhꜣy*	Amun	*nbt pr, wrt ḫnrt n nb wt Ḫnm sꜣ 3-nw*		mid Dyn. 21
319	*GꜤt-sšn*	Amun	*nbt pr, wrt ḫnrt tp n 3-nw n Ỉmn, ḥsyt Ꜥꜣ n Mwt*	Bab el Gusus	mid-late Dyn. 21
147	*ꜣst-m-ꜣḫ-bit*		*ḥsyt pꜣ* Ꜥ *n Mwt*	Bab el Gusus	mid-late Dyn. 21
151	*ꜣst-m-ꜣḫ-bit*	Amun	*ḥsyt pꜣ* Ꜥ *n Mwt*	Bab el Gusus	mid-late Dyn. 21
216	*Nsy-prw-nbw*	Amun	*ḥsyt* Ꜥ *Mwt nbt pt*	Bab el Gusus	mid-late Dyn. 21
230	*Tꜣ-ḫbt*	Amun	*ḥsyt n pꜣ* Ꜥ *n Mwt wr(t nbt) Ỉsrw*	Bab el Gusus	mid-late Dyn. 21
232	*Tꜣ-bꜣkt-Ḫnsw*	Amun Re	*ḥsyt n* Ꜥ *Mwt*	Bab el Gusus	mid-late Dyn. 21
316	*Tꜣ-šd-Ḫnsw*	Amun	*nbt pr, ḥsyt n pꜣ* Ꜥ *n Mwt nbt pt, ḥmt nṯr n Ỉmn-ipt, ḥmt nṯr n Mwt n pr ms, ḥmt nṯr Nḫbt ḥḏt n Nḫn*	Bab el Gusus	mid-late Dyn. 21
217	*Mrw-Ꜥḥ*	Amun Re	*nbt pr ḥsyt pꜣ Mwt wr(t nbt) Ỉsrw*		mid-late Dyn. 21
221	*Tꜣ-bꜣk(t)-n-Ḫnsw*	Amun Re	*ḥsyt n* Ꜥ *n Mwt wr(t) nbt Ỉsrw*		mid-late Dyn. 21
349	*ꜣst-m-ꜣḫbit*	Amun	*nbt pr, wrt ḫnrt n Ỉmn-wsr-ḥꜤt*		mid-late Dyn. 21
362	*Tꜣ...*	Amun	*nbt pr, (ḥsyt Ꜥꜣt)*		mid-late Dyn. 21
139	*ꜣst-m-ꜣḫ-bit*	Amun Re	*ḥst n pꜣ* Ꜥ *n Mwt wrt*	Bab el Gusus	mid-late Dyn. 21
150	*Ḥryw-wbn*	Amun Re	*nbt pr, wrt ḫnrt n Ỉmn m sꜣ 4-nw, wrt ḫnrt tpt, ḥm nṯr 2-nw n Mwt, ḥm nṯr 2-nw n Mwt n pr ms*	Bab el Gusus	late Dyn. 21
191	*Ṯnt-ḥn-f (Tꜣ-nt-ḥn.f)*	Amun	*wꜤb n Ỉmn?*	Bab el Gusus	late Dyn. 21
304	*Mryt-Ỉmn*	Amun Re	*nbt pr, ḥsyt n pꜣ* Ꜥ *n Mwt wrt nb(t) Ỉsrw, mnꜤt Ꜥꜣ n Ḫnsw pꜣ ḫrd*	Bab el Gusus	late Dyn. 21
225	*?*	Amun	*ḥsyt Ꜥꜣt*	Bab el Gusus	late Dyn. 21
128	*?*	Amun Re	*nbt pr, mnꜤt Ḫnsw pꜣ ḫrd*	Bab el Gusus?	late Dyn. 21

CHART 5: Other Titles

201	*Ḏd-Mwt-iw.s-ʿnḫ*	Amun	*ḥry wrt ḫnrt tp n Ỉmn, ḥmt nṯr n Ỉmn, p3 wr ḥk3w, ḥmt nṯr Ỉmn rḫt.f,?, ḥmt nṯr n Mwt ʿ3t ?, smt n t3 ḥwt Wsr-mʿ3t-rʿ mn-mʿ3t-Rʿ pr Ỉmn nṯrt, ḥry špstw*	TT60	late Dyn. 21
200	*Ḥnwt-t3wy*	Amun	*ḥsyt n p3 ʿ n Mwt wrt nbt Ỉšrw*		late Dyn. 21
340	*Ns-Ḫnsw*	Amun Re	*nbt pr, ḥsyt ʿ Mwt*		late Dyn. 21
386	*ʿnḫ-s-n-3st*	Amun	*nbt pr, ḥsyt n p3 ʿ n Mwt*		late Dyn. 21
396	*T3-b3kt-n-Ḫnsw*	Amun Re	*nbt pr, ḥsyt n p3 ʿ n Mwt*		late Dyn. 21
402	*T3-nḏm-Mwt*	Amun Re	*nbt pr, ḫnmt Ḫnsw*		late Dyn. 21
116	*Diw-Mwt-(r)-iwdw*	Amun Re	*mnʿt Ḫnsw p3 ḫrd, ḥsy(t) ḥr imnt w3st*		late Dyn. 21or early Dyn. 22
397	*Nsy-Ḫnsw-p3-ḫrd*	Amun Re	*nbt pr, wrt ḫnrt n Ỉmn ḥr s3 tp*		Dyn. 22
370	*Ḏd-Ḫnsw-iw-ʿnḫ*	Amun	*nbt pr, ḥry sšm pr Ỉmn*		early Dyn. 22
74	*Ns-ṯr-n-m3ʿt*	Montu, lord of Thebes	*ḥry šmʿyt, nbt pr*	Thebes	Third Intermediate Period
449	*3st-m-3ḫbit*	Amun Re	*nbt pr, rpʿt?, ḥsyt n ʿ n Mwt*		Third Intermediate Period
450	*3sty*	Amun Re	*rpʿt?*		Third Intermediate Period
415	*M3t?*	Amun	*iḥyt n Ỉmn Rʿ*	Ramesseum	Third Intermediate Period?
569	*N3-mnḫ-3st*	Amun	*iḥyt n Ỉmn*	TT33	Saite Period

CHAPTER 8 CONCLUSIONS

8.I Reiteration of questions raised

The goal of this study has been to elucidate the status and role of the *šmꜤyt*, or chantress, by addressing the questions posed in Chapter 1, which were:

Q. Does the title imply a religious vocation or was it an honorific title?
Q. How was the title obtained?
Q. Who were their families and what was their social status?
Q. What were the differences between the *šmꜤywt* and other musicians (i.e. *ḫnr, ḥsyt*)?
Q. Was there a similar male role?
Q. Which gods did they serve and in which cult centers?
Q. What were their responsibilities in cult practices?
Q. When did the title come into being and when did it cease to be used?
Q. Did those holding the title usurp the duties or role of a previously existing office or offices?
Q. Are there patterns in their depiction in art and writing (literature, private letters, tomb inscriptions) which give us clues to any of these questions?

The answers to these questions fall into roughly two areas of study; the family and the temple.

8.I.1 The Family

The first area of study concerns the family and the social status held by the families of *šmꜤywt* and therefore the status of the *šmꜤywt* themselves. By investigating the variety of cultic, administrative, and political titles held by the husbands and fathers of *šmꜤywt*, we can say they were a diverse group of women. During the Middle Kingdom, the title holders were middle class and evidence for them is very rare. *ŠmꜤywt* of the 18th Dynasty, however, belonged to wealthy families, either natal or marital, who were politically powerful. This wealthy upper class comprised the religious elite and those who were related to pharaoh or in his employ as advisors and administrators. The use of the title this time appears to have gained popularity during Hatshepsut's reign. The title was also largely a Theban phenomenon, coinciding with the ascendancy of Amun as the state god. There were no fluctuations in the use of the title until the Ramesside Period.

The Ramesside women were more socially diverse and more numerous. There were many women who belonged to more modest families – a wealthy middle class made up of landowners and "dependent specialists" (Trigger, 1993: 57), or those who worked for the nobility in specialized occupations. In the aftermath of the Amarna period there was an increase of personal and state piety (Assmann, 1989: 68-69). This is reflected in the rising numbers of women who were attached to local cults throughout Egypt as well as to the state cult of Amun.

During the Third Intermediate Period the numbers increased further, particularly during the tenure of the high priests of Amun during the mid-21st Dynasty. The women from this time period were from an economic cross-section of society similar to that of the Ramesside attestations, but they were overwhelmingly Theban and involved in the cult of Amun. This may suggest that the Theban priesthood was intervening by giving more women the opportunity to participate in the cult. Political reasons probably motivated this policy. As discussed previously, (Sections 5.IV.2.C, 5.V.2, 5.VII) the giving of titles could be seen as a political maneuver to favorably influence powerful families. This situation may also have heralded a devaluation of the status of the title since it seems to have lost some of its exclusivity, a process that may have begun as far back as the reign of Ramesses II.

The numbers of women who held the title *šmꜤyt* throughout time demonstrates that cult activities during the New Kingdom, Third Intermediate Period, and Late Period, were not solely the domain of royalty and elite men, although they were apparently dominated and dictated by them. While the system was run by men, women were needed to make it work (Robins, 1993b: 36). Although Robins was speaking of the royal women and their place in diplomacy, the evidence reviewed in this study suggests that it may also have been true of the elite non-royal woman's place in society. Entreating the favor of powerful families through women was one way in which the existing power structure could further solidify a base of loyal followers. Without the support of the female population of Egypt, an institution seeking political and economic power could not have a secure base of support. Women may not have held power through official posts in the administration, but they raised each new generation of officials. Their support of a particular cult was manifested in a very public way: they became chantresses.

Family influence appears to have been an important factor in a woman's decision to participate. The family's cult affiliations were also apparently a consideration in the woman's choice of cult in which she participated. However, the lack of consistency from generation to generation is suggestive of personal choice on the woman's part. There is no evidence to indicate that the title was hereditary, nor is there any evidence to show that the title was dependant on a woman's marital status or age.

8.II The Temple

The second area of study focuses on whether or not there were actual religious duties associated with the title and what those duties might have been. The evidence demonstrates that the title was a specialized position and not an honorific because *šmꜤywt*:

1. are represented shaven likes priests (tomb of Kheruef TT 192).
2. appear in contexts where only ritually pure people are allowed (Tuthmosis III's festival hall at Karnak, and near the king and royal family).
3. participated in standardized rites such as the Beautiful Feast of the Valley where the song is similar in each recorded case. The implication is that there was an apprenticeship or period of learning, perhaps a school such as the one shown in a Middle Kingdom Kom el Hisn tomb (Manniche, 1991a: fig. 74) where specialized knowledge of ritual music was taught.
4. were organized on the phyle system during the New Kingdom.
5. were directed by individuals (male and female) who held titles such as "overseer of chanters", indicating that they were organized and performed real duties. An overseer's position would hardly be necessary for a mere honorific or ranking title.
6. provided an important part of the daily offerings and the people who performed this role must have held some meaningful place in the temple hierarchy.

One of the essential elements of this study has been the presentation of evidence demonstrating the participation of the chantresses in formal cult settings. Because of the impersonal and timeless nature of official art, it can never be shown that a specific individual participated in a specific rite or festival. It is reasonably certain, however, that the anonymous women shown in scenes at Karnak and elsewhere were the middle and upper class women who are known from the monuments of their husbands, sons, and fathers.

Because there are so few women's titles in the relevant time periods, and few women held more than one title, it would be difficult to construct a hierarchy in which to place the *šmꜥyt* title. The variety of women who held the title, from king's daughters to the wives of temple scribes, further complicates the matter from a hierarchical point of view. The nature of the evidence suggests that women of high or middle-high status were the only ones to have held the title. This would naturally create the situation where having the title automatically presupposed a high status, and it became an indication of rank. If the title were truly an honorific, one would expect to see the title combined with a reference to the king, such as *ẖkrt nsw* and *špst nsw*.

A few men held the title "chanter" (see Appendix A). Their existence strengthens the position that the title was carried as a mark of service and not an honorific. Since the title was primarily associated with women, it would have been unsuitable as a mark of distinction for a man having no true place in the relative hierarchy of a ranking system. The men who held the title are usually shown engaged in musical activity. Their small numbers argue for a personal choice made by these men to participate in cult activities in a non-traditional way. The evidence cited in Appendix A demonstrates that it was probably a matter of piety, rather than societal factors that led them to become chanters.

Based on their representations in art and written media, it is clear that the *šmꜥywt* were vocalists. More specifically, they are usually associated with percussion instruments (drum, sistra, *menywt*, clappers) or are shown clapping. These circumstances lead to the conclusion that their style of vocalization was more rhythmic than melodic, and therefore the translation "chantress" is favoured over "singer". Less often, they were accompanied by stringed instruments, but their primary activities were probably *a capella*.

Their cultic function was to perform for the gods in a daily ritual setting and in public appearances of the gods. They also used their skills in the palace, although they were not as common as the *ḥsywt* in this context. The term *ḥsyt* implies melodic music that is often accompanied by stringed or wind instruments. It is the term more appropriately translated as "singer". Both *ḥsywt* and *šmꜥywt* may have made up the *ẖnrwt* so frequently mentioned in musical contexts. The differences between the words for musicians are subtle and difficult to interpret because they represent oral and aural phenomena.

8.III Summary

The results of this study show that the title was held by different numbers and classes of women over time, which indicates an evolution influenced by societal factors. Patterns emerging from an analysis of the database include the geographical dispersion of the title, a chronological evolution of the title, and social stratification of the title holders. The most important pattern to emerge is one of the social influence of local cults. The women buried at Thebes were heavily involved in the cult of Amun, regardless of their husband's occupation or their families' cultic affiliations. Women from other cult centers, or those with family ties to other places, could also be in the service of Amun, but were also likely to be involved in a local cult, such as that of Hathor, Lady of the Southern Sycamore in the Memphis area. Just as some men desired to be a part of the power structures of their time, so did some women. The prevalence of the title *šmꜥyt n(t) Ỉmn* is an outgrowth of that desire.

The formal participation of women in the religious hierarchy may have been a small part of the increasingly elaborate temple system of the New Kingdom, but the existence of titles such as *šmꜥyt* is important nonetheless. The result of collecting references to *šmꜥywt* and building the database presented in Appendix E has been a greater appreciation of how involved in public and community activities the women of ancient Egypt were. Although the title was a religious one, religion had such a pervasive presence in the lives of ancient Egyptians that any service to a deity would also have had a social dimension. The religious hierarchy functioned as a political and economic entity, controlling power and wealth. Political and economic power were related and complemented each other (Trigger, 1993: 55) and were intrinsically linked to the temple system in ancient Egypt. Therefore, the participation of women in cultic settings can be seen as social and political as well as pious.

APPENDIX A
MALE *Šmꜥw*

In the course of research it has become clear that there were men who held the title *šmꜥ* as individuals, or *šmꜥw* in groups. Although far fewer in number, their existence sheds light on their female counterparts. A database similar to the one used for the women is included at the end of this appendix.

Old Kingdom

The 6th Dynasty tomb of Djau from Deir el Gebrawi contains reliefs that may be the earliest reference to *šmꜥw* as a group (Davies, 1902: pl. VII). A row of men are depicted singing and dancing in the funeral procession. Nearby, a coffin is being dragged on sledges and borne on boats. The text above them reads *ḫbt in ḫnrt šmꜥ in šmꜥw* – "dancing by the *Khener*, chanting by the chanters". The men raise their hands as if clapping. Depicted above is a row of women dancing who probably represent the *Khener* and attest to the antiquity of the role of music in funeral settings. This procession is mirrored in many New Kingdom contexts where the women are labeled as *šmꜥywt* or *ḫnrt*.

Middle Kingdom

There are a few clear examples of men from the Middle Kingdom bearing the title, but not as many as Ward lists in his index.[1] All of these examples are also outlined in Chapter 5.

CG 20216 is a stela from Abydos divided into two registers. In the lower register there are two men and two women depicted standing in a line. Before the bodies or faces of the individuals are texts that give their names and titles. There seems to be some gender confusion in this regard. The woman on the right is called *mwt.f Wꜣḏt*: his mother Wadjet. This information is clearly associated with her. The next person in line is a man. In front of his face are the words *šmꜥw Sbk-sꜥnḫ* . *Sbk-sꜥnḫ* is the name of his wife given in the first register, but she does not bear any title there. Although the male version of the title seems to fit with who is pictured, the name does not. The title *šmꜥyt* spelled with an egg determinative stands before the face of the next man to his left, who otherwise has no designation. The clearly female title does not fit with the figure of the man. Perhaps the title belongs to the last woman in line, who is called *nbt pr Bby*: Lady of the House, Beby.

P Berlin 10021 is a Middle Kingdom letter from Illahun concerning what has been interpreted as a prison (*ḫnrt*) and some of its inmates (Scharff, 1924: 53), two of whom were musicians (one male *šmꜥ*, one female *šmꜥyt*). The text is fragmentary and difficult to interpret as a whole, but seems to be a list of people. A related text in P. Berlin 10081, from the same archive at Illahun, mentions the *šmꜥw S-nḫt, sꜣ Ḥtpi* (Kaplony-Heckel, 1971, vol. I: 36-37, #64).

The story of Sinuhe contains a reference to singers in both text B and the Ashmolean versions. The reference is plainly to a plural group and not a man as Ward implies (1982: #1514). While text B appears to refer only to men because of the masculine determinatives and the absence of the feminine "t", , the Ashmolean text does have the final "t" while using the same determinatives; .

A statue excavated at Saqqara in the valley temple of Unas bears the name and titles of the Overseer of the Granaries of the Two Lands in Memphis and Chanter of Ptah South of His Wall, Lord of the Two Lands, Sermaat, son of Kety (*šmꜥw n Ptḥ rsy inb.f nb tꜣwy, Sr-mꜣꜥt iri n Ḥty*). This title is not heretofore known, but a similar title dates to the reign of Amenhotep III; a *ḥry šmꜥw n pr Ptḥ, Ptḥ-ꜥnḫ* (Moussa and Altenmüller, 1975: 95).

New Kingdom

Miscellaneous Finds

A block statue of a man presenting a stela carries the identification *ḥry šmꜥw n pr Ptḥ, Ptḥ-ꜥnḫ* (Cramer, 1936: 91 [#10-13], pl. VI.1-2). From Tell Basta there are two[2] shabtis bearing the names and titles of men serving as *šmꜥ*, presumably in local cults (Bakr, 1992: n.36, n.84.1-3). Not surprisingly, the first is a *šmꜥ n Bꜥstt, Pꜣ-Rꜥ-ḥr-wṯs.f* (Chanter of Bastet, Paraherwetchesef) from the Ramesside period. The second is a *šmꜥ n nb pt, Mꜥiꜣ* (Chanter of the Lord of the Sky, Maia). A recently discovered shabti from Saqqara[3] bears the name and title of Bay, a *šmꜥywt* (sic) *n Ỉmn*. The hieratic is quite corrupt and awaits further interpretation, but may be Ramesside as it was found in the second courtyard of Horemhab's tomb. Palaeographically, a Ramesside date seems possible.

A further piece of evidence comes from the 20th Dynasty Tomb Robberies Papyri published by Peet. In BM 10052, one of the accused is identified as Amenkhau (*Ỉmn-ḫꜥw*), son of the *šmꜥt n wḏḥw, Ḥr*[4] (Peet, 1930:

[1] Ward (1982: 175), lists five sources, one of which is incorrect – CG 20023.

[2] There is a possible third man depending on the reading of the name *Ḥrtt* who was a *šmꜥ n ḥwt Bꜣstt* (Bakr, 1992: 151 n.547.1-11). This could be a female name as the final "t" in *šmꜥ* is sometimes left out for space considerations.

[3] van Walsem, et.al., 1999: 19-35, ills. Thanks to René van Walsem for providing information on this piece prior to its publication.

[4] The reading of the man's name, *Ḥr*, is not certain. The determinative at the end of the name is not clear, and while it is most commonly a

143ff, pls. XXVff). The word *šmʿ* in this case bears the feminine "t" at the end, leading to the conclusion that the title had become associated mainly with women and the spelling had crystallized in the feminine form.

Scenes of Festival Processions in Temples:

The festival procession of *Opet* at Luxor contains a scene of men labeled *šmʿw nty ḥr šmʿ ḥr ḥ3t nṯr pn špsy Ỉmn nb nsw t3wy*, "chanters who are chanting before this noble god, Amun lord of the thrones of the two lands" (Epigraphic Survey, 1994: pl. 91). Although there are no labeled representations of their female counterparts here, various groups of women shake sistra and dance.

Theban Tomb Material

Two individuals are known from the tomb of Nakhtamun (TT 341) (Davies and Gardiner, 1948: 35, pl. XXIV; KRI III, 361.12-.13). An interesting group of men on the north wall are making offerings to Ptah-Sokar-Osiris and asking him to protect the king, Ramesses II. The first three bear the title *sḏm-ʿš*, or "servant". The fourth is called *šmʿ n ḥwt Wsr-mʿ3-Rʿ-stp-n-Rʿ m (pr) Ỉmn, Nsw-niwt*: Chanter of the temple of User-Maat-Ra in the domain of Amun (the Ramesseum), Nesu-niwt. As a musician of the Ramesseum, it is natural for him to ask for divine intercession for the well being of the king. He and one other are interpreted as being foreigners because of the conical shape of the head, sometimes associated with Syrians (Davies and Gardiner, 1948: 35; Manniche, 1991b: 63). The last man in the group is called *šmʿ n Ptḥ-skr, Nfr-ʿḥʿ*: Chanter of Ptah-Sokar, Neferaha. Two unlabeled, seated men accompany them, one playing a lute and the other clapping. The text of a hymn to Ptah-Sokar-Osiris is recorded above the seated men.

A group of clapping men portrayed on the north wall of the tomb of Kheruef (TT 192) are labeled *šmʿw*. They are positioned above a group of women labeled *šmʿywt* (Epigraphic Survey, 1980: pls. 47, 59-63). The men are spatially oriented to imply that they were the "head of the parade" (i.e., they face backward toward the rest of the entourage). They are followed by dancers, offering bearers, *ḥsyw* who look and pose exactly like the *šmʿw*, and others. Their hymn is written in columns before them. Another group scene comes from the tomb of Kenamun (TT 93) (Davies, 1930: pl. 39-40). Among the people taking part in dragging the statue of Kenamun are male *šmʿw* marching with arms raised over their heads. Their caption says *ḫbt in šmʿw*, "dancing by the chanters" while the women bear the rubric *dḫn in šmʿ(y)wt*, "making rhythm by the chantresses".

Three men and another group of three women depicted in the tomb of Menkheperrasonb (TT 112) (Davies, 1933: pl. 17) are labeled *dḫnt šmʿw* "choir of chanters". They hold their arms out in a clapping gesture while the text of their hymn is spelled out before them (Davies, 1933: 14; Urk. IV, 935). This has been interpreted as part of the Beautiful Feast of the Valley procession and its festivities (Manniche, 1991a: 71-72).

A group of three men depicted in the tomb of Ramose (TT 55) stand before a group of butchers who are offering an ox head. They are labeled *šsp dḫn n šmʿ(w)*: choir of chanters (Davies, 1941: pl. XIII).

In addition to the man named in the Tomb Robberies Papyri, two other *šmʿw n wḏḥw* are known. Theban tomb 16 of Panehsy (Baud and Drioton, 1928: esp. fig. 16; KRI III, 396-399) shows the tomb owner and his brother, Pahesy, engaged in a procession of the sacred vases of Amun. Panehsy is described as the *ḥry šmʿ wḏḥw n Ỉmn* : overseer of the chanters of the offering table of Amun (see also KRI III, 397.11 and 398.15). His brother is a *šmʿ n wḏḥw n Ỉmn* (KRI III, 398.16). They hold their hands before them making a clapping gesture.

Late Period Evidence

Two individuals from Mariette's "nécropole des chanteuses" at Abydos were male *šmʿw*; stela 1296 bears an inscription of the *ḥry šmʿ(ywt) m pr Wsr n ḏdw 3bḏw ʿnḫ-wnn-nfr*, (Overseer of Chanters of the Domain of Osiris of Busiris and Abydos, Ankhwennefer) and the *šmʿ m pr Wsr* (Chanter of the Domain of Osiris, [name unclear]) (Mariette, 1880: 489).

Conclusions

The formula *šmʿ n* [deity or institution] was followed, just as it was followed for the women, although men were more likely to serve specific temples and royal institutions than women were. Men also seem absent from the cult of Amun, except for the very specific title *šmʿw n wḏḥw n Ỉmn* and the recent find from Saqqara, mentioned previously. Institutions that men were associated with included: *ḥwt B3stt* (temple of Bastet), *ḥwt Wsir* (temple of Osiris), *pr Wsir* (domain of Osiris), *pr Ptḥ* (domain of Ptah), *ḥwt Wsr-m3ʿt-Rʿ-stp-n-Rʿ* (the Ramesseum). There is nothing to indicate that men served only gods while women served only goddesses.

The existence of men bearing this title, one previously thought to belong solely to the realm of women, is interesting. While it is clear that the title was predominantly held by women, there was a male version, which is portrayed in the same manner as the feminine counterpart. They are shown in representations alongside women, apparently performing the same role. The occurrence of the title referring to individuals and groups of both sexes proves that it was not a gender specific role, and consequently rules out any question of whether the

man's name, its use as a female name is known (Ranke, 1935, vol. I: 245.18).

title was derived from, or contingent upon a husband's status or role in temple affairs.

The small numbers of men who held the title *šmꜥ* may suggest that personal piety or talent motivated them to become chanters. There was probably no prestige associated with the title for men as it was not a courtly title, nor an administrative one. As a religious title it carried no real power in the temple hierarchy. Most of the men who held the title did not have other recorded titles, indicating that they may have considered being a chanter their religious vocation. Surely other temple positions, however low, would have been open to them, but they chose to be chanters. Perhaps this is our only indication that talent was a factor in becoming a *šmꜥ*.

CHART 6: Male *šmꜥw*

NAME	DEITY	TITLES	DATE	PROV. & LOCATION	PUBLICATIONS
Ỉtiti	none given		Middle Kingdom	Illahun, P. Berlin 10021	Scharff, 1924, 53, autographed text 9; Ward, 1982, #1514
S-nḫt	none given		Middle Kingdom	Illahun, P. Berlin 10081	Kaplony-Heckel, 1971, vol. I, 36-37, #64; Ward, 1982, #1514
Sbk-sꜥnḫ?	none given		Dyn. 12	Abydos, CG 20216	Mariette, 1880, #986; Ward, 1982, #1514
Sr-mꜣꜥt	*Pth rsy-inb.f nb tꜣwy*	*imy-r pr ḥsb it mḥy m ꜥnḫ tꜣwy*	Dyn. 12	Saqqara, valley temple of Unas	Moussa and Altenmüller, 1975, 94-95; Ward, 1982, #1515
Ptḥ-ꜥnḫ	*ḥry šmꜥw n pr Ptḥ*		New Kingdom	Memphis?, Kestner Museum zu Hannover, #2946 (4)	Cramer, 1936, 91 (#10-13) pl. VI.1-2
Pꜣ-nḥsy	*ḥry šmꜥ n wḏḥw n Ỉmn*	*ḥm nṯr n Ỉmn-ḥtp-ḥr-wsḫt*	Rameses II	Thebes, TT16	Baud, et.al., 1928, fig. 16
Pꜣ-ḥsy	*wḏḥw n Ỉmn*		Rameses II	Thebes, TT16	Baud, et.al., 1928, fig. 16
Nsw-niwt	Ramesseum		Rameses II	Thebes, TT341	Davies, 1948, 35, pl. XXIV
Nfr-ꜥḥꜥ	Ptah-Sokar		Rameses II	Thebes, TT341	Davies, 1948, 35, pl. XXIV
Bꜣy	Amun?		Dyn. 19	Saqqara, tomb of Horemhab	van Walsem et. al., 1999, 19-35
Pꜣ-rꜥ-ḥr-wṯs.f	Bastet		Dyn. 19-20	Bubastis	Bakr, 1992, n. 36, n.84.1-3
Mꜥiꜣ	*nb pt*		Dyn. 19-20	Bubastis	Bakr, 1992, n. 36, n.84.1-3
Ḥr	*wḏḥw n Ỉmn*		Dyn. 20	Tomb Robberies Papyri; BM 10052	Peet, 1930, 143ff, pl. XXV ff.
ꜥnḫ-wnn-nfr?	Osiris		Saite Period	Abydos	Mariette, 1880, 489, #1296
not clear	Osiris		Saite Period	Abydos	Marriette, 1880, 489, #1296

APPENDIX B
THE EVIDENCE FROM ABYDOS

The so-called "nécropole des chanteuses" found by Mariette at Abydos provides some very interesting material for this study in the form of Middle and New Kingdom stelae. The fullest summary of this material is published in Mariette's two late nineteenth century volumes on his work there, *Abydos. Description des fouilles exécutées sur l'emplacement de cette ville* (1869-1880) and *Catalogue Général des Monuments d'Abydos* (1880). Mariette's focus was on the inscriptional material rather than the archaeological context of the stelae referred to therein. His description of the northern necropolis from which most of the items come is unfortunately brief (summarized from Mariette, 1880: 441-442): [1]

> Near the Shunet el Zebib lies a New Kingdom cemetery of women bearing the title *kema-t* [now transliterated *šmˁyt*]. These women can be recognized by their costumes on the stelae. Also found were small sarcophagi (of terra-cotta) with human fetuses. These sarcophagi were not buried in the ground, but rather within an ancient wall.[2] The name of Osiris here is *Wsir ms* (var. *nb ms, nb ˁ3 ms, ms nṯrw*) [Osiris of birth, lord of birth, great lord of birth, divine birth]. Could this title have to do with the gestation of children? What role did the chantresses fulfill here? The date of the necropolis seems to be year 27 of Ramesses XIII(sic).[3]

The individual stelae are not provenienced more specifically than to what quarter of the necropolis they came from. His general description of the cemetery refers to tombs, but no reference is made to what specific tomb individual items came from. There is also no map locating any individual tombs or objects of note.[4] The stelae from Mariette's excavations can, in part, be found in the Cairo Museum. Lacau's Catalogue General volume of New Kingdom stelae and Lange and Schäfer's volume of Middle Kingdom stelae give concordance lists of Mariette's field number to CG number. The others are dispersed throughout the world's collections.

The area is now usually associated with cenotaphs or offering chapels rather than tombs (Pouls, 1997-1998: 51; O'Connor, 1985: 161-177), which would account for the lack of detail about any actual burials or burial chambers. However, the cenotaph structures were not described by Mariette either.

Regarding the area in question, later authors have had to base their conclusions on the incomplete descriptions of excavations given by Mariette. The *Lexikon der Ägyptologie* describes the area as having been occupied "partly by tombs of songstresses of Osiris" and partly by tombs of the 18th-22nd Dynasties that had brick chapels associated with them (LÄ I, 36). Also, from the scanty information supplied by Mariette, Lise Manniche offers an interpretation of this cemetery:

> A section of the necropolis was set apart for songstresses (*šmˁyt*) of a number of deities... and their stillborn children. It is not known why these women had a separate burial place. It may indicate a favored status: perhaps it was a privilege for women dying in childbirth to be buried there. But the opposite may be equally well true; only one of the songstresses was accompanied by a husband[5], and possibly these women had no fathers in whose tomb they could be buried" (Manniche, 1991a: 124-25).

The stelae found at the site clearly indicate that these women had male relatives and husbands. If Mariette's suggestion that the unique epithet of Osiris used here (*nb ms*, and variations) related to childbirth and gestation, then Manniche's initial supposition about the favored status of women who died in childbirth would explain the situation better.

Other excavators have worked in the general area of Mariette's digging, but none specifically in the "nécropole des chanteuses". Their findings, however, may shed light on this area of the site.

Garstang worked at Abydos at the turn of the century, publishing his work in the Memoirs of the Egyptian Research Account as *El Arábah* (1901, reprinted 1989). Although his work concentrated on the temple area, he did find three shabtis of different *šmˁyt n Ỉmn* in the tombs he excavated (DB #s 572, 573, 574).

Peet published three volumes of *The Cemeteries of Abydos*, as part of the Egypt Exploration Fund memoirs. The second of these deals with the northern cemetery where Mariette worked, although no mention is made of the earlier excavator's work. Peet's characterization of the area ascribes the tombs to the Middle Kingdom and [Second] Intermediate period (1914: 54ff). The 18th

[1] The area is also dealt with summarily on p. 48-49 of *Description des fouilles* vol. 2, Section 267.
[2] Unfortunately, he does not specify what structure the wall was part of.
[3] One of the stelae excavated by Mariette is dated by inscription to Year 27 of the king then identified as Ramesses XIII but now numbered Ramesses XI, (pp. 442-443, No. 1173). The stelae of the chantresses are usually dated to late Dynasty XX - Dynasty XXI. (Fazzini, 2002, 358 n. 43).
[4] Peet's map of the site is somewhat useful in this regard (1913, vol. II: xiv, fig. 1).

[5] The stelae found at the site clearly bear the names of male relatives and husbands. If Mariette's suggestion that the unique epithet of Osiris used here (*nb ms*, and variations) related to childbirth and gestation, then Manniche's initial supposition about favored status of women who died in childbirth would explain the situation better.

Dynasty tombs are intrusive into those earlier tombs (1914: 70ff). The bodies mentioned are predominantly women who were buried with better quality grave goods: alabaster kohl pots, ceramic vessels, and jewelry of bronze, glass, and faience. Two children were also found in tombs rather than in walls as Mariette had found (1880: 442). 21st Dynasty material was also present in the form of fragments of a painted stucco coffin. A New Kingdom shabti of the *šmʿyt n Wsr, Kt-ḥr* (Chantress of Osiris, Kethor) was recovered from Peet's excavation of tomb D223 (DB #571; Peet, 1913, v. III: 32, pl. xii.10).

Recent work in the area by the University of Pennsylvania–Yale Institute of Fine Arts Expedition also furthers our understanding of the cult activities of the New Kingdom at Abydos. A recent article chronicling the work of the expedition sums up the difficulties in dealing with this material: "The methods that resulted in the dispersal of a great portion of the Abydene corpus pose significant obstacles to the understanding of this rich body of evidence for non-royal activity at the periphery of a major Egyptian temple.... the original archaeological context of this material remains unknown" (Pouls, 1997-1998: 59, n.4).[6]

Although this may be discouraging, the discovery of a temple of Tuthmosis III in the North cemetery area sheds light on the burial of the *šmʿywt* nearby. Its existence provides a possible venue of work for the women who served Osiris. The date also coincides with the increase in popularity of the title in the Theban area. A few stelae of *šmʿywt* were found in the area of the so-called Portal Temple of Rameses II which is close to the remains of the Tuthmosis III temple (Simpson, 1995: 57, 59, 61). Based on the architectural layout, the temple is believed to have been the terminus for processional ritual (Pouls, 1997-1998: 59, n. 6; Petrie, 1916: 174).

The history of the buildings at the site fits the pattern of *šmʿyt* attestations. The earliest stelae (Middle Kingdom) that mention *šmʿywt* are from Abydos.[7] Stela CG 20142 of the *šmʿyt Snw-ʿnḫ* (DB #580) is from the northern necropolis at Abydos. Stela CG 20216 (Lange and Schäfer, 1902, pt. 1: 238-239 and pt. 4: pl. XVII) is also from the northern necropolis and lists two individuals; *šmʿw Sbk-sʿnḫ*, and an unnamed male or female *šmʿ(yt)*.[8] None of these titles are connected with a god or goddess and the scenes depict the deceased as the recipient of offerings. However, the *ḥtp di nsw* formula contains the name of Osiris (*ḫnty imntiw* on 20142) *nb ȝbdw*. There was an Osiris-Khenti-Imentiu temple at Abydos during the Middle Kingdom that was torn down to make room for the New Kingdom structure (Kemp, 1968: 141). It may, therefore, be reasonable to assume the women were involved in that cult and were allowed to erect monuments nearby.

Database statistics

One hundred fifteen references are classified as having come from Abydos.[9] The women who served Osiris (23 references) were all from Abydos. Those women are mainly known from 20th Dynasty stelae recovered in Mareitte's excavations. The women themselves dedicated many of the stelae, rather than a husband or father. Ninety-two of the total 115 women from Abydos did not serve Osiris, but represented the cults of various gods- Amun, Hapi, Isis, Mut, Onuris, Hathor, Montu, Horus the Behedtite.[10] This may illustrate the presence of pilgrims at the site rather than Abydene *šmʿywt*.

The placement of such a large number of stelae representing *šmʿywt* at the site becomes an indication of the status that they had. Those dedicated by the women who served in the cult of Osiris are especially interesting because it indicates that it was the woman's position in the local cult that was the key factor in the placement of the tomb or stela.[11] The other family stelae can be viewed in the same light as the other dedications made by ancient Egyptians who wanted to leave their name at Abydos in order that their spirit could benefit from being represented at the holy site. They are difficult to interpret from a genealogical point of view, however, because the family relationships are not explicitly stated. It is hoped that continued work in the area of the Tuthmosis III temple may reveal more about the nature of the *šmʿywt*'s association with the cult of Osiris at Abydos, and the activities of pilgrims there.

[6] A list of other references to the expedition's work can be found there and in *LÄ* I, 28-41.
[7] These stelae are discussed in more detail in chapter 5.II.3-.4.
[8] The problems associated with this individual are discussed in chapter 5.II.3-.4.

[9] Twelve of those references were not securely attributed to Abydos, but can be assumed to come from there based on internal evidence of the objects.
[10] One woman served Osiris, Isis, and Horus, (DB ref. #555).
[11] An alternative view is that the women adopted the title because of the placement of the stelae; that is to say they took on a title relating to the particular god of the area – Osiris here – because of the placement of the stela in the domain of that god. This is not a view favored by the writer, but is within the realm of possibility.

APPENDIX C
LETTERS

The purpose of this appendix is to provide a summary of the elements relevant to the study of the *šmʿywt* that appeared in the numerous letters used for analysis in Chapter 4. They are not retranslated here. Most of them have been dealt with by Wente, 1990, *Letters from Ancient Egypt*, whose treatment of this material is far more comprehensive than what could be done here. Others sources are noted in the heading of each letter's description. They are arranged here in rough chronological order.

Northumberland papyrus no. 1: Barns, 1948, 35-46; Wente, 1990, 113-114; KRI I, 239-241. Rameses I-Seti I. This is a simple letter written by the Scribe Mahu to inquire about the health of the Scribe Yy the Younger and to ask him to look after the matter of the Captain Merymose. Also the *šmʿyt* of Amun, Isis-nefret sends Yy The Younger her greetings and wishes for his visit saying "I want to see you, my eyes being as big as Memphis because I am hungry to see you here" (line 12). The relationships between Isis-nefret, Mahu and Yy are unclear, but they are obviously close: perhaps Isis-nefret was the sister of one man and the wife or lover of the other.

A group of letters written by servants reflects a degree of familiarity between servants and those in higher positions. P. Leiden I, 364, 365, 366 concern the same group of people. They all date to the reign of Ramesses II.

P. Leiden I 360: Wente, 1990, 33-34; KRI III, 230
The servant Mersuiotef writes to his mistress the *šmʿyt* of Isis, the Noble Lady Tel inquiring about her and reassuring her that "the general is all right as well as his people and children. Don't worry".

P. Leiden I 364; Wente, 1990, 33; KRI III, 231-232
The servant Mermaat writes to the servant Rudefneheh, but greets the *šmʿyt* of Amun, Hathor first. The bulk of the letter is an invocation of the gods on her behalf, and the "other matter" is the message for Rudefneheh. This arrangement leads one to speculate that the *šmʿyt* was more important; perhaps she was Rudefneheh's employer and responsible for distributing the servants' mail.

P. Leiden I 365;[1] Wente, 1990, 32-33; KRI III, 232-233
The servant Meryiotef writes to the servant Rudefneheh and mentions the servant Mermaat (from letter 364 above). The letter includes an address to the *šmʿyt* of Amun Nubem..., and the *šmʿyt* of Amun Saupatjau.

P. Leiden I 366; Wente, 1990, 32; KRI II, 910-911
The servant Meryiotef writes to the *šmʿyt* of Amun, Ernute, chastising her for not writing sooner.

P. Leningrad 1118: Wente, 1990, 117; KRI III, 490. reign of Rameses II
This is a simple letter wherein the Scribe and Lector Priest Wernemty writes to the Master Chariot-maker Huy regarding his condition and that of his people. He also asks about the health of the *šmʿyt* of Amun, Naia.

P. Anastasi I (satirical letter): Wente, 1990, 100. reign of Rameses II [2]
Hori, the author of the letter, gives his mother's name as Tawosre from the region of Bilbeis,[3] a *šmʿyt* of Bastet in God's field.

Late Ramesside Letters

The late Ramesside period letters form a significant corpus of material. The main publication by Černý (1939), *Late Ramesside Letters*, and the Wente publications already cited have served as the main sources.[4] The letters have been identified by the numbers assigned to them in the original Černý and Wente publications as well as by their museum or collection numbers.

Nesamenope letters:

LRL 37- P. Geneva D 191: Černý, 1939, 57-60; Wente, 1967, 71-74; Černý, 1973, 213-214; Wente, 1990, 174-175. Rameses XI, year 2 of *wḥm-mswt*.

The *šmʿyt n Ỉmn-Rʿ nsw nṯrw* Henuttawy writes to the Scribe of the Necropolis Nesamenope.[5] It is a letter regarding grain transactions and a court case concerning the father of the addressee. It seems that Henuttawy was carrying out business for Nesamenope while he was unavailable. The letter implies he will return to take care of a problem arising from a disagreement concerning the measurement of grain. Černý speculates that Henuttawy may have been the wife of the scribe (1973: 214).

LRL 36- P. British Museum 10412: Černý, 1939, 55-56; Wente, 1967, 70-71; 1990, 175-176; Černý, 1973, 213-214. Rameses XI, year 2 of *wḥm-mswt*.

The same Nesamenope, Scribe of the Necropolis from *LRL* 37 writes to the *šmʿyt n Ỉmn-Rʿ*, Mutenipet. He

[1] This letter was recently (Spring 1999) in a traveling exhibit of items from Leiden. The website makes the following comments about this item: "This letter was found in a Memphite archive still rolled and sealed with a cord and clay seal. It may never have been delivered. It was sent by boat from Meriotef in Piramesse to Rudefneheh in Memphis" (http://icvc.imago.com.au/egypt/html/lifeitem4.html) (Western Australia exhibit showing).

[2] Bellion dates this piece to the reign of Seti II (1987: 8).
[3] Bubastis according to Wente (1990: 110, n.2).
[4] Letters 2, 5, 6, 7, 8, 9,14, 16, 17, 31, 30, 36, 37, 38, 39, 50.
[5] See also BM 10190 (Letter IV in Jansen, 1991), a fragmentary text dealing with domestic matters like cucumbers and a donkey which may involve the same people, and Černý (1973: 214) for a discussion of Nesamenope.

gives her instructions for a land transaction and its planting as well as the making of some weapons while he is in Nubia. The fact that he wrote to a different woman than the one who wrote to him may argue against Henuttawy being his wife. Both women were obviously close enough to be trusted with business dealings.

Butehamon letters:[6]

These letters were all written during the reign of Rameses XI. Three additional letters dealing with Butehamon and his associates are found in Janssen (1991). The women Hemisheri and Shedemdua are mentioned, but not by title.[7]

LRL 14 - BM 10417: Černý, 1939, 27-28; Wente, 1967, 46-47; Wente, 1990, 179.
year 6 of *wḥm-mswt*.
The Prophet of Amenhotep (l.p.h.) Amenhotep writes to Tuthmosis, Scribe of the Necropolis who is "south", probably in the military as he calls on the gods to give the addressee "favor with the general, your lord". Amenhotep assures Tuthmosis that the people he has inquired about in his last letter are safe and sound. One of those inquired about is the *šmꜤyt n Ỉmn-RꜤ nsw nṯrw*, Shedemdua. Amenhotep further states that he is bringing Tuthmosis's case before the oracle of Amenhotep whenever he is in procession (*r tnw ḫꜤy.f*) and that the god responds favorably every time.

LRL 5 - P. Leiden I 370: Černý, 1939, 9-11; Wente, 1967, 27-31; Wente, 1990, 180-181.
year 6 of *wḥm-mswt*.
This letter concerns some of the same people as letter 14; Tuthmosis writes to the Scribe Butehamon and the *šmꜤyt n Ỉmn-RꜤ nsw nṯrw* Shedemdua (who is inquired about in many letters). Tuthmosis expresses touching concern for the women and their children that they not lack anything. The rest is about business matters.

LRL 17- P. Geneva D 192: Černý, 1939, 33-34; Wente, 1967, 51; Wente, 1990, 185.
year 10 of *wḥm-mswt*.
The General's Singer (*ḥs*) Pentahures writes to the Scribe of the Necropolis Tuthmosis, the Singer (*ḥst*) Hemisheri,[8] and the *šmꜤyt n Ỉmn* Shedemdua. He expresses his wish for their health and that he may see them again soon.

LRL 8 - P. Geneva D 407: Černý, 1939, 13-17; Wente, 1967, 33-37; Wente, 1990, 187-188.
year 10 of *wḥm-mswt*.
Another letter from Tuthmosis to Butehamon assures him that things are going well with his affairs at home including the well being of the *šmꜤyt n Ỉmn* Shedemdua and Hemisheri (a *ḥsyt* in a previous letter). The General's Singer Pentahures is also addressed. Tuthmosis assures Pentahures, and others, that their people are fine.

LRL 7 - P. Bibliothèque Nationale 197,IV: Černý, 1939, 13; Wente, 1967, 32-33; Wente, 1990, 200. year 10 of *wḥm-mswt*.
The same scribe, Tuthmosis writes to the Guardian Khar. He asks him to look after Shedemdua and her children and prevent anyone from doing wrong to them. He also asks the addressee to pray to Amun for his safe return from "the wilds, the place where I am abandoned". He sends a further note to the *šmꜤyt n Ỉmn*, Tayuhenut asking her to let him know how she and her people are.

LRL 6 - P. Griffith: Černý, 1939, 12; Wente, 1967, 32; Wente, 1990, 201. no year, *wḥm-mswt*.
The Scribe Tuthmosis writes to the Necropolis Scribe Butehamun and the *šmꜤyt n Ỉmn* Hemisheri. "I am fine, pray for me to come back safely." He also asks after the *šmꜤyt n Ỉmn*, Baki and the *šmꜤyt n Ỉmn*, Shedemdua.

LRL 31 - P. Bibliothèque Nationale 196,III: Černý, 1939, 51-52; Wente, 1967, 67-68; Wente, 1990, 199. year 10 of *wḥm-mswt*.
The general's Singer Pentahu[res] writes to the Scribe Butehamun and others including the *šmꜤyt n Ỉmn-RꜤ nsw nṯrw* Hemisheri and another *šmꜤyt* whose name is lost (but probably Shedemdua as she appears in the other letters with these people). He exhorts the women to look after his father and the children. He also reports on a case submitted to an oracle of Khnum, which was decided favorably in front of the *šmꜤyt n Ỉmn*, Tuia, and the Scribe Hori. The nature of the case is not stated. The oracle seems to have taken place where the author is writing from, presumably Elephantine as it is mentioned previously and Khnum is the deity addressed. Tuia and Hori seem to act as witnesses at the oracle for Pentahures.

LRL 16 - P Turin 1971: Černý, 1939, 31-33; Wente, 1967, 49-51; Wente, 1990, 192-193.
year 10 of *wḥm-mswt*.
A letter to the Scribe of the Necropolis Tuthmosis (Tjaroy on the address) from Butehamon regards the health *šmꜤyt n Ỉmn RꜤ nsw nṯrw* Shedemdua and the *šmꜤyt n Ỉmn* Hemisheri. He also prays for Tuthmosis's safe return from Nubia.

LRL 2: P. Turin 1973: Černý, 1939, 2-5; Wente, 1967, 20-21; Wente, 1990, 188-189.
year 10 of *wḥm-mswt*.
The necropolis scribe Tuthmosis (Tjaroy on the address) writes to the Necropolis Scribe Buteh[amon and the *šmꜤyt n Ỉmn* Shedemdua]. He mentions the presence of Herere (Piankh's wife) at Elephantine as well as other personal topics including a reminder to make offering to the gods on his behalf.

[6] Background on Butehamon and his family is given in Černý (1973: Appendix D) and Bierbrier (1975: 39-44, 46, 51).
[7] The letters concerned are BM 10411, BM 10419, and BM 10440.
[8] This is undoubtedly the same Hemisheri who is referred to in many other letters where she is a *šmꜤyt*. Either she held both titles, or the writer of the letter confused the two.

LRL 50 - P. Turin 2026: Černý, 1939, 71-74; Wente, 1967, 83-85; Wente, 1990, 189-190
year 10 of *wḥm-mswt*.
[The scribe Tuthmosis writes to ... and the *šmꜥyt n Ỉmn* Shedem]dua. He inquires after the health of Hemisheri and a number of people, including Butehamon to whom he directs some business affairs.

LRL 9 - P. BM 10326: Černý, 1939, 17-21; Wente, 1967, 37; Wente, 1990, 190-192
year 10 of *wḥm-mswt*.
The Scribe Tuthmosis writes to the Scribe Butehamon, the *šmꜥyt n Ỉmn* Shedemdua, and Hemisheri. He calls upon the gods of the south (Horus of Kuban and Aniba) and Atum to give them long life. It is mainly a business letter.

Herere letters:
LRL 39 - P. Turin 2069: Černý, 1939, 61; Wente, 1967, 75.
year 10 of *wḥm mswt*?
The *wrt ḫnr, šmꜥyt n Ỉmn-Rꜥ nsw nṯrw* Herere writes to the Troop-Commander Peseg concerning rations for the men of the necropolis. This is the only letter that contains a reference to the *šmꜥyt* title, but the two following are included to show the position this woman had.

LRL 38 - P. Turin, unnumbered: Černý, 1939, 60-61; Wente, 1967, 74; Wente, 1990, 200. year 10 of *wḥm-mswt*.
The *wrt ḫnr n Ỉmn-Rꜥ, nsw nṯrw,* Herere writes to the Troop Captain Peseg. She writes to complain that the necropolis personnel have not received the rations she had previously written about. "Don't make them complain to me again" she says.

LRL 30- P. BM10100: Černý, 1939, 50-51; Wente, 1967, 65-67; Wente, 1990, 197.
year 10 of *wḥm-mswt*.
The General of Pharaoh writes to the two Foremen, the Scribe Butehamon, the Guardian Khar, and all the necropolis workmen: Necropolis Scribe Tjaroy (Tuthmosis), the Troop Captain, and a priest have reached him in the south to make a report on work being done (in Thebes?). He has left Herere in charge of five women servants for the work gang's use.

APPENDIX D CATALOGUE OF *Šmʿywt* KNOWN FROM THEBAN TOMBS OF THE 18-20TH DYNASTIES

The aim of this appendix is twofold: to gather the relevant publication information in one place, and to provide the reader with a sense of community and family relationships for the Theban noble class. Much of our understanding of the New Kingdom family and noble class comes from these tombs. By expanding upon the data given in the database, the information gathered will be of use to those researching any number of topics.

Although giving a bias toward evidence from the cult of Amun in the New Kingdom,[1] the importance of looking at the Theban tomb representations lies in their ability to give us an idea of family relationships. The Egyptian family was a close one, probably best demonstrated by the numerous family scenes on tomb walls and the numbers of people occasionally included on stelae found in the tombs. Tombs are one of the few places where extended family can be traced by name and title. Genealogical information about women is plentiful in the tombs that belonged to their husbands, sons, and fathers, although they are perhaps not as detailed as one would like them to be. Also, these tombs are often datable to a specific reign, giving an indication of the temporal distribution of the title.

The tomb numbers used here are those used by Porter and Moss. Not all sources listed contained references to the *šmʿyt* title, but supplied other information on the tomb or the people mentioned therein.

TT 6: Neferhotep and Nebnefer. Ramesses II; PM I.1, 14-15; KRI III, 577-587; Wild, 1979; Černý, 1949, 60. DB ref. #716.
Nebnefer was a chief workman in the Place of Truth like his father and grandfather. His wife was a *ḥsyt ʿ3t n Ḥwt-ḥr, šmʿyt n Ḫnmw Stt* [*ʿnḳt*] (Khnum, Satet [and Anukis]), *Ꞽi(-m-w3wt)* (Wild, 1979: pls. 4, 10). Her titles indicate a southern origin as these were the gods of the cataract region. In fact, the gods of the cataract play an important role in this tomb indicating some connection between the Theban occupants and the South. This is one of the few Deir el Medina tombs to mention a *šmʿyt*.[2]

TT 16: Panehsy. Ramesses II; PM I.1, 28-9; KRI III, 396-399; Baud and Drioton, 1928. DB ref. #678.
The wife of Panehsy was *šmʿyt n Ꞽmn T3-rnwt*. She is shown in many religious scenes with her husband, a Prophet of "Amenhotep of the Forecourt". He is also called the *ḥry šmʿ wdḥw n Ꞽmn* (overseer of the chanter(s) of the offering table of Amun) in a scene depicting the procession of the vases of Amun (Baud and Drioton, 1928: fig. 16). His brother is shown with him and labeled as a *šmʿ wdḥw n Ꞽmn*, obviously a subordinate. One other *šmʿ n wdḥw* is known from the Tomb Robberies Papyri.[3]

TT 19: Amenmes. Ramesses II; PM I.1, 32-4; KRI III, 390-396; Foucart, 1935. DB ref. #674, 717-718. (See also Section 3.III.5)
Amenmose was the first prophet of "Amenhotep of the Forecourt" so it is fitting that his wife Iwy was the *wrt ḫnrt n Ꞽmn-ḥtp* as well as a *šmʿyt n Ꞽmn-Rʿ-m-ipt-swt*. Two other *šmʿywt* appear in the tomb (KRI III, 395.16): *šmʿyt Ḥ3t-šps*, whose relationship to Amenmose is unknown, and *šmʿyt Ꞽmn Mʿkwi...*, also of an unknown relationship to Amenmose.

TT 23: Tjay. Merneptah; PM I, 38-41; KRI IV, 107-119; LD iii, 252-253; Collins, 1976, 34; Wilbour, 1936, 55-56. DB ref. #625-627, 719-722, 906.[4]
The two wives of the Royal Secretary Tjay were the *šmʿyt n Ꞽmn*, (sometimes *Ꞽmn-m-ipt-swt*) *Rʿi3*[5] and the *šmʿyt n Ꞽmn, Nb(t)-t3wy*. His mother Tamiu was also *šmʿyt n Ꞽmn*. Kitchen records the family of *Nb(t)-t3wy* (KRI IV, 117.9-118.3); her mother was a *šmʿyt n Ꞽmn, Mwt-nfrt*, her mother's mother was the *šmʿyt n Ꞽmn, Mḥt-ḫʿṯ*, her sisters were the *šmʿyt n Bʿstt, Ḥuy-n-r* and the *šmʿyt n Bʿstt, Mwt-nfrt*. A woman who may be Tjay's daughter (KRI IV, 116.3) was also a *šmʿyt n Ꞽmn*.

TT 31: Khonsu. Ramesses II; KRI III, 399-410; Davies and Gardiner, 1948. DB ref. #585-86, 599-605, 927. (Khonsu's family is also discussed in Section 3.III.5 and in Chapter 6)
Khonsu was the First Prophet of Tuthmosis III whose parents were Neferhotep, First Prophet of Amenhotep II, and Tausert, a *šmʿyt n Mnṯ*. She is frequently shown in the tomb taking part in the offerings and processions (Davies and Gardiner, 1948: pls. XII, XV). Given her prominence in the tomb, it is perhaps not surprising that her son married two women who were already *šmʿywt n Mnṯ*, like his mother, or became thus after marriage. The first wife,[6] a woman named Ruia, may have been a *šmʿyt*

[1] Evidence is weighted toward the Theban material partly because of Whale's work on the family in 18th Dynasty tombs, which details many unpublished tombs including the titles of the women depicted therein. The bias is also a product of the good preservation conditions in the area, and the interest of excavators and visitors in exploring the area.
[2] The other tombs at Deir el Medina are TT 211, TT 215, TT 267, and TT 359 (detailed below).

[3] For *wdḥw* vases, see Traunecker (1972: 195-236). Panehsy and his brother are also discussed in Section 3.III.5.
[4] Fayza Haikal provides recent documentation on the hymn in this tomb (1985: 361ff), but no full publication of the reliefs and texts has appeared.
[5] PM I.1, 38f calls her a "chief of the harîm of Sobk", but this title is not attested in the few publications relating to this tomb.
[6] The designations "first" and "second" are here used to clarify individuals (following Davies), but there is no real evidence to put them in a sequence.

n Mnṯ.[7] By this woman there were two or three children, one of whom was *šmˁyt n Mnṯ, šmˁyt n Ỉmn, Wỉ3y.*[8] One son was a Lector Priest of Montu, and later the High Priest of Sobek.

The second wife's titles were *šmˁyt n Ỉmn* and *šmˁyt n Mnṯ, ḥsy ˁ3 n Ḥwt-ḥr nbt Ỉwnt.*[9] Her name is a more difficult matter. There appear to be four different variants of the spelling; *Mwtỉ3, Mˁỉ3y, Mˁỉ, T3ỉ3y.* Davies assumes that the last versions are abbreviations of *Mwtỉ3.*[10] They had seven children. Three daughters have preserved titles: Aati, a *šmˁyt* of Montu (DB #604); Nesneb, a *šmˁyt* of Montu (DB #605); and Ru, a *ḥmt nṯr* of Tjenenet of On, the consort of Montu at Tod and Armant. One of Khonsu's sisters was a *šmˁyt* of Montu, and three other individuals named in the tomb were chantresses of Montu as well.[11] Their relationship to Khonsu is unknown, but perhaps they were the daughters of siblings shown in the tomb.

An interesting feature of this tomb is the presence of two women called *ḥmt nṯr* in the Montu procession; the one mentioned above and another woman whose name is lost and who served a cult also lost in the lacuna (Davies and Gardiner, 1948: XIV- XV). Both of these women were sisters of the *šmˁywt* listed in the database as children of Khonsu and Mutia. They are accompanied by their *šmˁywt* sisters in this register and the one above. They hold flowers, sistra, and a wand with a dish for incense offerings. The title *ḥmt nṯr* is relatively rare after the Middle Kingdom.[12]

TT 32: Djehutymose. Ramesses II; PM I.1, 49-50; KRI III, 316-319; Kákosy, 1988, 211-216. DB ref. #693, 723.
The owner of TT 32 was a Royal Scribe, Steward of Amun, Mayor of Esna, Overseer of the Fields of the Lord of the Two Lands, and Overseer of the Granary of Amun. His wife was the *nbt pr šmˁyt n Ỉmn, ḥsyt n Ḥwt-ḥr, 3st.* His mother was *šmˁyt n Nbt-wtt* [sic],[13] *šmˁyt n Ỉmn, Ḥnwt w3ḏbt.* There are only two devotees of *Nbt-ww* recorded in this study (DB #723 from this tomb and DB #854 from TT 183). Both date to the reign of Ramesses II.

TT 33: Padiamenipet. Saite; PM I.1, 50-56; LD iii, 244-245; Duemichen, 1884-1894.[14] DB ref. #568, 569.
Padiamenipet was the Chief Lector Priest of Nekhbet. His wife was *šmˁyt n imn, T3-di* and his mother was a *šmˁyt n Ỉmn, N3-mnḫ-3st.* This tomb contains references to two of the three Saite women in the database.

TT 39: Puimre. Tuthmosis III; PM I.1 71-75; *Urk.* IV, 520-527; Whale, 1989, 50-55; Davies, 1923a. DB ref. #260.
Of the two wives depicted, only one, Senseneb, bears titles: *dw3t nṯr* and *šmˁyt nt Ỉmn.* She is the more prominently portrayed of two wives (Whale, 1989: 52). This may be because she was most likely the daughter of Hepuseneb (TT67 and Gebel el Silsila shrine 15; see below), a High Priest of Amun and a powerful official under Hatshepsut. Puimre was Hepuseneb's subordinate during the building of Deir el Bahari (Grimal, 1992: 212, 219). Therefore it is likely that Puimre married the daughter of his superior. On her father's monuments, however, she is the only daughter without the title *šmˁyt n Ỉmn*, referred to only as a *dw3t nṯr*.

TT 40: Huy. Tutankhamun; PM I.1, 75-78; *Urk.* IV, 2064-2073 (792) esp. 2067.6; Hari, 1976, #294; (Nina) Davies and Gardiner, 1926. DB ref. #699.
The wife or sister of the Viceroy of Nubia, the King's Son, Huy, was a *šmˁyt n Ỉmn*, beloved of the good god, Kener (or Kel). There is no specified relationship between them, but she follows Huy's mother in the inscription, a place usually occupied by the wife.

TT 41: Amenemipet. Ramesses II; PM I.1, 78-81; KRI III, 308-316; Assmann, 1991b. DB refs. #880-882.
Amenemipet was a head steward in the temple of Amun. His wife and her mother were both *šmˁywt n Ỉmn*, and his mother was a *šmˁyt n Ỉmn, Mwt, Ḫnsw.*

TT 42: Amenmose. Tuthmosis III-Amenhotep II; PM I.1, 82-83; *Urk* IV, 1507-1508; Whale, 1989, 120-21; Davies and Davies, 1933. DB ref. #266.
Very few reliefs survive, but the texts remain somewhat more intact. The wife of Amenmose, Henuttawy was a *šmˁyt nt Ỉmn* and a *ḥsyt nt nbt Ỉwnt.*[15] She seems to have played an important role in the tomb. She is shown taking part in the ritual scenes of offering and adoring the gods with her husband.

[7] Her title is given as *šmˁyt n Mnṯ* in the family tree (Davies and Gardiner, 1948: 29), but it was not found in the published plates. Perhaps it appears on something not in the plates.
[8] Again, Davies has given her the title *šmˁyt n Ỉmn* (ibid.: 29), but it is not found in the published plates.
[9] *Ḥsy ˁ3* only appears in Davies and Gardiner (1948: pl. XI), in the lower register along with mother Tausert and her daughter Wia. Here she is not called a *šmˁyt*, just *ḥsy ˁ3*.
[10] This seems improbable, but no other solution presents itself. The variant *Mˁỉ3y* is found in contexts where only a wife's name would occur (ibid.: pl. XII, XIXa) and the representations indicate that they may be the same woman since the other people in the scenes with her are roughly the same. The rubrics for the women in the scenes of Tuthmosis's festival (ibid.: pl. XV) are mostly illegible but seem to refer to three different daughters named *Mˁỉ3*. Without better evidence it is impossible to draw futher conclusions.
[11] *T3y-sn, Wr-nr*, and *Ḥnwt-nfrt* (Davies and Gardiner, 1948: pl. XV).
[12] Two Third Intermediate Period examples are documented (DB #s 201, 150).
[13] The name of this goddess is usually *Nbt-ww* (Lanzone, 1974: I, 351 ff). The extra "*t*"s probably fills space or reflects the feminine aspect of the deity .
[14] This publication does not refer to the women or their titles in any detail.
[15] Whale translates both *šmˁyt* and *ḥsyt* as "priestess" in a general sense (1989: 120).

TT 44: Amenemhab. Ramesses II;[16] PM I.1, 84-85; El-Saady, 1996. DB ref. #503-511.
Amenemhab's wife and two daughters-in-law all bore the title *šmʿyt n Ỉmn*. All six daughters were also *šmʿywt* , but without a designated deity. His wife Isumut's full title was *nbt pr, šmʿyt n Ỉmn m Ỉpt-swt ḥr s3 šmʿ*.[17] The reference to *ḥr s3 šmʿ* is puzzling and is a designation otherwise unknown in this study. El Saady suggests that this means "the southern phyle" (1996: 43). Because this woman is from Thebes it is possible that "south" was meant here. However, in the interpretation favored by the writer, the designation may refer to a "phyle of singers" rather than the south phyle, since *šmʿ* can mean either (see also Section 7.I.)

TT 45: [Djehut. Amenhotep II] ~ usurped by Djehutyemhab in the reign of Ramesses II; PM I.1, 85-86; KRI III, 353-356; Davies and Gardiner, 1948. DB ref. #703-712.
The usurper Djehutyemhab completely redecorated one wall and inserted the names of his family everywhere else, including many *šmʿyt* . This had the effect of obscuring the names and titles of the original figures decorated for Djehut.

The wife of Djehutyemhab was Baketkhonsu, a *šmʿyt* of the Theban triad- Amun, Mut, and Khonsu (Davies and Gardiner, 1948: pl. IV). In the main scene, she is one of two women who offer or shake sistra before a goddess who is now lost (probably Mut or Sekhmet). Elsewhere she is simply called a *šmʿyt n Ỉmn*. The daughters who are shown in the banquet scene are all *šmʿywt*; Tyemheb, Nakhtmut, Henuttawy, Wer[nefert], Isisnefert, Irnefermut, Akhmut, and Isis. The last was named after Djehutyemhab's mother Isis, who was also a *šmʿyt n Ỉmn*.

Djehutyemhab's title "head of weavers" was apparently a modest occupation as only a small number of them are known to have had tombs. Those who did have tombs at Thebes had other titles that elevated their status (Davies and Gardiner, 1948: 3).

TT 46: Ramose. Amenhotep III-IV; PM I.1, 86-87; *Urk.* IV, 1995 (753); Hari, 1976, #193. DB ref. #698.
TT 46's owner, Ramose, held the titles steward, and overseer of the granaries of Upper and Lower Egypt. [18] Hari (1976: #193) gives the fullest account of his wife Neferetkha's titles; *šmʿyt n Ỉʿḥ-ms-Nfrt-iry, šmʿyt n Ỉ*[*tn*], *ḥsyt n Ḥwt-ḥr*.[19] This title is unusual in that she served the cult of the dead Queen and the Aten. This is the only example of a woman serving Ahmose-Nefertari. It is also one of the few references to the Aten.

TT 49: Neferhotep. Aye; PM I.1, 91-95; Davies, 1933. DB ref. #648-649.
Neferhotep was a superintendent of cattle and a chief scribe of Amun. Neferhotep's wife, Meryt-Ra and mother, Iwy, were both *šmʿywt n Ỉmn* (sometimes *Ỉmn-m-ipt-swt*). Meryt-Ra was also a *ḥsyt* of Hathor, Lady of Cusae.

TT 50: Neferhotep. Horemhab; PM I.1, 95-97; *Urk.* IV, 2177-2179 (853) esp. 2178.15; Hari, 1985. DB ref. #584, 615-622, 754-755.
Neferhotep's wife, her mother, her grandmother, and their daughter were all *šmʿyt n Ỉmn*. Two of Neferhotep's sisters were *šmʿyt n Ỉmn*, as well as his mother and her two sisters, (his aunts) and two of his grandfather's sisters (his great-aunts).

TT 51: Userhet. Seti I; PM I.1, 97-99; KRI I, 333-341; Davies, 1927; Mond, 1905, 70. DB ref. #4, 623-624, 756.
There are four women with the title *šmʿyt* in this tomb (Davies, 1927: 9-10). Userhet's wife was *nbt pr šmʿyt n Ỉmn, Ḥ3t-špswt* and his mother is identified as a *šmʿyt n Mnṯw T3-wsrt*. His mother-in-law was *nbt pr šmʿyt n Ỉmn-Rʿ nsw nṯrw, Ḥnwt-t3wy,* and a possible daughter-in-law, who is unnamed, was a *nbt pr šmʿyt n Ỉmn*.

TT 52: Nakht. Tuthmosis IV; PM I.1, 99-102; *Urk.* IV, 1603f. (528); Whale, 1989, 188-189; Davies, 1917. DB ref. #2.
Nakt was a scribe and hour priest whose wife was *nbt pr šmʿyt n Ỉmn T3wy*. The wife of Nakht has a prominent place in the decoration of the tomb, being present in every scene, and sharing in the offerings and rites depicted (Whale, 1989: 188-189). She is frequently shown holding a *menyt* and sistrum in these scenes.

TT 53: Amenemhet. Tuthmosis III; PM I.1, 102-104; *Urk.* IV, 1217-1225(362), esp. 1218.7; Whale, 1989, 97-100. DB ref. #264.
The tomb was fully decorated, but is now badly damaged and unpublished. The wife appears in many scenes, but had no titles (other than *nbt pr*). It was his mother, *Tti-m-nṯr* who was a *šmʿyt n Ỉmn*.

TT 55: Ramose. Amenhotep III-Akhenaton; PM I.1, 105-111; *Urk.* IV, 1776-1790 (634) esp. 1780; Davies, 1941. DB ref. #491, 701.
The tomb of Ramose is one of the most famous and beautiful in the Theban necropolis. As briefly mentioned in Section 5.IV.1, this tomb represents a transitional period from traditional to Amarna styles. Not only does the draftsmanship change, but so does the subject matter. It is only in the part of the tomb decorated under the reign of Amenhotep III that the family is depicted prominently. The absence of family and emphasis on the courtier's relationship to the king is characteristic of the new style and largely responsible for the lack of information on non-royal women in the Amarna age.

[16] The tentative date of El-Saady is based mainly on art historical grounds (1996: 49).
[17] This text is labeled 15a in the plates but called 15b in the text. The full version of her title only occurs here.
[18] See also *Urk* IV, 2110 for a stela from Giza mentioning Ramose.
[19] *Urk.* IV, 1995.12 (n. 753) publishes a slightly different restoration (*šmʿ n Ỉ*[*mn?*]) from incomplete block fragments found at Karnak. Because of the date of the piece it could be read either way.

Ramose's wife Merytptah was a *ḫkrt nsw,* and a *šmꜥyt n Ỉmn*, but everywhere the name of Amun has been effaced. Her parents were the *šmꜥyt n Ỉmn Mꜥy,*[20] and Amenhotep, whom Davies identifies with an important and well-known Memphite official[21] who held many titles.[22] Because of the mother's association with Amun, Hayes postulates she may have been Theban (1938: 23), while her husband was entirely Memphite. The name Merytptah also suggests a Memphite connection.

Ramose's father Neby was a northerner as well. His titles were superintendent of the cattle of Amun in the northern district and superintendent of the double granary of Amun in the nomes of the Delta. As a granary superintendent, Neby may have been a subordinate of Amunhotep who was a "granary overseer". Perhaps their children met and married with the influence of their parents. Amunhotep's close proximity to the king explains Merytptah's *ḫkrt nsw* title, and the high level of his position explains the women's involvement with the official cult of Amun at this early stage in the evolution of the title.

Also depicted in the tomb is a choir (*šspt dḫn n šmꜥ*) of three men followed by a butcher with a cow's head (Davies, 1941: 14, pl. XLVII). The song of the choir is recorded near them. Another group consisting of three women offer a *menyt* and two sistra. They are labeled *šspt [dḫn n šmꜥwt?]* followed by what were probably the words for sistra and *menywt.* The rubric ends with the words *nt Ỉmn-Rꜥ* (Davies, 1941: pl. XVIII). The tomb also preserves a funeral procession of the type discussed in Section 3.III.3, but the mourners and women who attend have no titles.

TT 61 and TT 131: User (Amenuser). Hatshepsut-Tuthmosis III; PM I.1, 123-125, 245-47;[23] *Urk.* IV, 1029-1043 (312-317); Whale, 1989, 55-58; Caminos, 1963, 57-63, pls. 45-47; Davies, 1943, ii, pl. 9; Davies and Gardiner, 1915, pl. 3c. DB ref. #261.
User was the mayor of Thebes and a vizier, as was his father before him. He had two tombs in the necropolis, an earlier tomb, TT 131, and TT 61. Just as in the tombs of Menkheperrasonb (TT 86 and 112), the earlier tomb focusses on the duties of vizier, and the later on his family life.

User's family is depicted on the walls of his contemporaries. As TT 61 is unpublished, one must rely on depictions from TT 100 (Rekhmire), TT 82 (Amenemhet), [24] and User's own Gebel el Silsila shrine (number 17, Caminos, 1963). Of the seven daughters known from various sources, only one was a *šmꜥyt nt (Ỉmn).*[25] The wife and mother of User both left no recorded titles. The sons of the family were mainly *wꜥb* priests. This tomb presents an interesting situation. User was an influential person, yet only one daughter held a title.[26] This indicates a personal choice made by a family member rather than the family's influence or tradition being the deciding factor.

TT 65: [Nebamun. Hatshepsut?]~ usurped by Imiseba, Ramesses IX; PM I.1, 129-132; KRI VI, 544-553; LD iii, 256. DB ref. #726, 789-791.
The wife of Imiseba was a woman who held a rather long string of titles: *šmꜥyt n Ỉmn-Rꜥ nsw nṯrw, sḫmt n Mwt m Ỉsrw, ḥsy(t) ꜥ3t n Ḥwt-ḥr ḥr ib ḏsrt, Ṯ(n)t-p3-st3*: the Chantress of Amun-Ra king of the gods, Sistrum Player of Mut in Isheru, Great Singer of Hathor of Deir el Bahari, Tjenetpasetja.

Imiseba's mother, Mutemeres, was also a *šmꜥyt n Ỉmn* (as well as Mut and Khonsu in another text) and a *ḥsyt n Ḥwt-ḥr*. Two grandmothers are also named in the tomb. His paternal[27] grandmother was the *šmꜥyt n Ỉmn-Rꜥ nsw nṯrw Wi3y* and his maternal grandmother was *šmꜥyt n Ỉmn nsw nṯrw nb pt, Tꜥ-mt* -[lost] .

TT 66: Hepu. Tuthmosis IV; PM I.1, 132-133; *Urk.* IV, 1576-1577 (517); Whale, 1989, 202-203; (Nina) Davies, 1963, pls. VIII-XIV. DB ref. #285.
The tomb is poorly preserved and bears traces of intentional damage (Whale, 1989: 202). Hepu's wife *Rn-n3y* was a *šmꜥyt nt (Ỉmn)* and is represented in many of those scenes that survive.

TT 67: Hepuseneb. Hatshepsut; PM I.1, 133; *Urk.* IV, 469-489 (150-156); Whale, 1989, 25-27; Caminos, 1963, 42-45, shrine 15. DB ref. #257-260.
Hepusenb (TT67) was an important official under Hatshepsut (Grimal, 1992: 212), his highest position being that of high priest of Amun. Correspondingly, the women of his family were of high rank. Because most of

---

[20] May is also mentioned on a stela now in Cairo and originally published by Quibell (1912: 6, 146, pl. lxxxiv).
[21] Hayes does not make the connection in his article dealing with Amenhotep which was published before Davies' work in TT 55 (1938: 9-24).
[22] His titles included: Attendant of the King, Overseer of Priests of the temple of Sekhmet, Leader of Festivals of Ptah-south-of-his-wall and of all the gods of Memphis, Overseer of works in *ḥnmt*-Ptah, Controller of Works, Treasurer of the House of Gold and Silver, Overseer of Craftsmen, Chief Steward, Granary Overseer, and Royal Scribe as well as variations of these titles and epithets that place him close to the king. It is interesting to note that none of these titles were ever present in the tomb of Ramose.
[23] Unfortunately, the PM citation for Säve-Söderbergh's *Private Tombs at Thebes*, was never published.
[24] Rekhmire was probably the mayor and vizier who followed User in the job. Amenemhet was probably User's steward, as he is called the counter of the grain of Amun and steward of the vizier.
[25] Her title is known from TT 82, TT 100, and Gebel el Silsila shrine 17, but not TT 61 or TT 131, which were owned by her father.
[26] This may be a result of preservation since the sources are so fragmentary and belong mainly to non-family members. The shrine may have recorded titles for daughters Amenemhab and Amenemweskhet, which are now lost, but they held no titles in any other source (TT 61, TT 82, TT 100).
[27] They are both clearly grandmothers, being the wives of *it it.f.* I have assumed that Wiay was the paternal grandmother since her husband shared Imiseba's titles as well as his father's. I have also assumed that the other couple represent the maternal grandparents rather than Imiseba's great-grandparents, although they could easily be the latter.

the scenes from this tomb are destroyed and unpublished, the information about his family comes from Gebel el Silsila, shrine 15 (Caminos, 1963: 42-52, pl. 35-39). Hepuseneb's daughters were among the first New Kingdom women to hold the title *šmʿyt*. From the shrine we know that three of his four daughters were *šmʿyt n Ỉmn*. The fourth, a *dw3t nṯr* (*nt Ỉmn*), is known from another tomb, TT 39 of Puiemre, where she is also a *šmʿyt n Ỉmn*. She is shown there as Puiemre's wife. This is a very interesting case because she is the earliest attested holder of the *dw3t nṯr* title, and it is the only 18th Dynasty non-royal attestation (Whale, 1989: 278, n. 23; Section 6.III.4.A).

TT 68: Paenkhemenu. Dynasty 20 ~ usurped in 21st Dynasty; PM I.1, 133-134; Seyfried, 1991; Černý, 1940, 235f. DB ref. #666-667.
Two phases of decoration reflect the original owner's and the usurper's wives' titles. The wife of Paenkhemenu, whose name is lost, was a *šmʿyt n Ỉmn, ḥsyt n Ỉmn-Rʿ*. This is interesting because *ḥsyt n Ỉmn* is not a common title; Hathor or Mut are usually named.[28] The usurper's wife was also a *šmʿyt n Ỉmn, ḥsyt n p3 ʿ n Mwt* named *T3-b3k-n-mwt*.

TT 69: Menna. Tuthmosis IV; PM I.1, 134-139; *Urk*. IV, 1607-1609 (530) esp. 1609.6; Whale, 1989, 206-209. DB ref. #286.
While the tomb was fully decorated and much survives, it has not been fully published except in bits in various publications.[29] Menna's wife *Ḥnwt-t3wy* was a *šmʿyt nt Ỉmn*. She plays a substantial role in the tomb, being represented in most of the scenes. In addition, she was depicted with scribal outfits in two scenes, implying a degree of literacy (Bryan, 1985: 21, pls. 6, 7). Two of their daughters held interesting designations as well. One was *ḥsyt nt Ḥwt-ḥr, ẖkrt nsw* and the other a *ḥsyt n Ỉmn*. Another woman, possibly one of the aforementioned daughters, was also a *šmʿyt* but her name and the name of the god she served are lost.

TT 74: Tjanuny. Tuthmosis III-Tuthmosis IV; PM I.1, 144-146; *Urk*. IV, 1002-1018 (298-302); Whale, 1989, 192-193; Brack and Brack, 1977. DB ref. #283.
The wife of Tjanuny, named Mutiry, figured prominently in the tomb. This is no surprise since she held a number of high titles; they were *ẖkrt nsw šmʿyt nt Ḏḥwty nb ḫmnw, ḥsyt nt Ḥwt-ḥr šmʿyt nt Nḥmt-ʿw3y ḥryt-ib ḫmnw*. Judging by her titles, she was probably from Hermopolis, although her husband does not seem to have any links to the town.

TT 75: Amenhotep-sa-s. Tuthmosis IV; PM I.1, 146-149; *Urk*. IV, 1207-1216 (360-361), esp. 1210.1, 1210.2, 1210.3, 1210.4 (360); Whale, 1989, 186-188; Davies, 1923b. DB ref. #278-281.
The tomb owner was a second prophet of Amun. His wife was a *ẖkrt nsw* and a *šmʿyt nt Ỉmn*. Their three daughters were all *šmʿywt nt Ỉmn*. All four are depicted in a procession on the occasion of their father's induction as the second prophet at the temple (Davies, 1923b: 9, pl. XIV). His wife and three daughters wait with *menywt* and sistra in the garden in front of the temple. They are larger than the others in the entourage, indicating their relationship to the inductee (see Section 3.III.7.)

TT 77: Ptahemhat. Tuthmosis IV; PM I.1, 150-152; *Urk*. IV, 1599-1601 (525); Manniche, 1988, 7-18. DB ref. #683.
Ptahemhat held many titles such as child of the nursery, overseer of works in the temple of Amun, and fan bearer. His wife Meryt was a *šmʿyt n Ỉmn*. Musicians and the Feast of the Valley are shown prominently in his tomb, but the wife is not part of the group of performers. Rather, she is the recipient of their musical blessings.

TT 78: Horemhab. Tuthmosis III-Amenhotep III; PM I.1, 152-156; *Urk*. IV, 1589-1596 (522) esp. 1596.19; Whale, 1989, 210-214; Brack and Brack, 1980. DB ref. #287.
The tomb was intentionally damaged, but it can still be seen that the wife was portrayed prominently. Itchwy was a *šmʿyt nt Ỉmn-m-Ỉpt-swt* (Brack and Brack, 1980: 82, abb.2). She is shown making offerings with her husband. The tomb also contains two groups of singers, one male, one female (neither are referred to by title), whose song seems to be related to the Beautiful Feast of the Valley (ibid.: 29-30; Schott, 1952: 126, 132).

TT 80: Djehutmose, called Djehutynefer. Amenhotep II; PM I.1, 157-159, 217-218; *Urk*. IV, 1475-1476 (455) esp. 1476.13; LD iii, 271; Whale, 1989, 170-175. DB ref. #482.
Djehutynefer, a treasury scribe, had two tombs at Thebes – TTs 80 and 104. His wife is known from TT 104 where she was identified as *ḥsyt n Ḥwt-ḥr nbt Ỉwnt, T3-ḫʿt*. In TT 80, Lepsius describes a small, unnamed figure as *sn.t.f ḥsyt n Ḥwt-ḥr nbt Ỉwnt šmʿyt n* [rest lost] (LD iii, 271). This may refer to a sister or a second wife named Meryt, who is also known from TT 80 and who is identified there specifically as a *ḥsyt nt Ḥwt-ḥr* but not as a *šmʿyt* in that inscription.

TT 82: Amenemhet. Tuthmosis III; PM I.1, 163-167; *Urk*. IV, 1043-1064 (318-322) esp. 1049.12; Whale, 1989, 60-68; Davies and Gardiner, 1915. DB ref. #262. (See also #261, a daughter of User (TT61) who is portrayed here.)
A large number of people in Amenemhet's extended family are recorded in this tomb, but it is from a statue (Berlin 2316; *Urk*. IV, 1049) that we know about one wife who held the title *šmʿyt nt Ỉmn*. This tomb shows four generations and illustrates the difficulty encountered

[28] One other *ḥsyt n Ỉmn* is known from the tomb of Menna (TT 69).
[29] See PM I.1, 134-139 for details of publications.

when dealing with Egyptian kinship terms and trying to unravel familial relationships.[30]

TT 85: Amenemhab. Tuthmosis III-Amenhotep II; *Urk.* IV, 889-922 (268-271) esp. 920.3; Whale, 1989, 123-128.[31] DB ref. #831.
Amenemhab was a lieutenant in the army. His wife Bak was a *šmʿyt n Ỉmn* and also a royal nurse and *ẖkrt nsw*. She held a series of "nurse" titles similar to the wife of Pesukher in TT 88: *mnʿt wrt n nb t3wy, ḥsyt nṯr nfr, šdt nṯr nfr, snḳ, ḫnm n Ḥr šnbt.s*: great nurse of the lord of the two lands, beloved of the good god, nurse of the good god, nurse, who nursed Horus with her breast. As a result of her relationship with the king, Bak has a prominent place in the tomb, and is even shown offering a bouquet directly to the king, as does her colleague in TT 88 (Whale, 1989: 124).

TT 86 and 112: Menkheperrasoneb. Tuthmosis III; PM I.1, 175-178, 229-230; *Urk.* IV, 926-936 (273, 274); Whale, 1989, 100-104; Davies and Davies, 1933. DB ref. #265.
The earlier tomb (TT 112) shows Menkheperrasoneb's family life whereas the later one (TT 86) shows only his official life as a high priest of Amun. Both male and female choirs of *šmʿyt* are shown in Beautiful Feast of the Valley processions. Both tombs depict the festival musicians and record their song (see Section 3.III.2.)

A statue of Menkheperrasoneb (CG 42125) says his mother was a *šmʿyt nt* [*Ỉmn-* name not preserved] (Legrain, 1906, vol. I, #42125).[32] However, the two women who are elsewhere called his mother did not have that title, and a solution as to who actually was his mother is not evident. The attribution of this statue to Menkheperrasoneb is in dispute (Whale, 1989: 102-103).

TT 88: Pehsukher. Tuthmosis III-Amenhotep II; PM I.1, 179-181; *Urk.* IV, 1459-1463 (448) esp. 1460.9-11; LD iii, 272; Whale, 1989, 128-129; Virey, 1891, 286-310. DB ref. #481.
Pehsukher was a lieutenant of the king and a standard bearer of the lord of two lands. His wife Neith was a *šmʿyt n Ỉmn* but her other titles and epithets emphasize her duties as a *mnʿt wrt n nb t3wy*. She also held the titles *ḥsy n nṯr nfr, šdt nṯr nfrt, snḳ ḫnm n šnbt.*beloved of the good god, nurse the good god, nurse, nurse of the breast.

If it is true that Pehsukher was the brother of Kenamun (TT 93) and possibly also Kaemheribsen (TT 98) (Whale, 1989: 158), then his mother would also have been a *mnʿt wrt*. This supports the idea that the mother was important in choosing a son's wife from among her own social circle.

TT 92: Suemnut. Amenhotep II; PM I.1, 187-189; *Urk.* IV, 1449-1452 (443) esp. 1451.20; Whale, 1989, 175-178. DB ref. #276.
The tomb was fully decorated but is now damaged and missing scenes. Suemnut was a royal cup bearer, "pure of hands". Suemnut's mother was a *šmʿyt n Ḏhwty*, which is interesting because most Theban attestations of the title include Amun. It is likely that the husband of this woman was connected to Hermopolis as the mayor of *Nfrwsy* [Balansurah] and hence her association with Thoth (Whale,1989: 178).

TT 93: Kenamun. Amenhotep II; PM I.1, 190-194; *Urk.* IV, 1385-1407 (421); Whale, 1989, 153-158; Davies, 1930. DB ref. #275.
This tomb is very damaged due to malice and structural defects although Kenamun's wife's name and titles are preserved: *šmʿyt n Ỉmn T3-ddt.s*. Kenamun's mother was a *mnʿt nsw*, which accounts for his closeness to the king and his important title, chief steward of the king. Pehsukher (TT 88) was probably the brother of Kenamun (Whale, 1989: 158) and therefore also the bother of Khaemheribsen (TT 98).

The figure of a man tentatively identified as Mayor of This, Overseer of Priests of Onuris, Amenhotep is also found in this tomb (Davies, 1930: pl. XXXVIII; Van Siclen, 1979: 19). He and his wife (a *šmʿyt n Ỉn-ḥrt*) are known from a British Museum stela and may have been the owners of now lost Theban tomb A19 (HTFES 8: 8-9, pl. 19; see below).

TT 96: Sennefer. Amenhotep II; PM I.1, 197-203; *Urk.* IV, 1417-1434 (432); Whale, 1989, 144-151; Virey, 1898, 1899, 1900. DB ref. #273, 277, 480.
Sennefer was a man with many connections in life and in the necropolis. The tombs of his father, the Royal Tutor Ahmose (TT 224) (Whale, 1989: 83-84; *Urk.* IV, 1432, 1434), and his brother the Vizier Amenemipet (TT 29), are both known. In addition, statues were found at Karnak that belonged to the family of Sennefer (Legrain, 1906, vol. I: 76, pl. LXXV; *Urk.* IV, 1435-1436 (433)).

Sennefer's female relatives held high titles. Two of his wives were called *mnʿt nsw*,[33] and the third was a *šmʿyt nt Ỉmn* named Meryt. She is the only one represented in the burial chamber, and does not appear in the vestibule. The other wives appear in the vestibule only. Two of his daughters were *šmʿywt nt Ỉmn*, and another was a *ẖkrt nsw*; a fourth remains unnamed. One of the daughters who held the *šmʿyt* title, Mut-tuy, may have been married to Kenamun (TT 162) who held the post of *ḥ3ty-ʿ n niwt rsyt* after Sennefer (see TT 162). Sennefer's mother, whose name and title are not known in the tomb of her husband Ahmose (TT 224), and a sister-in-law both held the title *ẖkrt nsw*.

[30] A number of works deal with the issue of kinship terms including Willems (1983); Robins (1979); and Černý (1956-1957).
[31] Whale does not include *šmʿyt* among her titles.
[32] *Urk* IV, 936.17 restores [*Ỉmn snt n nsw, Nbt-t3*], a rendering that is disputed (see Whale's discussion, 1989: 102-103).

[33] Whale postulates that these two were sisters (1989: 151).

TT 98: Kaemheribsen. Tuthmosis II-Amenhotep II?; PM I.1, 204; *Urk.* IV, 1500-1501 (472); Whale, 1989, 130-131; Fakhry, 1934, 83-86. DB refs. #267-269.
The tomb is badly damaged and information on it is incompletely published. The tomb owner was a third prophet of Amun, and all the women in his family had high titles. His mother was a *mnꜤt wrt nt nb-tꜢwy*, his wife was a *ḫkrt nsw, šmꜤyt nt Ỉmn*, and his two daughters were *šmꜤywt nt Ỉmn*. One was also a *šmꜤyt n pr Ꜥꜣ Ꜥꜣ-ḫpr-kꜣ-RꜤ*: chantress of the funerary estate of Tuthmosis I. It is speculated that Kaemheribsen was the brother of Kenamun (TT 93) which would give us his mother's name, Amenemipet, lost in TT 98 but known in TT 93 (Whale, 1989: 130-131). If he is the brother of Kenamun, then he is also the brother of Pehsukher (TT 88).

TT 100: Rekhmire. Tuthmosis II-Amenhotep II; PM I.1, 206-214; *Urk.* IV, 1071-1174; Whale, 1989, 131-135; Davies, 1943. DB refs. #270-272. (See also #261, a daughter of User (TT61) who is portrayed here.)
Rekhmire's wife and mother were both *ḫkrt nsw* and three of his daughters were *šmꜤyt nt Ỉmn*. The tomb focuses mainly on the duties of the vizier, rather than family life. One scene on the north wall of the passage portrays an assembly of women holding sistra and *menywt* (Davies, 1943: pl. LXXI), one of whom is called *sꜣt.f šmꜤyt n Ỉmn [Ḥnwt-tꜣwy?]*.

TT 106: Paser. Seti I; PM I.1, 219-224; KRI I, 285-301; KRI VII, 15-18, 107-108. DB ref. #919, 920.
There is some confusion as to who Tiy (DB ref. #919) is in relation to Paser, Overseer of the City and Vizier. Tiy is referred to twice as *sꜣt.f* (KRI I 296.4-.5, 298.2-.3), but PM I.1, 219 lists her as his wife, and Kitchen assumes that *sꜣt.f* is in error. Another chantress, Naia (DB ref. #920), is called *snt.s* (*.s* referring to Tiy). Paser's mother, on the other hand, is quite prominent in the tomb. Her name and title, *wrt ḫnrt n Ỉmn, Mryt-RꜤ*, is mentioned with regularity.

TT 108: Nebseny. Tuthmosis IV; PM I.1, 225-226; Whale, 1989, 195-196. DB ref. #284.
The tomb is unpublished and little remains of the decoration. He was a high priest of Onuris and his wife was a *ḫkrt nsw, šmꜤyt nt Ỉmn, Sn-snb*. She is shown prominently in the tomb taking part in offering rituals. This couple shows that the religious affiliation of the husband was not a deciding factor in the religious affiliation of the wife.

TT 111: Amenwahsu. Rameses II; PM I.1, 229; KRI III, 302-307. DB refs. #876-879.
Very little is left of the decoration in this tomb, but the names and titles of the women in Amenwahsu's family are intact. A stela from Tübingen (KRI III, 305-306) helps to complete the family information. His wife, mother, and daughter-in-law were all *šmꜤywt* as well as one other woman, whose relationship to the others is undefined. Amenwahsu was a scribe of divine writings in the temple of Amun and his father was an overseer of draughtsmen at Karnak.

TT 113: Kynebu. Ramesses VIII; PM I.1, 230-231; KRI VI, 440-447; Manniche, 1991a, 52-53, fig. 30; Cramer, 1936, 100f, pl. IX.1-2. DB ref. #727-730.
A statue group in Hanover gives the name and titles of the *wꜤb*-priest Kynebu's wife: *nbt pr šmꜤyt n Ỉmn-RꜤ nsw nṯrw, sššt n Mwt, Ꜣst* : Lady of the House, Chantress of Amun-Ra king of the gods, Sistrum player of mut, Isis (Cramer, 1936: 100ff). Three of his daughters depicted in his tomb, Mutemwia, Anwedjameset, and Mutemipet, were also *šmꜤywt n Ỉmn*.

TT 138: Nedjemger. Ramesses II; PM I.1, 251-252; KRI III, 383-387. DB ref. #724-725.
Nedjemger was the overseer of the garden in the Ramesseum in the estate of Amun. His wife Naushat, and daughter Baket-Mut, were both *šmꜤywt n Ỉmn*.

TT 149: Amenmose. Ramesses II; PM I.1, 260; KRI III, 218-219; HTFES 12, 10-11, pl. 23. DB ref. #77.
While data on the actual tomb are not published, two stelae in the British Museum (BM 142 and 107) are thought to come from this tomb. Amenmose was the son of Nefertari, a *šmꜤyt n Ỉmn*. He was a royal table scribe, overseer of huntsmen of Amun, and a steward of the temple of an unknown institution associated with Ramesses II (HTFES 12: 10-11).

TT 157: Nebwenenef. Ramesses II; KRI III, 282-291. DB ref. #731, 757.
Nebwenenef was the high priest of Amun, and high priest of Hathor Lady of Dendera, overseer of all the priests of all the gods, mayor, and hereditary nobleman. Nebwenenef's wife was a *wrt ḫnrt Ỉmn, sḫmyt n Mwt, wrt ḫnrt n Ḥwt-ḥr, šmꜤyt n Ꜣst wrt, Tꜣ-ḫꜤt*: Great One of the *Khener* of Amun, Sistrum Player of Mut, Great One of the *Khener* of Hathor, Chantress of Isis the Great, Takhat. The son and daughter of this couple served Hathor of Dendera as high priest and as *wrt ḫnrt*. An unnamed woman who is probably a sister or sister-in-law of Nebwenenef, is labeled *snt.f šmꜤyt n Ḥwt-ḥr*. She is in the company of two women who were both called *wrt ḫnrt n Ḥwt-ḥr*.

For a Theban family, they seem to have had many connections to the cult of Hathor at Dendera. Perhaps this was their home before Thebes. He left his mark on the west bank by building his own temple near the mortuary temple of Seti I (PM II^2, 421) in addition to his tomb. He must have been a man of significant political and economic stature.

TT 158: Tjanefer. Ramesses III; PM I.1, 268-271; KRI V, 400-412; LD iii, 240; Habachi, 1968, 107-113; Seele, 1959. DB ref. #628-635, 643, 681, 682, 785, 786, 788.
TT 148: Amenemipet. Ramesses V; PM I.1, 259-260; KRI V, 412-414; KRI VI, 90-94; Gaballa and Kitchen,

1981, 161-180. Other discussions of the people depicted in both tombs: Polz, 1998, esp. fig. 6; Bierbrier, 1975, 5f; Schott, 1957. Most of the database entries have been assigned a date of "Ramesses III or later" owing to the multi-generational nature of the entries. Many clearly lived in more than one reign.

The powerful family of Tjanefer included no less than 14 *šmʿywt* who were directly, or by marriage, related to him. The tomb of his son Amenemipet (TT 148) is included in this summary because some of the women are shown in both places. Also, the two women mentioned in the mortuary chapel of Paser at Medinet Habu (Schott, 1957) are included because they are related to Tjanefer's wife, Nefertari.

The parents of Tjanefer are known from a graffiti at Sehel left by Amenemipet, a brother of Tjanefer.[34] Their mother was a *šmʿyt n Ỉmn, Ḥnwt-mtr*, and their father is identified as the High Priest Amenhotep (Bierbrier, 1975: 6; Habachi, 1968: 110, fig. 3). The tomb of Tjanefer contains depictions of many *šmʿywt* including his wife Nefertari, a *wrt ḫnrt Ỉmn, šmʿyt n [Ỉmn]-m-Ỉpt-swt* (KRI V, 409.15; Seele, 1959: 5-10, pls. 4, 26). Her brother Paser, Mayor of Thebes, was married to a *šmʿyt n Ḥršf* and their daughter was a *šmʿyt n Ỉmn* (Schott, 1957: pl. 1). Tjanefer had three sisters who were *šmʿywt n Ỉmn,* and a sister-in-law who was a *šmʿyt n Ḫnm.*[35] Tjanefer and his siblings belong to the reign of Ramesses III or slightly before as Nefertari's other brother, Amenmose, Mayor of Thebes, is believed to have been born in year 50 or 60 of the reign of Ramesses II (Bierbrier, 1975: 5).

The son of Tjanefer and Nefertari, Amenemipet, was buried in TT 148. Ramesses V is named in the tomb giving an indication of the date of TT 148's decoration (Gaballa and Kitchen, 1981: 164). His immediate family also contained a few well-titled women. His main wife *T3-mrt* was a *wrt ḫnrt [Ỉmn], šmʿyt n Ỉmn-m-ipt-swt* and a daughter of the High Priest of Amun-Re Ramessesnakht and the *wrt ḫnrt Ỉmn*, Adjetau. The in-laws figure prominently in Amenemipet's tomb owing to Ramessesnakht's powerful position.[36] Amenemipet may have had a second wife who was the *šmʿyt n Ỉmn, T3-mit.*[37] His only recorded daughter was a *wrt ḫnrt Mwt.* Other female relatives depicted in the tomb include his sister-in-law Henut-tawy, *nbt pr šmʿyt n Ỉmn,* wife of Bakenkhonsu, Overseer of Cattle; his sister-in-law Sekhmet, *nbt pr šmʿyt n Ỉmn-m-Ỉpt-swt*[38]; his sister Tahenut-pameter, *wrt ḫnr Mnṯ nb Ỉwnt*; his sister Hutiay, *nbt pr wrt ḫnrt n Ỉmn m ḫnm-w3st* and his sister Heket (?) a *šmʿyt n Ỉmn.*

TT 162: Kenamun. Amenhotep II-Tuthmosis IV; PM I.1, 275-276; Whale, 1989, 183-186; Davies, 1963, 14f, pls. DB ref. #277.
While the tomb is very damaged, the name and title of the wife remains: *šmʿyt nt Ỉmn, Mwt-twy*. It is possible that she was the daughter of Sennefer (TT96) and through marriage to her, Kenamun came to be the mayor of Thebes after Sennefer (Whale, 1989: 184).

TT 163: Amenemhet. Merneptah or later; PM I.1, 276; Assmann, 1979, 54-77, pls. IX-X. DB ref. #641- 642.
Amenemhet was the mayor of Thebes. His wife was the *šmʿyt n Ỉmn, Nḏm-Mwt*. Another woman whose name is mostly lost,[39] but was probably Amenemhet's mother, was also a *šmʿyt n Ỉmn*. The tomb includes a scene of a harper singing to the deceased, his wife, and his parents.

TT 168: Any. Rameses II; PM I.1, 278; KRI III, 300. DB ref. #875.
Any, God's Father of Amun, *wʿb*, and Lector Priest was married to Mery-nebu, a *šmʿyt n Ỉmn-m-ipt-swt.* Although little more than their names and titles survive, it is clear from the inscriptions that they both served their god at Karnak.

TT 178: Neferronpet (called Kenro). Ramesses II; PM I.1, 283-285; KRI III, 321-331, esp. 321.10; Hoffman, 1995. DB ref. #670, 926.
Neferronpet was a scribe of the treasury of Amun. The doorjamb of his tomb displays his wife's name and titles; *nbt pr šmʿyt n Ỉmn, Mwt-m-wi3*. She figures prominently in decoration of the tomb. She is consistently shown holding a sistrum. Another woman depicted may be his mother.

TT 189: Nakht-Djehuty. Ramesses II; PM I.1, 295-297; KRI III, 348-353, esp. 349.7-.13 and VII, 139-140. DB refs. #732-733.
Both wives of this man, Niwtemheb and Tenetpaipt, were called *nbt pr šmʿyt n Ỉmn* in his tomb.

TT 194: Djehutyemhab. Ramesses II; PM I.1, 300-301; Seyfried, 1995. DB refs. #663-665, 702.
Djehutyemhab's wife, mother, mother-in-law, and a possible sister-in-law were all *šmʿywt nt Ỉmn*. In fact, his mother was described as a *šmʿyt n Ỉmn, Mwt, Ḫnsw*, and a *ḥryt šmʿywt nt Ỉmn* (see Section 7.I.). The tomb is unusual for the fact that Djehutyemhab depicted his father-in-law and mother-in-law.

[34] They are also depicted in TT 148 but not explicitly identified (Gaballa and Kitchen, 1981: 164).
[35] The husband's name is lost, but he could be the same brother who left the Sehel inscription. Since the woman's affiliation with Khnum can be seen as an indication of a southern origin, perhaps he met her while there on business.
[36] An article by Polz (1998) furthers the genealogy of the family of Ramessenakht.
[37] The identity of this woman is not certain. The author is inclined to see her as the wife of a brother or uncle as Gaballa and Kitchen speculate (Gaballa and Kitchen, 1981: 179-180). Her parents were likely the next couple in the scene: *wrt ḫnrt Ỉn-ḥrt, Tʿywnš* and *imy-ist n Šw Tfnwt, ḥm nṯr tpy Ỉn-ḥrt, S3-3st* (ibid.: 164-165).
[38] She was probably married to Amenhotep or Djehutyhotep, but it is unknown which.
[39] Assmann reconstructs *Wj3jj* (?) (1979: 66-67).

TT 206: Inpuemhab. Merenptah; PM I.1, 305-306; KRI IV, 179-180; Bruyère, 1952a. DB ref. #734.
Inpuemhab was a scribe of the royal necropolis and his wife was the *šmꜥyt n Ỉmn-Rꜥ, (Tnt)-Bdty*. Her title is actually known from a Deir el Medina stela (Bruyère, 1952a, season 1945-46: 58-59 and season 1946-47: 12, pl. 9).

TT 211: Paneb. Merenptah; PM I.1, 307-309; KRI IV, 189-193; Bruyère, 1952b, 82-87. DB ref. #655-656.
Paneb was a servant of the royal necropolis who lived at Deir el Medina. His wife was the *nbt pr šmꜥyt n Ỉmn, Wꜥbt*. Their daughter was the *nbt pr šmꜥyt n Ỉmn, Šrit-Rꜥ*.

TT 215: Amenemipet. Seti I; PM I.1, 311-312; KRI I, 381-389; Jourdain, 1939, 36, 48, pls. 29-30. DB ref. #657.
Amenemipet was a Gang Chief at Deir el Medina. His wife Hunero was a *šmꜥyt* of both Hathor and Amun.

TT 254: Amenmose. Ay-Horemhab; PM I.1, 338-339; Strudwick, 1996; Mond, 1905, 65-96. DB refs. #588-592.
Amenmose was a scribe of the treasury and a custodian of the estate of Queen Tiye in the estate of Amun. His wife was the *nbt pr šmꜥyt n Ỉmn, šmꜥyt n Ỉmn-m-Ỉpt-swt, Dwꜣt-nfrt* . At least one identified daughter was *šmꜥyt n Ỉmn, Mwt-m-wiꜣ*. Three guests shown at the feasts in the tombs who held the title *šmꜥyt n Ỉmn* may be other daughters or daughters-in-law.

TT 255: Roy. Horemhab; PM I.1, 339-340; *Urk.* IV, 2174 (851); Baud and Drioton, 1957. DB ref. #675-677.
The wife of Roy is consistently referred to as *nbt pr šmꜥyt n Ỉmn, Nbt-tꜣwy*. She is also once called *wrt ḫnrt Mwt, ḥsy ꜥꜣ n Ḥwt-ḥr* (Baud and Drioton, 1957: fig. 15-16, text 34). Nebtawy's husband was a royal scribe in the estates of Horemhab and Amun. In one scene she is shown with her husband offering to two god's wives, Ahmose Nefertari and Mutnedjmet, wife of Horemhab.

Another woman depicted in the tomb (either as Roy's sister or sister-in-law) was a *šmꜥyt n Ỉmn, wrt ḫnrt, Mwt-Bwy*. Her husband was the first prophet of Ahmose-Nefertari, providing a context for the family's veneration of the dead queen, as well as for the veneration of Mutnedjmet, the queen under whose reign she lived. A third couple is pictured in the tomb, but their relationship to Roy is unknown. The man was a royal scribe and overseer of the two granaries of the king, Amenemipet, and his wife was *nbt pr šmꜥyt n Ỉmn, Mwty*.

TT 257: Mahu. Ramesses II; PM I.1, 341-342; KRI III, 377-378; LD III, 250; Mostafa, 1995. DB ref. #583.
Mahu was a deputy of the Ramesseum, and a scribe of offerings. His wife was a *šmꜥyt n Ỉmn* named Tawert.

TT 263: Piay. Ramesses II; PM I.1, 344-345; KRI III, 380-383. DB ref. #735.
Piay was the chief of workshops of Amun in the Ramesseum. His wife was a *šmꜥyt n Ỉmn* named Webkhet.

TT 267: Hay. Ramesses III; PM I.1, 347-349; KRI V, 627-639; Valbelle 1975. DB ref. #653-654.
Hay was Deir el Medina villager and a maker of images of all the gods in the House of Gold, and a deputy of the workmen in the Place of Truth on the west of Thebes. His wife was the *nbt pr, šmꜥyt n Ỉmn, Ḥnwt-mtr*, and his daughter-in-law was *nbt pr šmꜥyt n Ỉmn m sꜣw tpy, Nbw-iiy*. This reference to the phyle system is discussed in Section 7.I.

TT 282: Nakht-Min/Anhernakht. Ramesses II; PM I.1, 364-365; KRI III, 115-116; Habachi, 1976a, 113-116; Habachi, 1968, 107f. DB ref. #643-645.
Habachi ascribes this tomb to a man called Anhernakht known from three graffiti found at Sehel, although there has been a good deal of speculation as to what the tomb owner's name should be.[40] The Sehel graffiti was left jointly by himself and a man named Amenemipet who was the brother of Tjanefer (TT 158). It is from this source alone that we know the name and titles of Tjanefer's mother's (DB ref. #643; see also TT 148 and TT 158).

Based on Habachi's reconstruction of events, there are two *šmꜥywt* associated with Nakht-min/Anhernakhte. His wife's name is lost in the tomb but her title was *šmꜥyt n Ỉmn* in the graffiti (Habachi, 1968: 113). *Tꜣ-nḏmt*, his mother who is known from other sources, was a *šmꜥyt n Ỉmn* as well (ibid.: 110).

TT 289: Setau. Ramesses II; PM I.1, 369-372; KRI III 80-111; Karkowski, 1981, 112-113; Habachi, 1981; Habachi, 1976a; Drenkhahn, 1975; Helck, 1975; Griffith, 1921, 87-88; Jacoby, 1900, 113-115. DB ref. #578, 607.
Setau is a well known figure from Ramesside times. He was the viceroy of Nubia under Ramesses II. Setau's mother was the *šmꜥyt n Ỉmn, ꜥ-n-wḏꜣ*. His wife was the *nbt pr ḥmt.f šmꜥyt n Nḫbt, šmꜥyt n Ỉmn, Nfrt-Mwt*. She was also a *wrt ḫnrt n Ỉmn*, and *wrt ḫnrt Nḫbt*. A number of sources including graffiti, stelae, and statues contribute to our knowledge of the variety of titles she held. The fact that she was part of so many large monuments along with her husband in the many places he dedicated things leads one to the conclusion that she enjoyed a high degree of respectability. Habachi speculates that she may have been related to Ramesses II because of a title held by Setau, "Father of the god and beloved of the god", which may have been the designation of the father or father-in-law of the reigning king (Karkowski, 1981: 137).

[40] PM I.1, 364 calls him Nakht, Fischer calls him Hekanakhte (Habachi, 1968: 107), Manniche calls him Nakhtmin (1987: 141) as does Kitchen (KRI III, 115). They all seem refer to the same person as the three main titles from the graffiti, head of bowmen, overseer of southern lands, and fan bearer, match those of the owner of TT 282 and are from the same time period.

TT 294: [Amenhotep]/Roma. early Ramesside; PM I.1, 376; Strudwick, 1996. DB ref. #587.
The *wꜥb*-priest Roma usurped the tomb of Amenhotep. Roma's wife was *nbt pr šmꜥyt n Ỉmn, Ḥwt-ḥr*. Nothing further is known about this family.

TT 295: Djehutmose. Tuthmosis IV-Amenhotep III; PM I.1, 376-377; Whale 1989, 218-226; Hegazy and Tosi, 1983. DB ref. #288.
Even though representations of a number of women are preserved, only Renutet, one of two wives of Djehutmose, carried the titles *šmꜥyt nt Ỉmn, ḥsyt nt Mwt*. An extended family is represented, including in-laws. The family tree is hypothetical, but Whale seems positive that Renutet was his cousin (1989: 224). She also believes there are only two wives, and not four as Hegazy and Tosi postulate (1983: 8).

TT 296: Nefersekheru. Ramesses II; PM I.1, 377-379; KRI VII, 145-153; Feucht, 1985. DB ref. #736-739, 832-833.
It seems that Nefersekheru, a royal scribe and deputy of the treasury, had three wives who were *šmꜥywt*: Nefertari, who is portrayed prominently (e.g., Feucht, 1985: pl. XXIII), Nedjem-Mut who is secondarily significant (e.g., ibid.: pl. XVII and XXX), and a third, Kah, who is only known from the entryway inscriptions (ibid.: 19, 21 and pls. VI, VII). A daughter, Aset, was also a *šmꜥyt n Ỉmn* and is shown mourning at the offering table of her father (ibid.: pl. XII). Two other daughters were *šmꜥywt n Ỉmn*: Her-pery and Hunero are shown receiving offerings with their father (ibid.: pl. XXVI).

TT 324: Hatiay. Ramesses VI; PM I.1, 395-396; KRI VI, 359-60; Habachi, 1965; Davies and Gardiner, 1948. DB refs. #637, #740. (See also DB #639, a daughter-in-law depicted in the tomb of Penne, TT 331.)
Hatiay's mother was the *nbt pr šmꜥyt n Ỉmn, ḥs(yt) n Ḥwt-ḥr, Nfrt-iri* (Davies and Gardiner, 1948: pl. XLI). His wife was the *nbt pr šmꜥyt n Ỉmn, šmꜥyt n Mnṯw nb Ỉwnt Ỉwy*.[41] Hatiay himself served Montu and Sobek. The wife is also mentioned in a Sehel grafito (grafitti no. 13c; see Habachi, 1965: 129, pl. 18.2, fig 6-c).

TT 331: Penne. Ramesses VII; PM I.1, 399; KRI VI, 418-421; Davies and Gardiner, 1948. DB ref. #639.
High Priest of Montu in Armant Penne and his wife Maiay, a *wrt ḫnrt n Mnṯw*, and a *šmꜥyt n (Ỉmn)*, seem to have been very active in the cult of Montu (Davies and Gardiner, 1948: pl. XXXVI- XXXVII). Her mother was a *wrt ḫnr n Ỉmn*. Her mother-in-law was a *šmꜥyt n Ỉmn* (#637) and the wife of Hatiay (TT 324) if we assume that Penne was the son of Hatiay (PM I.1, 399).
TT 341: Nakhtamen. Ramesses II; PM I.1, 408-409; KRI III, 359-364; Davies and Gardiner, 1948. DB refs. # 742, #743.
Nakhtamen was the overseer of the offering table of the Ramesseum. His tomb contains scenes of male *šmꜥw* in the act of performing (see Section 3.III.3). The wife *Kmnꜥ* is also a *šmꜥyt (n) Ỉmn,* although in most places her title is omitted.

There is also a *šmꜥyt n Ỉmn, Rꜥỉꜣ* depicted at the head of the mourning procession. She is dressed more elaborately than the other women in the procession. It is suggested that she was a professional mourner because the caption reads; *ḏd n nꜣ rmṯ nty m hiy ḥr ḥꜣt-* "said by the persons who wail at front" (Davies and Gardiner, 1948: p. 36 pl. XXVI).

One scene (ibid.: pl. XXVIII) shows the couple receiving offerings from their son and a group of musicians led by their daughter Bakenptah who plays the harp. They are followed by a small girl playing a gazelle-headed lyre. This figure has Bes tattoos on her legs and appears to be naked. Nakhtamen's family seems to have been very musically oriented.

TT 345: Amenhotep. Tuthmosis I or III; PM I.1, 413-414; *Urk.* IV, 105-108, (41, 42) esp. 106.1; Whale, 1989, 87-88. DB ref. #263.
The traditional date of this tomb has been the reign of Tuthmosis I, but has been redated to the reign of Tuthmosis III as the title of the husband refers to the funerary cult of Tuthmosis I (Whale, 1989: 87, 284 n. 68). His wife, the *nbt pr, šmꜥyt n Ỉmn, Rnꜣy* appears in many scenes with her husband. It is unpublished, and only partly decorated.

TT 359: Inherkha. Ramesses III-IV; PM I.1, 421-424; KRI VI, 183-199; Bruyère, 1933, 32-70, 84-90, pls. I, XXIV, fig. 17,18. DB refs. #744-747.
Inherkha was the pharaoh's foreman in the Place of Truth, and buried at Deir el Medina. His wife's name was *Wꜥbt* and she was a *šmꜥyt n Ỉmn-Rꜥ nb nsw tꜣwy*. In the tomb she is shown listening to a harper who is called a *ḥsy*. His mouth is open in one of the few scenes showing the performance aspect of the word *ḥsy*. Other women who appear in the tomb who held the title *šmꜥyt* may be friends or relatives of the tomb owner; *šmꜥyt n Ỉmn-Rꜥ nb nsw tꜣwy, Tꜣ-nḏm-mꜣꜥt-rꜥ, šmꜥyt n Ỉmn-Rꜥ nsw nṯrw, Nfrt-iry,* and *šmꜥyt n Ỉmn, Tꜣ-bꜣ-sꜣ.*

TT 369: Kaemwaset. Ramesses II; PM I.1, 432; KRI VII, 158-159. DB ref. #748.
The wife(?) of Kaemwaset, the high priest of Ptah and third prophet of Amun, was the *nbt pr šmꜥyt n Ỉmn, Tꜣ-iwnw.*

TT 372: Amenkhaw. Ramesses III; PM I.1, 432-433; KRI V, 419-420; Spiegel, 1950, 257-281, plates. DB refs. #749, #750.
Amenkhaw was an overseer of craftsmen in the royal palace. His mother was the *šmꜥyt n Ỉmn Mꜣꜥt-Nfrt*, and his wife was the *šmꜥyt n Ỉmn Nfrt-iry-m-ḥb*.

---

[41] Her Amun title is known only from the triple statue (KRI VI 359-5). In the tomb (on a restored section of the fishing scene and on the ceiling bandeaux) and in the Sehel graffiti she is called a *šmꜥyt n Mnṯw*.

TT 373: Amenmose. Ramesses II; PM I.1, 433-434; KRI III, 213-218; Seyfried, 1990; Habachi, 1976b, 83-103. DB refs. #668, #669.
In one text (Seyfried, 1990: [36(9)]) the royal scribe Amenmose's mother, Muteminet, bears the title *šmꜤyt n Ỉmn*. This woman was also called a *sḫmyt n Ỉmn Mwt Ḫnsw* on an ancestor bust and a statue of her son (HTFES 12, 10, pl. 24-25). It is interesting to note that she was not called a *šmꜤyt* on those two monuments, and that she is not called a *sḫmyt* where she is a *šmꜤyt*.

Amenmose's father's name indicates a connection with Tod (*Ḏrty*), while his mother's name points to a Theban origin (Habachi, 1976b: 93). Amenmose left a number of monuments throughout the country; Thebes, Memphis, Qantir, and one found in Libya may have been carried there at a later date from the Delta. Amenmose's title and epithets, "royal scribe, one whom the king made as head of the temples", may explain how his name came to be on so many monuments around the country (ibid.: 95).

The wife of the usurper of the tomb (whose name is unknown) was also a *šmꜤyt n Ỉmn, Ty-nt-....nw*. (Seyfried, 1990: text [92]). The usurpation was probably executed in Dynasty 20 (ibid.).

TT 384 Nebmehyt, Ramesses II; PM I.1, 436-437; KRI III 359; Fakhry, 1936, 124-126, tomb #1. DB ref. #751.
A ceiling text preserves the name and title of Nebmehyt's wife; *šmꜤyt n Ỉmn m ḫnm-wꜣst* (the Ramesseum), *BꜤkt-sḫmt*. Nebmehyt was also employed at the Ramesseum as a priest.

TT 385 Hunefer, Ramesses II; PM I.1, 437; KRI III, 163-164, esp. 163.15; Fakhry, 1936, tomb #2. DB ref. #752.
Hunefer was the mayor of Thebes and overseer of the granaries of the divine offerings of Amun. His wife Nehty was a *nbt pr, šmꜤyt n Ỉmn*.

TT 387: Meryptah. Ramesses II; PM I.1, 439; KRI III 319-320; Rogge, 1990, lieferung 6, 91-100. DB refs. #245, #753.
Scribe of the Table of the Lord of the Two Lands in Karnak, Meryptah's mother(?) Kafy is seen on a statue now in Vienna (DB ref. #245) and is also mentioned in the tomb, but without her title *šmꜤyt n Ỉmn* (KRI III, 320.10). Another woman, possibly his wife, is depicted in the tomb; *nbt pr šmꜤyt n Ỉmn, nb*[...] (DB ref. #753).
TT 409: Simut, called Kyky. Ramesses II; PM I.1, 461-462; KRI III, 331-345; Negm, 1997. DB ref. #804-807.
Simut was an overseer of the cattle counters of the domain of Amun, but he was particularly devoted to Mut, as two long inscriptions dedicated to her prove.[42] One of his wives held the title *šmꜤyt n Ỉmn, RꜤꜣy* (e.g. Negm, 1997: pl. VI-VII, X, XI) and also the variants *šmyt n Ỉmn n Mwt* (ibid.: XIV-XV) and *šmꜤyt n Mwt* (ibid.: XXXIV, XXXV). Amun is mentioned more often than Mut in the inscriptions dealing with her, but perhaps her husband's affection for the goddess Mut influenced Raia's decision to include service to Mut in her titles.

Another woman, perhaps his mother (ibid.: 47), is mentioned on one of the four statues in the tomb: [*nbt pr*] *šmꜤyt n Ỉmn, Twt-wiꜣ* (ibid.: pl. XXXIV-XXXV). A third woman, the *šmꜤyt n Ỉmn, Tꜣ-smnt*, may be a second wife. She is depicted with Simut in the frieze on walls E and G (ibid.: pl. XX-XXI, XXVI-XXVII) but not as frequently as Raia. A fourth woman may have been Simut's sister. The name *Tꜣ-wrt-ḥtpti* is found once with the title *šmꜤyt* (ibid.: pl. XX-XXI).

TT A17: Userhet. Ramesses III; PM I.1, 452; KRI V, 418;[43] Manniche, 1987, 78-79, fig. 68. DB ref. #815.
Userhet was a chief measurer of the granary of Amun. Fragments reconstructed in the Field Museum and Copenhagen show that his wife's name was Hathor and that she was a *šmꜤyt n Ỉmn* (Manniche, 1987: 78-79, fig. 68).

TT A19: Amenhotep. Tuthmosis IV- Amenhotep III?; PM I.1, 453; Van Siclen, 1979, 17ff; HTFES 8, 8-9. DB ref. #567.
The owners of this now-lost tomb recorded by Champollion (Not. Desc. I, 541) may be recorded in the tomb of Kenamun (TT 93)[44] and on a stela now in the British Museum (BM 902 in HTFES 8: 8-9, pl. 19). The husband was an important man, being the mayor of This, overseer of priests and high priest of Onuris. His wife was a *šmꜤyt* of Onuris named Henut. (See also above in the tomb of Kenamun, TT 93.)

TT A24: Simut. Amenhotep III; PM I.1, 454; *Urk*. IV, 1950 (733); Wilkinson, 1883, vol. i, 381, fig. 156, ii, 107, fig. 365. DB ref. #792.
A team from Waseda University, Japan rediscovered this tomb in their 1988-89 season.[45] Most of the decoration recorded by Wilkinson and Champollion has been lost. Only the fishing and fowling scene remains, but it is heavily soot damaged (www.waseda.ac.jp/projects/egypt/sites/TT-E.html#Dra' Abu_alNaga').

Simut's wife Baky, a *šmꜤyt n Ỉmn*, is also known from a statue found at the Mut complex of Karnak (CG 932, Borchardt, 1911-1936, pt. 3, 161) and another of unknown provenience (CG 1107, Borchardt, 1911-1936, pt. 4, 60-61). The latter piece indicates that she was also a *ḫkrt nsw*.

42 See Negm, 1997, 1-3 for a bibliography of works dealing with those texts.

43 Kitchen notes no title, but the figure in Manniche (1987: fig. 68) clearly shows it.
44 The man and his wife are pictured on the east wall of the outer transverse hall behind the right hand figures of Kenamun and his wife.
45 The Japanese designation for the tomb is W-6.

APPENDIX E
NOTES ON THE DATABASE AND REFERENCE LIST

The following table is a complete list of all the 860 references collected for this study. It is not meant to represent a comprehensive list of all known *šmꜥyt*, but rather a random sample group drawn from published data. The fields given in this appendix represent only the most basic information. Where other fields not shown in this chart have been relevant for this study (e.g. the familial information charts in Chapter 6), they have formed separate charts included in the chapters dealing with those topics. All references, regardless of whether they have previously appeared in any other chart are included here.

The list is meant to serve as a place to name all the *šmꜥywt* who did not appear in any other chart as well as a publication list. Multiple sources were sometimes used to fill in information about a woman and her family. Therefore, the publication information may contain references to works that make no mention of the *šmꜥyt* of that record, but rather to her family, and vice-versa.

The reference number (or DB #) assigned to each woman has no real significance other than to serve as a unique identifier for each entry. The reference list is arranged numerically by this identifier for ease of consultation. Some reference numbers are missing due to later deletions or the merging of entries.

An alphabetical list is also provided to aid in the search for known individuals who are cited in the database.

CHART 7: Reference list

Ref. #	NAME	DEITY	LOCATION	PROV.	DATE	PUBLICATIONS
2	*T3wy*	Amun	TT52	Thebes	Tuthmosis IV	Urk. IV, 1603; Whale, 1989, case 75; Davies, 1917
4	?	Amun	TT51	Thebes	Seti I	KRI I, 333-341, esp. 337.6; Davies, 1927, pl. V
6	*N3š3*	Amun		BM 9901	Seti I	KRI I, 306-307, esp. 306.15; Robins, 1993b, 153; Quirke, 1993, 89
7	*T3ʿ-ẖʿ*	Amun		Florence, Museo Archeologico di Firenze, 2591	Dyn. 19-20	Robins, 1993b, 170, fig. 73
9	*Ṯnt-Ỉmn (T3-nt-Ỉmn)*	Amun Re		Paris, Bibliotheque Nationale, 170-173; Louvre 2562; Marseilles, Musée Borely 253/1; Berlin, Agyptische Museum 8	mid Dyn. 21	Niwiński, 1989b, 352; ibid. 1988, nos. 21, 285, 339; Piankoff, 1936, 49ff
11	*Tity*	Amun		BM 183	Rameses II	KRI III, 56-57; HTFES 9, pl. XV
12	*Šri(t)-Rʿ*	Amun		BM 183	Rameses II	KRI III, 56-57; HTFES 9, pl. XV
13	*Mwt-nfrt*	Amun		BM 183	Rameses II	KRI III, 56-57; HTFES 9, pl. XV
14	*St-Mnty*	Amun		BM 183	Rameses II	KRI III, 56-57; HTFES 9, pl. XV
15	*Ḥwnry*	Hathor, lady of the southern sycomore	Sedment (CG 605)	BM 183 and Cairo CG 605	Rameses II	KRI III, 56-57; HTFES 9, pl. XV
16	*Pry*	Pre	Abydos or Memphis?	BM 139	Merenptah	PM II, 808; KRI IV, 124-125, esp. 124.13; HTFES 9, pl. XX
17	*T3-wr(t)-m-ḥb*	Pre	Abydos or Memphis?	BM 139	Merenptah	PM II, 808; KRI IV, 124-125, esp. 124.13-.14; HTFES 9, pl. XX
18	*Pry*	Amun	Abydos or Memphis?	BM 139	Merenptah	PM II, 808; KRI IV, 124-125, esp. 125.1; HTFES 9, pl. XX
19	*Ỉwy3*	Amun	Abydos or Memphis?	BM 139	Merenptah	PM II, 808; KRI IV, 124-125, esp. 125.2; HTFES 9, pl. XX
20	*B3k(t)-Ỉmn*	Pre	Abydos or Memphis?	BM 139	Merenptah	PM II, 808; KRI IV, 124-125, esp. 125.5; HTFES 9, pl. XX
21	*Ỉwnw-ry*	Pre	Abydos or Memphis?	BM 139	Merenptah	PM II, 808; KRI IV, 124-125, esp. 125.5; HTFES 9, pl. XX
22	*Ppy*	Amun	Abydos or Memphis?	BM 139	Merenptah	PM II, 808; KRI IV, 124-125, esp. 125.6; HTFES 9, pl. XX

CHART 7: Reference list

23	*Nbt-tꜣwy*	Pre	Memphis?	BM 164	Rameses II	HTFES 9, pl. XXIa-XXI; Cramer, 1936, 54
24	*Pi*	Pre	Memphis?	BM 164	Rameses II	HTFES 9, pl. XXIa-XXI; Cramer, 1936, 54
25	*Mrt-Rꜥ*	Pre		BM 166	Rameses II	HTFES 9, pl. XXII
26	*Wr-n-r*	Hathor, lady of the southern sycomore	Memphis?	BM 167 and BM 149	Rameses II	KRI III, 206.10, 207.11; HTFES 9, pl. XXIII
27	*Yy*	Hathor, lady of the southern sycomore	Memphis?	BM 167 and BM 149	Rameses II	KRI III, 206.9, 207.15; HTFES 9, pl. XXIII
29	*Pp*	Amun		BM 167 and BM 149	Rameses II	HTFES 9, pl. XXV
30	*Mwt-nfrt*	Mut		BM 167 and BM 149	Rameses II	KRI III, 207.12; HTFES 9, pl. XXV
31	*Ỉniw-hꜣy*	Hathor		BM 167 and BM 149	Rameses II	KRI III, 206.6; HTFES 9, pl. XXV
32	*Tꜣ-sw-ri*	Amun		BM 167 and BM 149	Rameses II	KRI III, 207.14; HTFES 9, pl. XXV
33	*Nfrt-iry*	Hathor, lady of the southern sycomore		BM 167 and BM 149	Rameses II	KRI III, 207.15; HTFES 9, pl. XXV
35	*P[wr]y*	Amun		BM 167 and BM 149	Rameses II	KRI III, 207.15; HTFES 9, pl. XXV
36	*Tꜣ-wr(t)-ḥtp-ṯ*	Amun		BM 167 and BM 149	Rameses II	KRI III, 207.15-.16; HTFES 9, pl. XXV
37	*Ḳꜣ-nḥbt*	Amun		BM 154	Merenptah	KRI IV, 123-124, esp. 123.11; HTFES 9, pl. XXVII; Brunner, 1959, 3-5
38	*Bꜣk-wrnr*	Bastet		BM 154	Merenptah	KRI IV, 123-124, esp. 123.11; HTFES 9, pl. XXVII; Brunner, 1959, 3-5
39	*Ḥnwt-Ỉwnw*	Bastet		BM 154	Merenptah	KRI IV, 123-124, esp. 123.12; HTFES 9, pl. XXVII; Brunner, 1959, 3-5
40	*Ỉwy*	Amun		BM 154	Merenptah	KRI IV, 123-124, esp. 123.12; HTFES 9, pl. XXVII; Brunner, 1959, 3-5
41	*Tꜣ-ḫꜥ(t)*	Bastet		BM 154	Merenptah	KRI IV, 123-124, esp. 123.16; HTFES 9, pl. XXVII; Brunner, 1959, 3-5
42	*Nfrt-iiṯ*	Bastet		BM 154	Merenptah	KRI IV, 123-124, esp. 123.16; HTFES 9, pl. XXVII; Brunner, 1959, 3-5
43	*Tꜣriꜣ*	Bastet		BM 154	Merenptah	KRI IV, 123-124, esp. 124.1; HTFES 9, pl. XXVII; Brunner, 1959, 3-5
44	*ꜣst*	Isis		BM 132	Dyn. 19	KRI III, 376.3-.4; HTFES 9, pl. XLV n.1

CHART 7: Reference list

45	*T3-wsr(t)*	Wepwawet		BM 792	Rameses IX	HTFES 10, pl. 44.2, 45.2; Lieblein, no. 1002
46	*3st*	Wepwawet		BM 792	Rameses IX	HTFES 10, pl. 44.2, 45.2; Lieblein, no. 1002
47	*T3-ʿḳy*	Wepwawet		BM 792	Rameses IX	HTFES 10, pl. 44.2, 45.2; Lieblein, no. 1002
48	*Ỉpt-nfrt*	Amun	Abydos?	BM 161	Dyn. 19	PM V, 96; HTFES 10, pl. 52-53
49	*Ḥnwt-ḏww*	Amun	Abydos?	BM 161	Dyn. 19	PM V, 96; HTFES 10, pl. 52-53
50	*Nšʿ*	Amun	Abydos?	BM 161	Dyn. 19	PM V, 96; HTFES 10, pl. 52-53
51	*T3-wrt*	Amun	Abydos?	BM 161	Dyn. 19	PM V, 96; HTFES 10, pl. 52-53
52	*Ỉy-nfr.ti*	Amun	Abydos?	BM 161	Dyn. 19	PM V, 96; HTFES 10, pl. 52-53
53	*T3-ʿḳ3y*	Amun	Abydos?	BM 161	Dyn. 19	PM V, 96; HTFES 10, pl. 52-53
54	*3st*	Amun	Abydos?	BM 161	Dyn. 19	PM V, 96; HTFES 10, pl. 52-53
55	*Mwt-m-wi3*	Amun	Abydos?	BM 161	Dyn. 19	PM V, 96; HTFES 10, pl. 52-53
56	*T3-n-shrry*	Amun	Abydos?	BM 161	Dyn. 19	PM V, 96; HTFES 10, pl. 52-53
57	*B3k(t)-ʿnḫt*	Isis	Memphis/ Saqqara or Iseum	BM 1465	Dyn. 19-20	PM III, 759; HTFES 10, pl. 93
58	*ʿš3t-nbw*	Khnum		BM 795	Dyn. 19	HTFES 10, pl. 94; Lieblein no. 995
59	*Ty*	Khnum		BM 795	Dyn. 19	HTFES 10, pl. 94; Lieblein no. 995
60	*Wrt-nfrt*	Khnum		BM 795	Dyn. 19	HTFES 10, pl. 94; Lieblein no. 995
61	*B3kti3*	Khnum		BM 795	Dyn. 19	HTFES 10, pl. 94; Lieblein no. 995
62	*Ḥry*	Khnum		BM 795	Dyn. 19	HTFES 10, pl. 94; Lieblein no. 995
63	*Nbt-wnw*	Khnum		BM 795	Dyn. 19	HTFES 10, pl. 94; Lieblein no. 995
64	*3st*	Khnum		BM 795	Dyn. 19	HTFES 10, pl. 94; Lieblein no. 995
65	*Nfrt-iry*	Thoth	Hermopolis?	BM 1680	Dyn. 19-20	HTFES 10, pl. 96-97
66	*Ỉs3y (Ḥn3y)*	Banebdjed	Mendes or Hermopolis Parva?	BM 312	Dyn. 19-20	HTFES 10, pl. 98; Lieblein no. 948
67	*T3-b3-s3*	Thoth, arbitrator of the two combatants	Mendes or Hermopolis Parva?	BM 312	Dyn. 19-20	HTFES 10, pl. 98; Lieblein no. 948

CHART 7: Reference list

68	*T3-bw-b3*	Pre		BM 1183	Rameses III	KRI V, 396, esp. 396.8-.9; HTFES 10, pl. 99
69	*Mwt-m-wi3*	Hathor, lady of the southern sycomore		BM 1183	Rameses III	KRI V, 396, esp. 396.8-.9; HTFES 10, pl. 99
70	*T3-wr(t)*	Amun		BM 327	Dyn. 19	HTFES 10, pl. 100; Lieblein no. 951
71	*ʿn-t3-ḫytw*	Amun		BM 327	Dyn. 19	HTFES 10, pl. 100; Lieblein no. 951
72	*Š...*	Amun		BM 35895	Third Intermediate Period	HTFES 11, pl. 4.1
73	*T3y-iw-šri*	Amun		BM 8447	Third Intermediate Period	PM II, 808; HTFES 11, pl. 10.1; Munro, 1973, 12, pl.1, abb. 2
74	*Ns-ṯr-n-m3ʿt*	Montu, lord of Thebes	Thebes	BM 8450	Third Intermediate Period	HTFES 11, pl. 16.1
75	*Dniw-n-Ḫnsw*	Amun Re		BM 27332	Third Intermediate Period	HTFES 11, pl. 18.1; James, 1985 no. 80
76	*Ḥwt-ḥr*	Horus of Behdet, Amun	Abydos	BM 1654 and Museo Egizio, 1465	Rameses II	KRI III, 444; HTFES 12, 10, pl. 21; Ruffle and Kitchen, 1979, 55-74; Frankfort, 1928, 243
77	*Nfrt-iry*	Amun	Thebes? TT149	BM 142 and 107	Rameses II	KRI III, 218-219, esp. 219.3; HTFES 12, 10-11, pl. 23
80	*Mryt-Ptḥ*	Amun	Abydos	BM 288	Dyn. 19-20	HTFES 12, pl. 59.1
81	*T3-nḥs*	Amun	Abydos	BM 288	Dyn. 19-20	HTFES 12, pl. 59.1
82	*T3-k3ri3*	Amun	Abydos	BM 288	Dyn. 19-20	HTFES 12, pl. 59.1
83	*T3-ʿnt-ḥr-twy-st?*	Amun		BM 292	Dyn. 19-20	HTFES 12, pl. 59.2
84	*Twy*	Hathor, lady of the (southern) sycomore	Abydos	BM 309	Dyn. 19-20	HTFES 12, pl. 61.1
85	*Wrt-w3ḥ-sw*	Amun		BM 349	Dyn. 19-20	HTFES 12, pl. 61.2
86	*Nfrt-iry*			BM 349	Dyn. 19-20	HTFES 12, pl. 61.2
87	*3st*			BM 349	Dyn. 19-20	HTFES 12, pl. 61.2
88	*Ḫʿt-b3ḥt*			BM 349	Dyn. 19-20	HTFES 12, pl. 61.2
89	*Ini-h3y*			BM 349	Dyn. 19-20	HTFES 12, pl. 61.2
90	*Ḥnr*	Amun		BM 549	Dyn. 19-20	HTFES 12, pl. 63
91	*Twy*	Amun		BM 351	Dyn. 19-20	HTFES 12, pl. 67.1
92	*Mwt-m-wi3*	Amun		BM 351	Dyn. 19-20	HTFES 12, pl. 67.1
93	*Bʿk-n-Imn*	Amun		BM 351	Dyn. 19-20	HTFES 12, pl. 67.1
94	*Tyi3y*	Amun		BM 351	Dyn. 19-20	HTFES 12, pl. 67.1
95	*...Mwt*	Amun		BM 351	Dyn. 19-20	HTFES 12, pl. 67.1
96	*Ḥnwt-t3-nb*	Amun		BM 700	Dyn. 19-20	HTFES 12, pl. 71.2; Moss, 1941, 9, pl.II
97	*T3-nfrt*	Amun		BM 474	Dyn. 19-20	HTFES 12, pl. 75; Vandier, 1958, 474 n.8;

CHART 7: Reference list

98	*Bʿk-wrn*	Montu		BM 474	Dyn. 19-20	HTFES 12, pl. 75; Vandier, 1958, 474 n.8;
99	*T3y-bs*	Thoth	Serabit el Khadim	BM 1831	Dyn. 19-20	HTFES 12, pl. 85.1; Gardiner, et.al., 1952-1955, vol. I, pl. lxxvi, vol. II, 193 n.295
100	*T3y-ʿḳy*	Thoth	Serabit el Khadim	BM 1831	Dyn. 19-20	HTFES 12, pl. 85.1; Gardiner, et.al., 1952-1955, vol. I, pl. lxxvi, vol. II, 193 n.295
101	*T3-wrt*	Wepwawet		BM 1184	Dyn. 19-20	HTFES 12, pl. 85.2
102	*Sḫmt*	Wepwawet		BM 1184	Dyn. 19-20	HTFES 12, pl. 85.2
103	*Ḥpt-disw*	Wepwawet		BM 1184	Dyn. 19-20	HTFES 12, pl. 85.2
104	*Ḥwt-ḥr*	Wepwawet		BM 1184	Dyn. 19-20	HTFES 12, pl. 85.2
105	*Nb(t)-t3wy*	Wepwawet		BM 1184	Dyn. 19-20	HTFES 12, pl. 85.2
106	*Dw3t*	Amun		BM 460	Dyn. 19	HTFES 12, pl. 92-95; Vandier, 1958, 442, 651; Helck,1960, 45
107	*T3-b3-st*	Amun Re		Aarhus, University collection	mid Dyn. 21 ?	Niwiński, 1988, no.1
108	*?*	Amun	Bab el Gusus	Alexandria, Graeco-Roman Museum, 461	mid Dyn. 21	Niwiński, 1988, no.4; D.L. A.75
109	*Ns-Ḫnsw*	Amun		Antwerp, Museum Vleeshuis, 79.1.465 AV	late Dyn. 21-early Dyn. 22	Niwiński, 1988, no.6
110	*T3-b3k-n-Mwt (T3-nt-b3k-n-Mwt)*	Amun	Bab el Gusus	Athens, National Archaeological Museum, 3335	mid Dyn. 21	Niwiński, 1988, no.8; D.L. A.76
111	*Ἰw.s-ʿnḫ*	Amun	Bab el Gusus	Athens, National Archaeological Museum, 3337	Dyn. 21	Niwiński, 1988, no.10; D.L. A.73
112	*Ṯnt-ry (T3-nt-ry)*	Amun		Athens, National Archaeological Museum, 3408, 3409, 3409a ANE	late Dyn. 21	Niwiński, 1988, no.14; D.L. A.72
113	*Ḥnwt-nfr*	Amun Re		Bergamo, Museo Civico	late Dyn. 21-early Dyn. 22	Niwiński, 1988, no.20
115	*T3yw-ḥrt*	Amun Re	Thebes	Berlin (east), Ägyptisches Museum, 28	mid Dyn. 21	Niwiński, 1988, no.22
116	*Diw-Mwt-(r)-iwdw*	Amun Re		Berlin (east), Ägyptisches Museum, 58 and 1075	late Dyn. 21-early Dyn. 22	Niwiński, 1988, no. 24
117	*3ḫ-Mwt-ʿwy*	Amun	Bab el Gusus	Berlin (east), Ägyptisches Museum, 11981-11983	mid-late Dyn. 21	Niwiński, 1988, no.34; D.L. A. 91
118	*Ἰ...*	Amun	Bab el Gusus	Berlin (east), Ägyptisches Museum, 11986	mid-late Dyn. 21	Niwiński, 1988, no.36; D.L. A.59

CHART 7: Reference list

119	*T3yw-ḥnwt*	Amun		Bolton, City Museum, 69.30	mid Dyn. 21	Niwiński, 1988, no.43
120	*Ḥnwt-t3wy*	Amun Re, Mut, Khonsu	TT60	Boston, MFA, 54.639-40	mid Dyn. 21	Niwiński, 1988, no.44
121	*Ỉ-t3-Mwt*	Amun		Bristol, City Museum and Art Gallery H.4633	late Dyn. 21-early Dyn. 22	Niwiński, 1988, no.46
122	*T3-wsrt-m-pr-nsw*	Amun	Bab el Gusus	Brussels, Musée du Cinquantenaire, E.5884, E.5909	mid Dyn. 21	Niwiński, 1988, no. 51; D.L. A.2
123	*Ỉḫy*	Amun	Bab el Gusus	Brussels, Musée du Cinquantenaire, E.5887	mid Dyn. 21	Niwiński, 1988, no. 52; D.L. A.51
124	?	Amun		Budapest, Szěpmüvěszeti Muzeum 51.2093	late Dyn. 21	Niwiński, 1988, no.59
125	*Ns-t3-nṯr*	Amun		Budapest, Szěpmüvěszeti Muzeum 51.2096	late Dyn. 21-early Dyn. 22	Niwiński, 1988, no.62
126	*T3yw-ḥryt*	Amun	Royal Cache at Deir el Bahari	Cairo, JdE 26196	early Dyn. 21	Niwiński, 1988, no.64
128	?	Amun Re	Bab el Gusus?	Cairo, 296Dyn. 22	late Dyn. 21	Niwiński, 1988, no.85; D.L. A. ...
130	*Nsy-Ḫnsw*	Amun	Bab el Gusus	Cairo , 29632, 29713 and S.R.IV.544=J36456, CG 6030-6031, 6040	mid-late Dyn. 21	Niwiński, 1989, 257; ibid., 1988 no. 90
131	*Ns-Mwt*	Amun	Bab el Gusus	Cairo, 29634, CG 6007	mid-late Dyn. 21	Niwiński, 1988 no.91; D.L. A.48
132	*3sty*	Amun	Bab el Gusus	Cairo, 29654, CG 6161, 6164-6165, 6198-6199	late Dyn. 21	Niwiński, 1988 no.99; D.L. A.66
133	*Nsy-t3-nb-tꜥwy*	Amun Re	Bab el Gusus	Cairo, 29656; CG 6048-6052	mid Dyn. 21	Niwiński, 1988, no.100; D.L. A.64
135	*Ḏd-m3ꜥt-iw.s-ꜥnḫ*	Amun	Bab el Gusus	Cairo, 29660; S.R.IV.542= J95645; S.R.IV.553= J95655; CG6213-6214, 6182-6184	mid Dyn. 21	Niwiński, 1989b, 256, 259; ibid., 1988, no. 103
136	*Ḫ3ꜥ.s*	Amun	Bab el Gusus	Cairo, 29665. CG 6115-6116, 6075-6077	mid-late Dyn. 21	Niwiński, 1988, no.108;D.L. A.102
137	*My-šm-rdwy-sḳtb?*	Amun Re	Bab el Gusus	Cairo, 29667, CG 6Dyn. 229-6232, 6238	mid Dyn. 21	Niwiński, 1988, no.110;D.L. A.111

CHART 7: Reference list

139	*ꜣst-m-ꜣḫ-bit*	Amun Re	Bab el Gusus	Cairo, 29671 and S.R.IV.555=J95657 CG 6123-6125, 6142-6143	mid-late Dyn. 21 or late Dyn. 21	Niwiński, 1989b, 259; ibid., 1988, no.114
141	*Ḏd-Mwt-iw.s-Ꜥnḫ*	Amun Re	Bab el Gusus	Cairo, 29679; CG 6113-6114, 6088-6090	early-mid Dyn. 21	Niwiński, 1988, no.117;D.L. A.150
142	*Nsy-tꜣ-nbt-tꜣwy*	Amun	Bab el Gusus	Cairo, 29685, CG 6055-6056, 6058-6060	mid Dyn. 21	Niwiński, 1988, no.121; D.L. A.77
144	*Ꜥnḫ.s-n-ꜣst*	Amun	Bab el Gusus	Cairo, 29708, CG 6032-6034	mid-late Dyn. 21	Niwiński, 1988, no.130; D.L. A.78
145	*Šbty*	Amun	Bab el Gusus	Cairo, 29711, CG 6027-6029	mid Dyn. 21	Niwiński, 1988, no.132;D.L. A.86
146	*Nsyt-tꜣ-nbt-tꜣwy*	Amun	Bab el Gusus	Cairo, 29716, CG 6245-48, 6237	mid Dyn. 21	Niwiński, 1988, no.134; D.L. A.88
147	*ꜣst-m-ꜣḫ-bit*		Bab el Gusus	Cairo, 29717, CG 6005, 6010	mid-late Dyn. 21	Niwiński, 1988, no.135; D.L. A.100
148	*Ḳꜣb-st-nbw?*	Amun	Bab el Gusus	Cairo, 29725, CG 6254, 6239, 6Dyn. 225, 6255	mid Dyn. 21	Niwiński, 1988, no.137; D.L. A.1
149	*Tꜣ-wḏꜣt-RꜤ*	the pure foundation of Ptah, Amun	Bab el Gusus	Cairo, 29737, CG 6278-6282	mid Dyn. 21	Niwiński, 1989b, pp 295, 297; ibid., 1988, no. 143
150	*Ḥryw-wbn*	Amun Re	Bab el Gusus	Cairo, 29738; and S.R.VII10254=J31986, S.R.VII.10256=14.7.35. 6, CG 6273-6277	late Dyn. 21	Niwiński, 1988, no.144; ibid., 1989, 284-285; Terrace and Fischer, 1970, n. 35
151	*ꜣst-m-ꜣḫ-bit*	Amun	Bab el Gusus	Cairo, 29740, CG 6006-6008	mid-late Dyn. 21	Niwiński, 1988, no.145; D.L. A.62
152	*Ḥnwt-tꜣwy*	Amun	TT 60	Cairo, 49100-49102	mid Dyn. 21	Niwiński, 1988, no.146
153	*ꜣst*	Amun	Bab el Gusus	Cairo (none), CG 6162-6163, 6195	mid Dyn. 21	Niwiński, 1988, no.151; D.L. A.130
154	*Tꜣyw-ḥnwt*	Amun	Bab el Gusus	Cairo (none)	early-mid Dyn. 21	Niwiński, 1988, no.155; D.L. A. ...
155	*?*	Amun	Bab el Gusus	Cleremont-Ferrand, Musée d'Art 3126-3127/894-426-1 & 8128/894-426-2	mid-late Dyn. 21	Niwiński, 1988, no.159; D.L. A.89
156	*Nsy-Ḫnsw*	Amun Re		Cleveland, Museum of Art CMA 14.714	early Dyn. 22	Niwiński, 1988, no.161
157	*Nsy-Ḫnsw*	Amun		Cleveland, Museum of Art CMA 21.1029	late Dyn. 21-early Dyn. 22	Niwiński, 1988, no.162

CHART 7: Reference list

158	*T3-n-pr-ms*	Amun		Cleveland, Museum of Art CMA 21.1029	late Dyn. 21-early Dyn. 22	Niwiński, 1988, no.162
159	*T3yw-ḥry*	Amun	Bab el Gusus	Copenhagen, National Muséet 3912	mid Dyn. 21	Niwiński, 1988, no.167; D.L. A.19
160	*Nsy-Ḫnsw*	Amun		Copenhagen, Ny Carlsberg Glyptotek AEIN 63	late Dyn. 21-early Dyn. 22	Niwiński, 1988, no.169
161	*Nsy-Ḫnsw*	Amun		Cracow, Muzeum Archeologiczne AS/2442	late Dyn. 21-early Dyn. 22	Niwiński, 1988, no.173
162	*Mwt-ipt*	Amun		Cracow, University Museum UJ.10628	late Dyn. 21-early Dyn. 22	Niwiński, 1988, no.174
163	*Ἰw.f-n-Ἰmn, ṯnt-wr-ḥk3t*	Amun	Akhmim?	Edinburgh, Royal Scottish Museum 1907.569 a-b	mid Dyn. 21	Niwiński, 1988, no.183
164	*Nsy-Mwt*	Amun	TT83	Edinburgh, Royal Scottish Museum 1956.354, 354a	late Dyn. 21-early Dyn. 22	Niwiński, 1988, no.184
165	*ʿnḫ.s-n-Mwt*	Amun	Bab el Gusus	Florence, Museo Archeologico 8523 and others	mid-late Dyn. 21	Niwiński, 1988, no.189; D.L. A.60
166	*?Ḏd-mwt-iw.s-ʿnḫ*	Amun	Bab el Gusus	Florence, Museo Archeologico 8524	Dyn. 21	Niwiński, 1988, no.190; D.L. A.15
168	*T3y-ḳ3y*	Amun	Thebes?	Frankfurt/Main, Liebieghaus 1651 a-f	Dyn. 19	Niwiński, 1988, no.195
169	*Bwt-[irw]-ḥʿr-Ḫnsw*	Amun	Bab el Gusus	Geneva, Musée d'Art et d'Histoire 163, 163 ter. (12454)	mid Dyn. 21	Niwiński, 1988, no.197; D.L. A.52
170	*Ṯnt...*	Amun		Grenoble, Musée des Beaux-arts, 1988,1003,3620	Dyn. 21	Niwiński, 1988, no.198
171	*T3-n3ḫt-n-t3-ḥʿʿt*	Amun		Grenoble, Musée des Beaux-arts, 1997, 2046, 3759, 3760	Dyn. 21	Niwiński, 1988, no.199
172	*Ḥnwt-t3-?-nb*	Amun		Grenoble, Musée des Beaux-arts, 2000	early Dyn. 21?	Niwiński, 1988, no.201
173	*Ḥnwt-t3wy*	Amun		Grenoble, Musée des Beaux-arts 2031	Dyn. 21	Niwiński, 1988, no.202
174	*Ḥ3t-špswt*	Amun		Grenoble, Musée des Beaux-arts 3572	mid Dyn. 21	Niwiński, 1988, no.203
175	*Nsy-Mwt*	Amun		Hildesheim, Pelizaeus-Museum 3100	Dyn. 21	Niwiński, 1988, no.206

CHART 7: Reference list

176	*Ḏd-Mwt-iw.s-ʿnḫ*	Amun	Bab el Gusus	Istanbul, Arkeoloji Muzeleri 10872	mid-late Dyn. 21	Niwiński, 1988, no.210; D.L. A.45
177	*Ḥryt-Mwt-iʿḥ-ms*	Amun		Jersey, Jersey Museum (none)	late Dyn. 21-early Dyn. 22	Niwiński, 1988, no.213
178	*G3wt-sšn*	Amun	Bab el Gusus	Leiden, Rijksmuseum van Oudheden, F.93/10.1a and Cairo, S.R.IV.1001and S.R.VII10Dyn. 221	late Dyn. 21	Niwiński, 1989b, 271, 273; ibid., 1988, no.Dyn. 228
179	*Nsy-t3-nb-t3wy*	Amun	Bab el Gusus	Leiden, Rijksmuseum van Oudheden, F.93/10.2a-b	late Dyn. 21	Niwiński, 1988, no.Dyn. 229; D.L. A.6
180	*Ṯnt-pn-hrw-nfr (T3-nt-p3-hrw-nfr)*	Amun	Bab el Gusus	Leiden, Rijksmuseum van Oudheden, F.93/10.3a-b	late Dyn. 21	Niwiński, 1988, no.231; D.L. A.47
181	*(Nsy)t3-nbt-išrw*	Amun		Leningrad, Hermitage 778	early Dyn. 22	Niwiński, 1988, no.235
182	*Šd-sw-t3-ipt*	Amun Re	Bab el Gusus	Lisbon, Sociedade de Geografia de Lisboa (none)	mid Dyn. 21	Niwiński, 1988, no.246; D.L. A.110
183	*Ḥnwt-t3wy*	Amun	Bab el Gusus	Lisbon, Sociedade de Geografia de Lisboa (none)	mid Dyn. 21	Niwiński, 1988, no.247;D.L. A.136
184	*Ḏd-Ḫnsw-iw.s-ʿnḫ*	Amun		Liverpool, Merseyside County Museum M.13994	late Dyn. 21-early Dyn. 22	Niwiński, 1988, no.249
185	*3st*	Amun		Liverpool, Merseyside County Museum M.13998	mid-late Dyn. 21	Niwiński, 1988, no.250
186	*K3t-bt*	Amun		BM 6665	late Dyn. 18	Niwiński, 1988, no. 254
187	*Mwt-n-ipt*	Amun		BM 15656	mid Dyn. 21	Niwiński, 1988, no.257
188	*Nsy...*	Amun		BM 15659	early Dyn. 21?	Niwiński, 1988, no.259
189	*Nsy-Ḫnsw*	Amun		BM Dyn. 22941	early Dyn. 22	Niwiński, 1988, no.262
190	*Ḥnwt-t3wy*	Amun		BM Dyn. 22941	early Dyn. 22	Niwiński, 1988, no.262
191	*Ṯnt-ḥn-f (T3-nt-ḥn.f)*	Amun	Bab el Gusus	BM 24791, 24791a, 24796	late Dyn. 21	Niwiński, 1988, no.265; D.L. A.44
192	*T3-ʿḥwty*	Amun	Bab el Gusus	BM 24793, 24794, 24795	mid-late Dyn. 21	Niwiński, 1988, no.267; D.L. A.32
193	*Mwt-ḥtp*	Amun		BM 29579	mid Dyn. 21	Niwiński, 1988, no.269
194	*Nsy-Mwt*	Amun		BM 35287, 36211	early Dyn. 22	Niwiński, 1988, no.271
195	*Ḥnwt-mḥyt*	Amun		BM 48001, 51101	Dyn. 19	Niwiński, 1988, no.274; Robins, 1997, fig. Dyn. 221

CHART 7: Reference list

196	*Rw-rw?*	Amun	Bab el Gusus	Madrid, Museo Arqueologico Nacional, 18254	mid Dyn. 21	Niwiński, 1988, no.281; D.L. A.14
197	*Ỉḫy (ȝst-m-ȝḫbit)*	Amun Re	Bab el Gusus	Madrid, Museo Arqueologico Nacional, 18257; Cairo, S.R.VII.11490=14.7.35. 1	late Dyn. 21	Niwiński, 1989b, 293; ibid., 1988, no.284; D.L. A.58
199	*Ḥryt-wbḫt*	Amun		Munich, Staatliche Sammlung Agyptischer Kunst, AS 12, 12b	early Dyn. 21	Niwiński, 1988, no.289
200	*Ḥnwt-tȝwy*	Amun		Munich, Staatliche Sammlung Ägyptischer Kunst, AS 57	late Dyn. 21	Niwiński, 1988, no.291
201	*Ḏd-Mwt-iw.s-ʿnḫ*	Amun	TT60	New York, Metropolitan Museum of Art, 25,3.1-3	late Dyn. 21	Niwiński, 1988, no.308
202	*ʿnḫ.s-Mwt*	Amun	TT60	New York, Metropolitan Museum of Art, 25.3.5, 25.3.13-14	mid-late Dyn. 21	Niwiński, 1988, no.309
203	*Tȝ-bȝkt-Mwt*	Amun	TT60	New York, Metropolitan Museum of Art, 25.3.10-12	mid-late Dyn. 21	Niwiński, 1988, no.311
204	*Ty*	Amun Re	TT60	New York, Metropolitan Museum of Art, 25.3.15-16	mid Dyn. 21	Niwiński, 1988, no.312
205	*Ḥnwt-tȝwy*	Amun	TT59	New York, Metropolitan Museum of Art, 25.3.182-184	mid Dyn. 21	Niwiński, 1988, no.313
208	*Ns-tȝ-wḏȝt-ȝḫ*	Amun	Bab el Gusus	coffin in Odessa, Archaeological Museum, 52976; papyri in Cairo, S.R.IV.558=J95660 and S.R.VII.11497	mid Dyn. 21	Niwiński, 1989b, 260, 296; ibid., 1988, no. 317
209	*Ḫnmm-Ḫnsw-pȝ-ḫrd*	Amun		Padova, Museo Civico, 84889	late Dyn. 21-early Dyn. 22	Niwiński, 1988, no.324
210	*Ṯnt-nȝw-ḥrrw*	Amun		Paris, Louvre,E13027, E13034, E13035, Edyn. 22343	early-mid Dyn. 21	Niwiński, 1988, no.328
212	*Ṯnt-šd-Mwt*	Amun		Paris, Louvre, 2612	late Dyn. 21	Niwiński, 1988, no.342

CHART 7: Reference list

213	*T3-Mwt-nfrt*	Amun		Paris, Louvre, N2571, N2598, N2620, N2623, N2631	Dyn. 19	Niwiński, 1988, no. 343
214	*Ḫnmm-Ḫnsw*	Amun		Paris, Louvre, AF9591	late Dyn. 21-early Dyn. 22	Niwiński, 1988, no.347
215	*Ḥnwt-nḫt*	Khnumet?		Schaffhousen, Museum zu Allerheiligen, (none)	late Dyn. 21-early Dyn. 22	Niwiński, 1988, no.354
216	*Nsy-prw-nbw*	Amun	Bab el Gusus	Stockholm, MedelhavsMuséet, NME 895 (=32003)	mid-late Dyn. 21	Niwiński, 1988, no.366; D.L. A....
217	*Mrw-ꜤḤ*	Amun Re		Sydney, University, Nicholson Museum 27	mid-late Dyn. 21	Niwiński, 1988, no.369
218	*Ḏd-Ḫnsw-iw.s-Ꜥnḫ*	Amun		Tubingen, Sammlung der Universitat 454	late Dyn. 21-early Dyn. 22	Niwiński, 1988, no.376
219	*Nsy-Ḫnsw*	Amun Re		Turin, Museo Egizio, Dyn. 2217, Cairo, CG 10110	mid Dyn. 21	Niwiński, 1988, no.378
220	*T3-b3k(t)-n-Ḫnsw*	Amun Re		Turin, Museo Egizio, Dyn. 2226, Cairo, CG 10104a-b, 10105	mid Dyn. 21	Niwiński, 1988, no.382
221	*T3-b3k(t)-n-Ḫnsw*	Amun Re		Turin, Museo Egizio, Dyn. 2227, Cairo, CG 10115	mid-late Dyn. 21	Niwiński, 1988, no.383
222	*T3-Mwt.f*	Amun		Turin, Museo Egizio, Dyn. 2228; Cairo, CG 10119a-b, 10120	late Dyn. 21	Niwiński, 1988, no.384
223	*Mwt-n-pr-Ỉmn*	Amun	Deir el Medina	Turin, Museo Egizio, suppl. 7715; CG 10108a-b	mid Dyn. 21	Niwiński, 1988, no.388
224	*Ḏd-Mwt-iw-Ꜥnḫ*	Amun		Uppsala, VictoriaMuséet B.59	late Dyn. 21-early Dyn. 22	Niwiński, 1988, no.394
225	*?*	Amun	Bab el Gusus	Uppsala, VictoriaMuséet VM 152 (NME893)	late Dyn. 21	Niwiński, 1988, no.396; D.L. A.80
226	*T3yw-ḥry*	Amun		Uppsala, Victoria Muséet VM 153	mid Dyn. 21	Niwiński, 1988, no.397
227	*Nsy-Ḫnsw*	Amun		Vatican, Museo Gregoriano Egizio	early Dyn. 22	Niwiński, 1988, no.400
228	*Ḫnmm-Ḫnsw-p3-ḫrd*	Amun		Vatican, Museo Gregoriano Egizio	early Dyn. 22	Niwiński, 1988, no.401

CHART 7: Reference list

229	*Ỉḫy*	Amun	Bab el Gusus	Vatican, Museo Gregoriano Egizio	mid-late Dyn. 21	Niwiński, 1988, no.403; D.L. A....
230	*T3-ḫbt*	Amun	Bab el Gusus	Vatican, Museo Gregoriano Egizio	mid-late Dyn. 21	Niwiński, 1988, no.404; D.L. A....
231	*T3-ḥmt-n-Mwt*	Amun		Vienna, Kunsthistorisches Museum, ÄOS Dyn. 228	Dyn. 21	Niwiński, 1988, no.407
232	*T3-b3kt-Ḫnsw*	Amun Re	Bab el Gusus	Vienna, Kunsthistorisches Museum, ÄOS 6264-6266; Cairo S.R.VII.10Dyn. 222	mid-late Dyn. 21	Niwiński, 1989b, 274; ibid., 1988, no. 414
233	*T3yw-3ḫ-ṯ*	Amun		Warsaw, Muzeum Narodowe, 141988	mid Dyn. 21	Niwiński, 1988, no.420
234	*T3-nt-Ḫnsw*	Amun	Bab el Gusus	Washington, National Museum of Natural History, 154953,154954, 365000	mid Dyn. 21	Niwiński, 1988, no.423; D.L. A.53
235	*T3-šd-Ḫnsw*	Amun Re	Bab el Gusus	unknown	Dyn. 21	Niwiński, 1988, no.434; D.L. A.138
236	*Ḥnwt-mr*	Amun	TT97	unknown	early Dyn. 21?	Niwiński, 1988, no.441
237	*Nfrt-iry*	Amun	TT97	unknown	early Dyn. 21	Niwiński, 1988, no.446
238	*T3-ist-it-Mwt-t3-wr*	Amun	TT97	unknown	early Dyn. 21?	Niwiński, 1988, no.447
239	*Šbty*	Amun			mid Dyn. 21	Niwiński, 1988, no.458
240	*?*	Amun Re		Cuba, La Habana, Museo Nacional 28	Third Intermediate Period	Lipinska, 1982, 66-67
241	*T3-šbt*		TT192	Cuba, La Habana, Museo Nacional 524/1-3	Dyn. 22	Lipinska, 1982, 132-137; Habachi, 1958, 338-341, 350
243	*Mwt-ir.t-di.s*	temple of Hathor	Dendera	Boston MFA, 98.1046	Saite	Leprohon, 1978, 45-48; Munro, 1973, 256; Petrie, 1900, pl. XXV
244	*Ns-Ḫnsw-p3-ẖrd*	Amun	Thebes	Boston, MFA 04.1763	Dyn. 22	D'Auria, et. al.,1988, 164-65. n. 118; Leprohon, 1978, 64-66
245	*Kˁfy*	Amun	TT387	Vienna, Kunsthistorisches Museum ÄOS 48	Rameses II	Rogge, 1990, Lfg. 6, 91-100
246	*T3-šryt-n(t)-3st*	Amun	Thebes?	Vienna, Kunsthistorisches Museum ÄOS 5912	Dyn. 21	Rogge, 1990, Lfg. 6, 179-182; Habachi, 1947, 261-283
247	*T3-mi3t*	Amun		Louvre, C.148	Rameses II	KRI III, 219-Dyn. 220, esp. Dyn. 220.7; Lowle, 1979, 50-54
248	*Nbwt-m-wsḫt*	Sobek		Louvre, C.148	Rameses II	KRI III, 219-Dyn. 220, esp. Dyn. 220.8; Lowle, 1979, 50-54

CHART 7: Reference list

249	*Pwyw*		Saqqara	Cairo, JdE 27958; R14, N6 on ground floor	Dyn. 19	Gaballa, 1979, 42-49.
250	*Tint...*	Amun	Saqqara	Cairo, JdE 27958; R14, N6 on ground floor	Dyn. 19	Gaballa, 1979, 42-49
251	*Mʿiꜣny*	Osiris, Isis	Abydos	Yale University Art Gallery, YPM 2657; Cairo, JdE 35258, JdE 32025, CG 34505; Louvre A.66	Seti I-Rameses II	KRI III, 447-463, esp. 450.7, 455.12; Scott, 1986, 124 n. 71; Gaballa, 1979, 42-49
253	*Twy*	Amun		Avignon, Musée Calvet, A4	Rameses II	KRI III, 191-195, esp. 192.16; Ruffle and Kitchen, 1979, 55-74
254	*Ỉyꜣ*	Sobek?	Dahamsha, Sobek temple	Luxor, J.149	Tuthmosis III?	Gaballa and Kitchen, 1981, p.136-7, pl. XXVIII; Luxor Museum, 1979, 79
257	*Tꜣ-m-rsfy*	Amun	TT67 and Gebel el Silsila, shrine 15	Thebes	Hatshepsut	Urk. IV, 471-489; Whale, 1989, case 9; Caminos, 1963, 42-52, esp. pl. 37-38
258	*Ḫnwt-tꜣwy*	Amun?	TT67 and Gebel el Silsila, shrine 15	Thebes	Hatshepsut	Urk. IV, 471-489; Whale, 1989, case 9; Caminos, 1963, 42-52, esp. pl. 37-38
259	*Ḫnwt-nfrt*	Amun?	TT67 and Gebel el Silsila, shrine 15	Thebes	Hatshepsut	Urk. IV, 471-489; Whale, 1989, case 9; Caminos, 1963, 42-52, esp. pl. 37-38
260	*Sn-snb*	Amun	TT39	Thebes	Hatshepsut-Tuthmosis III	Urk. IV, 520-527; Whale, 1989, case 19; Davies, 1923a
261	*Bꜣkt*	Amun?	TT61, TT131, TT82, TT100, Gebel el Silsilah, shrine 17	Thebes, Gebel el Silsilah	Hatshepsut-Tuthmosis III	Urk. IV, 1029-1043; Whale, 1989, case 20; Caminos, 1963, pl. 47; Davies, 1943, ii, pl. 9; Davies and Gardiner, 1915, pl. 3c
262	*Mryt-Ỉmn*	Amun	TT82	Thebes	Tuthmosis III	Urk. IV, 1049.12; Whale, 1989, case Dyn. 22; Davies and Gardiner, 1915
263	*Rnꜣy*	Amun	TT345	Thebes	Tuthmosis III	Urk. IV, 106.1; Whale, 1989, case 32
264	*Tti-m-nṯr*	Amun	TT53	Thebes	Tuthmosis III	Urk. IV, 1218.7; Whale, 1989, case 37
265	*?*	Amun		Cairo, CG 42125	Tuthmosis III	Urk. IV, 936.17; Whale, 1989, case 38; Legrain, 1906, vol. I, #42125

CHART 7: Reference list

266	*Ḥnwt-tꜣwy*	Amun	TT42	Thebes	Tuthmosis III-Amenhotep II	Urk. IV, 1507-1508; Whale, 1989, case 47; Davies and Davies, 1933 pl. xlvi.g
267	*Ḥnwt-tꜣwy*	Amun	TT98	Thebes	Tuthmosis III-Amenhotep II	Urk. IV, 1500.8; Whale, 1989, case 51
268	*Ỉmn-m-ỉpt*	Amun	TT98	Thebes	Tuthmosis III-Amenhotep II	Urk. IV, 1500.11; Whale, 1989, case 51
269	*Mwt-nfrt*	pharaoh *ꜥꜣ-ḫpr-kꜣ-Rꜥ*, Amun	TT98	Thebes	Tuthmosis III-Amenhotep II	Urk. IV, 1500.12-.14; Whale, 1989, case 51
270	*Tꜣ-ḫꜥt*	Amun	TT100	Thebes	Tuthmosis III-Amenhotep II	Urk. IV, 117-1175; Whale, 1989, case 52; Davies, 1943, pl. LXX
271	*Mꜣꜥt-nfrt*	Amun?	TT100	Thebes	Tuthmosis III-Amenhotep II	Urk. IV, 117-1175; Whale, 1989, case 52; Davies, 1943, pl. LXXI
272	*Mwt-nfrt*	Amun	TT100	Thebes	Tuthmosis III-Amenhotep II	Urk. IV, 117-1175; Whale, 1989, case 52; Davies, 1943, pl. LXXI?
273	*Mryt*	Amun	TT224, TT96 & KV40	Thebes	Tuthmosis III-Amenhotep II	Urk. IV 1434.1-.2; Whale, 1989, case 60
275	*Tꜣ-ddt.s*	Amun	TT93	Thebes	Amenhotep II	Urk. IV, 1385-1407; Whale, 1989, case 62; Davies, 1930
276	*Mryt*	Thoth	TT92	Thebes	Amenhotep II	Urk. IV, 1451.20; Whale, 1989, case 69
277	*Mwt-twy*	Amun	TT162 (and TT96)	Thebes	Amenhotep II-Tuthmosis IV	Whale, 1989, case 73 and 60
278	*Rꜣy*	Amun	TT75	Thebes	Tuthmosis IV	Urk. IV, 1210.1; Whale, 1989, case 74; Davies, 1923b
279	*Mwt-nfrt*	Amun	TT75	Thebes	Tuthmosis IV	Urk. IV, 1210.2; Whale, 1989, case 74; Davies, 1923b
280	*Ḥnwt-tꜣwy*	Amun	TT75	Thebes	Tuthmosis IV	Urk. IV, 1210.3; Whale, 1989, case 74; Davies, 1923b
281	*Ṯꜣ-ti*	Amun	TT75	Thebes	Tuthmosis IV	Urk. IV, 1210.4; Whale, 1989, case 74; Davies, 1923b
283	*Mwt-iry*	Thoth, lord of Herm-opolis, Nehemet-aawy, who is in Hermopolis	TT74	Thebes	Tuthmosis III-IV	Urk. IV, 1009.2-.5, 1010.13, 1011.14; Whale, 1989, case 77; Brack and Brack, 1977, 36

CHART 7: Reference list

284	*Sn-snb*	Amun	TT108	Thebes	Tuthmosis IV	Whale, 1989, case 79
285	*Rn-nꜣy*	Amun	TT66	Thebes	Tuthmosis IV	Urk. IV, 1576-1577; Whale, 1989, case 83; Davies, 1963, pls. VIII-XIV
286	*Ḥnwt-tꜣwy*	Amun	TT69	Thebes	Tuthmosis IV	Urk. IV, 1609.6; Whale, 1989, case 86
287	*Ỉtwy*	Amun	TT78	Thebes	Tuthmosis III-Amenhotep III	Urk. IV, 1596.19; Whale, 1989, case 87; Brack and Brack, 1980, 82
288	*Rnwtt*	Amun	TT295	Thebes	Amenhotep II-Tuthmosis IV?	Whale, 1989, case 89; Hegazy and Tosi, 1983
289	*Ḏd-mḥyt-is-Ꜥnḫ*	Amun Re		Berlin, Ägyptisches Museum, P.3009	late Dyn. 21-early Dyn. 22	Niwiński, 1989b, 245
290	*Ḏd-Ḫnsw-iw-Ꜥnḫ*	Amun Re		Berlin, Ägyptisches Museum, P.3125	late Dyn. 21-early Dyn. 22	Niwiński, 1989b, 248
291	*Mḥd-Mwt*	Amun		Berlin, Ägyptisches Museum, P.3126	late Dyn. 21	Niwiński, 1989b, 249
292	*Ṯnt-ḥm-n-Mwt*	Amun		Berlin, Ägyptisches Museum, P.3128	late Dyn. 21	Niwiński, 1989b, 249
293	*ꜣsty*	Amun		Berlin, Ägyptisches Museum, P.3143	late Dyn. 21-early Dyn. 22	Niwiński, 1989b, 250
294	*Mwt-m-wiꜣ*	Amun Re		Berlin, Ägyptisches Museum, P.3157	mid-late Dyn. 21	Niwiński, 1989b, 251
297	*Kꜣ-r-nḫt.s-n-Ḫnsw*	Amun		Cairo, S.R.IV.545=J95647	late Dyn. 21	Niwiński, 1989b, 257
298	*MꜤꜤt-kꜣ-RꜤ*	Amun	Bab el Gusus	Cairo, papyri-S.R.IV.548=J95650=14.7.35.8; coffins- JdE 29612, CG 6283, 6286-6289	late Dyn. 21	Niwiński, 1989b, 258; ibid., 1988, no. 80; D.L.A. 132
299	*Tꜣ-Ꜥꜣ-Ỉmn*	Amun	Bab el Gusus	Cairo, S.R.IV.552=J.95654	late Dyn. 21	Niwiński, 1989b, 258; D.L. A.127
303	*Ṯnt-sꜣ-rk-nꜣ-sti*	Amun Re		Cairo, S.R.IV.645=J.95712	late Dyn. 21	Niwiński, 1989b, 261
304	*Mryt-Ỉmn*	Amun Re	Bab el Gusus	Cairo, papyri-S.R.IV.933=J.95836, coffins- JdE 29704=29734, CG 6175-6176, 6197	late Dyn. 21	Niwiński, 1989b, 263; ibid., 1988, no. 128; D.L.A. 71
306	*Mry.f-n-Mwt*	Amun		Cairo, S.R.IV.957= J.95858	late Dyn. 21	Niwiński, 1989b, 266

CHART 7: Reference list

307	*ꜣst-m-ꜣḫt?*	Amun	Bab el Gusus	Cairo, S.R.IV.961=J.95861	late Dyn. 21	Niwiński, 1989b, 267; D.L. A.17
308	*Kꜥꜥ-sw-n-Ḫnsw*	Amun Re	Bab el Gusus?	Cairo, S.R.IV.1000=J.95892	late Dyn. 21	Niwiński, 1989b, 271
310	*Ḥnwt-tꜣwy*	Amun Re	Bab el Gusus	Cairo, S.R.IV.1531	mid Dyn. 21	Niwiński, 1989b, 272; D.L. A.64
311	*Ḏd-Mwt-is-s-ꜥnḫ*	Amun		Cairo, S.R.VII.10Dyn. 220	late Dyn. 21	Niwiński, 1989b, 273
314	*Ḏd-Mwt-is-s-ꜥnḫ*	Amun		Cairo, S.R.VII.10Dyn. 223	late Dyn. 21	Niwiński, 1989b, 274
315	*Ṯnt-diw-Mwt*	Amun Re,	Bab el Gusus	Cairo, S.R.VII.10234=J.35404 and S.R.VII10251	late Dyn. 21	Niwiński, 1989b, 278, 284; Piankoff and Rambova, 1957, 88-92
316	*Tꜣ-šd-Ḫnsw*	Amun	Bab el Gusus	Cairo, papyri-S.R.VII.10240, CG 40016, coffins- JdE 29625, CG 6129-6131	mid-late Dyn. 21	Niwiński, 1989b, 280; ibid., 1988, no. 88; Piankoff and Rambova, 1957, n. 18; D.L.A. 137
317	*Tꜣ-ꜥꜣ-pr-Ỉmn*	Amun		Cairo, S.R.VII.10242	late Dyn. 21	Niwiński, 1989b, 281; D.L. A.84
318	*Tꜣw-ḥnwt*	Amun Re	Bab el Gusus	Cairo, S.R.VII.10243=J.36464 and S.R.VII.10270	late Dyn. 21	Niwiński, 1989b, 281, 288
319	*Gꜥt-sšn*	Amun	Bab el Gusus	Cairo, his-S.R.VII.10244=J.33997 ; hers-S.R.IV.936=J.95838	mid-late Dyn. 21	Niwiński, 1989b, 264, 281-82; D.L. A.151 and A.152
320	*Ḏd-Ḫnsw-iw.s-ꜥnḫ*	Amun	Bab el Gusus	Cairo, S.R.VII.10247=J.33999 and 29658, CC 6065-6069	mid-late Dyn. 21	Niwiński, 1989b, 283; ibid, 1988, no. 101; D.L. A.83
323	*ꜥnḫ.s-n-Mwt*	Amun Re	Bab el Gusus	Cairo, papyri-S.R.VII.10255, coffins-JdE 29675, CG 6147-6149, 6158-6159	mid Dyn. 21	Niwiński, 1989b, 285; ibid., 1988, no 115; D.L.A. 38
325	*Dyr-pw-(sti?)*	Amun Re	Bab el Gusus	Cairo, papyri-S.R.VII.10257, coffins-JdE 29669, CG 6617-6618, 6083-6085	mid-late Dyn. 21	Niwiński, 1989b, 286; ibid., 1988, no. 112; D.L.A. 123
327	*Ḥnwt-tꜣwy*		Bab el Gusus	Cairo, S.R.VII.10653=23.4.40.1	mid Dyn. 21	Niwiński, 1989b, 290-91; D.L. A.87
329	*Nsy-tꜣ-nbt-tꜣwy*	Amun Re	Bab el Gusus	Cairo, S.R.VII.11493	mid Dyn. 21	Niwiński, 1989b, 294; D.L. A.9

CHART 7: Reference list

333	*S3-Ḫnsw*	Amun Re	Bab el Gusus	Cairo, S.R.IV.943=J.95845=C G58006	late Dyn. 21	Niwiński, 1989b, 301; D.L. A.59
334	*3sty*	Amun Re	Bab el Gusus	Chicago, Field Museum, 31326	late Dyn. 21	Niwiński, 1989b, 303; D.L. A.66
335	*Bw-irw-ḥꜤr-Mwt?*	Amun Re		Cleveland, Museum of Art, 14.725	late Dyn. 21	Niwiński, 1989b, 304
336	*Nsy-(t3)-nb(t)-išrw*	Amun Re		Edinburgh, Royal Scottish Museum, 1958.850	late Dyn. 21	Niwiński, 1989b, 307
337	*Ṯmḥd-ḫhsw*	Amun Re		Florence, Museo Archeologico, 3663	mid-late Dyn. 21	Niwiński, 1989b, 308
338	*Nsy-Mwt*	Amun Re		Hamm, Stadtisches Gustav-Lubcke-Museum, Dyn. 2236	late Dyn. 21-early Dyn. 22	Niwiński, 1989b, 309
339	*Mi3Ꜥ-nḥm*	Amun	Thebes?	Havana, Museo Nacional (no number)	mid Dyn. 21	Niwiński, 1989b, 309; Lipinska, 1982, 137-142
340	*Ns-Ḫnsw*	Amun Re		Houston, Museum of Fine Arts, 31-73	late Dyn. 21	Niwiński, 1989b, 309
341	*T3yw-ḥryt*	Amun Re		Leiden, Rijksmuseum van Oudheden, AMS 40	mid Dyn. 21	Niwiński, 1989b, 310
342	*T3-r-stit*	Amun		Leiden, Rijksmuseum van Oudheden, AMS 34	early-mid Dyn. 21	Niwiński, 1989b, 311-312
343	*Nsty-Ḫnsw-tp*	Amun Re		Leiden, Rijksmuseum van Oudheden, CI.10	late Dyn. 21	Niwiński, 1989b, 312
344	*Nsy-Ḫnsw-p3-ḫrd*	Amun		Leiden, Rijksmuseum van Oudheden, AMS 43	late Dyn. 21-early Dyn. 22	Niwiński, 1989b, 312
345	*Ṯnt-RꜤ-ss*	Amun		Leiden, Rijksmuseum van Oudheden, AMS 39	late Dyn. 21-early Dyn. 22	Niwiński, 1989b, 312-313
346	*Nsy-Ḫnsw*	Amun Re		Leiden, Rijksmuseum van Oudheden, AMS 35	late Dyn. 21-early Dyn. 22	Niwiński, 1989b, 313
347	*Mwt-ip*	Amun Re		Leiden, Rijksmuseum van Oudheden, AMS 42	late Dyn. 21-early Dyn. 22	Niwiński, 1989b, 314
348	*Ḏd-Ḫnsw-iw-st-Ꜥnḫ*	Amun		Leningrad, Hermitage 1108	late Dyn. 21	Niwiński, 1989b, 317

CHART 7: Reference list

349	*ꜣst-m-ꜣḫbit*	Amun		BM 9903	mid-late Dyn. 21	Niwiński, 1989b, 320
350	*ꜣst-m-ꜣḫbit*	Amun		BM 9904	mid-late Dyn. 21	Niwiński, 1989b, 320
351	*Ṯnt-sꜣ-rk-nꜣ-sti?*	Amun Re		BM 9919	late Dyn. 21	Niwiński, 1989b, 321
352	*Ṯnt-šdy-Ḫnsw*	Amun		BM 9938	mid-late Dyn. 21	Niwiński, 1989b, 321
353	*Diw-sw-n-Mwt*	Amun		BM 9948	mid-late Dyn. 21	Niwiński, 1989b, 322
354	*Ṯnt-mḥd-Mwt*	Amun		BM 9970	late Dyn. 21	Niwiński, 1989b, 322
355	*Ḏd-Ḫnsw*	Amun		BM 9983	late Dyn. 21	Niwiński, 1989b, 324
356	*Ns-Mwt*	Amun Re		BM 9984	late Dyn. 21-early Dyn. 22	Niwiński, 1989b, 324-325
358	*Mḥ-Mwt-ḥꜥt*	Amun		BM 10005 and 10035	late Dyn. 21-early Dyn. 22	Niwiński, 1989b, 327, 332
359	*Pꜣ-šb-wbḫt-n-Mwt*	Amun Re		BM 10007	late Dyn. 21	Niwiński, 1989b, 328
360	*Tꜣ-mni*	Amun		BM 10002, 10008	mid Dyn. 21	Niwiński, 1989b, 326, 328
361	*Mwt-ḥtp-ti*	Amun		BM 10010	mid Dyn. 21	Niwiński, 1989b, 328
362	*Tꜣ...*	Amun		BM 10012	mid-late Dyn. 21	Niwiński, 1989b, 329
364	*ꜣst-m-ꜣḫ-bit*	Amun		BM 10019	late Dyn. 21	Niwiński, 1989b, 330
366	*Špst-ns-Mwt-ꜥnḫ-ti*	Amun (Re)		BM 10036	late Dyn. 21-early Dyn. 22	Niwiński, 1989b, 332
367	*Ḏd-Ḫnsw-iw.s-ꜥnḫ*	Amun Re		BM 10044	early Dyn. 22	Niwiński, 1989b, 333
368	*ꜣst-(m)-ꜣḫ-bit*	Amun Re		BM 10062	early Dyn. 22	Niwiński, 1989b, 333
369	*ꜥnḫ-s*	Amun Re		BM 10203	late Dyn. 21	Niwiński, 1989b, 335
370	*Ḏd-Ḫnsw-iw-ꜥnḫ*	Amun		BM 10328	early Dyn. 22	Niwiński, 1989b, 336
371	*Nsy-Ḫnsw*	Amun Re		BM 10329	Dyn. 22	Niwiński, 1989b, 336
372	*Ḏd-ṯnt-di-ipt-wrt*	Amun		BM 10330	Dyn. 22	Niwiński, 1989b, 336
373	*Ỉnhꜣy*	Amun		BM 10472	mid Dyn. 21	Quirke, 1993, n. 14; Niwiński, 1989b, 336-337
374	*Tfrr-wꜣst*	Amun		BM 10094	late Dyn. 21	Niwiński, 1989b, 339
375	*Ḏd-Ỉmnt-iw-st-ꜥnḫ*	Amun		BM 10307	Dyn. 22	Niwiński, 1989b, 340
376	*...Ỉmnt*	Amun		BM 10448	late Dyn. 21	Niwiński, 1989b, 341
377	*Ṯnt-wsrt.s-n-pr-nsw*	Amun	Bab el Gusus	Luxor Museum, J.24 (Cairo S.R.VII.10253)	mid Dyn. 21	Niwiński, 1989b, 341; D.L. A.2; Luxor Museum, 1979, 248
378	*Ns-Ḫnsw*	Amun	Bab el Gusus	Luxor, City Museum J.25 (Cairo S.R.VII.10252)	mid-late Dyn. 21	Niwiński, 1989b, 341; Luxor Museum, 1979, 251; Piankoff and Rambova, 1957, vol. 1, 80-81 and vol. II no. 4
379	*ꜣst*			Manchester, John Rylands University Library, Heiratic 2	early Dyn. 22	Niwiński, 1989b, 342

CHART 7: Reference list

380	*Ḥnwt-t3wy*	Amun		Marseille, Musée Borely, 292	Dyn. 22 or later	Niwiński, 1989b, 342
381	*Nsyt-3st*	Amun Re	Thebes, tomb MMA 60	New York, Metropolitan Museum of Art, 25.3.30	late Dyn. 21	Niwiński, 1989b, 345-346
382	*Gʿwt-sšn*	Amun Re	Thebes, tomb MMA 60	New York, Metropolitan Museum of Art, papyri-25.3.31, coffins-26.3.6-8	late Dyn. 21	Niwiński, 1989b, 346; ibid., 1988, no. 315
383	*Ty*	Amun Re	Thebes, tomb MMA 60	New York, Metropolitan Museum of Art, 25.3.33	late Dyn. 21	Niwiński, 1989b, 346-347
384	*Nʿw-ny*	Amun Re	TT358	New York, MMA, 30.3.31 and 30.3.23-25	early Dyn. 21	Niwiński, 1989b, 347; ibid. 1988, no. 316
385	*Ḥnwt-nṯrw*	Amun		Paris, Biblioteque Nationale, 38-45	early Dyn. 21	Niwiński, 1989b, 350
386	*ʿnḫ-s-n-3st*	Amun		Paris, Biblioteque Nationale, 62-88	late Dyn. 21	Niwiński, 1989b, 351
388	*Bʿw-Mwt-r-nḫtyw*	Amun Re		Paris, Louvre, N.3069	late Dyn. 21	Niwiński, 1989b, 352
389	*Tfrr-w3st*	Amun Re		Paris, Louvre, N.3119	late Dyn. 21-early Dyn. 22	Niwiński, 1989b, 355
390	*Šb-n-3st (špt-n-3st)*	Amun		Paris, Louvre, N.3131	Dyn. 22	Niwiński, 1989b, 356
391	*Nsy-Ḫnsw-p3-ḫrd*	Amun Re		Paris, Louvre, N. 3140 (and 3141)	late Dyn. 21	Niwiński, 1989b, 356
392	*Nsy-t3-nbt-išrw*	Amun Re		Paris, Louvre, N.3Dyn. 227	late Dyn. 21-early Dyn. 22	Niwiński, 1989b, 357-358
393	*Ḏd-Ḫnsw-iw.s-ʿnḫ*	Amun Re		Paris, Louvre, N.3276	late Dyn. 21	Niwiński, 1989b, 358
394	*Ḏd-Ḫnsw-iw.s-ʿnḫ*	Amun Re		Paris, Louvre, N.3280	late Dyn. 21	Niwiński, 1989b, 359
395	*Ṯnt-šdt-Mwt*	Amun Re		Paris, Louvre, N. 3286	late Dyn. 21	Niwiński, 1989b, 359
396	*T3-b3kt-n-Ḫnsw*	Amun Re		Paris, Louvre, N.3287	late Dyn. 21	Niwiński, 1989b, 359
397	*Nsy-Ḫnsw-p3-ḫrd*	Amun Re		Paris, Louvre, E.31856	Dyn. 22	Niwiński, 1989b, 364
398	*Mwt-m-(ḫʿy?)-mw.s*	Amun		Paris, Louvre, N.3132	late Dyn. 21	Niwiński, 1989b, 364
399	*Ḥnwt-t3wy*	Amun Re		Richmond, Virginia Museum, 54-10 and BM 10018	late Dyn. 21	Niwiński, 1989b, 330, 364
400	*Msʿ-Sbḳ*	Amun		Turin, Museo Egizio, 1769 (& Deir el Bahari A.111)	late Dyn. 21	Niwiński, 1989b, 365

CHART 7: Reference list

401	*Ns-sw-ꜣst*			Turin, Museo Egizio, 1782	late Dyn. 21-early Dyn. 22	Niwiński, 1989b, 368
402	*Tꜣ-nḏm-Mwt*	Amun Re		Turin, Museo Egizio, 1784	late Dyn. 21	Niwiński, 1989b, 369
403	*Mwt-rwḏ*	Amun		Turin, Museo Egizio, 1787	late Dyn. 21	Niwiński, 1989b, 369-370
404	*Tꜣ-mry*	Amun Re		Turin, Museo Egizio, 1849	late Dyn. 21	Niwiński, 1989b, 370
405	*Nsṯ-Ỉmn (Ns-tꜣ-nbt-išrw)*	Amun		Turin, Museo Egizio, 1850	late Dyn. 21	Niwiński, 1989b, 371
406	*Gꜥt-sšny*	Amun		Turin, Museo Egizio, 1852	late Dyn. 21-early Dyn. 22	Niwiński, 1989b, 371
407	*Ḏd-Mwt-iw.s-ꜥnḫ*	Amun		Turin, Museo Egizio, 1855	Dyn. 22	Niwiński, 1989b, 372
408	*ꜣst-m-bit*	Amun (Re)		Vienna, Papyrussammlung der O.N., Aeg. 12000	late Dyn. 21-early Dyn. 22	Niwiński, 1989b, 375
409	*Tꜣ-ḥmt-n-Mwt*	Amun		Warsaw, Muzeum Narodowe, 199628 MN	late Dyn. 21	Niwiński, 1989b, 375
410	*Dni?-n-Bꜥstt*	Amun		Location unknown	Dyn. 22	Niwiński, 1989b, 378
411	*Ỉn-iw-hꜣdꜣ?*	Hathor, lady of the (southern) sycomore		Musée G. Labit, Toulouse, Inv. 49.278	New Kingdom	Ramond, 1977, 51-54, pl. XI
412	*ꜣsty*	Bastet		Musée G. Labit, Toulouse, Inv. 49.278	New Kingdom	Ramond, 1977, 51-54, pl. XI
413	*Tꜣ-rnnt*	Amun		Musée G. Labit, Toulouse, Inv. 49.278	New Kingdom	Ramond, 1977, 51-54, pl. XI
414	*Wb-ḫt*	Amun	Ramesseum	Manchester museum 4588?	Dyn. 19	Quibell, 1989, 15, pl. X.3
415	*Mꜥt?*	Amun	Ramesseum		Third Intermediate Period?	Quibell, 1989, 19, pl. XXV.14
416	*Tꜣ-wrt-m-ḥb*	Amun	Ramesseum		Dyn. 19-20?	Quibell, 1989, 19, pl. XXVI.9
417	*Nfr(t)-iy*	Isis	Ramesseum		Rameses II	KRI III, 389-390, esp. 390.1; Quibell, 1989, 19-20, pl. XXVII.2
418	*Ḏd-Mwt-iw.s-ꜥnḫ*	Amun	Ramesseum		Third Intermediate Period?	Quibell, 1989, 18, pl. XXII
419	*Mwt-m-wiꜣ*	Amun	possibly Qantir or Ramesseum	Philadelphia, University Museum 61-13-1	Rameses II	KRI III, 267.14-.15; Schulman, 1966, 124
420	*ꜥ-n-Mwt*	Amun	possibly Qantir or Ramesseum	Philadelphia, University Museum 61-13-1	Rameses II	KRI III, 267.15; Schulman, 1966, 124

CHART 7: Reference list

421	*Nfrt-iry*	Amun	possibly Qantir or Ramesseum	Philadelphia, University Museum 61-13-1	Rameses II	KRI III, 267.15-.16; Schulman, 1966, 124
422	*Ḥwt-ḥr*	Amun	possibly Qantir or Ramess-eum	Philadelphia, University Museum 61-13-1	Rameses II	KRI III, 267.16; Schulman, 1966, 124
423	*ꜣst-m-ḥb*	Amun	possibly Qantir or Ramess-eum	BM 290	Rameses II	KRI III, 260.12; Schulman, 1966, 125
424	*?*	Amun Re	possibly Qantir or Ramess-eum	Budapest, Hungarian Museum of Fine Arts 51.2145	Rameses II	KRI III, 268; Schulman, 1966, 126
425	*Pwyꜣ*	Amun Re	possibly Qantir or Ramess-eum	Philadelphia, University Museum 61-13-1	Rameses II	KRI III, 267.13; Schulman, 1966, 124
426	*ꜣst-nfr(t)*	Amun		Northumberland collection, letter 1	late Dyn. 18-early Dyn. 19	Barns, 1948, 36-37
427	*Tꜣ-ibḥt-Rʿ*	Amun		Florence	Dyn. 30?	Bosse, 1936, 62-63
428	*Nꜣ-nfr; Rn-nfr*	Seth	Ihnasya el Medina	Gardiner's collection?	Rameses XI	Gardiner, 1940, 23-29
429	*Tꜣyw-ḥry*	Seth	Ihnasya el Medina	Gardiner's collection?	Rameses XI	Gardiner, 1940, 23-29
430	*Tnt-Nepthys*	Nemty	Ihnasya el Medina	Gardiner's collection?	Rameses XI	Gardiner, 1940, 23-29
431	*ꜣst*	Montu-m-tawy	Qantir	Hildesheim, 0380	Rameses II	KRI II, 451.9; Sadek, 1987, 15 n.12
433	*Tnt?-ipt*	Montu-m-tawy	Horbeit or Qantir?		Rameses II	KRI II, 451.13; Sadek, 1987, 16; Clère, 1950, 33 & n.3
435	*Kiy*	Amun	Memphis		Dyn. 18	Sadek, 1987, 19; Petrie, 1909-1913, pl. 15p
436	*Tꜣ-...*	Amun		Deir el Bahari	Dyn. 18	Sadek, 1987, 57
437	*Nbw-ḥsbdw*	Osiris	Abydos		Dyn. 20	Sadek, 1987, 96; Mariette, 1880, 448-449, no.1192
438	*Ḥnwt-mḥyt*	Amun Re,		Deir el Bahari	Merenptah	KRI V, 433-434, esp. 434.13-.14; Sadek, 1987, 225
439	*Tꜣ-kꜣ(t); ḫnsw-wp-nfrt*	Amun		Deir el Bahari	Merenptah	KRI V, 433-434, esp. 434.7-.8; Sadek, 1987, 227
440	*Tyt*	Amun		Deir el Bahari	Dyn. 18	Sadek, 1987, Dyn. 227
441	*Ỉnhy*	Hathor, lady of heaven, lady of the southern sycomore	Memphis?	Baltimore, Walters Art Gallery, Dyn. 22.106	Dyn. 19	Capel and Markoe, 1996, 96-98

CHART 7: Reference list

442	*Ns-ḫnsw-p3-ḫrd*	Amun	Thebes?	Berkeley, U. of C. Phoebe Hearst Museum of Anthropology, 6-19929	late Dyn. 22	Capel and Markoe, 1996, 167-168
443	*Ḥnwt-wdbw*	Amun	Thebes, tomb of Hatiay, no number	St. Louis, Washington U. Gallery of Art, Dyn. 2292	Amenhotep III	Capel and Markoe 1996, 168-169; Kozloff, et. al., 1992, 312-317, no. 61
444	*Rnnwtt*	Amun Re, Wepwawet, Hathor of Medjedny	Asyut?	New York, Metropolitan Museum 15.2.1 and 33.2.1	Seti I	Capel and Markoe 1996, 172-174; Karig, 1969, 27-34; Hayes, 1959, vol. II, 349; Kamal, 1916, 86-89
445	*Iʿy*	Wepwawet	Asyut?	Yale U. Gallery of Art, 1947.81	Rameses III or later	Capel, and Markoe, 1996,174; Scott, 1986, no. 73
446	*Ḥ3t-šryt*	Aten	Abydos?	BM 8644	Amenhotep IV	Manniche, 1991a, 95; Martin, 1986, 115-116, pl. 11; Schneider, 1977, I, 292
447	*3st*	Aten		New York, Metropolitan Museum of Art 66.99.38	Amenhotep IV	Manniche, 1991a, 95; Martin, 1986, 116, pl. 12; Schneider, 1977, I, 292
448	*Ir-mwt-p3-nfr*	Amun Re		Cairo, JdE 86125	Dyn. 21	Habachi, 1947, 261ff
449	*3st-m-3ḫbit*	Amun Re		BM 10743	Third Intermediate Period	Quirke, 1993, no. 33
450	*3sty*	Amun Re		BM 10084	Third Intermediate Period	Quirke, 1993, no. 38
451	*3st*	Thoth		Hildesheim?	Third Intermediate Period	Chappaz, BSEG 11, 145-6
452	*ʿnḫy-n-3st*	Amun			Third Intermediate Period	Chappaz, BSEG 11, 145-6
453	*Gʿwt-sšnw*	Amun			Third Intermediate Period	Chappaz, BSEG 11, 145-6
454	*In-h3y*	Amun			New Kingdom	Chappaz, BSEG 12, 83-96
455	*Bʿkt-3st*				New Kingdom	Chappaz, BSEG 12, 83-96
456	*Bʿk-n-wrl*	Amun Re			New Kingdom	Chappaz, BSEG 12, 83-96
457	*Sbk-ḫnt*	Amun			Third Intermediate Period	Chappaz, BSEG 12, 83-96
458	*3st*	Thoth			New Kingdom	Chappaz, BSEG 14, 89-104
459	*Iwy*	Amun			New Kingdom	Chappaz, BSEG 14, 89-104
460	*In-h3y*	Amun			New Kingdom	Chappaz, BSEG 14, 89-104
461	*Py-pwy*				New Kingdom	Chappaz, BSEG 14, 89-104

CHART 7: Reference list

462	*Mʿy*	Thoth			New Kingdom	Chappaz, BSEG 14, 89-104
463	*N3-š3-ʿ3*	Amun			New Kingdom	Chappaz, BSEG 14, 89-104
464	*T3-wḏ3t*	Amun			New Kingdom	Chappaz, BSEG 14, 89-104
465	*Mwt-m-wi3*	Amun			Third Intermediate Period	Chappaz, BSEG 14, 89-104
466	*?*	Amun		Sotheby's NY 2.12.88 n. 323	Third Intermediate Period	Chappaz, BSEG 14, 97
467	*P3-ṯ3w*	Isis	Abydos tomb 36	Boston, 03.17-46-54, 1769	Dyn. 19	Chappaz, BSEG 14, 89-104; D'Auria, et. al., 1988, n. 105
468	*Sḫmt-m-ḥb*			Leiden CI 24	Dyn. 19	Schneider, 1977, ii, 43
469	*Šd(t)-sy-Mwt*	Amun	Thebes	Leiden AH 101f	Dyn. 20	Schneider, 1977, ii, 3.1.1.32, pg. 44
470	*?*	Amun		Leiden AH 199e	Dyn. 19-20	Schneider, 1977, ii, 49 (3.1.2.8)
471	*Nb-...*	Amun		Leiden BA 235	Dyn. 19-20	Schneider, 1977, ii, 49 (3.1.2.9)
472	*Ỉp3y*	Amun	Saqqara	Leiden, AST 15	late Dyn. 18	Schneider, 1977, ii, 57 (3.2.1.4)
473	*T3-dy(.t)-Mwt*	Amun	Deir el Bahari cache II	Leiden F 93/10.87-88	Dyn. 21	Schneider, 1977, ii, 135-6 (4.3.1.77-78)
474	*Nsy-t3-nbt-išrw*	Amun	Thebes	Leiden F 1970/1.2	Dyn. 21	Schneider, 1977, ii, 146 (4.5.1.21)
475	*W3y-k3*			Leiden RO II 183	Dyn. 19-20	Schneider, 1977, ii, 98-99 (3.3.1.9)
476	*B3kt-3st*			Leiden AF 131	early Dyn. 19	Schneider, 1977, ii, 99
477	*B3k-wrt?*			Leiden AF 140a,b, BA 267	Dyn. 19-20	Schneider, 1977, ii, 105 (3.3.2.3-.5)
480	*Mwt-nfrt*	Amun	Karnak, also in TT96?	Cairo, CG 42126	Amenhotep II-Tuthmosis IV	Urk., IV, 1435.12; Legrain, 1906, vol. I, 76, pl. 75
481	*Nyt*	Amun	TT88	Thebes	Tuthmosis III-Amenhotep II	Urk. IV, 1460.9-11; LD iii, 272; Whale case 50; Virey, 1891, 286-310
482	*Mryt?*	Amun?	TT80	Thebes	Amenhotep II	Urk. IV, 1476.13; LD iii, 271 [59]; Whale, 1989, case 68, 170-175
487	*Ḥnwt-wrt*	Amun		BM 31	Amenhotep II	Urk. IV, 1503.16; HTFES 8, 7
491	*Mryt-Ptḥ*	Amun Re	TT55	Thebes	Amenhotep III-IV	Urk. IV, 1780.3; Daives, 1941
492	*Mʿnwn3*	Bastet	Bubastis	Cairo, E. 87911	Amenhotep III	Urk. IV, 1931.11; Habachi, 1957, 105, pl. 39-41
493	*B3t3*	Amun *ḥr s3 4-nw*	Abydos	Cairo, CG 34117	Amenhotep III	Urk. IV, 1940.5; Lacau, 1918, fasc. 2,169-170, fasc 1 pl. LIII; Mariette, 1880, n.1108

CHART 7: Reference list

496	*Tiy*	Osiris, Isis	Abydos	Yale University Art Gallery, YPM 2657; Cairo, JdE 35258, JdE 32025, CG 34505; Louvre A.66	Seti I-Rameses II	KRI III, 447-463, esp. 450.7, 455.12; Scott, 1986, 124 n. 71; Gaballa, 1979, 42-49
497	*Ms*	Osiris	Abydos?	Petrie collection, UC 14419	Second Intermediate Period	Stewart, 1979, 33 no. 138, pl. 34.3
498	*Sḫ3-nfr*	Re		Petrie collection, UC 14495	Dyn. 20	Stewart, 1976, 33, pl. 25
499	*...t3wy*	Osiris	Abydos?	Petrie collection, UC 14406	Dyn. 19-20	Stewart, 1976, 43, pl. 34.1
500	*Wrt...*	Amun	Buhen, block B- courtyard B		Dyn. 19-20	Smith, 1976, 95-96, pl. xii.4
501	*?*	Horus, lord of Buhen	Buhen, block F		Dyn. 19-20?	Smith, 1976, 116, pl. xxiii.2
502	*?*		Buhen, pavement of south temple		Rameses II	KRI III, 135.1; Smith, 1976, 145, 216, pl. xxxix.1; lxxvii.5
503	*Ỉsw-mwt*	Amun of Karnak	TT44	Thebes	Rameses II	El-Saady, 1996, 43-6
504	*Ḥwt-ḥr*	Amun	TT44	Thebes	Rameses II	El-Saady, 1996, 43-6
505	*?*	Amun	TT44	Thebes	Rameses II	El-Saady, 1996, 43-6
506	*?*		TT44	Thebes	Rameses II	El-Saady, 1996, 43-6
507	*Nfrt-iry*		TT44	Thebes	Rameses II	El-Saady, 1996, 43-6
508	*T3-my(t)*		TT44	Thebes	Rameses II	El-Saady, 1996, 43-6
509	*Ỉryt-nfrt*		TT44	Thebes	Rameses II	El-Saady, 1996, 43-6
510	*?*		TT44	Thebes	Rameses II	El-Saady, 1996, 43-6
511	*?*		TT44	Thebes	Rameses II	El-Saady, 1996, 43-6
513	*Ỉry-tḫ*	Khnum	Amarah West, temple		Dyn. 19-20	Helck, 1960, 239; Fairman, 1938, 155, pl. II.3
514	*T3-mḥyt*	Horus of Aniba	Amarah West, temple		Dyn. 19-20	Helck, 1960, 239; Fairman, 1938, 155, pl. II.3
515	*Ỉw-ns-nb-t3wy*	Bastet, lady of Bubastis		New York, MMA 62.186	Dyn. 18	Fischer, 1977, 139-140
517	*Mwt-mnw*	Hapi	Abydos		Dyn. 19	Mariette, 1880, 425-426, n. 1139
518	*Nht-m-wi3*	Hathor	Abydos		Rameses II	Mariette, 1880, 418-419, n. 1128
519	*Mwty*	Hathor	Abydos		Rameses II	Mariette, 1880, 418-419, n. 1128
520	*Nfrt-iry*	Amun	Abydos		Rameses II	Mariette, 1880, 418-419, n. 1128
521	*N3-ty*	Amun	Abydos		Rameses II	Mariette, 1880, 418-419, n. 1128

CHART 7: Reference list

522	*Tȝ-kmȝy*	Amun	Abydos		Rameses II	Mariette, 1880, 418-419, n. 1128
523	*Dwȝt-nfr*	Amun	Abydos		Rameses II	Mariette, 1880, 418-419, n. 1128
524	*Tiȝ*	Amun	Abydos		Rameses II	Mariette, 1880, 418-419, n. 1128
525	*Bȝk-Ỉmn*	Amun?	Abydos		Rameses II	Mariette, 1880, 418-419, n. 1128
526	*Mwt-nḏm*	Amun	Abydos		Rameses II	Mariette, 1880, 418-419, n. 1128
527	*Ỉ-y*	Amun	Abydos		Rameses II	Mariette, 1880, 418-419, n. 1128
528	*Twiȝ*	Amun	Abydos		Rameses II	Mariette, 1880, 418-419, n. 1128
529	*Nȝ-ṯyi*	Amun	Abydos		Rameses II	Mariette, 1880, 418-419, n. 1128
530	*ȝst-nfrt*	Amun	Abydos		Dyn. 19	Mariette, 1880, 421-422, n. 1135
531	*ʿwrti*	Amun	Abydos		Dyn. 19	Mariette, 1880, 421-422, n. 1135
532	*Rwḳȝšȝ*	Amun	Abydos		Dyn. 19	Mariette, 1880, 421-422, n. 1135
533	*Wȝḏt-rnpt*	Amun	Abydos		Seti I	KRI I, 321, esp. 321.8; Mariette, 1880, 423-424, n. 1137
534	*Ḥwt-ḥr*	Amun	Abydos		Dyn. 19	Mariette, 1880, 428-429, n. 1144
535	*Mwt-wnš*	Onuris	Abydos		Dyn. 19	Mariette, 1880, 428-429, n. 1144
536	*Ḏʿ-ȝst*	Onuris	Abydos		Dyn. 19	Mariette, 1880, 428-429, n. 1144
537	*Wty-rnw?*	the king?	Abydos		Dyn. 19	Mariette, 1880, 430, n. 1148
538	*Ỉ?ȝ*	Amun	Abydos	Cairo, JdE 19775	Rameses II	KRI III, 52.4; Mariette, 1880, 435, n. 1160
539	*Tȝ-mr-pn-ʿs*	Osiris	Abydos		Rameses XI	KRI VI, 701; Mariette, 1880, 442-443, n. 1173
540	*Tȝ-mrit*	Amun	Abydos		Dyn. 20	Mariette, 1880, 442, n. 1174
541	*?*	Osiris	Abydos		Dyn. 20	Mariette, 1880, 443-444, n. 1175
542	*Šbwti-wsri*	Osiris	Abydos		Dyn. 20	Mariette, 1880, 444, n. 1176
543	*Nṯm-ȝst*	Osiris	Abydos		Dyn. 20	Mariette, 1880, 444, n. 1176
544	*ȝst*	Osiris	Abydos		Dyn. 20	Mariette, 1880, 445, n. 1179
545	*Ṯnt-bḥw-ȝḫ*	Osiris	Abydos		Dyn. 20	Mariette, 1880, 446, n. 1182
546	*Tȝ-wr-ḥḳȝt*	Osiris	Abydos		Dyn. 20	Mariette, 1880, 446, n. 1184
547	*Tȝ-ʿšt-wšbw*	Osiris	Abydos		Dyn. 20	Mariette, 1880, 446-447,n. 1185
548	*Ḥnwt-tȝwy*	Osiris	Abydos		Dyn. 20	Mariette, 1880, 447, n. 1187

CHART 7: Reference list

549	*T3-Mwt-nfr*	Isis	Abydos		Dyn. 20	Mariette, 1880, 448, n. 1189
550	*Šf3y?*	Mut	Abydos		Dyn. 20	Mariette, 1880, 448, n. 1190
551	*Pr-ms-m-?*	Osiris	Abydos		Dyn. 20	Mariette, 1880, 448, n. 1191
553	*T3-?*	Amun	Abydos		Dyn. 20	Mariette, 1880, 449, n. 1193
554	*T3-Mwt*	Amun	Abydos		Dyn. 20	Mariette, 1880, 450. n. 1195
555	*Mr-?*	Osiris, Horus, (Isis?)	Abydos		Dyn. 20	Mariette, 1880, 450, n. 1196
556	*Pr?*	Amun	Abydos		Dyn. 20	Mariette, 1880, 450, n. 1197
558	*T3-Mwt-nfrt*	Amun	Abydos		Late pd.	Mariette, 1880, 478, n. 1268
559	*Ỉ-t3wy*	Amun	Abydos		Third Intermediate Period	Mariette, 1880, 465, n. 1229
560	*Nst-Ỉmn*	Amun	Abydos		Third Intermediate Period	Mariette, 1880, 466, n. 1231
561	*Tiy*	Isis	Abydos		Dyn. 19	Mariette, 1880, 41, n. 374
562	*Šrit-Rʿ*	Osiris	Abydos		Dyn. 20	Mariette, 1880, 555-556, n. 1429
563	*T3-b3k-n-3st*	Osiris	Abydos		Dyn. 20	Mariette, 1880, 555-556, n. 1429
564	*T?-s3???ṯ*	Osiris	Abydos		Dyn. 20	Mariette, 1880, 555-556, n. 1429
565	*Bw-wy3?*	Herishef	Sedment		Rameses II	KRI III, 224.12; Petrie and Brunton, 1924, pl. lxviii
566	*?*	Seth	Dakhla		Sheshonq I	Gardiner, 1933, 29-30, fig. 1; Spiegelberg,1899, 12-21
567	*Ḥnwt*	Onuris	Thebes, TT A19?	BM 902	Tuthmosis IV	Urk. IV 1616.13; HTFES 8, pl. 9; Van Siclen, 1979, 19
568	*T3-di*	Amun	TT33	Thebes	Saite	PM I.1, 50; LD iii, 244-245 [20]
569	*N3-mnḫ-3st*	Amun	TT33	Thebes	Saite	PM I.1, 50; LD iii, 244-245 [20]
570	*?*	Osiris	Abydos		New Kingdom	Peet, 1914, vol.II, 116, fig. 74, pl. xxvi.1
571	*Kt-ḫr?*	Osiris	Abydos, tomb D223		Dyn. 18	Peet, 1913, vol. III, 32, pl. xii.10
572	*ʿnḫ-s-3st*	Amun	Abydos		New Kingdom-Third Intermediate Period	Garstang, 1989, 43, pl. XIV
573	*Rʿ*	Amun	Abydos		New Kingdom-Third Intermediate Period	Garstang, 1989, 43

CHART 7: Reference list

574	*Ššn*	Amun	Abydos		New Kingdom-Third Intermediate Period	Garstang, 1989, 43
575	*Ỉ-pw-y*	Amun	Memphis	Munich, Staatiliche Sammlung, ÄS 11	Amenhotep III	Müller, 1966, n. 47
577	*Mrwt-ti*	Hathor	Faras, temple at Hathor rock	Khartoum Museum, 4451	late Dyn.18-early 19	Karkowski, 1981, 87-89
578	*Nfrt-Mwt*	Nekhbet, Amun	Faras, Qasr Ibrim, TT289, Sehel	Khartoum Museum	Rameses II	KRI III, 80-111, esp. 85.9, 86.11, 107.5; Karkowski, 1981, 112-113; Drenkhhahn, 1975, 47; Jacoby, 1900, 113-115
579	*Ḥr-iy*	Amun	Abydos	Cairo, CG 34099 and CG 34101	Dyn. 18	Lacau, 1918, fasc. 2, 153-155, fasc. 1, pl.XLIX, XLVIII; Mariette, 1880, n.1085 and 1086
580	*Snw-ʿnḫ*		Abydos	Cairo, CG 20142	Middle Kingdom	Lange and Schafer, 1902, 167-168, pl. 13; Mariette, 1880, 909
581	*S3t-tp-iḥw*		Illahun	Berlin, P.10021	Middle Kingdom	Scharff, 1924, *9
582	*Ỉwy*	Amun *ḥr s3 2-nw*	Karnak cachette (statue)	Cairo, CG 42122; Louvre C.50	Seti I-Rameses II	KRI I, 327-331, esp 328.2; Lowle, 1976, 97-98; Legrain, 1906, 71-73, pl. 72
583	*T3-wrt*	Amun	TT257	Thebes	Rameses II	KRI III, 377-378; Mostafa, 1995
584	*Rnwtt*	Amun	TT50	Thebes	Horemheb	Urk. IV, 2178.15; Hari, 1985
585	*T3-wsrt*	Montu	TT31	Thebes	Rameses II	KRI III, 399-410, esp. 402.2; Davies and Gardiner, 1948, pl. X.2
586	*Mwtiʿy (Mʿy)*	Amun, Montu	TT31	Thebes	Rameses II	KRI III, 399-410; esp. 404.15; Davies and Gardiner 1948 pls. XII, XVI
587	*Ḥwt-ḥr*	Amun	TT294	Thebes	early Dyn. 19	Strudwick, 1996, 17
588	*Dw3t-nfrt?*	Amun of Karnak	TT254	Thebes	Horemheb	Strudwick, 1996, 57-59
589	*Mwt-m-wi3*	Amun	TT254	Thebes	Horemheb	Strudwick, 1996, 57-59
590	*...i3w*	Amun	TT254	Thebes	Horemheb	Strudwick, 1996, 57-59
591	*Ty*	Amun	TT254	Thebes	Horemheb	Strudwick, 1996, 57-59
592	*?*	Amun	TT254	Thebes	Horemheb	Strudwick, 1996, 57-59
593	*Šri-Rʿ*	Amun		Bologna 1094	Dyn. 19-20	Caminos, 1954, 20-21
594	*K3i3*	Pre		Bologna 1094, line 8.6	Dyn. 19-20	Caminos, 1954, 22-23
595	*S3-kt*	Thoth		Bologna 1094, line 9.7	Dyn. 19-20	Caminos, 1954, 26
596	*Nsw-m-ḥ3b*	Thoth		Bologna 1094, line 10.6	Dyn. 19-20	Caminos, 1954, 22-23

CHART 7: Reference list

597	*Styky*	Hathor, lady of the southern sycomore		P. Sallier IV vs.	Rameses II	Caminos, 1954, 333-335
598	*Sḫm-nfr*	Amun		P. Sallier IV vs.	Rameses II	Caminos, 1954, 333-335
599	*T3y-sn*	Montu	TT31	Thebes	Rameses II	KRI III, 399-410, esp. 407.1; Davies and Gardiner, 1948, pl. XV
600	*Wr-nrw*	Montu	TT31	Thebes	Rameses II	KRI III, 399-410; Davies and Gardiner, 1948, pl. XV
601	*Ḥnwt-nfrt*	Montu	TT31	Thebes	Rameses II	KRI III, 399-410, esp. 407.2; Davies and Gardiner, 1948, pl. XV
602	*Rwi3*	Montu	TT31	Thebes	Rameses II	KRI III, 399-410; Davies and Gardiner, 1948, 29
603	*Wi3y*	Montu, Amun	TT31	Thebes	Rameses II	KRI III, 399-410, esp. 400.7; Davies and Gardiner, 1948, 29
604	*ʿ3ti*	Montu	TT31	Thebes	Rameses II	KRI III, 399-410, esp. 402.7; Davies and Gardiner, 1948, 29
605	*Ns-nb*	Montu	TT31	Thebes	Rameses II	KRI III, 399-410, esp. 402.6; Davies and Gardiner, 1948, 29
606	*T3...*	Amun	Heliopolis		Dyn. 19-20	El-Saady, 1995, 101-104
607	*ʿ-n-wḏ3*	Amun	Kom el Ahmar?	Mulhouse Museum	Rameses II	KRI III, 80-111, esp. 85.10; Jacoby, 1900, 113-115
608	*Mwt-nfrt*	Amun	Zawyet el Sultan		Seti I	Osing, 1992
609	*Ḳ3-(ḳ3)*	Amun	Zawyet el Sultan		Seti I	Osing, 1992
610	*Ry*	Amun Re	Gurob		Dyn. 19	Loat, 1904, pl. xvii.1
611	*T3-wrt-ḥtpt*	Amun	el Mashayikh	el-Mashayikh and Cairo, CG 582, 1093	Merenptah	KRI IV, 141-147, esp. 146.7; Ockinga and al-Masri, 1988, 11-12
612	*Sḫmt-nfrt*	Amun Re	el Mashayikh	el-Mashayikh and Cairo, CG 582, 1093	Merenptah	KRI IV, 141-147, esp. 142.3; Ockinga and al-Masri, 1988, 11-12
613	*ʿn-m-mr*	Amun	Faqus region	Tell Basta storehouse, n. 399	Dyn. 19-20	Radwan, 1987, 223f, pl. II
614	*Wr-n-r*	Amun	Faqus region	Tell Basta storehouse, n. 398	Dyn. 19-20	Radwan, 1987, 223f, pl. III
615	*Bʿk-mwt*	Amun	TT50	Thebes	Horemheb	Urk. IV, 2177-2179; Hari, 1985
616	*Mwt-nfrt*	Amun	TT50	Thebes	Horemheb	Urk. IV, 2177-2179; Hari, 1985
617	*T3-ḫʿt*	Amun	TT50	Thebes	Horemheb	Urk. IV, 2177-2179; Hari, 1985
618	*T3-ḫʿt*	Amun	TT50	Thebes	Horemheb	Urk. IV, 2177-2179; Hari, 1985

CHART 7: Reference list

619	*Pikˁ?*	Amun	TT50	Thebes	Horemheb	Urk. IV, 2177-2179; Hari, 1985
620	*Ṯ3pwy?*	Amun	TT50	Thebes	Horemheb	Urk. IV, 2177-2179; Hari, 1985
621	*Ty*	Amun	TT50	Thebes	Horemheb	Urk. IV, 2177-2179; Hari, 1985
622	*Imn-sˁh*	Amun	TT50	Thebes	Horemheb	Urk. IV, 2177-2179; Hari, 1985
623	*Ḥ3t-špswt*	Amun	TT51	Thebes	Seti I	KRI I, 333-341, esp. 338.12, 338.15; Davies, 1927, 9, pl. X
624	*T3-wsrt*	Montu?	TT51	Thebes	Seti I	KRI I, 333-341, esp. 338.8; Davies, 1927, 16, pl. Xb
625	*T3-miw*	Amun	TT23	Thebes	Merenptah	PM I.1, 38f; KRI IV, 107-119, esp. 116.10; LD iii, 252-253 [38]; Wilbour, 1936, 55-56
626	*Rˁi3*	Amun of Karnak	TT23	Thebes	Merenptah	PM I.1, 38f; KRI IV, 107-119, esp. 111.6, 118.15-.16; LD iii, 252-253 [38]; Wilbour, 1936, 55-56
627	*Nbt-t3wy*	Amun	TT23	Thebes	Merenptah	PM I.1, 38f; KRI IV, 107-119, esp. 116.10; LD iii, 252-253 [38]; Wilbour, 1936, 55-56
628	*Ḥnwt*	Amun	TT158	Thebes	Rameses III or later	KRI V, 400-412; Seele, 1959, 5-10, pls. 4, 26
629	*Šri(t)-Rˁ*	Amun	TT158	Thebes	Rameses III or later	KRI V, 400-412, esp. 403.4; Seele, 1959, 5-10, pls. 4, 26
630	*(Ḥ?)ḳrt*	Amun	TT158	Thebes	Rameses III or later	KRI V, 400-412, esp. 403.4; Seele, 1959, 5-10, pls. 4, 26
631	*Ḥnwt-t3wy*	Amun	TT158, TT148	Thebes	Rameses III or later	KRI V, 400-412, esp. 403.3; Gaballa and Kitchen, 1981, 161-180; Seele, 1959, 5-10, pls. 4, 26
632	*T3y-ḥnwt-p3-mtr*	Amun	TT158	Thebes	Rameses III or later	KRI V, 400-412, esp. 403.3; Seele, 1959, 5-10, pls. 4, 26
633	*T3y-nḏmt*	Amun	TT158, TT148	Thebes	Rameses III or later	KRI V, 400-412, esp. 403.2; Gaballa and Kitchen 1981, 161-180; Seele, 1959, 5-10, pls. 4, 26
634	*Nfrt-iry*	Amun of Karnak	TT158	Thebes	Rameses III or later	KRI V, 400-412, esp. 402.5; Seele, 1959, 5-10, pls. 4, 26
635	*Sḫmt*	Khnum	TT158	Thebes	Rameses III or later	KRI V, 400-412, esp. 409.13; Seele, 1959, 5-10, pls. 4, 26

CHART 7: Reference list

636	*Nfrt-iry*	Montu, Amun			Dyn. 19-20	Habachi, 1965, 123-136
637	*Ỉwy*	Montu, Amun	TT324 among others	Thebes, Sehel, etc.	Rameses VI	KRI VI, 360.5-.6; Habachi, 1965, 123-136; Davies and Gardiner, 1948
638	*Tȝ-Mwt-nfrt*	Khnum, lord of the cataract			Dyn. 19-20	Habachi, 1965, 123-136
639	*Mˁiȝy*	Montu, Amun	TT331	Thebes	Rameses VII	KRI VI, 418-421; Habachi, 1965, 123-136; Davies and Gardiner, 1948, 53-55
640	*Mwt-ir-di.s*	Anukis			Dyn. 19-20	Habachi, 1965, 123-136
641	*Wiȝy(?)*	Amun	TT163	BM 55337	mid-late Dyn. 19	Assman, 1979, 54-77, pl. 9,10
642	*Nḏmt-niwt*	Amun	TT163	BM 55337	mid-late Dyn. 19	Assman, 1979, 54-77, pl. 9,10
643	*Ḥnwt-mtr*	Amun	Sehel, (TT158)	Thebes, Sehel	Rameses II	KRI III, 250.5 and V, 400-412, esp. 403.5, 409.12; Habachi, 1968, 107-113
644	*Tȝ-nḏmt*	Amun	TT282, Sehel		Rameses II	KRI III, 250, esp. 250.5-.6; Habachi, 1968, 107-113
645	*?*	Amun	TT282, Sehel		Rameses II	Habachi, 1968, 107-113
646	*Nwbt-nṯr-nfr*	Sobek	El Kab		New Kingdom	Sayce, 1898, 111-112
647	*?*	Amun	Thebes, Dra Abu el Naga, K 91.10		Dyn. 18	Leclant and Clerc, 1993, 240-241
648	*Mryt-Rˁ*	Amun of Karnak	TT49	Thebes	Amenhotep IV-Aye	Davies, 1933
649	*Ỉwy*	Amun	TT49	Thebes	Amenhotep IV-Aye	Davies, 1933
650	*Ḫˁyt*	Mehyt	Bubastis	Cairo or Zagazig	Rameses III	Habachi, 1957, 101 pl.37
651	*Tȝ-mrt*	Bastet, lady of Bubastis	Bubastis	Cairo or Zagazig	New Kingdom	Habachi, 1957, 102, pl.38
652	*Ḫbwy-nw-ns*	Bastet	Bubastis	Cairo, 87085	Amenhotep III	Habachi, 1957, 95-96, pl.28-29
653	*Ḥnwt-mtr*	Amun	TT267	Thebes, (Deir el Medina)	Rameses III	KRI V, 627-639, esp. 630.10-.11, 632.14; Valbelle, 1975, 24, pl. XVII
654	*Nbw-iiy*	Amun	TT267	Thebes (Deir el Medina)	Rameses III	KRI V, 627-639, esp. 631.16-632.1; Valbelle, 1975, 28
655	*Wˁbt*	Amun	TT211	Thebes, (Deir el Medina)	Merenptah	KRI IV, 189-193, esp. 191.3, and 436.7; Bruyère, 1952b, 82
656	*Šrit-Rˁ*	Amun	TT211	Thebes, (Deir el Medina)	Merenptah	KRI IV, 189-193, esp. 189.11; Bruyère, 1952b, 83

CHART 7: Reference list

657	*Ḥwy-n-r (Ḥwt-ḥr)*	Hathor?, Amun	TT215	Thebes (Deir el Medina)	Seti I	KRI I, 381-389, esp. 382.1; Jourdain, 1939, 36, 48 pl. 29-30
659	*Wrt-nfrt*	Isis	Abydos	Boston, 00.690	Rameses II	KRI III, 465-467, esp. 465.12; D'Auria, et. al., 1988, n. 108; Randall-MacIver, et.al., 1902, 64, pl. 37
660	*Ṯy*	Amun Re	Heliopolis	Boston, 12.1004	Dyn. 20	D'Auria, et.al., 1988, n. 110
661	*Ꞽwy*	Amun	Saqqara	Boston, 1977.717	late Dyn. 18	D'Auria, et. al. 1988, n. 98
662	*Tȝ-Ꞽmn*	Amun	Saqqara	Boston, 92.2582	Ptolemaic	D'Auria, et. al. 1988, n. 134
663	*Nḏm-Mwt*	Amun	TT194	Thebes	Rameses II	Seyfried, 1995, text 22, 23, 24, 75, 114, 117
664	*Mwt?*	Amun, Mut, Khonsu	TT194	Thebes	Rameses II	Seyfried, 1995, text 2, 49
665	*Nfr-Mwt*	Amun	TT194	Thebes	Rameses II	Seyfried, 1995, text 34, 35
666	*Tȝ-bȝk-n-Mwt*	Amun	TT68	Thebes	Dyn. 21	Seyfried, 1991, 69; Černý, 1940, 235f
667	*...?*	Amun	TT68	Thebes	Dyn. 20	Seyfried, 1991
668	*Mwt-m-int*	Amun	TT373	Thebes and BM 1198	Rameses II	Seyfried, 1990; HTFES 12, 10, pl. 24-25
669	*Tnt-...nw*	Amun	TT373	Thebes	Dyn. 20	Seyfried, 1990, text 92, fig. 114
670	*Mwt-m-wiȝ*	Amun	TT178	Thebes	Rameses II	KRI III, 321-331, esp. 321.10; Hofmann, 1995
671	*Tȝ-wr(t)-m-ḥb*	Amun	Deir el Medina	Turin, Museo Egizio, n. 50225	Dyn. 20	Tosi and Roccati, 1971-1972
672	*Ꞽi-y*	Mut	Deir el Medina	Turin, Museo Egizio, n. 50219	Dyn. 19-20	Tosi and Roccati, 1971-1972
673	*Sȝt-Rˁ*	Atum Re	Heliopolis-Matareyyeh	Cairo?	Dyn. 19-20	Bakry, 1974, 70-78
674	*Ꞽwy*	Amun Re of Karnak	TT19	Thebes	Rameses II	KRI III, 390-396, esp. 393.15; Foucart, 1935
675	*Nbt-tȝwy*	Amun	TT255	Thebes	Horemheb	Urk. IV, 2174; Baud and Drioton, 1957, 46
676	*Bwy*	Amun	TT255	Thebes	Horemheb	Urk. IV, 2174.20; Baud and Drioton, 1957, 47
677	*Mwty*	Amun	TT255	Thebes	Horemheb	Urk. IV, 2174.15; Baud and Drioton, 1957, 14
678	*Tȝ-rnwt*	Amun	TT16	Thebes	Rameses II	KRI III, 396-399, esp. 397.8-9 and 399.5; Baud and Drioton, 1928
679	*Ṯȝy-nb-nḫt-rw*	Osiris	Abydos	Vienna, ÄOS 157	Late pd.	De Meulenaere, 1975-76, 150; Munro 1973, 262, pl. 26, abb. 96
680	*Ḏd-ȝst-n-imw*	Osiris	Abydos	Cairo, JdE 20240	Late pd.	De Meulenaere, 1975-76, 151; Munro, 1973, 98f, 278, abb. 125; Mariette, 1880, 476, n. 1259

CHART 7: Reference list

681	*Ṯ3-tiy*	Herishef	Medinet Habu	Thebes	Rameses III	KRI V, 384-390, esp. 388.6-.7; Schott, 1957, pl. 1 lines 63-65
682	*?*	Amun	Medinet Habu	Thebes	Rameses III	KRI V, 384-390, esp. 388.6-.7; Schott, 1957, pl. 1 lines 63-65
683	*Mryt*	Amun	TT77	Thebes	Tuthmosis IV	Urk. IV, 1599-1601; Manniche, 1988, 7-18
684	*[T?]3-miy*	Neith	Bubastis	Cairo, JdE 38709, CG 53263	Merenptah	KRI IV, 372-373, esp. 373.7; El-Sayed, 1982, 379-380
685	*Mwt-nfrt*	Atum		Vienna, 53	New Kingdom	von Bergmann, 1887, 42-43
686	*Sḫmt*	Atum		Vienna, 53	New Kingdom	von Bergmann, 1887, 42-43
687	*Ỉsriḫ*			Vienna, 53	New Kingdom	von Bergmann, 1887, 42-43
688	*Ỉʿi*	Wepwawet		Vienna, 53	New Kingdom	von Bergmann, 1887, 42-43
689	*Ḥwt-ḥr*	Amun	Coptos	Cairo	Dyn. 19-20	Weigall, 1908, 112
690	*S3t-Ỉmn*	Montu of Medamud	Abydos	Vienna, Kunsthistorisches Musuem, ÄOS 132	Middle Kingdom	Rogge, 1990, v. 4, 34-38; von Bergmann, 1892, 16
691	*W3ḏ-h3w*	Montu of Medamud	Abydos	Vienna, Kunsthistorisches Musuem, ÄS 132	Middle Kingdom	Rogge, 1990, v. 4, 34-38; von Bergmann, 1892, 16
692	*Mwt-nfrt*	Amun of the lake, Amun of Diospolis Parva	Diospolis Parva	Cairo?	Horemheb	Legrain, 1907, 269-275
693	*3st*	Amun	TT32	Thebes and Cairo, CG 549	Rameses II	KRI III, 316-319, esp. 317.5; Kákosy, 1988; Borchardt, 1911-1936, pt. 2, 94-96
694	*Ty*	Thoth		BM 1042	Dyn. 18	HTFES 8, 43-47, pls. 37-38
695	*Mwty*	Isis		BM 1222	New Kingdom	HTFES 8, 52-53, pl. 44
696	*Bi3*	Amun	Abydos	BM 1062	late Dyn. 18-early Dyn. 19	HTFES 7, 14, pl. 49
697	*Mwt-nfrt*	Khnum, lord of Her-weret	Balansurah	Cairo?	Amenhotep III-IV	Urk. IV, 2020.20; Hari, 1976, #144; Daressy, 1919, 53-57
698	*Nfrt-ḫʿ*	Ahmose-Nefertari, the Aten	TT46	Thebes	Amenhotep III-IV	Urk. IV, 1995 (753); Hari, 1976, #193
699	*Knr*	Amun	TT40	Thebes	Tutankh-amun	Urk. IV, 2067.6; Hari, 1976, #294; Nina Davies and Gardiner, 1926, 15, pl. XI
700	*Typwy*	Amun	Saqqara	Musée du Leyde	Amenhotep III-IV	Hari, 1976, #307; Hari, 1964, 30
701	*Mʿy*	Amun	TT55	Thebes	Amenhotep III-IV	Urk. IV, 1784.2; Davies, 1941

CHART 7: Reference list

702	*?*		TT194	Thebes	Rameses II	Seyfried, 1995, text 41, 42
703	*ꜣst*	Amun	TT45	Thebes	Rameses II	KRI III, 353-356, esp. 353.14; Davies and Gardiner, 1948, pl. II
704	*Bʿk(t)-Ḫnsw*	Amun, Mut, Khonsu	TT45	Thebes	Rameses II	KRI III, 353-356, esp. 345.2-3; Davies and Gardiner, 1948, pl. III-V
705	*Ty-m-ḥb*	Amun	TT45	Thebes	Rameses II	KRI III, 353-356, esp. 355.12; Davies and Gardiner, 1948, pl. IV
706	*Nḫt-Mwt*	Amun	TT45	Thebes	Rameses II	KRI III, 353-356, esp. 354.15; Davies and Gardiner, 1948, pl. III
707	*Ỉr-nfrw-Mwt*	Amun	TT45	Thebes	Rameses II	KRI III, 353-356, esp. 356.1; Davies and Gardiner, 1948, pl. IV
708	*Ḥnwt-tꜣwy*	Amun	TT45	Thebes	Rameses II	KRI III, 353-356, esp. 356.1; Davies and Gardiner, 1948, pl. IV
709	*wr-[nfr]*	Amun	TT45	Thebes	Rameses II	KRI III, 353-356, esp. 356.2; Davies and Gardiner, 1948, pl. IV
710	*ꜣst-nfrt*	Amun	TT45	Thebes	Rameses II	KRI III, 353-356, esp. 356.4; Davies and Gardiner, 1948, pl. IV
711	*ꜣḫ-Mwt*	Amun	TT45	Thebes	Rameses II	KRI III, 353-356, esp. 356.4; Davies and Gardiner, 1948, pl. IV
712	*ꜣst*	Amun	TT45	Thebes	Rameses II	KRI III, 353-356, esp. 356.5; Davies and Gardiner, 1948, pl. IV
713	*ꜣst*		Sehel	Sehel	Rameses II	KRI III, 847.12-.13
714	*Mʿiꜣ*		Sehel	Sehel	Rameses II	KRI III, 847.12-.13
715	*ꜣst-nfrt*		Sehel	Sehel	Rameses II	KRI III, 847.12-.13
716	*Ỉy*	Khnum, Satis, Anukis	TT6	Thebes (Deir el Medina)	Rameses II	KRI III 577-587, esp. 579.6; Wild, 1979, pl. 4; Černý, 1949, 60
717	*Ḥꜣt-šps(t)*		TT19	Thebes	Rameses II	KRI III, 390-396, esp. 395.16
718	*Mʿkwỉ*	Amun	TT19	Thebes	Rameses II	KRI III, 390-396, esp. 396.1
719	*Mwt-nfrt*	Amun	TT23	Thebes	Merenptah	KRI IV, 107-119, esp. 117.12
720	*Mhyt-ḫʿṯ*	Amun	TT23	Thebes	Merenptah	KRI IV, 107-119, esp. 117.13-.14
721	*Ḥwy-n-r*	Bastet	TT23	Thebes	Merenptah	KRI IV, 107-119, esp. 118.3
722	*Mwt-nfrt*	Bastet	TT23	Thebes	Merenptah	KRI IV, 107-119, esp. 118.3

CHART 7: Reference list

723	*Ḥnwt-w3ḏbt*	Nebet-ww, Amun	TT32	Thebes and Cairo, CG 549	Rameses II	KRI III, 316-319, esp. 316.15-16, 317.5; Kákosy, 1988, 211-216; Borchardt, 1911-1936, pt. 2, 94-96
724	*N3w-š3ʿt*	Amun Re	TT138	Thebes	Rameses II	KRI III, 383-387, esp. 384.11
725	*B3kt-Mwt*	Amun	TT138	Thebes	Rameses II	KRI III, 383-387, esp. 387.4
726	*Ṯnt-p3-sṯ3*	Amun Re	TT65	Thebes	Rameses XI	KRI VI, 544-553; LD iii, 256
727	*3st*	Amun Re	Thebes? (temple or TT113)	Kestner-Museum, Hannover 2945	Rameses VIII	KRI VI, 440-447; Cramer, 1936, 100f, pl. IX1.-.2
728	*Mwt-m-wi3*	Amun	TT113	Thebes	Rameses VIII	KRI VI, 440.11
729	*ʿ-n-wḏ3-mst*	Amun	TT113	Thebes	Rameses VIII	KRI VI, 440.11
730	*Mwt-m-ipt*	Amun	TT113	Thebes	Rameses VIII	KRI VI, 440-447; Manniche, 1991a, 53, fig. 30
731	*?*	Hathor	TT157	Thebes	Rameses II	KRI III 286.5, 282-291
732	*Niwt-m-ḥb*	Amun	TT189	Thebes	Rameses II	KRI III, 348-353, esp 349.7, VII, 139-140
733	*Tnt-p3-ipt*	Amun	TT189	Thebes	Rameses II	KRI III, 348-353, esp. 349.13, VII 139-140
734	*(Tnt)-Bdty*	Amun Re	TT206	Thebes, (Deir el Medina)	Merenptah	KRI IV, 179-180, esp. 180.3; Bruyère, 1952a season 1945-1946, 58-59 and season 1946-1947, 12, pl. 9
735	*Wbḫt*	Amun	TT263	Thebes	Rameses II	KRI III, 380-383, esp. 381.16
736	*Nfrt-iry*	Amun, Mut, Khonsu	TT296	Thebes	Rameses II	KRI VII, 145-153; Feucht, 1985, c.f. text 19, pl. XXIII
737	*Nḏm-Mwt*	Amun, Mut, Khonsu	TT296	Thebes	Rameses II	KRI VII, 145-153; Feucht, 1985, pl. XVII, XXX
738	*3st*	Amun	TT296	Thebes	Rameses II	KRI VII, 145-153; Feucht, 1985, text 31
739	*K3ḥ*	Amun	TT296	Thebes	Rameses II	KRI VII, 145-153; Feucht, 1985, texts 10, 13, pls. VI, VII
740	*Nfrt-iry*	Amun	TT324	Thebes	Rameses VI	KRI VI, 359-360; Davies and Gardiner, 1948
742	*Kmnʿ*	Amun	TT341	Thebes	Rameses II	KRI III 359-364; Davies and Gardiner, 1948, 31-41 and plates
743	*Rʿi3*	Amun Re	TT341	Thebes	Rameses II	KRI III 359-364, esp. 363.2; Davies and Gardiner, 1948, 31-41 and plates
744	*Wʿbt*	Amun Re	TT359	Thebes	Rameses IV	KRI VI, 183-199
745	*T3-nḏm-m3ʿt-rʿ*	Amun Re	TT359	Thebes	Rameses IV	KRI VI, 183-199
746	*Nfrt-iry*	Amun Re	TT359	Thebes	Rameses IV	KRI VI, 183-199

CHART 7: Reference list

747	*Tꜣ-bꜣ-sꜣ*	Amun	TT359	Thebes		Rameses IV	KRI VI, 183-199
748	*Tꜣ-iwnw*	Amun	TT369	Thebes		Rameses II	KRI VII, 158-159
749	*Nfrt-iry-m-ḥb*	Amun	TT372	Thebes		Rameses III	KRI V, 419-420, esp. 420.4-.5
750	*Mᶜᶜt-nfrt*	Amun	TT372	Thebes		Rameses III	KRI V, 419-420, esp. 420.4
751	*Bᶜkt-Sḫmt*	Amun of the Ramess-eum	TT384	Thebes		Rameses II	KRI III 359.11; Fakhry, 1936, tomb #1
752	*Nhty*	Amun	TT385	Thebes		Rameses II	KRI III, 163.15; Fakhry, 1936, tomb #2
753	*Nb[-ḫni?]-tw*	Amun	TT387	Thebes		Rameses II	KRI III, 319-320, esp. 320.3
754	*Ỉmn-sᶜh*		TT50	Thebes		Horemheb	Urk. IV, 2177-2179; Hari, 1985, 65
755	*Ty*		TT50	Thebes		Horemheb	Urk. IV, 2177-2179; Hari, 1985, 65
756	*Ḥnwt-tꜣwy*	Amun Re	TT51	Thebes		Seti I	KRI I, 333-341, esp. 337.6, 340.8; Davies, 1927, 10
757	*Tꜣ-ḫᶜt*	Isis	TT157	Thebes		Rameses II	KRI III 285.6, 282-291
758	*Ḫᶜt-nsw*	Onuris	el Mashayikh, Abydos	various		Rameses II	KRI III, 470-477, esp. 472. 8, 473.8; Bryan, 1986, 5-30
759	*?*	Seth	Dakhla			Sheshonq I	Gardiner, 1933, 29-30, fig. 1; Spiegelberg,1899, 12-21
760	*Wrty*	Thoth			Field Museum of Natural History #31283	late Dyn. 18-early Dyn. 19?	Allen, 1936, 32
762	*Tꜣ-kꜣ-mn-(wḏꜣ?)*	Amun	Thebes?		Pushkin Museum n. 86 I.1.a.5633 (4074)	Dyn. 19	Hodjash and Berlev, 1982, 144-145, n. 86
763	*Ḥwy-n-r*	Amun	Thebes?		Pushkin Museum n. 86 I.1.a.5633 (4074)	Dyn. 19	Hodjash and Berlev, 1982,144-145, n. 86
764	*Tꜣ-pr?*	Amun			Athens, National Archaeological Museum, X 199	Dyn. 22	Tzachou-Alexandri, 1995, 152-153
765	*Hꜣny*	Amun			Athens, National Archaeological Museum, X 187	Dyn. 22 or later	Tzachou-Alexandri, 1995, 154
766	*Ḏd-ꜣst-iw.s-ᶜnḫ*	Amun			Athens, National Archaeological Museum, 3424	Dyn. 22-30	Tzachou-Alexandri, 1995, 168-169
767	*Ryᶜ*	Amun	probably Thebes		Bologna, KS 1815-16	late Dyn. 18	Pernigotti, 1980, # 13
768	*Mryt*	Amun	probably Thebes		Bologna, KS 1814	late Dyn. 18-early Dyn. 19	Pernigotti, 1980, # 14
769	*Tꜣ-ḫᶜt*	Amun	probably Thebes		Bologna, KS 1814	late Dyn. 18-early Dyn. 19	Pernigotti, 1980, # 14
770	*Nfrt-iry*	Amun	probably Thebes?		Bologna, KS 1813	Dyn. 19	Pernigotti, 1980, # 19

CHART 7: Reference list

771	*Wr-n-r*	Amun		Bologna, KS 1905	Dyn. 18	Bresciani, 1985, #14
772	*Pwy*	Amun		Bologna KS 19Dyn. 22	late Dyn. 18	Bresciani, 1985, #23
773	*Tꜣ-wsr*	Amun		Bologna, KS 1906	early Dyn. 19	Bresciani, 1985, #24
774	*Mwt-nfrt*	Amun		Bologna, KS 1905	Dyn. 18	Bresciani, 1985, #14
775	*Biꜣt*	Amun	Abydos, near Portal Temple of RII	Cairo, JdE 91252	Dyn. 18	Simpson, 1995, 57, fig. 95, pl. 3
776	*Kꜥiꜣ*	Amun	Abydos, near Portal Temple of RII	Cairo, JdE 91254 or 91247	New Kingdom	Simpson, 1995, 59, fig. 98, pl. 14b
777	*Twt-wiꜣ*	Amun	Abydos, near Portal Temple of RII	University Museum, Philadelphia UM 69-29-60	New Kingdom	Simpson, 1995, 61, fig. 100
778	*Tꜣy-sn-nfr*	Wepwawet	Asyut?	Pushkin Museum n. 89, I.1.a 5636 (4145)	Rameses II or Merenptah	Hodjash and Berlev, 1982, 149, n. 89
779	*Mhyt-ḫꜥṯ*	Wepwawet	Asyut?	Pushkin Museum n. 89, I.1.a 5636 (4145)	Rameses II or Merenptah	Hodjash and Berlev, 1982, 149, n. 89
780	*Nfr-ꜣst*	Wepwawet	Asyut?	Pushkin Museum n. 89, I.1.a 5636 (4145)	Rameses II or Merenptah	Hodjash and Berlev, 1982, 149, n. 89
781	*Wnp*	Wepwawet	Asyut?	Pushkin Museum n. 89, I.1.a 5636 (4145)	Rameses II or Merenptah	Hodjash and Berlev, 1982, 149, n. 89
782	*Tꜣ-kt*	Wepwawet	Asyut?	Pushkin Museum n. 89, I.1.a 5636 (4145)	Rameses II or Merenptah	Hodjash and Berlev, 1982, 149, n. 89
783	*Rnnwtt*	Amun Re, Wepwawet	Asyut, tomb of Amenhotep		Seti I	Capel and Markoe 1996, 172-174; Karig, 1969, 27-34; Hayes, 1959, vol. II, 349; Kamal, 1916, 86-89
784	*Tꜣ-imnt-snb*	Khenti-amentiu	Akhmim	Cairo, CG Dyn. 22054	Ptolemaic pd.	Munro, 1973, 302
785	*Tꜣ-mryt*	Amun of Karnak	TT148	Thebes	Rameses III or later	Gaballa and Kitchen, 1981, 161-180
786	*Tꜣ-mit*	Amun	TT148	Thebes	Rameses III or later	Gaballa and Kitchen, 1981, 161-180
787	*Ḏd-Ḥr-iw.s-ꜥnḫ*	Amun		Leningrad, Hermitage 778	early Dyn. 22	Niwiński, 1988, no.235
788	*Sḫmt*	Amun of Karnak	TT148	Thebes	Rameses III or later	Gaballa and Kitchen, 1981, 161-180
788	*Nsy-tꜣ-nb-išrw*	Amun		BM 35287, 36211	early Dyn. 22	Niwiński, 1988, no.271
789	*Mwt-m-mr.s*	Amun Re, Mut, Knonsu	TT65	Thebes	Rameses XI	KRI VI, 545.14; LD iii, 256
790	*Wiꜣy*	Amun Re	TT65	Thebes	Rameses XI	KRI VI, 545.14; LD iii, 256

CHART 7: Reference list

791	*Tꜣ-mt...*	Amun Re	TT65	Thebes	Rameses XI	KRI VI, 544-553, esp. 545.14; LD iii, 256
792	*Bꜣky*	Amun	TT A24 (Waseda U. # W-6), Mut temple at Karnak	Thebes, Cairo, CG 932, CG 1107	Amenhotep III	Urk. IV, 1950; Wilkinson, 1883, 107, fig. 365; Borchardt, 1911-1936, pt. 3, 161 and pt. 4, 60-61
793	*Tꜣyw-nḏmt*	Nekhbet	El Kab tomb 4	El Kab	Rameses III	KRI V, 430 (207) and VI, 555 (41); personal observation
794	*Ns-w-m-sbꜣ?*	Nekhbet	El Kab tomb 4	El Kab	Rameses III	KRI V, 430 (207) and VI, 555 (41); personal observation
795	*Mryt-RꜤ*			Wiesbaden Museum, SNA Dyn. 2293	Tuthmosis III	Schlick-Nolte, 1984, vol. 1, 127-128
796	*Ꞽw.s-m-ḥswt-Mwt*	Amun Re		Darmstadt, Hessisches Landesmuseum, O. Nr	Third Intermediate Period	Schlick-Nolte, 1984, vol. 1, 25-26
797	*Ty*	Hathor, lady of the (southern) sycomore	Saqqara	Linköping, Sweden	late Dyn. 18-early Dyn. 19	Martin, 1987, vol. 1, #38, pl. 13
798	*MꜤiꜣ*	Amun Re	Saqqara	East Berlin, 7278	late Dyn. 18-early Dyn. 19	Martin, 1987, vol. 1, #42, pl. 15
799	*Sꜣt-Ꞽmn*	Amun Re	Saqqara	Saqqara, Antiquities magazine	late Dyn. 18-early Dyn. 19	Martin, 1987, vol. 1, #47, pl. 16
800	*Tꜣyw.sn*	Amun	Thebes	Bodleian Library Oxford, B9	Dyn. 19-20	Currelly, et.al. 1913, 11, #B9
801	*Nfr...*	Amun	Thebes	Bodleian Library Oxford, B9	Dyn. 19-20	Currelly, et.al. 1913, 11, #B9
802	*...ḫbw-šꜤt*	Amun	Thebes	Bodleian Library Oxford, B9	Dyn. 19-20	Currelly, et.al. 1913, 11, #B9
803	*Nfrt-iry*		Saqqara, tomb of Ameneminet	Cairo, S.R. 12002 section IV (on display in room 13); Munich Gl. 298	late Dyn. 18	Löhr, 1970, 467-474
804	*RꜤiꜣy*	Amun Re, Mut	TT409	Thebes	Rameses II	KRI III, 331-345, esp. 341.16; Negm, 1997
805	*Twt-wiꜣ*	Amun	TT409	Thebes	Rameses II	KRI III, 331-345, esp. 345.15; Negm, 1997
806	*Tꜣ-smnt*	Amun	TT409	Thebes	Rameses II	KRI III, 331-345, esp. 343.5-.6; Negm, 1997
807	*Tꜣ-wrt-ḥtp-ti*	Amun	TT409	Thebes	Rameses II	KRI III, 331-345, esp. 342.15; Negm, 1997
808	*ꜣḫ.s?*	Hathor?	Saqqara, tomb of Iurudef	Saqqara	Rameses II	Raven, 1991, 5

CHART 7: Reference list

809	*Nbw-ii*	Amun		Boston MFA, temp. #85.1998	Dyn. 19	unpublished; information courtesy MFA
810	*Ṯr-(?nḫt)-Mwt?*	Amun?	Thebes	Boston MFA, temp. #154.1994	Dyn. 19	unpublished; information courtesy MFA
811	*T3y*	Hathor, lady of the southern sycomore		Cambridge, Fitzwilliam Museum E55.49	Dyn. 19-20	Delvaux and Warmenbol, 1991, fig.27
812	*Wrt-nfrt*	Khnum		BM 795	Dyn. 19	HTFES 10, pl. 94; Lieblein no. 995
813	*Ṯi3*	Amun, great of victories		Toronto, ROM 955.79.2; Florence Cat. no. 15988	Rameses II	KRI III, 366-372, esp. 368.5, .8; Kitchen, 1973, 426; Cooney, 1956, 27-28, pl. 51
814	*Mwt-m-wi3*	Amun	Saqqara, tomb chapel of Raia	Saqqara	Rameses II	KRI VII, 167.16 (486); Martin, 1991, 124-30; Martin, 1985, 10-19, pl. 19
815	*Ḥwt-ḥr*	Amun	TT A17	Chicago, Field Museum or Copenhagen?	Rameses III	KRI V, 418.9; Manniche, 1987, 78-79, fig. 68
816	*Nfrt-iry*	Amun	TT323	Thebes, Turin N: 22025 (=suppl. 6261)	Seti I-Rameses II	KRI I, 392-396, esp. 393.3; also KRI III, 650, esp. 650.11
817	*Ḥmt-nṯr*	Amun	TT323	Thebes	Seti I	KRI I, 392-396, 392.10
818	*T3-k3*	Amun		Louvre, Inv. 4011	Seti I	KRI I, 331, esp. 331.12
820	*T3-swrḫ?*	Amun		Musée Guimet	Seti I	KRI I, 325, VII, 430
821	*T3-mit*	Amun		Musée Guimet	Seti I	KRI I, 325, VII, 430
822	*Ṯw-iw*	Amun		British Museum 10473 and 10471	Seti I	KRI I, 321, esp. 321.14-.15
823	*Mʿyʿ*	Isis	Saqqara	Berlin 7274	Seti I	KRI I, 309-319, esp. 311.3
824	*Sḫmt*	Amun		Louvre C.92	Seti I	KRI I, 307-308, esp. 307.15
825	*Rnnwt*	Amun		Louvre C.92	Seti I	KRI I, 307-308, esp. 308.5
826	*Ḫnt-iwnw*	Amun		Louvre C.92	Seti I	KRI I, 307-308, esp. 308.9
827	*Mwt-nfrt*	Amun			Amenhotep III?	Urk. IV, 1930.5
828	*Ṯwyw*	Amun			Amenhotep III-IV	Urk. IV, 1895
829	*Nfrt-iry*	Amun			late Dyn. 18	Urk. IV, 2077.18
830	*Mryt.f*	Thoth			Amenhotep II	Urk. IV, 1454.11 [443]
831	*B3k*	Amun	TT85	Thebes	Tuthmosis III-Amenhotep II	Urk. IV, 920.3; Whale, 1989, case 49
832	*Ḥr-pry*	Amun	TT296	Thebes	Rameses II	KRI VII, 145-153; Feucht, 1985, text 88, pl. XXVI
833	*Ḥwy-n-r*	Amun?	TT296	Thebes	Rameses II	KRI VII, 145-153; Feucht, 1985, text 87-88, pl. XXVI
834	*Nwb-mt*	Amun	Abydos		Rameses II	KRI III, 36-46, esp. 37.6
835	*B3kt-wr-n-r*	Amun	TT156	Thebes	Rameses II	KRI III, 113-115, esp. 114.8
836	*Mʿi3*	Amun	TT156	Thebes	Rameses II	KRI III, 113-115, esp. 114.6

CHART 7: Reference list

837	*T3-nḏmt*	Amun	Aniba	University Museum, Philadelphia, E.14232	Rameses II	KRI III, 118.6,.8
838	*Bꜥkti*	*Mn-ḫpr-Rꜥ* (no cartouche)		Louvre (no. number)	Rameses II	KRI III, 120 esp 120.16
839	*Nb-m-wsḫt*		Aniba		Rameses II	KRI III, 124-126, esp. 124.15
840	*Mrwt-t3-dy*	Amun	Buhen or Aniba?	BM 476	Rameses II	KRI III, 126-129, esp. 127.14
841	*Ḥnwt-n-m3ꜥt*	Amun	Buhen or Aniba?	BM 476	Rameses II	KRI III, 126-129, esp. 127.14-.15
842	*Ḥnwt-bw-tm-mt.s*	Amun	Buhen or Aniba?	BM 476	Rameses II	KRI III, 126-129, esp. 127.15
843	*Ḥ3t-špst*	Amun	Buhen or Aniba?	BM 476	Rameses II	KRI III, 126-129, esp. 127.15-.16
844	*Ꞽi-m-wnwt*	Amun	Buhen or Aniba?	BM 476	Rameses II	KRI III, 126-129, esp. 128.2
845	*Ḥwt-ḥr*	Amun	Buhen or Aniba?	BM 476	Rameses II	KRI III, 126-129, esp. 128.3
846	*T3-bs*		Abu Simbel?	Cairo, Temp. no. 25/8/15/1	Rameses II	KRI III, 130-131, esp. 131.4
847	*T3-n*[...]		Buhen (Wadi Halfa)	BM 1188	Rameses II	KRI III, 132-135, esp. 133.6-.7
848	*Mryt-nbw*		Buhen (Wadi Halfa)	BM 1188	Rameses II	KRI III, 132-135, esp. 133.6-.7
849	*?ḥ-di.s*		Buhen (Wadi Halfa)	BM 1188	Rameses II	KRI III, 132-135, esp. 133.6, 135.1
850	*Mry(t)*	Amun	TT184	Thebes	Rameses II	KRI III, 162-163, esp. 162.10-.11
851	*Ꞽni-hty*	Hathor, lady of the sycomore	Saqqara		Rameses II	KRI III, 171-180, esp. 180.15
852	*Bꜥkt-Mwt*	Amun	TT183	Thebes	Rameses II	KRI III, 182-185, esp. 183.4-.5 and VII, 114
853	*Twi3*	Amun	TT183	Thebes	Rameses II	KRI III, 182-185, esp. 183.4 and VII, 114
854	*3st*	Nebet-ww	TT183	Thebes	Rameses II	KRI III, 182-185, esp. 184.2 and VII, 114
855	*Ty*	Amun	Saqqara	Cairo, JdE 43276A	Rameses II	KRI III, 187-191, esp. 188.10-.11
856	*Twy*	Hathor, lady of the southern sycomore		Brussels E.5183	Rameses II	KRI III, 198-199, esp. 198.15-.16

CHART 7: Reference list

857	*Twy*	Hathor, lady of the (southern) sycomore	Qurnah		Rameses II	KRI III, 202, esp. 202.13-.14
858	*Nht-m-wiꜣ*	Hathor	Abydos	Cairo, CG34517	Rameses II	KRI III, 220-221
859	*Mwt-twy*	Hathor	Abydos	Cairo, CG34517	Rameses II	KRI III, 220-221
860	*Ty-ty*	Amun	Abydos	Cairo, CG34517	Rameses II	KRI III, 220-221
861	*Tꜣ-kmꜥy*	Amun	Abydos	Cairo, CG34517	Rameses II	KRI III, 220-221
862	*Sbꜣt(wnt)-nfr*	Amun	Abydos	Cairo, CG34517	Rameses II	KRI III, 220-221
863	*Tiꜣ*	Amun	Abydos	Cairo, CG34517	Rameses II	KRI III, 220-221
864	*Bꜣkt*	Amun	Abydos	Cairo, CG34517	Rameses II	KRI III, 220-221
865	*Tꜣ-nḏm(t)*	Amun	Abydos	Cairo, CG34517	Rameses II	KRI III, 220-221
866	*Ỉ-y*	Amun	Abydos	Cairo, CG34517	Rameses II	KRI III, 220-221
867	*Twiꜣ*	Amun	Abydos	Cairo, CG34517	Rameses II	KRI III, 220-221
868	*Nꜣty*	Amun	Abydos	Cairo, CG34517	Rameses II	KRI III, 220-221
869	*Ntibpꜣrtiꜣ?*	Amun	Abydos		Rameses II	KRI III, 246, esp. .10
870	*Tꜣ-wsrt*	Amun	Abydos		Rameses II	KRI III, 246, esp. 246.12
871	*Ḥnwt-mḥyt*	Amun		Naples Museum, 1069	Rameses II	KRI III 272-274, esp. 274.2
872	*Wiꜣy*	Amun		Naples Museum, 1069	Rameses II	KRI III 272-274, esp. 274.3
873	*Nfrt-iry*	Amun		Naples Museum, 1069	Rameses II	KRI III 272-274, esp. 274.4
874	*Tꜣ-kꜣ-ꜥnti*	Pre		Cairo, temp. no. 14-10-69-1	Rameses II	KRI III, 280-281, esp. 281.2
875	*Mry-nbw*	Amun of Karnak	TT168	Thebes	Rameses II	KRI III, 300, esp. 300.15
876	*Wiꜣy*	Amun	TT111	Thebes	Rameses II	KRI III, 302-307, esp. 304.2
877	*Ỉwy*	Bastet, lady of Ankh-tawy	TT111	Thebes, Louvre C.210	Rameses II	KRI III, 302-307, esp. 304.5-.6, 307.4
878	*Bꜣkt-wr-n-r*	Amun	TT111?	Tübingen	Rameses II	KRI III, 305-306, esp. 305.15-.16
879	*Ḥnwt*	Amun Re	TT111	Thebes	Rameses II	KRI III, 302-307, esp. 304.16
880	*Ỉny*	Amun, Mut, Khonsu	TT41	Thebes	Rameses II	KRI III, 308-316, esp. 309.2-.3; Assmann, 1991b
881	*Nḏmt*	Amun	TT41	Thebes	Rameses II	KRI III, 308-316, esp. 309.3-.4; Assmann, 1991b
882	*Mꜥy?*	Amun	TT41	Thebes	Rameses II	KRI III, 308-316, esp. 314.5; Assmann, 1991b
883	*Wr-nw-r-iꜣ*	Amun		Copenhagen, B.5 (A.A. a22)	Rameses II	KRI III, 370.5
884	*?*		el Mashayikh	Cairo , CG 1141	Rameses II	KRI III, 463-464, esp. 463.11; Borchardt, 1911-1936, pt. 4, 78-79
885	*Bꜣk(t)-ꜣst*	Amun	Gadra (s. of Abydos)	Cairo, JdE 29332 [temp. no. 21/3/25/11]	Rameses II	KRI III, 467, esp. 467.14-.15

CHART 7: Reference list

886	*Twy*	Amun	TT360	Thebes (also BM 144, 191)	Rameses II	KRI III, 598-609, esp. 602.5
887	*T3-nḏmt*	Amun	Deir el Bahari	Deir el Bahari, Tuthmosis III temple	Rameses III	KRI V, 417-418
888	*Rny*	Mut	Sehel	Sehel	Rameses III	KRI V, 420-421, esp. 421.1-.2
889	*Špst-nfrt-rnpt*	(Hathor) lady of the sycomore	Deir el Bahari	Deir el Bahari	Rameses III	KRI V, 423-424, esp. 423.10-.11
890	*3st-nfrt*	(Hathor) lady of the sycomore	Qantir	Cairo?	Rameses III	KRI V, 426-427, esp. 426.8
891	*T3-k3rt (ḫʿ-Bʿstt)*	Amun		Vienna, 63	Rameses III	KRI V, 432-433, esp. 433.2
892	*ʿnḫ-i3-iw-nbw*	Amun		Vienna, 63	Rameses III	KRI V, 432-433, esp. 433.4
893	*W3ḏyt-m-ḥb*	Amun		Vienna, 63	Rameses III	KRI V, 432-433, esp. 433.7
894	*Mwt-m-mnw*	Amun		Vienna, 63	Rameses III	KRI V, 432-433, esp. 433.7-.8
895	*Bʿk(t)-Swtḫ*	Amun	Deir el Medina	Turin, N.57150 (Sp. 6628)	Rameses III	KRI V, 471, esp. 471.7
896	*3st-nfrt*	Amun		Leicester City Museum, No. 2	Merenptah	KRI IV, 98-99
897	*T3-miw*	Amun		Leicester City Museum, No. 2	Merenptah	KRI IV, 98-99
898	*T3-ḳ3i*	Amun		Leicester City Museum, No. 2	Merenptah	KRI IV, 98-99
899	*ʿ-n-wd3-mwt*	Amun		Leicester City Museum, No. 2	Merenptah	KRI IV, 98-99
900	*Kʿi3y*	Amun		Leicester City Museum, No. 2	Merenptah	KRI IV, 98-99
901	*Ìwn-nw-n3*	Amun		Leicester City Museum, No. 2	Merenptah	KRI IV, 98-99
902	*3st-nfrt*	Amun	Abydos	Cairo, temp. no. 12-6-24-17	Merenptah	KRI IV, 103, esp. 103.7
903	*ʿwrti*	Amun	Abydos	Cairo, temp. no. 12-6-24-17	Merenptah	KRI IV, 103, esp. 103.8
904	*R3-ḳ3-š3*	Amun	Abydos	Cairo, temp. no. 12-6-24-17	Merenptah	KRI IV, 103, esp. 103.9-.10
905	*3st*	Amun		Musée de Vienne (Isère), NE. 1555	Merenptah	KRI IV, 104-106, esp. 105.16
906	*Ìwy*	Amun	TT23	Thebes	Merenptah	KRI IV, 107-119, esp. 116.13
907	*Ḥwt-ḥr*			Vienna, 140	Merenptah	KRI IV, 121-122, esp. 122.9
908	*Nfrt-iry*	Amun of Karnak		Paris, Louvre, A.68	Merenptah	KRI IV, 136-137, esp. 136.11, 137.4-.5
909	*T3-miw*	Amun		Cambridge, Fitzwilliam Museum E.195.1899	Merenptah	KRI IV, 138, esp. 138.9-.10

CHART 7: Reference list

910	*T3-wrt-hrṯ*	Amun Re	Aniba, tomb SA.7	Aniba	Merenptah	KRI IV, 282-285, esp. 284.2
911	*Nsy-Mwt*	Amun	Aniba, tomb SA.7	Aniba	Merenptah	KRI IV, 282-285, esp. 284.3-.4
912	*3st-nfrt*	Amun?	Surarieh, chapel of Merneptah	Surarieh	Merenptah	KRI IV, 289-292, esp. 289.15
913	*3st-t3...*	Amun	Surarieh, chapel of Merneptah	Surarieh	Merenptah	KRI IV, 289-292, esp. 289.15-.16
914	*T3-[...]-p3-3st*	Amun	Surarieh, chapel of Merneptah	Surarieh	Merenptah	KRI IV, 289-292, esp. 289.16
915	*K3t*	(Hathor) lady of the southern sycomore	Memphis	Collection Michaelides	Merenptah	KRI IV, 292-293, esp 292.13
916	*Nfrt-Mwt*	Amun	Gurob	Petrie collection or Cairo?	Merenptah	KRI IV, 339, esp. 339.15-.16
917	*3st-[...]*	Isis	Abydos	Cairo?	Merenptah	KRI IV, 377-378, esp. 378.3
918	*Ἰr...*		Memphis, tomb	Cairo?; Anthes field number 9	Merenptah	KRI IV, 379-381, esp. 380.7
919	*Tiy*	Amun	TT106	Thebes	Seti I	KRI I, 285-301, esp. 296.4-.5, 298.2-.3
920	*N3i3*	Amun	TT106	Thebes	Seti I	KRI I, 285-301 [VII, 15-18, 107-108]
921	*P3[...]t3ʿg3yt?*	Amun	Deir el Bahari	Deir el Bahari	Rameses VI	KRI VI, 361.15
922	*T3-diw-Mwt*	Amun Re		Cairo, JdE 35410	Rameses XI	KRI VI, 850.2
923	*T3-wsr(t)*	Amun	Abydos	Berlin 2081	Rameses VIII	KRI VI, 439-441, esp. 440.6
924	*Ḥwy-n-r*	Amun	Abydos	Berlin 2081	Rameses VIII	KRI VI, 439-441, esp. 440.6
925	*Nbw-ḫʿti*	Amun	Abydos	Berlin 2081	Rameses VIII	KRI VI, 439-441, esp. 440.9
926	*Wi3y*	Amun	TT178	Thebes	Rameses II	KRI III, 321-331, esp. 321.10; Hofmann, 1995
927	*Tnt-iwnt*	Montu	TT31	Thebes	Rameses II	KRI III, 399-410, esp. 406.13; Davies and Gardiner, 1948, pl. XV
928	*Ty*	Amun Re	Saqqara, tomb of Mose	Saqqara	Rameses II	KRI III, 418-435, esp. 421.5
929	*Mwt-nfrt*	Bastet, lady of Ankh-tawy	Saqqara, tomb of Mose	Saqqara	Rameses II	KRI III, 418-435, esp. 420.9-.10

CHART 8: Alphabetical cross reference list

REF #	NAME
711	*ꜣḫ-Mwt*
117	*ꜣḫ-Mwt-ꜥwy*
808	*ꜣḫ.s?*
458	*ꜣst*
447	*ꜣst*
54	*ꜣst*
44	*ꜣst*
64	*ꜣst*
431	*ꜣst*
713	*ꜣst*
854	*ꜣst*
738	*ꜣst*
693	*ꜣst*
703	*ꜣst*
712	*ꜣst*
905	*ꜣst*
87	*ꜣst*
544	*ꜣst*
727	*ꜣst*
46	*ꜣst*
153	*ꜣst*
185	*ꜣst*
379	*ꜣst*
451	*ꜣst*
917	*ꜣst-*[...]
412	*ꜣsty*
132	*ꜣsty*
334	*ꜣsty*
293	*ꜣsty*
450	*ꜣsty*
147	*ꜣst-m-ꜣḫ-bit*
151	*ꜣst-m-ꜣḫ-bit*
349	*ꜣst-m-ꜣḫ-bit*
350	*ꜣst-m-ꜣḫ-bit*
139	*ꜣst-m-ꜣḫ-bit*
364	*ꜣst-m-ꜣḫ-bit*
449	*ꜣst-m-ꜣḫ-bit*
368	*ꜣst-(m)-ꜣḫ-bit*
307	*ꜣst-m-ꜣḫt?*
408	*ꜣst-m-bit*
423	*ꜣst-m-ḥb*
426	*ꜣst-nfr(t)*
530	*ꜣst-nfrt*
715	*ꜣst-nfrt*
710	*ꜣst-nfrt*
902	*ꜣst-nfrt*
912	*ꜣst-nfrt*
896	*ꜣst-nfrt*
890	*ꜣst-nfrt*
913	*ꜣst-tꜣ...*
118	*Ꞽ...*
538	*Ꞽ?ꜣ*
688	*Ꞽꜣi*
445	*Ꞽꜣy*
672	*Ꞽi-y*
844	*Ꞽi-m-wnwt*
254	*Ꞽyꜣ*
527	*Ꞽ-y*
866	*Ꞽ-y*
716	*Ꞽy*
52	*Ꞽy-nfr.ti*
459	*Ꞽwy*
515	*Ꞽw-ns-nb-tꜣwy*
649	*Ꞽwy*
661	*Ꞽwy*
582	*Ꞽwy*
877	*Ꞽwy*
674	*Ꞽwy*
906	*Ꞽwy*
40	*Ꞽwy*
637	*Ꞽwy*
19	*Ꞽwyꜣ*
163	*Ꞽw.f-n-Ꞽmn ṯnt-wr-ḥkꜣt*
901	*Ꞽwn-nw-nꜣ*
21	*Ꞽwnw-ry*
111	*Ꞽw.s-ꜥnḫ*
796	*Ꞽw.s-m-ḥswt-Mwt*
472	*Ꞽpꜣy*
575	*Ꞽ-pw-y*
48	*Ꞽpt-nfrt*
268	*Ꞽmn-m-ipt*
622	*Ꞽmn-sꜥh*
754	*Ꞽmn-sꜥh*
31	*Ꞽniw-hꜣy*
89	*Ꞽni-hꜣy*
411	*Ꞽn-iw-hꜣḏꜣ?*
851	*Ꞽni-hty*
880	*Ꞽny*
454	*Ꞽn-hꜣy*
460	*Ꞽn-hꜣy*
441	*Ꞽnhy*
373	*Ꞽnhꜣy*
918	*Ꞽr...*
509	*Ꞽryt-nfrt*
513	*Ꞽry-tḫ*
448	*Ꞽr-mwt-pꜣ-nfr*
707	*Ꞽr-nfrw-Mwt*

123	*Ỉḫy*
229	*Ỉḫy*
197	*Ỉḫy (ꜣst-m-ꜣḫbit)*
66	*Ỉsꜣy (Ḥnꜣy)*
503	*Ỉsw-mwt*
687	*Ỉsriḫ*
559	*Ỉ-tꜣwy*
121	*Ỉ-tꜣ-Mwt*
287	*Ỉṯwy*
27	*Yy*
604	*ꜥꜣti*
531	*ꜥwrti*
903	*ꜥwrti*
607	*ꜥ-n-wḏꜣ*
899	*ꜥ-n-wdꜣ-mwt*
729	*ꜥ-n-wḏꜣ-mst*
420	*ꜥ-n-Mwt*
613	*ꜥn-m-mr*
892	*ꜥnḫ-iꜣ-iw-nbw*
452	*ꜥnḫy-n-ꜣst*
369	*ꜥnḫ-s*
572	*ꜥnḫ-s-ꜣst*
202	*ꜥnḫ.s-Mwt*
144	*ꜥnḫ.s-n-ꜣst*
386	*ꜥnḫ-s-n-ꜣst*
323	*ꜥnḫ.s-n-Mwt*
165	*ꜥnḫ.s-n-Mwt*
71	*ꜥn-tꜣ-ḫytw*
58	*ꜥšꜣt-nbw*
475	*Wꜣy-kꜣ*
893	*Wꜣḏyt-m-ḥb*
691	*Wꜣḏ-hꜣw*
533	*Wꜣḏt-rnpt*
876	*Wiꜣy*
926	*Wiꜣy*
603	*Wiꜣy*
872	*Wiꜣy*
641	*Wiꜣy(?)*
790	*Wiꜣy*
655	*Wꜥbt*
744	*Wꜥbt*
414	*Wb-ḫt*
735	*Wbḫt*
781	*Wnp*
883	*Wr-nw-r-iꜣ*
709	*Wr-[nfr]*
60	*Wrt-nfrt*
812	*Wrt-nfrt*
659	*Wrt-nfrt*
771	*Wr-n-r*
26	*Wr-n-r*
614	*Wr-n-r*
600	*Wr-nrw*
500	*Wrt...*
760	*Wrty*
85	*Wrt-wꜣḥ-sw*
537	*Wty-rnw?*
388	*Bꜣw-Mwt-r-nḫtyw*
831	*Bꜣk*
525	*Bꜣk-Ỉmn*
792	*Bꜣky*
98	*Bꜣk-wrn*
38	*Bꜣk-wrnr*
477	*Bꜣk-wrt?*
615	*Bꜣk-mwt*
93	*Bꜣk-n-Ỉmn*
456	*Bꜣk-n-wrl*
261	*Bꜣkt*
864	*Bꜣkt*
455	*Bꜣkt-ꜣst*
476	*Bꜣkt-ꜣst*
885	*Bꜣk(t)-ꜣst*
838	*Bꜣkti*
61	*Bꜣktiꜣ*
20	*Bꜣk(t)-Ỉmn*
57	*Bꜣk(t)-ꜥnḫt*
878	*Bꜣkt-wr-n-r*
835	*Bꜣkt-wr-n-r*
725	*Bꜣkt-Mwt*
852	*Bꜣkt-Mwt*
704	*Bꜣk(t)-Ḫnsw*
895	*Bꜣk(t)-Swtḫ*
751	*Bꜣkt-Sḫmt*
493	*Bꜣtꜣ*
696	*Biꜣ*
775	*Biꜣt*
676	*Bwy*
335	*Bw-irw-ḥꜥr-Mwt?*
565	*Bw-wyꜣ?*
169	*Bwt-[irw]-ḥꜥr-Ḫnsw*
359	*Pꜣ-šb-wbḫt-n-Mwt*
467	*Pꜣ-ṯꜣw*
921	*Pꜣ[...]tꜣꜥgꜣyt?*
24	*Pi*
619	*Pikꜥ?*
461	*Py-pwy*
772	*Pwy*
425	*Pwyꜣ*
249	*Pwyw*
35	*P[wr]y*

29	*Pp*
22	*Ppy*
556	*Pr?*
16	*Pry*
18	*Pry*
551	*Pr-ms-m-?*
271	*Mꜣꜥt-nfrt*
750	*Mꜣꜥt-nfrt*
298	*Mꜣꜥt-kꜣ-Rꜥ*
415	*Mꜣt?*
339	*Miꜣꜥ-nḥm*
137	*My-šm-rdwy-sḳtb?*
798	*Mꜥiꜣ*
714	*Mꜥiꜣ*
836	*Mꜥiꜣ*
639	*Mꜥiꜣy*
251	*Mꜥiꜣny*
462	*Mꜥy*
701	*Mꜥy*
882	*Mꜥy?*
823	*Mꜥyꜥ*
492	*Mꜥnwnꜣ*
718	*Mꜥkwi*
664	*Mwt?*
586	*Mwtiꜥy* (*Mꜥy*)
347	*Mwt-ip*
162	*Mwt-ipt*
283	*Mwt-iry*
243	*Mwt-ir.t-di.s*
640	*Mwt-ir-di.s*
695	*Mwty*
677	*Mwty*
519	*Mwty*
535	*Mwt-wnš*
730	*Mwt-m-ipt*
668	*Mwt-m-int*
589	*Mwt-m-wiꜣ*
55	*Mwt-m-wiꜣ*
419	*Mwt-m-wiꜣ*
814	*Mwt-m-wiꜣ*
670	*Mwt-m-wiꜣ*
92	*Mwt-m-wiꜣ*
69	*Mwt-m-wiꜣ*
728	*Mwt-m-wiꜣ*
294	*Mwt-m-wiꜣ*
465	*Mwt-m-wiꜣ*
894	*Mwt-m-mnw*
789	*Mwt-m-mr.s*
517	*Mwt-mnw*
398	*Mwt-m-(ḫꜥy?)-mw.s*
187	*Mwt-n-ipt*
223	*Mwt-n-pr-Ỉmn*
685	*Mwt-nfrt*
774	*Mwt-nfrt*
272	*Mwt-nfrt*
269	*Mwt-nfrt*
480	*Mwt-nfrt*
279	*Mwt-nfrt*
827	*Mwt-nfrt*
697	*Mwt-nfrt*
692	*Mwt-nfrt*
616	*Mwt-nfrt*
608	*Mwt-nfrt*
929	*Mwt-nfrt*
13	*Mwt-nfrt*
30	*Mwt-nfrt*
719	*Mwt-nfrt*
722	*Mwt-nfrt*
526	*Mwt-nḏm*
403	*Mwt-rwḏ*
193	*Mwt-ḥtp*
361	*Mwt-ḥtp-ti*
277	*Mwt-twy*
859	*Mwt-twy*
555	*Mr-?*
306	*Mry.f-n-Mwt*
875	*Mry-nbw*
273	*Mryt*
482	*Mryt?*
276	*Mryt*
683	*Mryt*
768	*Mryt*
850	*Mry(t)*
262	*Mryt-Ỉmn*
304	*Mryt-Ỉmn*
491	*Mryt-Ptḥ*
80	*Mryt-Ptḥ*
830	*Mryt.f*
848	*Mryt-nbw*
795	*Mryt-Rꜥ*
648	*Mryt-Rꜥ*
25	*Mrt-Rꜥ*
217	*Mrw-ꜥḥ*
840	*Mrwt-tꜣ-dy*
577	*Mrwt-ti*
291	*Mḥd-Mwt*
358	*Mḥ-Mwt-ḥꜥt*
779	*Mḥyt-ḫꜥṯ*
720	*Mḥyt-ḫꜥṯ*
497	*Ms*

400	*Mšꜥ-Sbḳ*
920	*Nꜣiꜣ*
384	*Nꜣw-ny*
569	*Nꜣ-mnḫ-ꜣst*
428	*Nꜣ-nfr; Rn-nfr*
6	*Nꜣšꜣ*
463	*Nꜣ-šꜣ-ꜥꜣ*
724	*Nꜣw-šꜣꜥt*
521	*Nꜣ-ty*
868	*Nꜣṯy*
529	*Nꜣ-ṯyi*
732	*Niwt-m-ḥb*
481	*Nyt*
834	*Nwb-mt*
646	*Nwbt-nṯr-nfr*
471	*Nb-...*
809	*Nbw-ii*
654	*Nbw-iiy*
437	*Nbw-ḥsbdw*
925	*Nbw-ḫꜥti*
248	*Nbwt-m-wsḫt*
839	*Nb-m-wsḫt*
753	*Nb[-ḫni?]-tw*
63	*Nbt-wnw*
675	*Nbt-tꜣwy*
23	*Nbt-tꜣwy*
627	*Nbt-tꜣwy*
105	*Nb(t)-tꜣwy*
801	*Nfr...*
780	*Nfr-ꜣst*
665	*Nfr-Mwt*
42	*Nfrt-iiṯ*
417	*Nfr(t)-iy*
003	*Nfrt-iry*
829	*Nfrt-iry*
770	*Nfrt-iry*
816	*Nfrt-iry*
520	*Nfrt-iry*
421	*Nfrt-iry*
77	*Nfrt-iry*
736	*Nfrt-iry*
507	*Nfrt-iry*
33	*Nfrt-iry*
873	*Nfrt-iry*
908	*Nfrt-iry*
65	*Nfrt-iry*
86	*Nfrt-iry*
636	*Nfrt-iry*
746	*Nfrt-iry*
634	*Nfrt-iry*
740	*Nfrt-iry*
237	*Nfrt-iry*
749	*Nfrt-iry-m-ḥb*
578	*Nfrt-Mwt*
916	*Nfrt-Mwt*
698	*Nfrt-ḫꜥ*
752	*Nhty*
518	*Nht-m-wiꜣ*
858	*Nht-m-wiꜣ*
706	*Nḫt-Mwt*
188	*Nsy...*
216	*Nsy-prw-nbw*
911	*Nsy-Mwt*
175	*Nsy-Mwt*
338	*Nsy-Mwt*
164	*Nsy-Mwt*
194	*Nsy-Mwt*
219	*Nsy-Ḫnsw*
130	*Nsy-Ḫnsw*
157	*Nsy-Ḫnsw*
160	*Nsy-Ḫnsw*
161	*Nsy-Ḫnsw*
346	*Nsy-Ḫnsw*
371	*Nsy-Ḫnsw*
156	*Nsy-Ḫnsw*
189	*Nsy-Ḫnsw*
227	*Nsy-Ḫnsw*
133	*Nsy-tꜣ-nb-tꜥwy*
179	*Nsy-tꜣ-nb-tꜣwy*
391	*Nsy-Ḫnsw-pꜣ-ẖrd*
344	*Nsy-Ḫnsw-pꜣ-ẖrd*
397	*Nsy-Ḫnsw-pꜣ-ẖrd*
788	*Nsy-tꜣ-nb-išrw*
474	*Nsy-tꜣ-nbt-išrw*
336	*Nsy-(tꜣ)-nb(t)-išrw*
392	*Nsy-tꜣ-nbt-išrw*
181	*(Nsy)tꜣ-nbt-išrw*
381	*Nsyt-ꜣst*
142	*Nsy-tꜣ-nbt-tꜣwy*
329	*Nsy-tꜣ-nbt-tꜣwy*
146	*Nsyt-tꜣ-nbt-tꜣwy*
596	*Nsw-m-ḥꜣb*
794	*Ns-w-m-sbꜣ?*
131	*Ns-Mwt*
356	*Ns-Mwt*
605	*Ns-nb*
378	*Ns-Ḫnsw*
340	*Ns-Ḫnsw*
109	*Ns-Ḫnsw*
244	*Ns-Ḫnsw-pꜣ-ẖrd*

442	*Ns-Ḫnsw-pꜣ-ẖrd*
401	*Ns-sw-ꜣst*
208	*Ns-tꜣ-wḏꜣt-ꜣẖ*
125	*Ns-tꜣ-nṯr*
560	*Nst-Ỉmn*
405	*Nsṯ-Ỉmn* (*Ns-tꜣ-nbt-išrw*)
343	*Nsty-Ḫnsw-tp*
74	*Ns-ṯr-n-mꜣꜥt*
50	*Nšꜥ*
869	*Ntibpꜣrtiꜣ?*
543	*Nṯm-ꜣst*
663	*Nḏm-Mwt*
737	*Nḏm-Mwt*
881	*Nḏmt*
642	*Nḏmt-niwt*
278	*Rꜣy*
904	*Rꜣ-ḳꜣ-šꜣ*
610	*Ry*
767	*Ryꜥ*
573	*Rꜥ*
743	*Rꜥiꜣ*
626	*RꜥỈꜣ*
804	*Rꜥiꜣy*
602	*Rwiꜣ*
196	*Rw-rw?*
532	*Rwḳꜣšꜣ*
263	*Rnꜣy*
888	*Rny*
288	*Rnwtt*
584	*Rnwtt*
285	*Rn-nꜣy*
825	*Rnnwt*
783	*Rnnwtt*
444	*Rnnwtt*
765	*Hꜣny*
843	*Ḥꜣt-špst*
174	*Ḥꜣt-špswt*
623	*Ḥꜣt-špswt*
717	*Ḥꜣt-šps(t)*
446	*Ḥꜣt-šryt*
763	*Ḥwy-n-r*
657	*Ḥwy-n-r* (*Ḥwt-ḥr*)
833	*Ḥwy-n-r*
721	*Ḥwy-n-r*
924	*Ḥwy-n-r*
15	*Ḥwnry*
534	*Ḥwt-ḥr*
587	*Ḥwt-ḥr*
76	*Ḥwt-ḥr*
845	*Ḥwt-ḥr*
422	*Ḥwt-ḥr*
504	*Ḥwt-ḥr*
907	*Ḥwt-ḥr*
689	*Ḥwt-ḥr*
104	*Ḥwt-ḥr*
815	*Ḥwt-ḥr*
103	*Ḥpt-disw*
817	*Ḥmt-nṯr*
567	*Ḥnwt*
879	*Ḥnwt*
628	*Ḥnwt*
39	*Ḥnwt-Ỉwnw*
723	*Ḥnwt-wꜣḏbt*
487	*Ḥnwt-wrt*
443	*Ḥnwt-wḏbw*
842	*Ḥnwt-bw-tm-mt.s*
195	*Ḥnwt-mḥyt*
871	*Ḥnwt-mḥyt*
438	*Ḥnwt-mḥyt*
236	*Ḥnwt-mr*
643	*Ḥnwt-mtr*
653	*Ḥnwt-mtr*
113	*Ḥnwt-nfr*
601	*Ḥnwt-nfrt*
259	*ḥnwt-nfrt*
841	*Ḥnwt-n-mꜣꜥt*
215	*Ḥnwt-nẖt*
385	*Ḥnwt-nṯrw*
96	*Ḥnwt-tꜣ-nb*
172	*Ḥnwt-tꜣ-?-nb*
49	*Ḥnwt-ḏww*
266	*Ḥnwt-tꜣwy*
267	*Ḥnwt-tꜣwy*
286	*Ḥnwt-tꜣwy*
280	*Ḥnwt-tꜣwy*
756	*Ḥnwt-tꜣwy*
708	*Ḥnwt-tꜣwy*
548	*Ḥnwt-tꜣwy*
631	*Ḥnwt-tꜣwy*
173	*Ḥnwt-tꜣwy*
183	*Ḥnwt-tꜣwy*
310	*Ḥnwt-tꜣwy*
327	*Ḥnwt-tꜣwy*
152	*Ḥnwt-tꜣwy*
205	*Ḥnwt-tꜣwy*
120	*Ḥnwt-tꜣwy*
200	*Ḥnwt-tꜣwy*
399	*Ḥnwt-tꜣwy*
380	*Ḥnwt-tꜣwy*
190	*Ḥnwt-tꜣwy*

258	*Ḥnwt-tꜣwy*
826	*Ḥnt-iwnw*
90	*Ḥnr*
579	*Ḥr-iy*
62	*Ḥry*
150	*Ḥryw-wbn*
199	*Ḥryt-wbḫt*
177	*Ḥryt-Mwt-iꜥḥ-ms*
832	*Ḥr-pry*
630	*(Ḥ?)ḳrt*
136	*Ḫꜣꜥ.s*
650	*Ḫꜥyt*
88	*Ḫꜥt-bꜣḥt*
758	*Ḫꜥt-nsw*
652	*Ḫbwy-nw-ns*
214	*Ḫnmm-Ḫnsw*
209	*Ḫnmm-Ḫnsw-pꜣ-ẖrd*
228	*Ḫnmm-Ḫnsw-pꜣ-ẖrd*
333	*Sꜣ-Ḫnsw*
595	*Sꜣ-kt*
690	*Sꜣt-Ỉmn*
799	*Sꜣt-Ỉmn*
673	*Sꜣt-Rꜥ*
581	*Sꜣt-tp-iḥw*
862	*Sbꜣt(wnt)-nfr*
457	*Sbḳ-ḥnt*
498	*Sḫꜣ-nfr*
598	*Sḫm-nfr*
686	*Sḫmt*
824	*Sḫmt*
102	*Sḫmt*
788	*Sḫmt*
635	*Sḫmt*
400	*Sḫmt-m-ḥb*
612	*Sḫmt-nfrt*
580	*Snw-ꜥnḫ*
260	*Sn-snb*
284	*Sn-snb*
597	*Styky*
14	*St-Mnty*
72	*Š...*
542	*Šbwti-wsri*
390	*Šb-n-ꜣst (špt-n-ꜣst)*
145	*Šbty*
239	*Šbty*
889	*Špst-nfrt-rnpt*
366	*Špst-ns-Mwt-ꜥnḫ-ti*
550	*Šfꜣy?*
593	*Šri-Rꜥ*
12	*Šri(t)-Rꜥ*
656	*Šrit-Rꜥ*
562	*Šrit-Rꜥ*
629	*Šri(t)-Rꜥ*
574	*Ššn*
182	*Šd-sw-tꜣ-ipt*
469	*Šd(t)-sy-Mwt*
609	*Ḳꜣ-(ḳꜣ)*
148	*Ḳꜣb-st-nbw?*
37	*Ḳꜣ-nḥbt*
776	*Kꜣiꜣ*
594	*Kꜣiꜣ*
900	*Kꜣiꜣy*
308	*Kꜣꜥ-sw-n-Ḫnsw*
245	*Kꜣfy*
297	*Kꜣ-r-nḫt.s-n-Ḫnsw*
739	*Kꜣḥ*
915	*Kꜣt*
186	*Kꜣt-bt*
435	*Kiy*
742	*Kmnꜥ*
699	*Knr*
571	*Kt-ḥr?*
178	*Gꜣwt-sšn*
382	*Gꜣwt-sšn*
453	*Gꜣwt-sšnw*
319	*Gꜣt-sšn*
406	*Gꜣt-sšny*
436	*Tꜣ-...*
606	*Tꜣ...*
553	*Tꜣ-?*
362	*Tꜣ...*
427	*Tꜣ-ibḥt-Rꜥ*
662	*Tꜣ-Ỉmn*
820	*Tꜣ-isrḫ?*
238	*Tꜣ-ist-it-Mwt-tꜣ-wr*
748	*Tꜣ-iwnw*
784	*Tꜣ-imnt-snb*
811	*Tꜣy*
73	*Tꜣy-iw-šri*
100	*Tꜣy-ꜥḳy*
233	*Tꜣyw-ꜣḫ-ṯ*
793	*Tꜣyw-nḏmt*
154	*Tꜣyw-ḥnwt*
119	*Tꜣyw-ḥnwt*
429	*Tꜣyw-ḥry*
159	*Tꜣyw-ḥry*
226	*Tꜣyw-ḥry*
126	*Tꜣyw-ḥryt*
341	*Tꜣyw-ḥryt*
115	*Tꜣyw-ḥrt*

800	*Tꜣyw.sn*
99	*Tꜣy-bs*
632	*Tꜣy-ḥnwt-pꜣ-mtr*
633	*Tꜣy-nḏmt*
168	*Tꜣy-ḳꜣy*
599	*Tꜣy-sn*
778	*Tꜣy-sn-nfr*
299	*Tꜣ-ꜥꜣ-Ỉmn*
317	*Tꜣ-ꜥꜣ-pr-Ỉmn*
192	*Tꜣ-ꜥḥwty*
7	*Tꜣꜥ-ḫꜥ*
83	*Tꜣ-ꜥnt-ḥr-twy-st?*
547	*Tꜣ-ꜥšt-wšbw*
53	*Tꜣ-ꜥḳꜣy*
47	*Tꜣ-ꜥḳy*
2	*Tꜣwy*
318	*Tꜣw-ḥnwt*
546	*Tꜣ-wr-ḥḳꜣt*
51	*Tꜣ-wrt*
70	*Tꜣ-wr(t)*
583	*Tꜣ-wrt*
101	*Tꜣ-wrt*
17	*Tꜣ-wr(t)-m-ḥb*
416	*Tꜣ-wrt-m-ḥb*
671	*Tꜣ-wr(t)-m-ḥb*
910	*Tꜣ-wrt-hrṯ*
611	*Tꜣ-wrt-ḥtpt*
807	*Tꜣ-wrt-ḥtp-ti*
36	*Tꜣ-wr(t)-ḥtp-ṯ*
773	*Tꜣ-wsr*
624	*Tꜣ-wsrt*
870	*Tꜣ-wsrt*
585	*Tꜣ-wsrt*
923	*Tꜣ-wsr(t)*
45	*Tꜣ-wsr(t)*
122	*Tꜣ-wsrt-m-pr-nsw*
464	*Tꜣ-wḏꜣt*
149	*Tꜣ-wḏꜣt-Rꜥ*
67	*Tꜣ-bꜣ-sꜣ*
747	*Tꜣ-bꜣ-sꜣ*
107	*Tꜣ-bꜣ-st*
563	*Tꜣ-bꜣk-n-ꜣst*
666	*Tꜣ-bꜣk-n-Mwt*
110	*Tꜣ-bꜣk-n-Mwt (Tꜣ-nt-bꜣk-n-Mwt)*
203	*Tꜣ-bꜣkt-Mwt*
220	*Tꜣ-bꜣk(t)-n-Ḫnsw*
221	*Tꜣ-bꜣk(t)-n-Ḫnsw*
396	*Tꜣ-bꜣkt-n-Ḫnsw*
232	*Tꜣ-bꜣkt-Ḫnsw*
68	*Tꜣ-bw-bꜣ*
846	*Tꜣ-bs*
764	*Tꜣ-pr?*
247	*Tꜣ-miꜣt*
625	*Tꜣ-miw*
897	*Tꜣ-miw*
909	*Tꜣ-miw*
821	*Tꜣ-mit*
786	*Tꜣ-mit*
508	*Tꜣ-my(t)*
554	*Tꜣ-Mwt*
222	*Tꜣ-Mwt.f*
549	*Tꜣ-Mwt-nfr*
558	*Tꜣ-Mwt-nfrt*
213	*Tꜣ-Mwt-nfrt*
638	*Tꜣ-Mwt-nfrt*
514	*Tꜣ-mḥyt*
360	*Tꜣ-mni*
404	*Tꜣ-mry*
540	*Tꜣ-mrit*
785	*Tꜣ-mryt*
539	*Tꜣ-mr-pn-ꜥs*
257	*Tꜣ-m-rsfy*
651	*Tꜣ-mrt*
791	*Tꜣ-mt...*
847	*Tꜣ-n[...]*
171	*Tꜣ-nꜣḫt-n-tꜣ-ḥꜣꜥt*
158	*Tꜣ-n-pr-ms*
97	*Tꜣ-nfrt*
81	*Tꜣ-nḥs*
56	*Tꜣ-n-shrry*
234	*Tꜣ-nt-Ḫnsw*
745	*Tꜣ-nḏm-mꜣꜥt-rꜥ*
402	*Tꜣ-nḏm-Mwt*
865	*Tꜣ-nḏm(t)*
837	*Tꜣ-nḏmt*
644	*Tꜣ-nḏmt*
887	*Tꜣ-nḏmt*
43	*Tꜣriꜣ*
678	*Tꜣ-rnwt*
413	*Tꜣ-rnnt*
342	*Tꜣ-r-stit*
231	*Tꜣ-ḥmt-n-Mwt*
409	*Tꜣ-ḥmt-n-Mwt*
270	*Tꜣ-ḫꜥt*
617	*Tꜣ-ḫꜥt*
618	*Tꜣ-ḫꜥt*
769	*Tꜣ-ḫꜥt*
757	*Tꜣ-ḫꜥt*
41	*Tꜣ-ḫꜥ(t)*

230	*Tꜣ-ḫbt*
32	*Tꜣ-sw-ri*
806	*Tꜣ-smnt*
241	*Tꜣ-šbt*
246	*Tꜣ-šryt-n(t)-ꜣst*
235	*Tꜣ-šd-Ḫnsw*
316	*Tꜣ-šd-Ḫnsw*
818	*Tꜣ-ḳꜣ*
898	*Tꜣ-ḳꜣi*
874	*Tꜣ-kꜣ-ʿnti*
82	*Tꜣ-kꜣriꜣ*
762	*Tꜣ-kꜣ-mn-(wḏꜣ?)*
891	*Tꜣ-kꜣrt (ḫʿ-Bꜣstt)*
439	*Tꜣ-ḳꜣ(t); ḥnsw-wp-nfrt*
522	*Tꜣ-kmꜣy*
861	*Tꜣ-kmʿy*
782	*Tꜣ-kt*
568	*Tꜣ-di*
922	*Tꜣ-diw-Mwt*
473	*Tꜣ-dy(.t)-Mwt*
275	*Tꜣ-ddt.s*
914	*Tꜣ-[...]-pꜣ-ꜣst*
684	*[T?]ꜣ-miy*
524	*Tiꜣ*
863	*Tiꜣ*
561	*Tiy*
919	*Tiy*
496	*Tiy*
250	*Tint...*
11	*Tity*
694	*Ty*
591	*Ty*
621	*Ty*
766	*Ty*
797	*Ty*
59	*Ty*
855	*Ty*
928	*Ty*
204	*Ty*
383	*Ty*
94	*Tyiꜣy*
700	*Typwy*
705	*Ty-m-ḥb*
440	*Tyt*
860	*Ty-ty*
528	*Twiꜣ*
867	*Twiꜣ*
853	*Twiꜣ*
886	*Twy*
857	*Twy*
253	*Twy*
856	*Twy*
84	*Twy*
91	*Twy*
777	*Twt-wiꜣ*
805	*Twt-wiꜣ*
374	*Tfrr-wꜣst*
389	*Tfrr-wꜣst*
927	*Tnt-iwnt*
433	*Tnt?-ipt*
734	*(Tnt)-Bdty*
733	*Tnt-pꜣ-ipt*
430	*Tnt-Nbt-ḥwt*
669	*Tnt-...nw*
264	*Tti-m-nṯr*
564	*T?-sꜣ???ṯ*
679	*Ṯꜣy-nb-nḫt-rw*
620	*Ṯꜣpwy?*
281	*Ṯꜣ-ti*
681	*Ṯꜣ-tiy*
813	*Ṯiꜣ*
660	*Ṯy*
822	*Ṯw-iw*
828	*Ṯwyw*
337	*Ṯmḥd-ḫhsw*
170	*Ṯnt...*
9	*Ṯnt-Imn (Tꜣ-nt-Imn)*
377	*Ṯnt-wsrt.s-n-pr-nsw*
545	*Ṯnt-bḥw-ꜣḫ*
726	*Ṯnt-pꜣ-sṯꜣ*
180	*Ṯnt-pn-hrw-nfr (Tꜣ-nt-pꜣ-hrw-nfr)*
354	*Ṯnt-mḥd-Mwt*
210	*Ṯnt-nꜣw-ḥrw*
345	*Ṯnt-Rʿ-ss*
112	*Ṯnt-ry (Tꜣ-nt-ry)*
292	*Ṯnt-ḥm-n-Mwt*
191	*Ṯnt-ḥn-f (Tꜣ-nt-ḥn.f)*
303	*Ṯnt-sꜣ-rk-nꜣ-sti*
351	*Ṯnt-sꜣ-rk-nꜣ-sti?*
352	*Ṯnt-šdy-Ḫnsw*
212	*Ṯnt-šd-Mwt*
395	*Ṯnt-šdt-Mwt*
315	*Ṯnt-diw-Mwt*
810	*Ṯr-(?nḫt)-Mwt?*
116	*Diw-Mwt-(r)-iwdw*
353	*Diw-sw-n-Mwt*
325	*Dyr-pw-(sti?)*
106	*Dwꜣt*
523	*Dwꜣt-nfr*

588	*Dwꜣt-nfrt?*
410	*Dni?-n-Bꜣstt*
75	*Dniw-n-Ḫnsw*
536	*Ḏꜥ-ꜣst*
766	*Ḏd-ꜣst-iw.s-ꜥnḫ*
680	*Ḏd-ꜣst-n-imw*
375	*Ḏd-Ỉmnt-iw-st-ꜥnḫ*
135	*Ḏd-mꜣꜥt-iw.s-ꜥnḫ*
224	*Ḏd-Mwt-iw-ꜥnḫ*
166	*?Ḏd-mwt-iw.s-ꜥnḫ*
201	*Ḏd-Mwt-iw.s-ꜥnḫ*
311	*Ḏd-Mwt-is-s-ꜥnḫ*
314	*Ḏd-Mwt-is-s-ꜥnḫ*
407	*Ḏd-Mwt-iw.s-ꜥnḫ*
418	*Ḏd-Mwt-iw.s-ꜥnḥ*
141	*Ḏd-Mwt-iw.s-ꜥnḫ*
176	*Ḏd-Mwt-iw.s-ꜥnḫ*
289	*Ḏd-mḥyt-is-ꜥnḫ*
787	*Ḏd-Ḥr-iw.s-ꜥnḫ*
355	*Ḏd-Ḫnsw*
290	*Ḏd-Ḫnsw-iw-ꜥnḫ*
370	*Ḏd-Ḫnsw-iw-ꜥnḫ*
320	*Ḏd-Ḫnsw-iw.s-ꜥnḫ*
393	*Ḏd-Ḫnsw-iw.s-ꜥnḫ*
394	*Ḏd-Ḫnsw-iw.s-ꜥnḫ*
184	*Ḏd-Ḫnsw-iw.s-ꜥnḫ*
218	*Ḏd-Ḫnsw-iw.s-ꜥnḫ*
367	*Ḏd-Ḫnsw-iw.s-ꜥnḫ*
348	*Ḏd-Ḫnsw-iw-st-ꜥnḫ*
372	*Ḏd-ṯnt-di-ipt-wrt*
849	*?ḥ-di.s*
590	*...iꜣw*
499	*...tꜣwy*
802	*...ḫbw-šꜥt*
95	*...Mwt*
376	*...Ỉmnt*

N.B. Twenty-eight references where none of the woman's name is preserved have been omitted from this list.

LIST OF ABBREVIATIONS USED

Journal abbreviations follow the standard used in the *Lexikon der Ägyptologie* (LÄ)

BM	British Museum
CAA	*Corpus Antiquitatum Aegyptiacarum*
CAT. MON.	Mariette, A. 1880. *Catalogue général des Monuments d'Abydos découverts pendant les fouilles de cette ville.* Paris: L'imprimerie nationale.
CG	Catalogue général des antiquités égyptiennes du Musée du Caire.
Chicago Assyrian Dictionary	Oriental Institute. 1956. *The Assyrian Dictionary of the Oriental Institute of the University of Chicago.* Chicago: Oriental Institute.
DB # or DB #s	a reference or references to individuals named in the database
D.L. A.	Daressy's list number from Bab el Gusus cache
EEF/EES	Egypt Exploration Fund/Society
ERA	Egyptian Research Account
HTFES	*Hieroglyphic Texts from Egyptian Stelae etc.* vols 7-12
KRI	*Ramesside Inscriptions,* K.A. Kitchen. Oxford
LÄ	*Lexikon der Ägyptologie* W. Helck and E. Otto, eds., 7 vols. Wiesbaden: Otto Harassowitz.
Lieblein no.	entry number in Lieblein, J. 1979. *Dictionaire de Noms Hiéroglyphiques/ Hieroglyphisches Namen-Wörterbuch.* Hildesheim: Olms. Originally published 1871/1892, Leipzig.
LD	*Denkmaeler aus Aegypten und Aethiopien.* C.R. Lepsius. 6 vols.
LRL	Wente, E. 1967a. *Late Ramesside Letters.* SAOC 33. Chicago: University of Chicago Press. and Černý, J. 1939. *Late Ramesside Letters.* Brussels: Fondation Égyptologique Reine Élisabeth.
OMRO	*Oudheidkundige Mededelingen uit het Rijksmuseum van Oudheden*
PM	*Topographical Bibliography of Ancient Egyptian Hieroglyphic Texts, reliefs, and Paintings.* B. Porter and R.L.B. Moss 2nd ed. 7 vols.
Bruyère, Rapport	Bruyère, B. 1933. *Rapport sur les fouilles de Deir el Médineh (1930)* and 1952 *(1945-1946, 1946-1947).* Cairo: IFAO.
TT	designation for Theban tombs (followed by number)
Urk. II	Sethe, K., 1904. *Hieroglyphische Urkunden der Griechisch-Römischenzeit II.* Leipzig: J. C. Hinrichs'sche.
Urk. IV	Sethe, K. and W. Helck. 1906-1958. *Urkunden der 18. Dynastie. Urkunden des aegyptische Altertums,* vol. IV. Leipzig: J.C. Hinrichs'sche.
Wb	Erman, A., and H. Grapow. 1926. *Wörterbuch der Aegyptische Sprache.* Leipzig: J. C. Hinrichs Buchhandlung.

BIBLIOGRAPHY

ABD EL-RAZIK, M. 1974. The Dedicatory and Building Texts of Ramesses II in Luxor Temple. I: The Texts. *JEA* 60: 142-160.

ABD EL-RAZIK, M. 1975. The Dedicatory and Building Texts of Ramesses II in Luxor temple. II: Interpretation. *JEA* 61: 125-136.

ABDUL-QADER MUHAMMED, M. 1966. *The Development of the Funerary Beliefs and Practices Displayed in the Private Tombs of the New Kingdom at Thebes*. Cairo: Ministry of Culture and National Guidance.

ALDRED, C. 1987. *The Egyptians*. Revised ed. London: Thames and Hudson.

ALLAM, S. 1970. Zur Stellung der Frau im Alten Ägypten (in der Zeit des Neuen Reiches, 16.-10. Jahrhundert v. u. Z.). *Das Altertum* 16: 67-81.

ALLAM, S. 1990. A new look at the Adoption Papyrus (reconsidered). *JEA* 76: 189-191.

ALLEN, T. G. 1936. *Egyptian Stelae in the Field Museum of Natural History*. Chicago: Field Museum of Natural History.

ALLEN, T. G. 1974. *The Book of the Dead or Going Forth by Day: Ideas of the Ancient Egyptians Concerning the Hereafter as Expressed in Their Own Terms*. SAOC, vol. 37. Chicago: University of Chicago Press.

ALTENMÜLLER, H. 1972-1992. "Löschen der Fackeln in Milch", in *LÄ* III, col. 1078-1079.

El-AMIR, M. 1953. Further Notes on Egyptian Marriage and Divorce. *BIE* XXXIV: 139-150.

El-AMIR, M. 1972. Monogamy, Polygamy, Endogamy and Consanguinity in Ancient Egyptian Marriage. *BIFAO* 72: 103-107.

ANDERSON, R. 1996. Ancient Egyptian Music: Some Literary Evidence. *BACE* 7: 7-14.

ASSMANN, J. 1979. Harfnerlied und Horussöhne. *JEA* 65: 54-77.

ASSMANN, J. 1984. *Ägypten - Theologie und Frömmigkeit einer frühen Hochkultur*. Stuttgart: Verlag W. Kohlhammer.

ASSMANN, J. 1989. "State and Religion in the New Kingdom," in *Religion and Philosophy in Ancient Egypt*. Yale Egyptological Studies 3. New Haven: Yale University.

ASSMANN, J. 1991a. "Das ägyptische Prozessionsfest," in *Das Fest und Das Heilige*. J. Assmann and T. Sundermeier. pp. 105-122. Studien zum Verstehen fremder Religionen, band 1. Gütersloh: Gerd Mohn.

ASSMANN, J. 1991b. *Das Grab des Amenemope, TT 41*. in *Theben*, band 3. Mainz: P. von Zabern.

BADAWY, A. M. 1975. The Approach to the Egyptian Temple in the Late and Graeco-Roman Periods. *ZÄS* 102: 79-90.

BAER, K. 1960. *Rank and Title in the Old Kingdom*. Chicago: University of Chicago Press.

BAIKIE, J. 1932. *Egyptian Antiquities in the Nile Valley*. London: Methuen and Co.

BAINES, J. 1985. *Fecundity Figures. Egyptian Personification and the Iconology of a Genre*. Warminster: Aris and Phillips.

BAINES, J., AND C. J. EYRE. 1983. Four notes on literacy. *GM* 61: 65-96.

BAKIR, A. 1952. *Slavery in Pharaonic Egypt*. Cairo: IFAO.

BAKR, M. I. 1992. *Tell Basta*. Zagazig: University of Zagazig, Institute of Near Eastern Studies.

BAKRY, H. S. K. 1974. The Discovery of a Sarcophagus of Sat-Re' at Heliopolis. *Studi Classici e Orientali* 23: 70-78.

BARGUET, P. 1962. *Le Temple d'Amon-Rê à Karnak*. Cairo: IFAO.

BARNS, J. 1948. Three Hieratic Papyri in the Duke of Northumberland's Collection. *JEA* 34: 35-46.

BARNS, J. 1952. *The Ashmolean Ostracon of Sinuhe*. London: Griffith Institute, Oxford University Press.

BARTHELMESS, P. 1992. *Der Übergang ins Jenseits in den thebanischen Beamtengräbern der Ramessidenzeit*. Heidelberg: Heidelberger Orientverlag.

BAUD, M. AND E. DRIOTON. 1928. *Le tombeau de Panehsy*, in *Tombes Thébaines. Nécropole de Dira' Abu'n-Naga. MIFAO* LVII.2. Cairo: IFAO.

BAUD, M. AND E. DRIOTON. 1957. *Le tombeau de Roy*. in *Tombes Thébaines. Nécropole de Dira' Abu'n-naga. MIFAO* LVII.1 Cairo: IFAO.

BECKERATH, J. VON. 1972-1992. "Abydos", in *LÄ* I, col. 28-42.

BEGELSBACHER-FISCHER, B. L. 1981. *Untersuchungen zur Götterwelt des Alten Reiches im Spiegel der Privatgräber der IV. und V. Dynastie.* Göttingen: Vandenhoeck and Ruprecht.

BELL, L. 1985. Luxor Temple and the Cult of the Royal Ka. *JNES* 44: 251-294.

BELL, L. 1997. "The New Kingdom "Divine" Temple: The Example of Luxor", in *Temples of Ancient Egypt.* B. Shafer, ed. Ithaca, New York: Cornell University Press.

BELLION, M. 1987. *Egypte ancienne. Catalogue des manuscrits hiéroglyphiques et hiératiques et des dessins, sur papyrus, cuir, ou tissu, publiés ou signalés.* Paris: Epsilon Reproduction.

BENNETT, J. 1939. The Restoration Inscription of Tut'ankhamun. *JEA* 25: 8-15.

BENSON, M., AND J. GOURLAY. 1899. *The Temple of Mut in Asher.* London: J. Murray.

von BERGMANN, E. 1887. Inschriftliche Denkmäler der Sammlung Ägyptischer Alterthümer des österreichischen Kaiserhauses. *RdT* 9: 32-63.

von BERGMANN, E. 1892. Inschriftlische Denkmäler der Sammlung Ägyptischer Alterthümer der österreichischen Kaiserhauses. *RdT* 12: 1-23.

BIERBRIER, M. L. 1973. Hrere, Wife of the High Priest Paiankh. *JNES* 32: 311.

BIERBRIER, M. L. 1975. *The Late New Kingdom in Egypt (c. 1300-664 B.C.).* Warminster: Aris and Phillips.

BIERBRIER, M. L. 1982a. *Hieroglyphic Texts from Egyptian Stelae etc.,* Part 10. London: British Museum. (abbr. HTFES 10)

BIERBRIER, M. L. 1982b. *The Tomb-Builders of the Pharaohs.* Cairo: AUC Press.

BIERBRIER, M. L. 1987. *Hieroglyphic Texts from Egyptian Stelae etc.,* Part. 11. London: British Museum. (abbr. HTFES 11)

BIERBRIER, M. L. 1993. *Hieroglyphic Texts from Egyptian Stelae etc.,* Part. 12. London: British Museum. (abbr. HTFES 12)

BLACKMAN, A. M. 1912. The Significance of Incense and Libations in Funerary and Temple Ritual. *ZÄS* 50: 69-75.

BLACKMAN, A. M. 1921. On the Position of Women in the Ancient Egyptian Hierarchy. *JEA* 7: 8-30.

BLACKMAN, A. M., and W. V Davies. 1988. *The Story of King Kheops and the Magicians Transcribed from Papyrus Westcar (Berlin Papyrus 3033).* Reading: J. V. Books.

BLACKMAN, W. S. 1927. *The Fellahin of Upper Egypt.* London: G.G. Harrap and Co. Ltd.

BLEEKER, C. J. 1967. *Egyptian Festivals.* Leiden: E. J. Brill.

BLEEKER, C. J. 1973. *Hathor and Thoth. Two Key figures of the Ancient Egyptian Religion.* Leiden: E. J. Brill.

BLEIBERG, E. 1988. The Redistributive Economy in New Kingdom Egypt: An Examination of *B3kw(t).* *JARCE* 25: 157-168.

BONNET, H. 1952. *Reallexikon der Ägyptischen Religionsgeschichte.* Berlin: de Gruyter.

BORCHARDT, L. 1911-1936 . *Statuen und Statuetten von Königen und Privatleuten im Museum von Kairo.* Cairo: IFAO.

BORCHARDT, L. 1981. *Das Grabdenkmal des Königs Sa3hu-Re'.* Osnabrück: Otto Zeller Verlag. Originally published 1913, Berlin.

BOSSE, K. 1936. *Die Menschliche Figur in der Rundplastik der Ägyptischen Spätzeit von der XXII. bis zur XXX. Dynasties.* Glückstadt: J.J. Augustin.

BOTHMER, B., H. DE MEULENAERE, AND H. MÜLLER. 1960. *Egyptian Sculpture of the Late Period. 700 B.C. to A.D. 100.* New York: Brooklyn Museum.

BRACK, A., AND A. BRACK. 1977. *Das Grab des Tjanuni. Theben Nr. 74.* Mainz am Rhein: DAIK.

BRACK, A., AND A. BRACK. 1980. *Das Grab des Haremhab. Theben Nr. 78.* Mainz am Rhein: DAIK.

BREASTED, J. H. 1959. *Development of Religion and Thought in Ancient Egypt.* New York: Harper.

BREASTED, J. H. 1967. *A History of Egypt.* New York: Scribner. Originally published 1912, New York.

BRESCIANI, E. 1985. *Le Stele Egiziane del Museo Civico Archeologico di Bologna.* Bologna: Instituto per la Storia di Bologna.

BRUNNER, H. 1959. An Honoured Teacher of the Ramesside Period. *JEA* 45: 3-5.

BRUNNER-TRAUT, E. 1992. *Der Tanz im Alten Ägypten.* 3rd ed. Glückstadt: J. J. Augustin. Originally published 1937, Munich.

BRUNNER-TRAUT, E. 1972-1992. "Gesten", in *LÄ* II, col. 573-585.

BRUYÈRE, B. 1933. *Rapport sur les fouilles de Deir el Médineh (1930)*. Cairo: IFAO.

BRUYÈRE, B. 1952a. *Rapport sur les fouilles de Deir el Médineh (1945-1946, 1946-1947)*. Cairo: IFAO.

BRUYÈRE, B. 1952b. *Tombes Thébaines de Deir el Médineh à décoration monochrome*. Cairo: IFAO.

BRYAN, B. 1982. The etymology of *Ḫnr* "Group of Musical Performers". *BES* 4: 35-53.

BRYAN, B. 1985. Evidence for female literacy from Theban tombs of the New Kingdom. *BES* 6: 17-32.

BRYAN, B. 1986. The Career and Family of Minmose, High Priest of Onuris. *CdE* 61: 5-30.

BUCK, A. de. 1951. *The Egyptian Coffin Texts IV: Index of Spells 268-354*. Chicago: Oriental Institute.

CAMINOS, R. A. 1954. *Late-Egyptian Miscellanies*. Oxford: Oxford Press.

CAMINOS, R.A. 1963. *Gebel es-Silsilah*, volume 1, The Shrines. London: EES.

CAPEL, A. K., AND G. E. MARKOE. 1996. *Mistress of the House, Mistress of Heaven: Women in Ancient Egypt*. Cincinnati: Cincinnati Art Museum.

CENIVAL, F. de. 1977. Deux papyrus inédits de Lille avec une révision du P.dém.Lille 31. *Enchoria* VII: 1-49.

ČERNÝ, J. 1927. Le culte d'Amenophis Ier chez les ouvriers de la nécropole Thébaine. *BIFAO* 27: 159-203.

ČERNÝ, J. 1939. *Late Ramesside Letters*. Bruxelles: Fondation Égyptologique Reine Élisabeth.

ČERNÝ, J. 1940. Usurpation d'une tombe à Thèbes. *ASAE* 40: 235-240.

ČERNÝ, J. 1949. *Répertoire Onomastique de Deir el-Médineh*. Cairo: IFAO.

ČERNÝ, J. 1956-1957. "A Note on the Ancient Egyptian Family," in *Studi in Onore di Aristide Calderini e Roberto Paribeni*, volume 2, Studi di Papirologia e Antichitá Orientali. pp. 52-55. Milan: Casa Editrice. Ceschina.

ČERNÝ, J. 1958. *Egyptian Stelae in the Bankes Collection*. Oxford: Griffith Institute.

ČERNÝ, J. 1973. *A Community of Workmen at Thebes in the Ramesside Period*. Cairo: IFAO.

ČERNÝ, J., AND S. I. GROLL. 1984. *A Late Egyptian Grammar*. 3rd. ed. Rome: Biblical Institute Press.

CHAPPAZ, J. 1988. Répertoire annuel des figurines funéraires 1. *BSEG* 11: 141-151.

CHAPPAZ, J. 1989. Répertoire annuel des figurines funéraires 2. *BSEG* 12: 83-96.

CHAPPAZ, J. 1991. Répertoire annuel des figurines funéraires 4. *BSEG* 14: 89-104.

CLÈRE, J. J. 1950. Nouveaux documents relatifs au culte des colosses de Ramsès II dans le Delta. *Kêmi* 11: 24-46.

COLE, S. 1981. Could Greek Women Read and Write? in *Reflections of Women in Antiquity*. H. P. Foley, ed., pp. 219-245. New York: Gordon and Breach Science Publishers.

COLLINS, L. 1976. The Private Tombs of Thebes: Excavations by Sir Robert Mond 1905 and 1906. *JEA* 62: 18-40.

COONEY, J.D. 1956. *Five Years of Collecting Egyptian Art 1951-1956*. Brooklyn: Brooklyn Museum.

CRAMER, M. 1936. Ägyptische Denkmäler im Kestner-Museum zu Hannover. *ZÄS* 72: 81-108.

CRUZ-URIBE, E. 1988. A New Look at the Adoption Papyrus. *JEA* 74: 220-223.

CURRELLY, C. T., A. H. GARDINER, H. THOMPSON, AND J. G. MILNE. 1913. *Theban Ostraca Edited from the Originals, Now Mainly in the Royal Ontario Museum of Archaeology, Toronto, and the Bodleian Library, Oxford.* London: Oxford University Press.

DARESSY, G. 1919. Deux Statues de Balansourah. *ASAE* 18: 53-57.

DAUMAS, F. 1969. Les propylées du temple d'Hathor à Philae et le culte de la deésse. *ZÄS* 95: 1-17.

D'AURIA, S., P. LACOVARA, AND C. ROEHRIG. 1988. *Mummies and Magic. The Funerary Arts of Ancient Egypt*. Boston: MFA Boston.

DAVID, R. 1981. *A Guide to Religious Ritual at Abydos*. Warminster: Aris and Phillips.

DAVIES, Nina de G. 1963. *Scenes from some Theban Tombs (Nos. 38, 66, 162, 81)*. Private Tombs at Thebes 4. Oxford: University Press.

DAVIES, Nina de G. and A. H. GARDINER. 1926. *The Tomb of Huy, Viceroy of Nubia in the Reign of*

Tutankhamen (No. 40). The Theban Tomb series, mem. 4. London: EEF

DAVIES, Norman de G. 1902. *The Rock Tombs of Deir el Gabrawi: Part 2. Tomb of Zau and tombs of the Northern group*. London: EEF.

DAVIES, Norman de G. 1906. *The Rock Tombs of el Amarna*. volume 4. London: Memoirs of the Archaeological Survey of Egypt.

DAVIES, Norman de G. 1908. *The Rock Tombs of el Amarna*. volume 8. London: Memoirs of the Archaeological Survey of Egypt.

DAVIES, Norman de G. 1917. *The Tomb of Nakht at Thebes*. New York: Metropolitan Museum of Art.

DAVIES, Norman de G. 1923a. *The Tomb of Puyemre at Thebes*. 2vols. New York: Metropolitan Museum of Art.

DAVIES, Norman de G. 1923b. *The Tombs of Two Officials of Tuthmosis IV*. London: EES.

DAVIES, Norman de G. 1927. *Two Ramesside Tombs at Thebes*. New York: Metropolitan Museum of Art.

DAVIES, Norman de G. 1930. *The Tomb of Ken-amun at Thebes*. New York: Metropolitan Museum of Art.

DAVIES, Norman de G. 1933. *The Tomb of Nefer-Hotep at Thebes*. New York: Metropolitan Museum of Art.

DAVIES, Norman de G. 1941. *The Tomb of the Vizier Ramose*. London: EES.

DAVIES, Norman de G. 1943. *The Tomb of Rekhmire at Thebes*. 2 vols. New York: Metropolitan Museum of Art.

DAVIES, Norman de G. AND Nina de G. DAVIES. 1933. *The Tombs of Menkheperrasonb, Amenmose, and Another*. London: EES.

DAVIES, Norman. AND Nina. de G. DAVIES. 1939. Harvest Rites in a Theban Tomb. *JEA* 25/2: 154-156, plates.

DAVIES, Norman de G. AND A. H. GARDINER. 1915. *The Tomb of Amenemhēt*. London: EEF.

DAVIES, Norman de G. AND A. H. GARDINER. 1920. *The Tomb of Antefoker, vizier of Sesostris I, and his wife Senet (n. 30)*. London: EES.

DAVIES, Norman de G. AND A. H. GARDINER. 1948. *Seven Private Tombs at Kurnah*. London: EES.

DELVAUX, L., AND E. WARMENBOL. 1991. *Les Divins Chats d'Égypte: Un air subtil, un dangereux parfum*. Leuven: Peeters.

DERCHAIN, P. 1962. L'adoration du Soleil levant dans le temple de Psammétique Ier à El Kab. *CdE* 37: 257-271.

DESROCHES-NOBLECOURT, C. 1986. *La Femme au temps des pharaons*. Paris: Stock Pernoud.

DÉVAUD, E. 1910. Varia. *Sphinx* 13: 103-108.

DEVERIA, T. 1980. *Catalogue des manuscrits égyptiens au Musée Egyptien du Louvre*. Hildesheim: Georg Olms. Originally published 1881, Paris.

DONADONI, S. ed. 1997. *The Egyptians*. Chicago: University of Chicago Press.

DOXEY, D. 1995. *A Social and Historical Analysis of Egyptian Non-Royal Epithets in the Middle Kingdom*. Ph.D. dissertation, University of Pennsylvania. Philadelphia.

DRENKHAHN, R. 1975. Eine Privatstiftung des Vizekönigs Setau in El-Kab. *SAK* 3: 43-48.

DUEMICHEN, J. 1884-1894. *Der Grabpalast des Patuamenap in der Thebanische Nekropolis*. Leipzig: J.C. Hinrichs.

EDGERTON, W. F. 1931. *Notes on Egyptian Marriage Chiefly in the Ptolemaic Period*. Chicago: University of Chicago Press.

EDWARDS, I. E. S. 1939. *Hieroglyphic Texts from Egyptian Stelae, etc. in the British Museum*, part VIII. London: British Museum. (abbr. HTFES 8)

EGYPTIAN CULTURE CENTER, WASEDA UNIVERSITY, JAPAN. 1996-2000. Excavations of the Private Tombs in the Theban Necropolis. Online publication: www.waseda.ac.jp/projects/egypt/sites/TT-E.html.

ENGLUND, G. 1989. *Cognitive Structures and Popular Expressions*. Boreas 20, Uppsala, Sweden: Acta Universitatis Upsaliensis.

EPIGRAPHIC SURVEY. 1930. *Medinet Habu. Festival Scenes of Rameses III*. Volume 4. Oriental Institute Publications, Vol. 51. Chicago: University of Chicago Press.

EPIGRAPHIC SURVEY. 1936. *Reliefs and Inscriptions at Karnak*. Volume 2. Oriental Institute Publications Vol 35. Chicago: University of Chicago Press.

EPIGRAPHIC SURVEY. 1979. *The Temple of Khonsu*. Volume 1. *Scenes of King Herihor in the Court*. Oriental Institute Publications, Vol. 100. Chicago: University of Chicago Press.

EPIGRAPHIC SURVEY. 1980. *The Tomb of Kheruef. Theban Tomb 192.* Oriental Institute Publications, Vol. 102. Chicago: Oriental Institute of the University of Chicago.

EPIGRAPHIC SURVEY. 1994. *The Festival Procession of Opet in the Colonnade Hall.* Oriental Institute Publications, Vol. 112. Chicago: University of Chicago Press.

ERMAN, A. 1890. *Die Märchen des Papyrus Westcar.* Berlin: W. Spemann.

ERMAN, A., AND H. GRAPOW. 1926. *Wörterbuch der Aegyptische Sprache.* Leipzig: J. C. Hinrichs Buchhandlung.

EYRE, C. J. 1992. The Adoption Papyrus in Social Context. *JEA* 78: 207-221.

FÁBIÁN, Z. I. 1997. Report on the first Two Seasons in the Theban Tomb 184 (Nefermenu). *SAK* 24: 81-102.

FAIRMAN, H. W. 1938. Preliminary Report on the Excavations at Sesebi (Sudla) and ‘Amarah West, Anglo-Egyptian Sudan. *JEA* 24: 151-156, pls. VII-XI.

FAKHRY, A. 1934. Tombeau de Kaemheribsen à Thèbes. *ASAE* 34: 83-86, and plates.

FAKHRY, A. 1936. Three Unnumbered Tombs at Thebes. *ASAE* 36: 124-130.

FAKHRY, A. 1942. A Note on the Tomb of Kheruef at Thebes. *ASAE* 42: 449-508.

FAULKNER, R. O. 1972. *The Ancient Egyptian Book of the Dead.* Austin, Texas: University of Texas Press.

FAULKNER, R. O. 1973. *The Ancient Egyptian Coffin Texts. Spells 1-354.* Warminster: Aris and Phillips.

FAULKNER, R. O. 1975. *Egypt From the Inception of the Nineteenth Dynasty to the Death of Ramesses III*, in *History of the Middle East and the Aegean Region c. 1380-1000 B.C.*, 3rd ed., I.E.S. Edwards, et. al., eds. Cambridge: Cambridge University Press.

FAULKNER, R. O. 1991. *A Concise Dictionary of Middle Egyptian.* Oxford: Griffith Institute.

FAZZINI, R. A. 2002. “Some Reliefs of the Third Intermediate Period in the Egyptian Museum, Cairo” in *Egyptian Museum Collections around the World.* Vol. 1. M. Eldamaty and M. Trad, eds., pp 351-362. Cairo: American University Press.

FEUCHT, E. 1985. *Das Grab des Nefersecheru (TT 296).* Mainz: P. von Zabern.

FEUCHT, E. 1997. “Women,” in *The Egyptians.*, S. Donadoni, ed., pp. 315-346. Chicago: University of Chicago Press.

FISCHER, H. G. 1968. *Dendera in the 3rd Millennium B.C.* Locust Valley, NY: J.J. Augustin.

FISCHER, H. G. 1976. *Egyptian Studies I: Varia.* New York: Metropolitan Museum of Art.

FISCHER, H. G. 1977. “The Mark of a Second Hand on Ancient Egyptian Antiquities,” in *Ancient Egypt in the Metropolitan Museum Journal, Volumes 1-11 (1968-1976).*, pp. 113-142. New York: Metropolitan Museum of Art.

FISCHER, H. G. 1989. *Egyptian Women of the Old Kingdom and of the Heracleopolitan Period.* New York: Metropolitan Museum of Art.

FISCHER, H. G. 1972-1992. “Priesterin”, in *LÄ* IV, col. 1100-1105.

FOUCART, G. 1930. *La belle fête de la vallée. BIFAO* 24. Cairo: IFAO.

FOUCART, G. 1935. *Le tombeau de Amonmos,* in *Tombes Thébaines. Nécropole de Dira’ Abu’n-Naga. MIFAO* LVII.3, pts. i and iv. Cairo: IFAO.

FRANKFORT, H. 1928. The Cemeteries of Abydos: Work of the Season 1925-26. *JEA* 14: 235-245.

GABALLA, G. A. 1979. “Monuments of Prominent Men of Memphis, Abydos, and Thebes,” in *Glimpses of Ancient Egypt.* J. Ruffle et. al., eds., pp. 42-49. Warminster: Aris and Phillips.

GABALLA, G. A., AND K. A. KITCHEN. 1981. Ramesside Varia IV. The Prophet Amenemope, His Tomb and Family. *MDAIK* 37: 161-180.

GALVIN, M. 1981. *Priests and Priestesses of Hathor in the Old Kingdom and First Intermediate Period.* Ph.D. dissertation, Brandeis University.

GALVIN, M. 1984. The Hereditary Status of the Titles of the Cult of Hathor. *JEA* 70: 42-49.

GARDINER, A. H. 1932. *Late Egyptian Stories.* Brussels: Édition de la Fondation Égyptologique Reine Élisabeth.

GARDINER, A. H. 1933. The Dakhleh Stela. *JEA* 19: 19-30.

GARDINER, A. H. 1937. *Late-Egyptian Miscellanies.* Bruxelles: Édition de la Fondation Égyptologique Reine Élisabeth.

GARDINER, A. H. 1940. Adoption Extraordinary. *JEA* 26: 23-29.

GARDINER, A.H. 1941. Ramesside Texts on Taxation, etc. of Corn. *JEA* 27: 19-73.

GARDINER, A. H. 1948. *Ramesside Administrative Documents*. London: Oxford University Press.

GARDINER, A. H., T. E. PEET, and J. ČERNÝ. 1952-1955. *The Inscriptions of Sinai.* 2 volumes. Oxford: 45th memoir of the EES.

GARSTANG, J. 1989. *El Arâbah.* London: History and Mysteries of Man Ltd. Originally published 1901, London.

GILLAM, R. 1991. *Topographical, Prosopographical and Historical Studies in the 14th Upper Egyptian Nome.* Ph.D. dissertation, University of Toronto.

GILLAM, R. 1995. Priestesses of Hathor: Their Function, Decline and Disappearance. *JARCE* 32: 211-237.

GITTON, M. 1976. La résiliation d'une fonction religiuese: Nouvelle interprétation de la stéle de donation d'Ahmes Néfertary. *BIFAO* 76: 65-89.

GITTON, M. 1979. "Le Clergé féminin au Nouvel Empire," in *First International Congress of Egyptology Acts*. W. F. Reineke. pp. 225-228. Schriften zur Geschichte und Kultur des alten Orients. Akademie der Wissenschaften der DDR Zentral Institut für alte Geschichte und Archäologie. Berlin: Akademie verlag.

GITTON, M. 1984. *Les divines épouses de la 18e dynastie*. Paris: Belles Lettres.

GOEDICKE, H. 1971. *Re-Used Blocks from the Pyramid of Amenemhet I at Lisht.* New York: Metropolitan Museum of Art.

GOFF, B. 1979. *Symbols of Ancient Egypt in the Late Period: the 21st Dynasty*. The Hague: Mouton.

GOHARY, J. 1992. *Akhenaten's Sed-festival at Karnak.* London: Kegan Paul International.

GRAEFE, E. 1981. *Untersuchungen zur Verwaltung und Geschichte der Institution der Gottesgemahlin des Amun vom Beginn des Neuen Reiches bis zur Spätzeit.* Wiesbaden: Harrassowitz.

GRIFFITH, F. Ll. 1921. Oxford excavations in Nubia. *LAAA* 8: 65-104, pl. IXf.

GRIMAL, N. 1992. *A History of Ancient Egypt.* Oxford: Blackwell.

GUEST, E. M. 1926. Women's Titles in the Middle Kingdom. *Ancient Egypt* 1926: 46-50.

GUGLIELMI, W. 1991. *Die Göttin Mr.t.* Leiden: E.J. Brill.

HABACHI, L. 1947. A Statue of Osiris Made for Ankhefenamun, Prophet of the House of Amun in Khapu and his Daughter. *ASAE* 47: 261-282.

HABACHI, L. 1957. *Tell Basta.* Cairo: IFAO.

HABACHI, L. 1958. Clearance of the Tomb of Kheruef at Thebes (1957-1958). *ASAE* 55: 325-350.

HABACHI, L. 1965. A Family from Armant in Aswan and in Thebes. *JEA* 51: 123-136.

HABACHI, L. 1968. The Owner of Tomb 282 in the Theban Necropolis. *JEA* 54: 107-113.

HABACHI, L. 1969. *Features of the Deification of Ramesses II.* Glückstadt: J. J. Augustin.

HABACHI, L. 1976a. Miscellanea on Viceroys of Kush and their Assistants Burried in Dra' Abu el-Naga South. *JARCE* 13: 113-116.

HABACHI, L. 1976b. "The Royal Scribe Amenmose, Son of Penzerti and Mutemonet: His Monuments in Egypt and Abroad," in *Studies in Honor of George R. Hughes*. pp. 83-104. SAOC 39. Chicago: Oriental Institute.

HABACHI, L. 1981. *Sixteen Studies on Lower Nubia.* Cairo: IFAO.

HAIKAL, F. 1985. "Preliminary studies on the tomb of Thay in Thebes: The hymn to the light." in *Mélanges Gamal Eddin Mokhtar,* vol. I. P. Posener-Krieger, ed. pp. 361-372. Cairo: IFAO.

HALL, H. R. 1925. *Hieroglyphic Texts from Egyptian Stelae, etc., in the British Museum,* part VII. London: British Museum. (abbr. HTFES 7)

HANNIG, R. 1995. *Grosses Handwörterbuch Ägyptisch-Deutsch (2800-950 v. Chr.)*. Mainz: P. von Zabern.

HARI, R. 1964. *Horemheb et la Reine Moutnedjemet ou la fin d'une Dynastie*. Geneva: Impr. La Sirène.

HARI, R. 1976. *Repertoire Onomastique Amarnien.* Geneva: Aegyptiaca Helvetica 4.

HARI, R. 1985. *La Tombe Thébaine du Père divin Neferhotep (TT50).* Geneva: Éditions de Belles Lettres.

HARRIS, J.R. ed. 1987. *The Legacy of Egypt*, 2nd ed. Oxford: Oxford University Press.

HAYES, W. C. 1938. A Writing-Palette of the Chief Steward Amenhotpe and Some Notes on its Owner. *JEA* 24: 9-24.

HAYES, W. C. 1959. *The Scepter of Egypt*, 2 vols. New York: Metropolitan Museum of Art.

HEGAZY, E. A. AND M. TOSI. 1983. *A Theban Private Tomb. Tomb No. 295*. Mainz am Rhein: DAIK.

HEIN, I., AND H. SATZINGER. 1989. *Corpus Antiquitatum Aegypticarum: Kunsthistorisches Museum Wien. Stelen des Mittleren Reiches I.* Mainz am Rhein: P. von Zabern.

HELCK, W. 1960. *Materialen zur Wirtschaftsgeschichte des Neuen Reiches*. Wiesbaden: Akademie der Wissenschaften und der Literatur.

HELCK, W. 1975. Die Grosse Stele des Vizekönigs *Stꜣw* aus Wadi es-Sabua. *SAK* 3: 85-112.

HELCK, W. AND E. OTTO. 1972-1992. *Lexikon der Ägyptologie*. 7 vols. Wiesbaden: Harassowitz. (abbr. *LÄ*)

HICKMANN, H. 1952. Le Métier de Musicien au Temps des Pharaons. *Cahiers d'Histoire Egyptienne* Série IV: 79-101.

HICKMANN, H. 1954. Dieux et Déesses de la Musique. *Cahiers d'Histoire Egyptienne* Série VI, Mars: 31-59.

HICKMANN, H. 1958. La chironomie dans l'Egypte pharaonique. *ZÄS* 83: 96-127.

HICKMANN, H. 1961. *Ägypten. Musikgeschichte in Bildern.* Leipzig: Deutscher Verlag für Musik.

HOCH, J. 1994. *Semitic Words in Egyptian Texts of the New Kingdom and Third Intermediate Period.* Princeton: Princeton University Press.

HODJASH, S., AND O. BERLEV. 1982. *The Egyptian Reliefs and Stelae in the Pushkin Museum of Fine Arts, Moscow.* Leningrad: Aurora Art.

HOFMANN, E. 1995. *Das Grab des Neferrenpet. Gen. Kenro (TT178).* Mainz am Rhein: P. von Zabern.

HOLTHOER, R. 1984. "The Hamboula-group Tombs at Khokha," in Boreas 13. *Sundries in Honour of Torgny Säve-Söderbergh.* pp. 73-96. Uppsala: Acta Universitatis Upsaliensis.

HORNUNG, E. 1997. "The Pharaoh," in *The Egyptians*, S. Donadoni ed., pp. 283-314. Chicago: University of Chicago Press.

HORNUNG, E. AND E. STAEHELIN. 1974. *Studien zum Sedfest.* Geneva: Aegyptiaca Helvetica I.

van der HORST, P. W. 1982. "The Way of Life of the Egyptian Priests According to Chaeremon," in *Studies in Egyptian Religion Dedicated to Professor Jan Zandee*, M. Heerma van Voss, ed., pp. 61-71. Leiden: E. J. Brill.

JACOBY, A. 1900. Eine inedirte Statue des Prinzen Setau. *RdT* 22: 113-115.

JAMES, T. G. H. 1970. *Hieroglyphic Texts from Egyptian Stelae etc.*, part IX. London: British Museum.

JAMES, T. G. H. 1973. *Egypt: From the expulsion of the Hyksos to Amenophis I.* in *History of the Middle East and the Aegean Region c. 1380-1000 B.C.*, 3rd ed., I.E.S. Edwards, et. al., eds. Cambridge: Cambridge University.

JAMES, T. G. H. 1985. *Egyptian Painting and Drawing in the British Museum.* London: British Museum.

JANSSEN, J. J. 1991. *Hieratic Papyri in the British Museum VI. Late Ramesside Letters and Communications.* London: British Museum.

JANSSEN, R. M., AND J. J. JANSSEN. 1990. *Growing up in Ancient Egypt.* London: Rubicon Press.

JANSSEN, R. M., AND J. J. JANSSEN. 1996. *Getting Old in Ancient Egypt.* London: Rubicon Press.

JOHNSON, J. 1998. "Women, Wealth, and Work in Egyptian Society of the Ptolemaic Period," in *Egyptian Religion. The Last Thousand Years. Studies Dedicated to the Memory of Jan Quaegebeur,* W. Clarysse, et.al. eds. *OLA* 84. pp. 1393-1421. Leuven: Peeters.

JOURDAIN, G. 1939. "La Tombe du Scribe Royal Amenemopet," in *Deux Tombes de Deir el Medineh*, J. Vandier d'Abbadie, G. Jourdain, eds. *MIFAO* LXXIII. Cairo: IFAO.

KÁKOSY, L. 1988. Ungarische Grabungen in Theben; TT 32. *BSAK* 2: 211-216.

KANAWATI, N. 1976. Polygamy in the Old Kingdom. *SAK* 4: 149-160.

KANAWATI, N. 1977. *The Egyptian Administration in the Old Kingdom.* Warminster: Aris and Phillips.

KANAWATI, N. 1979. The Provincial Movement in the Sixth Dynasty of Egypt. in *Acts, 1st ICE.* pp. 353-358.

KAMAL, A.B. 1904-1905. *Stèles: Ptolémaiques et Romaines.* Cairo: IFAO.

KAMAL, A. B. 1916. Fouilles à Deir Dronka et à Assiout (1913-1914). *ASAE* 16: 65-114.

KAPLONY, P. 1963. *Inschriften der aegyptischen Frühzeit.* Wiesbaden: Harrassowitz.

KAPLONY-HECKEL, U. 1971. *Ägyptische Handschriften*. Wiesbaden: Franz Steiner Verlag.

KARIG, J. S. 1969. Die Kultkammer des Amenhotep aus Deir Durunka. *ZÄS* 95: 27-34.

KARKOWSKI, J. 1981. *Faras V: The Pharaonic Inscriptions from Faras*. Warsaw: PWN.

KEES, H. 1912. *Das Opfertanz des ägyptischen Königs*. Munich.

KEES, H. 1948. Die Phylen und ihre Vorsteher im Diest der Tempel und Totenstiftung. *Or* 17: 71-90 and 314-325.

KEES, H. 1953. *Das Priestertum im Äegyptischen Staat vom neuen Reich bis zur Spätzeit*. Leiden: E. J. Brill.

KEES, H. 1961. Ein bedeutende Amonspriesterfamilie der Ramessidenzeit. *OLZ* 56: 5-10.

KEES, H. 1964. *Die Hohenpriesters des Amun von Karnak von Herihor bis zum Ende der Äthiopenzeit*. Leiden: E. J. Brill.

KEMP, B. 1968. The Osiris Temple at Abydos. *MDAIK* 23: 138-155.

KEMP, B. 1978a. The Harim-Palace at Medinet Ghurab. *ZÄS* 105: 122-133.

KEMP, B. 1978b. "Imperialism and Empire in New Kingdom Egypt (c. 1575-1087 B.C.)," in *Imperialism in the Ancient World*, P. Garnsey nd C. Whittaker, eds., pp. 7-57, 284-297. Cambridge: Cambridge University Press.

KEMP, B. 1983. "Old Kingdom, Middle Kingdom and Second Intermediate Period c. 2686-1552 BC," in *Ancient Egypt: A Social History*. B. G. Trigger, et. al., pp. 71-182. Cambridge: Cambridge University Press.

KEMP, B. 1989. *Ancient Egypt: Anatomy of a Civilization*. London: Routledge.

KITCHEN, K. A. 1969-1990. *Ramesside Inscriptions: Historical and Biographical*. Volumes I-VIII Oxford: Blackwell.

KITCHEN, K. A. 1973. *The Third Intermediate Period in Egypt (1100-650 B.C.)*. Warminster: Aris and Phillips.

KOCH, R. 1990. *Die Erzählung des Sinuhe*. Bibliotheca Aegyptiaca 17. Bruxelles: Fondation Égyptologique Reine Élisabeth.

KOLARI, E. 1947. *Musikinstrumente und ihre Verwendung im alten Testament*. Helsinki.

KOZLOFF, A., B. BRYAN, AND L. BERMAN. 1992. *Egypt's Dazzling Sun: Amenhotep III and his World*. Cleveland: Cleveland Museum of Art.

KUENTZ, C. 1971. *La face sud du massif est du pylône de Ramses II à Louxor*. Cairo: Centre de documentation et d'études sur l'ancienne Égypte.

LACAU, P. 1918. *Stèles du Nouvel Empire*. Cairo: IFAO.

LACAU, P., AND H. CHEVRIER. 1977. *Une Chapelle d'Hatshepsout à Karnak*. 2 vols. Cairo: IFAO.

LANGE, H. O., AND H. SCHÄFER. 1902, 1908. *Grab- und Denksteine des Mittleren Reiches*. Cairo: IFAO.

LANZONE, R. V. 1974. *Dizionario di Mitologia Egizia*. Amsterdam: John Benjamins B.V.

LECLANT, J., AND G. CLERC. 1993. Fouilles et Travaux en Égypte et au Soudan. 1991-1992. *Or* 62: 240-241.

LEFEBVRE, G. 1914. Fouilles à Abydos. *ASAE* 13: 193-214 and plates.

LEFEBVRE, G. 1929. *Histoire des Grands Prêtres d'Amon de Karnak jusqu'à la XXIe Dynastie*. Paris: P. Geuthner.

LEGRAIN, G. 1906. *Statues et statuettes de rois et particuliers*. Catalogue Général vol. 30. Cairo: IFAO.

LEGRAIN, G. 1907. Notes d'Inspection. *ASAE* 8: 248-275.

LEPROHON, R. J. 1978. *Corpus Antiquitatum Aegyptiacarum. Museum of Fine Arts, Boston: Loose Leaf Catalogue of Egyptian Antiquities*. fasc. 2-3. *Stelae II: The New Kingdom to the Coptic Period*. Mainz: P. von Zabern.

LEPROHON, R. J. 1978. The Personnel of the Middle Kingdom Funerary Stelae. *JARCE* 15: 33-38.

LEPROHON, R. J. 1985. The Reign of Akhenaten Seen Through the Later Royal Decrees. in *Mélanges Gamal Eddin Mokhtar*, vol. 2, P. Posener-Kriéger, ed., pp. 93-104. Cairo: IFAO.

LEPROHON, R.J. 1988. Cultic Activities in the Temple at Amarna. in D. Redford, *The Akhenaten Temple Project. Volume 2: Rwd-mnw, Foreigners and Inscriptions*. ch. 5, p. 47-51. Toronto: Akhenaten Temple Project and the University of Toronto Press.

LEPSIUS, C. R. 1972-1973. *Denkmaeler aus Aegypten und Aethiopien. Band I-VI*. Geneva: Editions de Belles Lettres. Originally published 1849, Berlin. (abbr. LD)

LESKO, B., ed. 1987. *Women's Earliest Records from Ancient Egypt and Western Asia: Proceedings of the Conference on Women in the Ancient Near East, Brown University*. Atlanta: Scholar's Press.

LESKO, L. H., ed. 1998. *Ancient Egyptian and Mediterranean Studies in Memory of William A. Ward*. Providence, R.I: Department of Egyptology, Brown University.

LIEBLEIN, J. 1979. *Dictionaire de Noms Hiéroglyphiques/Hieroglyphisches Namen-Wörterbuch*. Hildesheim: Olms. Originally published 1871/1892, Leipzig.

LIPIŃSKA, J. 1982. *Corpus Antiquitatum Aegypticarum: Monuments de l'Egypte ancienne au Palacio de Belles Artes à la Havane et du Museo Bacardí à Santiago de Cuba*. Mainz am Rhein: P. von Zabern.

LOAT, L. 1904. *Gurob*. London: Egyptian Research Account.

LÖHR, B. 1970. Ein Memphitisches Grab vom Ende der 18. Dynastie (um 1320 v. Chr). *Pantheon* XXVIII/6: 467-474.

LOWLE, D. A. 1976. A Remarkable Family of Draughtsmen-Painters from Early Nineteenth-Dynasty Thebes. *Oriens Antiquus* XV: 91-196.

LOWLE, D. A. 1979. "A Nineteenth Dynasty Stela in the Louvre," in *Glimpses of Ancient Egypt*. J. Ruffle et. al., eds., pp. 50-54. Warminster: Aris and Phillips.

LÜDDECKENS, E. 1943. Untersuchungen über Religiösen Gehalt, Sprache und Form der Ägyptischen Totenklagen. *MDAIK* 11.

LUXOR MUSEUM. 1979. *Luxor Museum of Ancient Egyptian Art. Catalogue*. Cairo: American Research Center in Egypt.

MÁLEK, J. 1974. Two Monuments of the Tias. *JEA* 60: 161-167.

MANNICHE, L. 1987. *The Tombs of the Nobles at Luxor*. Cairo: AUC Press.

MANNICHE, L. 1988. *The Wall Decorations of Three Theban Tombs (TT 77, 175, 249)*. Copenhagen: Museum Tusculanum Press.

MANNICHE, L. 1991a. *Music and Musicians in Ancient Egypt*. London: British Museum Press.

MANNICHE, L. 1991b. Music at the Court of the Sun-Disk. *Amarna Letters* 1: 62-65.

MARIETTE, A. 1869-1880. *Abydos. Description des Fouilles exécutées sur l'emplacement de cette ville*. Paris: L'imprimerie nationale.

MARIETTE, A. 1880. *Catalogue général des Monuments d'Abydos découverts pendant les fouilles de cette ville*. Paris: L'imprimerie nationale.

MARTIN, G. T. 1983. The Tomb of Tia and Tia: Preliminary report on the Saqqâra excavations, 1982. *JEA* 69: 25-29.

MARTIN, G. T. 1984. The Tomb of Tia and Tia: Preliminary report on the Saqqâra excavations, 1983. *JEA* 70: 5-12.

MARTIN, G. T. 1985. *The Tomb Chapels of Paser and Ra'ia at Saqqâra*. Egypt Exploration Society, 52nd Memoir. London: EES.

MARTIN, G. T. 1986. Shabtis of Private Persons in the Amarna Period. *MDAIK* 42: 109-129.

MARTIN, G. T. 1987. *Corpus of Reliefs of the New Kingdom from the Memphite Necropolis and Lower Egypt*. London: Keagan Paul International.

MARTIN, G. T. 1991. *The Hidden Tombs of Memphis*. London: Thames and Hudson.

MEEKS, D. 1980. *Année Lexicographique. 1977-1979*. Paris: D. Meeks.

de MEULENAERE, H. 1975-76. Le Clergé abydénien d'Osiris à la Basse Époque. *Orientalia Lovaniensia Periodica* 6/7: 133-151.

MOND, M. R. 1905. Report of Work in the Necropolis of Thebes during the Winter of 1903-1904. *ASAE* 6: 65-96.

MONTET, P. 1949. Les Divinités du temple de Behbeit el Hagar. *Kemi* 10: 43-48.

MORENZ, S. 1973. *Egyptian Religion*. Ithaca: Cornell University Press.

MORET, A. 1988. *Le Rituel du Culte Divin Journalier en Egypte*. Geneva: Slatkine Reprints. Originally published 1902, Annales du Musée Guimet, Bibliothèque d'Etudes, Paris.

MOSS, R. 1941. Some Rubbings of Egyptian Monuments Made a Hundred Years Ago. *JEA* 27: 7-11, pls. II-III.

MOSTAFA, M. F. 1995. *Das Grab des Neferhotep und des Meh (TT 257)*. Mainz am Rhein: P. von Zabern.

MOUSSA, A. M., AND H. A. ALTENMÜLLER. 1975. Ein Denkmal zum Kult des Königs Unas am Ende der 12. Dynastie. *MDAIK* 31.1: 93-97.

MÜLLER, H. 1937. Darstellungen von Gebärden auf Denkmälern des Alten Reiches. *MDAIK* 7: 57-118.

MÜLLER, H. 1966. *Die Ägyptische Sammlung des Bayerisches Staates*. Munich.

MUNRO, P. 1973. *Die spätägyptischen Totenstelen*. Glückstadt: J. J. Augustin.

MYŚLIWIEC, K. 1985. *Eighteenth Dynasty Before the Amarna Period*. Leiden: E. J. Brill.

NAGUIB, S. 1990. *Le Clergé Féminin d'Amon Thébain à la 21e Dynastie*. Leuven: Peeters.

NAVILLE, E. 1882. Le Decret de Phtah Totunen en faveur de Ramsés II et de Ramsés III. *TSBA* VII: 119-138.

NAVILLE, E. 1892. *The Festival Hall of Osorkon II in the Great Temple of Bubastis*. London: EEF.

NEGM, M. 1997. *The Tomb of Simut Called Kyky. Theban Tomb 409 at Qurnah*. Warminster, England: Aris and Phillips.

NEWBERRY, P. AND F. WILLOUGHBY. 1893. *Beni Hasan*. Archaeological Survey of Egypt, memoir no. 12. London: K. Paul and EEF

NIMS, C. 1957. "Popular Religion in Ancient Egyptian Temples," in *Proceedings of the 23rd International Congress of Orientalists*. London.

NIWIŃSKI, A. 1984. Butehamon - Schreiber der Nekropolis. *SAK* 11: 135-156.

NIWIŃSKI, A. 1988. *21st Dynasty Coffins From Thebes*. Mainz am Rhein: P. von Zabern.

NIWIŃSKI, A. 1989a. Some Remarks on Rank and Titles of Women in the Twenty-first Dynasty Theban "Sate of Amun". *DE* 14: 79-89.

NIWIŃSKI, A. 1989b. *Studies on the Illustrated Theban Funerary Papyri of the 11th and 10th Centuries B.C.* Freiburg, Switzerland: Freiburg University.

NIWIŃSKI, A. 1992. "Ritual Protection of the Dead or Symbolic Reflection of his Special Status in Society?", in *The Intellectual Heritage of Egypt*. U. Luft ed. Budapest: Studia Aegyptiaca XIV.

NORD, D. 1975. Der königliche Harim im alten Ägypten und seine Verwaltung, by Elfriede Reiser. [review] in *JNES* 34, pp. 142-145.

NORD, D. 1981. "The Term *ẖnr*: 'Harem' or 'Musical Performers'?" in *Studies in Honor of Dows Dunham. Studies in Ancient Egypt, the Aegean, and the Sudan*, W.K. Simpson and W. Davis, eds., pp. 137-145. Boston: Museum of Fine Art.

OCKINGA, B. AND Y. AL-MASRI. 1988. *Two Ramesside Tombs at El-Mashayikh*. Sydney: The Ancient History Documentation Center, Macquaire University.

O'CONNOR, D. 1985. "The <Cenotaphs> of the Middle Kingdom at Abydos," in *Mélanges Gamal Eddin Mokhtar*, P. Posener-Kriéger, ed., pp. 161-177. Cairo: IFAO.

O'CONNOR, D. AND E.H. CLINE, eds. 1998. *Amenhotep III. Perspectives on His Reign*. Ann Arbor: University of Michigan Press.

OMLIN, J. 1973. *Der Papyrus 55001 und seine Satirisch-erotischen Zeichnungen und Inschriften*. Turin: Edizioni d'arte fratelli Pozzo.

ORIENTAL INSTITUTE. 1956. *The Assyrian Dictionary of the Oriental Institute of the University of Chicago*. Chicago: Oriental Institute.

OSING, J. 1992. *Das Grab des Nefersecheru in Zawyet Sultan*. Mainz am Rhein: DAIK.

PARKINSON, R.B. 1991. *Voices from Ancient Egypt. An Anthology of Middle Kingdom Writings*. Norman, Oklahoma: University of Oklahoma Press.

PEET, T. E. 1913. *The Cemeteries of Abydos*. London: EEF.

PEET, T. E. 1914. *The Cemeteries of Abydos,* part II, 1911-1912. London: EEF.

PEET, T. E. 1930. *The Great Tomb-Robberies of the Twentieth Egyptian Dynasty*. Oxford: Clarendon Press.

PENDLEBURY, J. D. S. 1951. *The City of Akhenaten. The Central City and the Official Quarters*. London: EES.

PERNIGOTTI, S. 1980. *La Statuaria Egiziana nel Museo Civico Archeologico di Bologna*. Bologna: Instituto per la Storia di Bologna.

PESTMAN, P. W. 1961. *Marriage and Matrimonial Property in Ancient Egypt*. Leiden: E. J. Brill.

PETRIE, W. M. F. 1900. *Denderah, 1898*. London: EES.

PETRIE, W. M. F. 1909-1913. *Memphis*, vols. I-V. London: Egyptian Research Account.

PETRIE, W. M. F. 1916. A Cemetery Portal. *Ancient Egypt:* 174f.

PETRIE, W. M. F., AND G. BRUNTON. 1924. *Sedment II*. London: Egyptian Research Account.

PETRIE. W. M. F., E. AYRTON, C. CURRELLY, AND A. WEIGALL. 1902-1904. *Abydos*. 3 vols. London: EEF.

PIANKOFF, A. 1936. The Funerary Papyrus of Tent-Amon. *Egyptian Religion* IV: 49-79.

PIANKOFF, A., AND N. RAMBOVA. 1957. *Mythological Papyri*. New York: Pantheon Books.

POLZ, D., 1998. The Ramsesnakht Dynasty and the Fall of the New Kingdom: A New Monument in Thebes. *SAK* 25: 257-293.

POMEROY, S. 1984. *Women in Hellenistic Egypt: From Alexander to Cleopatra*. New York: Schocken Books.

PORTER, B., AND R. MOSS. 1937. *Topographical Bibliography of Ancient Egyptian Hieroglyphic Texts, Reliefs, and Paintings*. Vol. V. *Upper Egypt: Sites*. Oxford: Clarendon Press. (abbr. PM V)

PORTER, B., AND R. MOSS. 1960. *Topographical Bibliography of Ancient Egyptian Hieroglyphic Texts, Reliefs, and Paintings*, Vol. I. *The Theban Necropolis*. Part 1 *Private Tombs*. 2nd ed. Oxford: Clarendon Press. (abbr. PM I.1)

PORTER, B., AND R. MOSS. 1972. *Topographical Bibliography of Ancient Egyptian Hieroglyphic Texts, Reliefs, and Paintings*. Vol. II. *Theban Temples*. 2nd ed. Oxford: Clarendon Press. (abbr. PM II)

PORTER, B., AND R. MOSS. 1974-1978. *Topographical Bibliography of Ancient Egyptian Hieroglyphic Texts, Reliefs, and Paintings*. Vol. III. *Memphis*. Parts 1 and 2. 2nd ed. Oxford: Clarendon Press. (abbr. PM III.1, III.2)

POSENER, G. 1957. Le conte de Néferkarè et du général Siséné. *RdE* 11: 119-137.

POULS, M. A. 1997-1998. A Newly Discovered Temple of Thutmose III at Abydos. *KMT* 8: 48-59.

QUIBELL, J. E. 1989. *The Ramesseum and the tomb of Ptah-hetep*. London: Histories and Mysteries of Man, Ltd. Originally published 1896: Egyptian Research Account, vol. 2.

QUIBELL, J. E. 1912. Excavations of Saqqara (1908-9, 1909-10): The Monastery of Apa Jeremias. Cairo: IFAO.

QUIRKE, S. 1993. *Owners of Funerary Papyri in the British Museum*. London: British Museum Press.

RADWAN, A. 1985. "The *ʿnḫ* Vessel and its Ritual Function," in *Mélanges Gamal Eddin Mokhtar*. P. Posener-Kriéger, ed., pp. 211-217. Cairo: IFAO.

RADWAN, A. 1987. Six Ramesside Stelae in the Popular Pyramidion-Form. *ASAE* 71: 223-228 (6 plates).

RAMOND, P. 1977. *Les stèles égyptiennes du Musée G. Labit à Toulouse*. Cairo: IFAO.

RANDALL-MACIVER, D., A. C. MACE, AND F. L. GRIFFITH. 1902. *El Arabah and Abydos, 1899-1901*. London: Egypt Exploration Fund.

RANKE, H. 1935. *Die Aegyptischen Personennamen*. Glückstadt: J. J. Augustin.

RAVEN, M. 1991. *The Tomb of Iurudef. A Memphite Offiicial in the Reign of Ramesses II*. London: Egypt Exploration Society.

REDFORD, D.B. 1988. *The Akhenaten Temple Project. Volume 2: Rwd-mnw, Foreigners and Inscriptions*. Toronto: Akhenaten Temple Project and the University of Toronto Press.

REDFORD, D. B. 1992. *Egypt, Canaan, and Israel in Ancient Times*. Cairo: AUC.

REISER, E. 1972. *Der Königliche Harim im alten Ägypten und seine Verwaltung*. Vienna: Verlag Notrig.

REYMOND, E. A. E. 1981. *From the Records of a Priestly Family from Memphis*. vol. 1. Wiesbaden: Harrassowitz.

REYNDERS, M. 1998. *Sšš.t* and *sḫm*: Names and Types of the Egyptian Sistrum. in *Egyptian Religion. The Last Thousand Years*. part 1. Clarysse, W. et. al., eds., p. 1013-1026. Leuven: Peeters.

RITNER, R. 1994. "Denderite Temple Hierarchy and the Family of Theban High Priest Nebwenenef: Block Statue OIM 10729," in *For his Ka; Essays offered in memory of Klaus Baer*, D. P. Silverman, ed. SAOC 55. Chicago: Oriental Institute of the University of Chicago.

RITNER, R. 1998. Fictive Adoptions or Celibate Priestesses? *GM* 164: 85-90.

ROBERTS, A. 1997. *Hathor Rising*. Rochester, Vt.: Inner Traditions International.

ROBINS, G. 1979. The Relationships specified by Egyptian Kinship Terms of the Middle and New Kingdoms. *CdE* LIV: 197-217.

ROBINS, G. 1993a. The God's Wife of Amun in the 18th Dynasty in Egypt. in *Images of Women in Antiquity*. revised ed. A. Cameron and A. Kuhrt, ed., pp. 65-78. London: Routledge.

ROBINS, G. 1993b. *Women in Ancient Egypt*. Cambridge: Harvard University Press.

ROBINS, G. 1994. Some Principles of Compositional Dominance and Gender Hierarchy in Egyptian Art. *JARCE* 31: 33-40.

ROBINS, G. 1997. *The Art of Ancient Egypt*. Cambridge: Harvard University Press.

de ROCHEMONTEIX, M. AND E. CHASSINAT. 1987. *Le Temple d'Edfou,* tome 1, 3rd fasc. 2nd ed. Cairo: IFAO.

ROEDER, G. 1909. Der Isistempel von Behbet. *ZÄS* 46: 68

ROEDER, G. 1952. Zwei hieroglyphischen Inschriften aus Hermopolis (Ober-Ägypten). *ASAE* 52: 315-442.

ROGGE, A. 1990. *Corpus Antiquitatum Aegypticarum: Statuen des Neuen Reiches und der Dritten Zwischenzeit. Kunsthistorisches Museum Wien. Ägyptisch-Orientalische Sammlung*. Mainz am Rhein: P. von Zabern.

ROTH, A. M. 1991. *Egyptian Phyles in the Old Kingdom: The Evolution of a System of Social Organization*. Chicago: Oriental Institute.

RUFFLE, J., AND K. A. KITCHEN. 1979. "The Family of Urhiya and Yupa, High Stewards of the Ramesseum," in *Glimpses of Ancient Egypt*. J. Ruffle, et. al., eds., pp. 55-74. Warminster: Aris and Phillips.

RUFFLE, J., G. GABALLA, AND K.A. KITCHEN, eds. 1979. *Glimpses of Ancient Egypt. Studies in honor of H. W. Fairman*. Warminster: Aris and Phillips.

El-SAADY, H. 1995. Two Heliopolitan Stelae of the New Kingdom. *ZÄS* 122: 101-104.

El-SAADY, H. 1996. *The Tomb of Amenemhab; no. 44 at Qurnah*. Warminster: Aris and Phillips.

SADEK, A. I. 1987. *Popular Religion in Egypt during the New Kingdom*. Hildesheim: Gerstenberg Verlag.

SAUNERON, S. 1960. *The Priests of Ancient Egypt*. New York: Grove Press, Inc.

SAUNERON, S. 1968. Les inscriptions ptolémaïques de Mout à Karnak. *BIE* 45: 45-52.

SÄVE-SÖDERBERGH, T. 1957. *Four Eighteenth Dynasty Tombs*. Oxford: University Press.

SAYCE, A. H. 1898. Gleanings from the land of Egypt. *RdT* 20: 111-112.

El-SAYED, R. 1982. *La Déesse Neith de Saïs*. Cairo: IFAO.

SCHARFF, A. 1924. Briefe aus Illahun. *ZÄS* 59: 20-51.

SCHNEIDER, H. D. 1977. *Shabtis: An introduction to the history of ancient Egyptian funerary statuettes with a catalogue of the collection of shabtis in the National Museum of Antiquities at Leiden*. Leiden: Rikjsmuseum van Oudheden.

SCHLICK-NOLTE, B. 1984. *Corpus Antiquitatum Aegypticarum. Museen der Rhein-Mainz-Region*. Mainz am Rhein: P. von Zabern.

SCHOTT, S. 1937. Das Löschen von Fackeln in Milch. *ZÄS* 73: 1-25.

SCHOTT, S. 1952. *Das schöne Fest vom Wüstentale. Festbräuche einer Totenstadt*. Wiesbaden: Akademie der Wissentschaften und der Literatur in Mainz.

SCHOTT, S. 1957. *Wall Scenes from the Mortuary Chapel of the Mayor Paser at Medinet Habu*. Chicago: University of Chicago Press.

SCHULMAN, A. R. 1966. *Mhr* and *Mškb*, Two Egyptian Military Titles of Semitic Origin. *ZÄS* 93: 123-132.

SCOTT, G. D. I. 1986. *Ancient Egyptian Art at Yale*. New Haven: Yale University Art Gallery.

SEELE, K. 1959. *The Tomb of Tjanefer at Thebes*. Chicago: University of Chicago.

SETHE, K. 1904. *Hieroglyphische Urkunden der Griechisch-Römischenzeit II*. Leipzig: J. C. Hinrichs'sche.

SETHE, K. AND W. HELCK. 1906-1958. *Urkunden der 18. Dynastie. Urkunden des aegyptische Altertums, IV*. Leipzig: J.C. Hinrichs'sche.

SEYFRIED, K.-J. 1990. *Das Grab des Amonmose (TT373)*. Mainz am Rhein: P. von Zabern.

SEYFRIED, K.-J. 1991. *Das Grab des Paenkhemenu (TT68) und die Anlage TT 227*. Mainz am Rhein: P. von Zabern.

SEYFRIED, K.-J. 1995. *Das Grab des Djehutiemhab (TT194)*. Mainz am Rhein: P. von Zabern.

SHAFER, B., L. LESKO, D. SILVERMAN, AND J. BAINES. 1991. *Religion in Ancient Egypt. Gods, Myths, and Personal Practice*. Ithaca: Cornell University Press.

SHAFER, B., ed. 1997. *Temples of Ancient Egypt*. Ithaca: Cornell University Press.

SILIOTTI, A. 1996. *Guide to the Valley of the Kings and to the Theban Necropolises and Temples*. Luxor: A. A. Gaddis and Sons.

SIMPSON, W. K. 1974a. Polygamy in Egypt in the Middle Kingdom. *JEA* 60: 100-105.

SIMPSON, W. K. 1974b. *The Terrace of the Great God at Abydos: The offering chapels of Dynasties 12 and 13*. New Haven and Philadelphia: Yale Univserity Press and University of Pennsylvania Press.

SIMPSON, W. K. 1995. *Inscribed Material from the Pennsylvania-Yale Excavations at Abydos*. New Haven and Philadelphia: Yale Univserity Press and University of Pennsylvania Press.

SMITH, H. S. 1976. *The Fortress of Buhen:Volume I, The Inscriptions*. London: Egypt Exploration Society.

SMITH, R. W. AND D. B. REDFORD. 1976. *The Akhenaten Temple Project. Volume 1: Initial Discoveries*. Warminster: Aris and Phillps Ltd.

SPALINGER, A. 1998. The Limitations of Formal Ancient Egyptian Religion. *JNES* 57: 241-260.

SPENCER, A.J. 1982. *Death in Ancient Egypt*. London, New York: Penguin.

SPIEGEL, J. 1950. Ptah-Verehrung in Theben (grab 372). *ASAE* 40: 257-281.

SPIEGELBERG, W. 1899. Eine stele aus der Oase Dachel. *RdT* 21: 12-21.

SPIEGELBERG, W. 1922. *Der demotische Text der Priesterdekrete von Kanopus und Memphis (Rosettana)*. Heidelberg: C. Winter.

STEWART, H. M. 1976. *Egyptian Stelae, Reliefs and Paintings from the Petrie Collection. Part 1. The New Kingdom*. Warminster: Aris and Phillips.

STEWART, H. M. 1979. *Egyptian Stelae, Reliefs and Paintings from the Petrie Collection. Part 2. Archaic Period to the Second Intermediate Period*. Warminster: Aris and Phillips.

STRUDWICK, N. 1996. *The Tombs of Amenhotep, Khnummose, and Amenmose at Thebes*. Oxford: Griffith Institute and Ashmolean Museum.

TEETER, E. 1993. "Female Musicians in Pharaonic Egypt," in *Rediscovering the Muses. Women's Musical Traditions*. K. Marshall, ed., pp. 68-91. Boston: Northeastern University Press.

TERRACE, E., AND H.G. FISCHER. 1970. *Treasures of Egyptian Art from the Cairo Museum*. Boston: Museum of Fine Arts.

THAUSING, G., AND H. GOEDICKE. 1971. *Nofretari; A Documentation of her Tomb and its Decoration*. Graz, Austria: Akademische Druck- u. Verlagsanstalt.

THÉODORIDOS, A. 1964. La stèle juridique d'Amarah. *RIDA* XI: 45-80.

TOSI, M., AND A. ROCCATI. 1971-1972. *Stele e Altre Epigrafi di Deir el Medina. n. 50001-50262*. Turin: Edizioni d'arte Fratelli Pozzo.

TRAUNECKER, C. 1972. Les Rites de l'Eau à Karnak d'après les textes de la rampe de Taharqa. *BIFAO* 72: 195-236.

TRIGGER, B. 1993. *Early Civilizations. Ancient Egypt in Context*. Cairo: AUC Press.

TRIGGER, B. G., B. KEMP, D. O'CONNOR, AND A. B. LLOYD. 1983. *Ancient Egypt. A Social History*. Cambridge: Cambridge University Press.

TROY, L. 1986. *Patterns of Queenship in Ancient Egyptian Myth and History*. Boreas 14. Uppsala, Sweden: Acta Universitatis Upsaliensis.

TYLDESLEY, J. 1994. *Daughters of Isis. Women in Ancient Egypt*. Harmondsworth: Viking.

TYLDESLEY, J. 1996. *Hatchepsut. The Female Pharaoh*. London, New York: Viking.

TZACHOU-ALEXANDRI, O. ed. 1995. *The World of Egypt in the National Archaeological Museum*. Athens: Greek Ministry of Culture.

UPHILL, E. 1965. The Egyptian Sed-Festival Rites. *JNES* 24: 365-383.

VALBELLE, D. 1975. *La Tombe de Hay à Deir el-Medineh [n. 267]*. Cairo: IFAO.

VANDIER, J. 1958. *Manuel d'Archéologie Egyptienne*, vol. III. Paris: Éditions A. et J. Picard et Cie.

VANDIER, J. 1964. *Manuel d'Archéologie Egyptienne*, vol IV. Paris: Éditions A. et J. Picard et Cie.

VAN SICLEN, C. 1979. Identity of a Figure in the Tomb of Kenamun. *Serapis* 5: 17-20.

VIREY, P. 1887. Le Tombeau d'un Seigneur de Thini dans la Nécropole de Thèbes. *RdT* 9: 27-32.

VIREY, P. 1891. *Sept Tombeaux Thébains. MIFAO* 5.2. Cairo: IFAO.

VIREY, P. 1898. La Tombe des Vignes à Thèbes ou Tombe de Sennofri, Directeur des Greniers des Troupeaux et des Jardins d'Ammon. *RdT* 20: 211-23.

VIREY, P. 1899. La Tombe des Vignes à Thèbes ou Tombe de Sennofri, Directeur des Greniers des Troupeaux et des Jardins d'Ammon. *RdT* 21: 137-49.

VIREY, P. 1900. La Tombe des Vignes à Thèbes ou Tombe de Sennofri, Directeur des Greniers des Troupeaux et des Jardins d'Ammon. *RdT* 22: 83-97.

van WALSEM, R., G. T. MARTIN, B. G. ASTON, E. STROUHAL, AND L. HORÁKOVÁ. 1999. Preliminary report on the Saqqara excavations, season 1999. *Oudheidkundige Mededelingen uit het Rijksmuseum van Oudheden*, 79: 19-35, ills.

WARD, W. 1982. *Index of Egyptian Administrative and Religious Titles of the Middle Kingdom.* Beirut: American University in Beirut.

WARD, W. 1983. Reflections on Some Egyptian Terms Presumed to Mean "Harem, Harem-woman, Concubine". *Berytus* 31: 67-74.

WARD, W. 1986. *Essays on Feminine Titles of the Middle Kingdom and Related Subjects.* Beirut: American University in Beirut.

WATTERSON, B. 1991. *Women in Ancient Egypt.* New York: St. Martin's Press.

WEIGALL, A. E. P. 1908. Upper Egyptian Notes. *ASAE* 9: 105-112.

WENTE, E. 1967a. *Late Ramesside Letters.* SAOC 33. Chicago: University of Chicago Press.

WENTE, E. 1967b. On the Chronology of the Twenty-First Dynasty. *JNES* 26: 155-176.

WENTE, E. 1969. Hathor at the Jubilee. *Studies in Honor of John A. Wilson. SAOC* 35. G. E. Kadish, ed., pp. 83-91. Chicago: University of Chicago Press.

WENTE, E. 1990. *Letters from Ancient Egypt.* Atlanta: Scholars Press.

WESTERMANN, W. L. 1924. The Castanet Dancers of Arsinoe. *JEA* 10: 134-144.

WHALE, S. 1989. *The Family in the Eighteenth Dynasty of Egypt: A Study of the Representations of the Family in Private Tombs.* Sydney: The Australian Centre for Egyptology.

WILBOUR, C. E. 1936. *Travels in Egypt.* J. Capart, ed. Brooklyn: Brooklyn Museum.

WILD, H. 1963. Les Danses Sacrées de l'Égypte Ancienne. *Sources Orientales* 6: 36-117.

WILD, H. 1979. *La Tombe de Néfer-Hotep (I) et Neb-Néfer à Deir el Médîna [N°. 6] et autres documents les concernant.* Cairo: IFAO [*MIFAO* CIII/2].

WILDUNG, D. 1997. *Egypt. From Prehistory to the Romans.* Cologne: Taschen.

WILKINSON, J.G. 1883. *The Manners and Customs of the Ancient Egyptians.* 3 vol. Boston: S. E. Cassino and Company. S. Birch, ed. 2nd Edition.

WILKINSON, R.H. 1994. *Symbol and Magic in Egyptian Art.* London: Thames and Hudson.

WILLEMS, H. O. 1983. A Description of Egyptian Kinship Terminology of the Middle Kingdom c. 2000-1650 B.C. *Bijdragen tot de Taal-, Land- en Volkenekunde* 139.1: 152-168.

WOLF, W. 1931. *Das schöne Fest von Opet.* Leipzig: J. C. Hinrisch'sche.

YOYOTTE, J. 1961. Les vierges consacrées d'Amon thébain. *CRAIBL*: 43-52.